MODERN ELOQUENCE
VOLUME ELEVEN
MASTERPIECES

MODERN ELOQUENCE

IN TWELVE VOLUMES

The outstanding After-Dinner Speeches, Lectures and Addresses of Modern Times, by the most eminent speakers of America and Europe

VOLUME

    I—AFTER DINNER SPEECHES, A-D

    II—AFTER DINNER SPEECHES, E-M

    III—AFTER DINNER SPEECHES, N-Z

    IV—ADDRESSES—Business and Industry

    V—ADDRESSES—Tributes to Great Men

    VI—ADDRESSES—Literary, Educational, Professional

    VII—ADDRESSES—Church, Cause, Country

    VIII—FAMOUS LECTURES—Humorous, Inspirational, Scientific

    IX—MASTERPIECES—European

    X—MASTERPIECES—American

    XI—MASTERPIECES—World War

    XII—FIVE HUNDRED BEST ANECDOTES—INDEX

Introductory Essays by Eminent Authorities giving a Practical Course of Instruction on the Important Phases of Public Speaking

Modern Eloquence
Founded by THOMAS B. REED
VOLUME ELEVEN - MASTERPIECES

ASHLEY H. THORNDIKE, Editor
Professor of English, Columbia University

Advisory Editorial Board

BRANDER MATTHEWS, Chairman
Professor, Dramatic Literature, Columbia University

SIR ROBERT LAIRD BORDEN
Formerly Prime Minister of Canada

NICHOLAS MURRAY BUTLER
President, Columbia University

JOHN W. DAVIS
Formerly U. S. Ambassador to England

HENRY CABOT LODGE
Senator from Massachusetts

ELIHU ROOT
Formerly Secretary of State, Secretary of War, Senator

OSCAR S. STRAUS
Formerly Secretary of Commerce, Ambassador to Turkey

AUGUSTUS THOMAS
Playright, Chairman, Producing Managers' Association

HENRY van DYKE
*Professor of English Literature, Princeton University
Formerly U. S. Minister to the Netherlands*

Modern Eloquence Corporation
NEW YORK

Copyright 1923, by
MODERN ELOQUENCE CORPORATION

Entered at Stationers' Hall, London
All rights reserved

PRINTED IN U. S. A.

CONTENTS

	PAGE
INTRODUCTION: The Oratory of the World War A. H. THORNDIKE	xvii
CHRONOLOGY OF THE WORLD WAR	xxiii

ALBERT, KING OF BELGIUM
    Belgium Ready 36

ANNUNZIO, GABRIELE D'
    To the Officers on the Piave 148

ASQUITH, HERBERT HENRY
    England Supports Belgium 51

BAKER, NEWTON DIEHL
    The March Toward Liberty 249

BALFOUR, ARTHUR JAMES
    The Fourth of July in London 233
    At the Washington Conference 390

BARNES, GEORGE NICOLL
    At the Peace Conference 343

BEATTY, ADMIRAL
    Comrades of the Mist 415

BECK, JAMES MONTGOMERY
    America and the Allies 117

BETHMANN-HOLLWEG, THEOBALD VON
    Germany Begins the War 31

BORAH, WILLIAM EDGAR
    The League of Nations 365

BORDEN, SIR ROBERT LAIRD
    The Voice of the Empire 92

BOURGEOIS, LÉON
    At the Peace Conference 324, 333

CONTENTS

                                                    PAGE

BRIAND, ARISTIDE
    The German Peace Proposal 136
    At the Washington Conference 397

CECIL, LORD ROBERT
    At the Peace Conference 338

CLEMENCEAU, GEORGES
    One Aim: Victory 169
    At the Peace Conference 315

CROWDER, ENOCH HERBERT
    Begin Now! 303

DAVISON, HENRY P.
    The American Red Cross 296

FOCH, MARSHAL
    To the French Academy 422

FRENCH OFFICER, A
    To the First Americans Who Fell in France . . . 414

GINISTY, BISHOP
    Verdun 413

GOMPERS, SAMUEL
    Labor's Attitude 271

GREY, SIR EDWARD
    England's Position 12

HADLEY, ARTHUR TWINING
    Commemoration Address 418

HARDING, PRESIDENT WARREN G.
    At the Washington Conference 379

HOOVER, HERBERT
    Food Control: A War Measure 285

HUGHES, CHARLES E.
    At the Washington Conference 383

ISHII, VISCOUNT
    To the United States Senate 238

CONTENTS

JAURÈS, JEAN
    Socialists and the War 6
    Last Speech 11

KATO, BARON
    At the Washington Conference 396

KERENSKY, ALEXANDER
    Declaration of the Labor Party 61
    Addresses to Workingmen and Soldiers 174

KIPLING, RUDYARD
    The American Invasion of England 300

KITCHENER OF KHARTUM
    More Men 86

KOO, WELLINGTON
    At the Peace Conference 346

KORNILOFF, GENERAL
    Appeal to His Soldiers 176

LANE, FRANKLIN K.
    The Message of the West 254

LAURIER, SIR WILFRID
    "Ready, Aye, Ready" 63

LENINE, NIKOLAI
    A Dictatorship of the Proletariat 181
    The Peasants 187

LLOYD GEORGE, DAVID
    An Appeal to the Nation 70
    Victory or Defeat: No Half-Way House . . . 156
    To American Comrades in Arms 200
    At the Peace Conference 313, 322

MAKINO, BARON
    At the Peace Conference 342

MEIGHEN, ARTHUR
    The Glorious Dead 431

MERCIER, CARDINAL
    Coronation Day Sermon 129

CONTENTS

	PAGE
MILLERAND, PRESIDENT	
Semi-Centennial of the French Republic	423
NICHOLAS II, CZAR OF RUSSIA	
Russia Enters the War	60
ORLANDO, PREMIER	
At the Peace Conference	323, 341
PAGE, WALTER HINES	
The Fourth of July in London	231
PERSHING, GENERAL	
To the United States Senate	420
To the Unknown British Warrior	433
POINCARÉ, RAYMOND	
Declaration of War by France	38
At the Peace Conference	306
REDMOND, JOHN	
Ireland and the War	29
ROOSEVELT, THEODORE	
National Duty and International Ideals	99
ROOT, ELIHU	
The War and Discussion	241
SONNINO, BARON	
At the Peace Conference	314
TAFT, WILLIAM HOWARD	
The League of Nations	348
TROTSKY, LEON	
To the Red Army	178
VENISELOS, ELEUTHERIOS	
Greece Enters the War	138
At the Peace Conference	345
VIVIANI, RENÉ RAPHAEL	
Declaration of War by France	40
The Spirit of France	82
Addresses in America	208, 210

CONTENTS

WHITLOCK, BRAND
    Lafayette, Apostle of Liberty 224

WILHELM II, EMPEROR OF GERMANY
    Moses and Amalek 1
    Address to the German People 6

WILSON, WOODROW
    Declaration of War by the United States 190
    Flag Day Address 217
    The Fourteen Points 264
    Force to the Utmost 280
    At the Peace Conference 312, 318, 327

CONTENTS

Arranged Chronologically

INTRODUCTION: The Oratory of the World War A. H.
    THORNDIKE xvii
CHRONOLOGY OF THE WORLD WAR xxiii

1. THE OPENING OF THE WAR
    WILHELM II, EMPEROR OF GERMANY
        Moses and Amalek 1
        Address to the German People 6
    JAURÈS, JEAN
        Socialists and the War . . . July 25, 1914   6
        Last Speech . . . . . . July 29, 1914   11
    GREY, SIR EDWARD (NOW VISCOUNT)
        England's Position . . . . August 3, 1914   12
    REDMOND, JOHN
        Ireland and the War . . . August 3, 1914   29
    VON BETHMANN-HOLLWEG, THEOBALD
        Germany Begins the War . . August 4, 1914   31
    ALBERT, KING OF BELGIUM
        Belgium Ready . . . . . August 4, 1914   36
    POINCARÉ, RAYMOND
        Declaration of War by France . August 4, 1914   38
    VIVIANI, RENÉ RAPHAEL
        Declaration of War by France . August 4, 1914   40
    ASQUITH, HERBERT HENRY
        England Supports Belgium . August 6, 1914   51
    NICHOLAS II, CZAR OF RUSSIA
        Russia Enters the War . . . August 8, 1914   60
    KERENSKY, ALEXANDER
        Declaration of the Labor Party . August 8, 1914   61

CONTENTS

II. THE PROGRESS OF THE WAR
   LAURIER, SIR WILFRID
      "Ready, Aye, Ready" . . . August 19, 1914 63
   LLOYD GEORGE, DAVID
      An Appeal to the Nation . September 19, 1914 70
   VIVIANI, RENÉ RAPHAEL
      The Spirit of France . . December 22, 1914 82
   KITCHENER OF KHARTUM
      More Men . . . . July 9, 1915 86
   BORDEN, SIR ROBERT LAIRD
      The Voice of the Empire . . August 4, 1915 92
   ROOSEVELT, THEODORE
      National Duty and International Ideals
                                   April 29, 1916 99
   BECK, JAMES MONTGOMERY
      America and the Allies . . . July 5, 1916 117
   MERCIER, CARDINAL
      Coronation Day Sermon . . . July 21, 1916 129
   BRIAND, ARISTIDE
      The German Peace Proposal. December 13, 1916 136
   VENISELOS, ELEUTHERIOS
      Greece Enters the War . . . August, 1917 138
   ANNUNZIO, GABRIELE D'
      To the Officers on the Piave . December, 1917 148
   LLOYD GEORGE, DAVID
      Victory or Defeat . . . December 14, 1917 156
   CLEMENCEAU, GEORGES
      One Aim: Victory . . . . June 4, 1918 169

III. THE RUSSIAN REVOLUTION
   KERENSKY, ALEXANDER
      To Workingmen and Soldiers . March, 1917 174
   KORNILOFF, GENERAL
      Appeal to His Soldiers . September 10, 1917 176

CONTENTS

	PAGE
TROTSKY, LEON	
To the Red Army . . . . . April, 1919	178
LENINE, NIKOLAI	
A Dictatorship of the Proletariat . March, 1919	181
The Peasants . . . . April, 1919	187

IV. THE UNITED STATES IN THE WAR

WILSON, WOODROW
    Declaration of War by the U. S. April 2, 1917   190

LLOYD GEORGE, DAVID
    To American Comrades in Arms . April 12, 1917   200

VIVIANI, RENÉ RAPHAEL, Addresses in America
    I. At Mt. Vernon . . . April 29, 1917   208
    II. At the Auditorium, Chicago, May 4, 1917   210

WILSON, WOODROW
    Flag Day Address . . . . June 14, 1917   217

WHITLOCK, BRAND
    Lafayette, Apostle of Liberty . July 4, 1917   224

PAGE, WALTER HINES
    The Fourth of July in London . July 4, 1917   231

BALFOUR, ARTHUR JAMES
    The Fourth of July in London . July 4, 1917   233

ISHII, VISCOUNT
    To the United States Senate . August 30, 1917   238

ROOT, ELIHU
    The War and Discussion . September 14, 1917   241

BAKER, NEWTON DIEHL
    The March Toward Liberty . October 8, 1917   249

LANE, FRANKLIN K.
    The Message of the West . October 18, 1917   254

WILSON, WOODROW
    The Fourteen Points . . . January 8, 1918   264

GOMPERS, SAMUEL
    Labor's Attitude . . . . February 22, 1918   271

CONTENTS

WILSON, WOODROW
    Force to the Utmost . . . April 6, 1918 280
HOOVER, HERBERT
    Food Control: A War Measure . April 18, 1918 285
DAVISON, HENRY P.
    The American Red Cross . . May 18, 1918 296
KIPLING, RUDYARD
    American Invasion of England July 21, 1918 300
CROWDER, ENOCH HERBERT
    Begin Now! . . . . . September, 1918 303

V. THE PEACE CONFERENCE 305
  1. OPENING SESSION, January 18, 1919
    PRESIDENT POINCARÉ, Inaugural 306
    PRESIDENT WILSON, Nomination of Georges Clemenceau as President of the Conference . 312
    MR. LLOYD GEORGE 313
    BARON SONNINO 314
    M. CLEMENCEAU, Opening Address . . . 315
  2. SESSION January 25, 1919
    PRESIDENT WILSON 318
    MR. LLOYD GEORGE 322
    PREMIER ORLANDO 323
    M. LÉON BOURGEOIS 324
  3. SESSION February 15, 1919
    PRESIDENT WILSON 327
    M. LÉON BOURGEOIS 333
    LORD ROBERT CECIL 338
    PREMIER ORLANDO OF ITALY 341
    BARON MAKINO OF JAPAN 342
    MR. BARNES 343
    M. VENISELOS OF GREECE 345
    MR. WELLINGTON KOO OF CHINA . . . 346

TAFT, WILLIAM HOWARD
    The League of Nations . . March 4, 1919 348
BORAH, WILLIAM EDGAR
    The League of Nations . November 19, 1919 365

VI. THE WASHINGTON CONFERENCE ON THE LIMITATION
OF ARMAMENTS
 PRESIDENT HARDING . . . November 12, 1921 379
 SECRETARY HUGHES . . . November 12, 1921 383
 MR. BALFOUR . . . . . November 15, 1921 390
 BARON KATO . . . . . November 15, 1921 396
 M. BRIAND . . . . . . November 21, 1921 397

VII. MEMORIALS
 GINISTY, BISHOP
  Verdun . . . . . . February 17, 1917 413
 FRENCH OFFICER, A
  To the First Americans Who Fell in France
        November 6, 1917 414
 BEATTY, ADMIRAL
  Comrades of the Mist . . December 1, 1918 415
 HADLEY, ARTHUR TWINING
  Commemoration Address . . June 15, 1919 418
 PERSHING, GENERAL
  To the U. S. Senate . . September 18, 1919 420
 FOCH, MARSHAL
  To the French Academy . . February 5, 1920 422
 MILLERAND, PRESIDENT
  Semi-Centennial of the French Republic
        November 19, 1920 423
 MEIGHEN, ARTHUR
  The Glorious Dead . . . . July 3, 1921 431
 PERSHING, GENERAL
  To the Unknown British Warrior
        October 17, 1921 433

ILLUSTRATIONS

	PAGE
Edward Grey	12
Woodrow Wilson	190
René R. Viviani	208
William E. Borah	365
Ferdinand Foch	422
Arthur Meighen	431

INTRODUCTION

ORATORY OF THE WORLD WAR

By Ashley H. Thorndike

Oratory has always flourished in time of war. Though the orator and the soldier are often cited as representing opposite temperaments, the man of words and the man of action, yet both types are called to their best efforts in the intense emotion of national crises. Passions that stir nations find expression in both words and deeds, in eloquence and in battle. Many of the world's most famous orations were occasioned by war. The Philippics of Demosthenes and the Philippics of Cicero were delivered during wars that threatened the existence of Athens and Rome. In modern times the American Revolution, the French Revolution, the Napoleonic wars, and the American Civil War have produced the masterpieces of Chatham, Burke, Mirabeau, Pitt and Lincoln given in volumes IX and X in this series. Debates on the issues that lead to war, appeals to nations and soldiers to carry on the war, discussion of the purpose and significance of peace and victory, memorials to the fallen soldiers—these make up a large part of the oratory that survives through the ages and holds an assured place in permanent literature.

The World War, which in every comparison dwarfs all earlier wars, far surpasses them in the quantity of its oratory. While the War lasted there was nothing else to talk about. Before the War began many of its issues—militarism, closer union between one nation and another, hopes and projects for disarmament and permanent peace—were already favorite themes for public discussion. Since the War closed, the terms of peace and their sequels have been the principal subjects of both national and international debate. There is probably no orator of distinction of the present time who has not spoken on issues of the War. It could almost be said that every public speaker of our time has made his most effective and most memorable speech on some issue of the War. Most of us, if asked what speech has moved us most, would select one made in connection with the War. The volume of war speeches is enormous, and there is good reason to believe that among them there are some worthy of very high rank among the masterpieces of eloquence.

This War has surpassed all past wars in the variety, as well as in the quantity of its oratory. There has been opportunity for eloquence to attempt whatever it has essayed before. It would be difficult to find a single oration of the past for which some parallel in its subject matter or in the occasion of its delivery could not be found in the oratory of the World War. Moreover there have been many new occasions and unheard-of subjects. It was a war of peoples. Popular support, whether by enlistment in the armies or subscription to government loans, was maintained by a vast amount of speech making. Nothing just like our four-minute speakers has been known before in history. It was a war of allies. Envoys journeyed not from one court to another but from one people to another. The United States sent a delegation headed by Mr. Root to offer greetings to the Russian people after the revolution. The many special embassies to this country included orators of such high though contrasting quality as Balfour and Viviani. The War engaged the entire resources of the combatant nations. In the United States, industrial organization and efficiency were manifest keys to our successful coöperation, and in consequence the themes of many addresses. Business men as well as the clergy, the bar and political leaders found themselves making speeches. It would prove an almost endless task to enumerate the many new ways to which public speaking was put to service during the War.

One particular difference between the oratory of this War and all those that preceded it, with the partial exception of our Civil War, may be called to mind. Major Pond relates that once when Wendell Phillips faced a hostile and noisy audience he continued in a moderate tone of voice speaking directly to the newspaper reporters in the orchestra just below the platform. The audience, piqued by curiosity, gradually became quiet and tried to hear what he was saying to the reporters. Phillips faced the crowd and said, "Go on, gentlemen, go on. I do not need your ears. Through these pencils I speak to thirty millions of people."

By the time of our own Civil War an orator could speak through the press to many millions. Lincoln's address might cause no great commotion on the field of Gettysburg, but in a little time it had reached the hearts of his countrymen. The publicity given to a speech then is vastly increased now. Viscount Grey's great speech in the British House of Commons, preparing for England's entry into the War, and Bethmann-Hollweg's defense of Germany in the Reichstag were at once read by every thoughtful American, and they influenced the reader in his decision as to the right and wrong of the contending nations. President Wilson's speeches were delivered really before world-wide audiences speaking many languages. The orator must often be conscious of the two audiences one immediate, responsive to gesture and to tone of voice, and the other distant, immense, but reached almost instantaneously through cable and telegraph. What effects this widening audience has on public speaking need not be discussed here. But manifestly the oratory of the World War, while comprising many addresses to small groups on special occasions, when the speaker was in the most intimate and personal relation with his audience, also includes speeches that were really addressed to audiences of enormous size far beyond the reach of the author's voice.

Such of the more important and representative speeches as can be included within the scope of this volume offer many points of interest to both the reader of history and the student of public speaking. This volume supplies a survey of the history of the War. Its causes are set forth in parliamentary addresses from the points of view of the different nations. Its progress may be marked by the exhortations for popular support and the impassioned declarations of purpose and determination. The story of the American participation may be read in speeches made before our entry as well as those made during the War and after the Armistice. The negotiations for peace, causes of so many expectations and disappointments, may be studied through the debate and discussion which they aroused. These pages echo again with the ideals and hopes, the valor and sacrifice, the victories and the deaths of the appalling struggle.

Although a large space is given to speakers of the English tongue, the volume is markedly international in character. Nearly all the nations of Europe, the dominions of the British Empire, China and Japan are represented. And the expression of opinion is unrestricted. Bethmann-Hollweg is heard on the causes of the War as well as Grey and Viviani. Socialism and nationalism, pacificism and imperialism, the supporters and the opponents of the League of Nations, all have their spokesmen. Great commanders speaking to their soldiers, revolutionists proclaiming destruction to an ancient stability, venerable leaders of parliaments and youths the hopes of new nations, all raise their voices in this amazing forum whither it seems as if every human passion had sent its advocate.

The selection of speeches has inevitably been determined partly by the occasions on which they were delivered. Among these are the meetings of the national parliaments to support the declarations of war, the appeals of monarchs or leaders to great public meetings, the receptions of special envoys to foreign nations, the sessions of the Peace Conference in Paris and the Disarmament Conference at Washington. Many of these were historical occasions of such magnitude that they must have lent impressiveness to any words that were spoken. But often the oration met or transcended the occasion, and sometimes the oration made its own opportunity. Such was the case in Cardinal Mercier's great sermon preached in accord with the strict letter of German prohibition, but defying its intention and with his opening sentence storming the hearts of the Belgian audience. A test of the great oratorical power of many of the addresses gathered here may be found in the vividness with which they recall the momentous occasions and crucial decisions of the War.

In the variety as well as in the excellence of these orations the student of public speaking will find considerations worthy of his attention. Here are men of different nationalities, of varied temperaments, with contrasting opinions, discussing the same subject. Here is exposition, debate, eulogy, defiance, appeal and proclamation. Here is Lloyd George putting before a great public audience the causes of the war and ridiculing and denouncing the enemy in a speech, every word of which wins an immediate response. Here is Clemenceau defying and taunting the riotous opposition in the French Deputies, interrupted, overwhelmed for a moment by the cries of both parties, but returning again to reassert his single purpose, to win the war. Here is Wilson, before our Congress, calling the nation to arms in lofty terms of responsibility and duty. The three occasions are very different; the three speakers are worlds apart in qualities of temperament and mind; the three speeches are quite unlike, but there is no question that they are examples of most extraordinary, perhaps unforgettable, eloquence.

In the mere matter of oratorical excellence there is an unfairness in bringing into comparison speakers who can be represented only in translation. But Viviani's fervor by no means disappears in an English dress. His marvelous power of lifting his hearers on the wings of his first paragraph into the high altitudes of emotion and imagination will not be unfelt by the reader of the printed pages. Nor does the harshly phrased but heavily massed argument of Lenine fail in translation to disclose something of his uncompromising personality. Among the speakers native to the English language it is indeed easy for the student of oratorical art to make comparisons. They are all discussing the same subject, often they are expressing similar ideas but never in the same manner. We may find each method of the art of speaking illustrated, each quality of eloquence exemplified, every type of orator represented. Never before and perhaps never again will there be the same opportunity for public speaking as the Great War provided.

We may indeed devoutly hope that oratory will never again be excited by a world war. But the emotions which inspired the best eloquence of this War were those centering upon home, friendship, country, liberty, humanity, justice, and all that is worthiest in civilization. So long as men hold these dear they will find stirring and winged words in these war speeches, words which will not let us forget the tyrannies they denounce, the liberties they exalt or the unknown soldiers whom they commemorate.

CHRONOLOGY OF THE WORLD WAR

1914.

June 28. Archduke Francis Ferdinand and his wife assassinated at Serajevo, Bosnia.

July 23. Austrian note presented at Belgrade.
24. Sir Edward Grey proposed Four-Power mediation in Austro-Serbian conflict.
25. At 6 P. M. Serbian reply given to Austrian Minister who left Belgrade at 6:30 P. M.
Austrian mobilization ordered.
Serbia mobilized.
Russia prepared to mobilize on Austrian frontier.
26. Germany threatened mobilization if Russia did not suspend her military preparations.
28. Austria refused mediation and declared war on Serbia.
29. German Chancellor instructed by Kaiser to offer that Germany would not annex French territory if England remained neutral.
30. Sir Edward Grey repudiated Germany's "infamous proposal."
31. France replied to England's inquiry that she would respect Belgian neutrality; no answer from Germany.
Germany asked whether France would remain neutral; Viviani replied that France would act as her interests dictated.
Russian general mobilization.
Austrian general mobilization.

Aug. 1. Mobilization in Belgium.
General mobilization ordered in France.
Germany declared war on Russia.
2. Germany demanded right of way through Belgium.
3. Sir Edward Grey in Commons defined British attitude.
Belgium rejected Germany's ultimatum.
Germany declared war on France.
4. German troops entered Belgium.
Chancellor in Reichstag announced invasion of Luxembourg and Belgium: "Necessity knows no law."
England declared war on Germany.
5. Austria-Hungary declared war on Russia.
10. France declared war on Austria-Hungary.
12. England declared war on Austria-Hungary.
23. Japan declared war on Germany.

Sept. 6. First Marne battle begun; German advance stopped.

	13.	Battle of the Aisne; Rheims and Soissons, captured by Allies.
Oct.	15.	First battle of Ypres.
Nov.	3.	Dardanelles forts bombarded.

1915.

Mar.	5.	New Dardanelles attack opened.
	10.	Battle of Neuve-Chapelle; British attack.
	22.	Russians took Przemysl, Galicia.
April	22.	Second Battle of Ypres; German attack using asphyxiating gas.
	25.	Allied landing in Gallipoli.
May	7.	*Lusitania* torpedoed and sunk.
	23.	Italy declared war on Austria-Hungary.
June	3.	Przemysl retaken by Germans and Austrians.
Aug.	5.	Germans entered Warsaw.
Sept.	25.	Battle of Loos; French offensive in Champagne.
	15.	Bulgaria declared war on Serbia.

1916.

Jan.	8.	Gallipoli evacuated.
Feb.	21.	Battle of Verdun begun by Germans.
May	24.	Great Battle at Verdun—two armies engaged on whole front.
	31.	Battle of Jutland; Admiral Beatty intercepted German ships.
June	5.	Lord Kitchener and Staff lost on H. M. S. *Hampshire*.
July	1.	Battle of the Somme; Franco-British offensive.
Aug.	6.	Italian offensive on the Isonzo.
Sept.	3.	Great Anglo-French Somme attack.
Oct.	24.	French victory at Verdun.
Dec.	12.	Peace proposals from Germany announced by Chancellor in the Reichstag.
	15.	French victory at Verdun.
	30.	Allies negatived German proposals.

1917.

Feb.	1.	Unrestricted U-boat war begun by Germany.
	3.	U. S. broke diplomatic relations with Germany.
Mar.	12.	Revolution in Russia; provisional government elected.
	15.	Abdication of Czar.
	17.	Allied advance in Somme region.
	19.	German retreat on Cambrai.
April	2.	President Wilson asked Congress to declare that a state of war existed with Germany.
May	18.	President Wilson signed Conscription Act: to raise 500,000 men by selective drafts.
June	7.	First stage of Flanders Battle; British attack. General Pershing, American Commander-in-Chief, arrived in London.
Aug.	20.	French attack at Verdun.

Sept.	8.	Korniloff, dismissed by Kerensky, marched on Petrograd.
	15.	Russia a republic; M. Kerensky, head.
Oct.	23.	Battle of La Malmaison; French victory across Soissons-Laon road.
	24.	Austro-German attack on Isonzo; Italians forced to retreat.
Nov.	7.	Lenine's coup d'état in Petrograd.
Dec.	9.	Fall of Jerusalem to General Allenby.

1918.

Jan.	8.	President Wilson's "14 Points" message to Congress.
Mar.	3.	Soviet Russia signed Peace of Brest-Litovsk with Central Powers.
	21.	German offensive begun: First Assault; Second Battle of the Somme.
	23.	Paris bombed by long range gun.
	28.	General Pershing offered General Foch all available U. S. forces.
April	9.	German offensive; Second Assault.
	14.	General Foch's appointment as Allied Commander-in-Chief in France announced.
	23.	Naval raid on Zeebrugge.
May	1.	Americans on Amiens front near Montdidier.
	27.	German offensive; Third Assault on Aisne front between Soissons and Rheims.
	31.	Americans at Chateau-Thierry.
June	9.	Battle of Noyon; German offensive; Fourth Assault.
	23.	Italians regained the initiative.
		Austrians defeated; pursued by Italians.
	25.	U. S. Marine Brigade's success at Belleau Wood.
July	1.	Americans carried Vaux near Chateau-Thierry.
	15.	German offensive; Fifth Assault; Second Battle of the Marne.
	18.	Allied offensive; First Assault; Battle of Tardenois.
		General Foch's great counter-stroke on 27-mile front; recovery of Chateau-Thierry and Soissons.
Aug.	8.	Allied offensive; Second Assault; Battle of Amiens.
Sept.	2.	Allied offensive; Third Assault.
	12.	Battle of St. Mihiel; Pershing attacked with First American Army.
	19.	British attack in Palestine.
	26.	Battle of Champagne and Argonne; Franco-American attack.
		Battle of Cambrai; Hindenburg line broken.
Oct.	4.	Franco-American advance between Rheims and Verdun.
		German note to President Wilson proposing Armistice.
	9.	Allied attack; fall of Cambrai to the Canadians.
	29.	Italian armies progressed on 30-mile front.
		Allied offensive; Last assault.

Nov. 8. Marshal Foch presented Armistice terms to German delegates.
      9. Kaiser abdicated; Revolution in Berlin.
     11. At 5 A. M. Armistice signed at Rethondes Station. At 11 A. M. fighting ceased all along front.
     17. Allied armies began march to Rhine in accordance with Armistice.
     21. Main installment of German High Sea Fleet surrendered for internment to Admiral Beatty.

1919.

Jan. 18. Paris Conference, opened by Poincaré. Clemenceau permanent President of the Conference.
June 28. Peace signed at Versailles.
Nov. 19. U. S. Senate rejected Peace Treaty.

1920.

Jan. 10. Formal ratification of Peace with Germany in Paris signed by M. Clemenceau, Mr. Lloyd George, Signor Nitti, Mr. Matsui, and German Baron von Lersner. U. S. stood out.

MASTERPIECES
WORLD WAR

I. THE OPENING OF THE WAR

EMPEROR WILLIAM II OF GERMANY

MOSES AND AMALEK

[The following sermon was addressed by the Emperor to his men on board the royal yacht in August 1900. It may be taken as fairly representative of the Kaiser's many speeches—all in the same tone of assurance: "My policy is good and I am in the hands of God as one of His chief instruments." Although this sermon has no direct connection with the World War and though it was delivered fourteen years before its commencement, it may stand as a sample of the German attitude which was really the chief cause of the world conflagration. The elevation of militarism and imperialism as a sort of religion—this is the theme of the sermon and this was the false gospel which led Germany to the war. Following the sermon, we print the ex-Kaiser's address to the German people at the beginning of the war, dated August 6, 1914.

William II, German Emperor and King of Prussia, was born in 1859. He ascended the throne in 1888 and fled from his country to Holland in 1918. The results of his reign are too well known for comment. The Emperor aspired to distinction in many fields; among them, oratory.]

IT is a most impressive picture that our text to-day brings before our souls. Israel wanders through the desert from the Red Sea to Mount Sinai. But suddenly the heathen Amalekites stop them and want to prevent their advance, and a battle ensues. Joshua leads the young men of Israel to the fight, the swords clash together, and a hot and bloody struggle begins in the valley of Rephidim. But, see! whilst the fight is going on, the pious men of God, Moses, Aaron, and Hur, go to the top of the hill. They lift up their hands to heaven; they pray. Down in the valley the fighting hosts; at the top of the mountain the praying men. This is the holy battle picture of our text. Who does not understand to-day what it tells us? Again, a heathenish Amalekite has stirred in distant Asia with great power and much cunning. By burning and murder it is sought to prevent the entrance of European trade and European genius, the triumphal march of Christian morals and Christian faith. Again the command of God has been issued: "Choose us out men, and go out, fight with Amalek." A hot and bloody struggle has begun. Many of our brothers stand already under fire, many are on their way to the enemy's coasts, and you have seen them, the thousands who at the call, "Volunteers to the fore! Who will be the guardian of the Empire?" now assemble, to enter the fight with flying colors. But you, who remain behind at home, who are bound by other sacred duties, say, do you not hear God's call, which He makes to you, and which says to you, "Go up on the mountain; raise up thy hands to the heavens"? The prayer of the just can do much if it be earnest.

Thus let it be. Yonder, far away, the hosts of fighters; here at home, the hosts of praying men. May this be the holy battle picture of our days. May this peaceful morning hour remind us—may it remind us of the sacred duty of intercession, of the sacred power of intercession. The sacred duty of intercession! Certainly it is an enthusiastic moment when a ship with young men on board weighs anchor. Did you not see the warriors' eyes flash? Did you not hear their many-voiced hurrahs? But when the native shores vanish, when one enters the glowing heat of the Red Sea or the heavy waters of the ocean, how easily brightness and enthusiasm grow weary! Certainly it is a sublime moment when, after a long voyage, in the distance the straight lines of the German forts can be seen, and the black, red, and white flags of the German colony become visible, and comrades in arms stand on the shore waiting to give a hearty reception. But the long marches in the burning sun, the long nights of bivouac in the rain! How easily gayety and strength vanish! Certainly it is a longed-for moment when at last the drums beat to the charge and the bugles are blown to advance when a command is given: "Forward! At the enemy!" But then, when amid the roar of the guns and the flashing of the shells, comrades fall to the right and left, and hostile batteries still refuse to yield—how easily at such a moment the bravest hearts begin to tremble!

Christians, in order that our brothers over yonder may remain gay even in the greatest distress, faithful in the most painful duty, courageous in the greatest danger, they want something more than ammunition and sharp weapons—more even than youthful courage and fiery enthusiasm. They want a blessing from above, vital power from above; otherwise, they cannot win and remain victorious. And the heavenly world opens only to prayer. Prayer is the golden key to the treasury of our God. But he who has it has also the promise that to him who asks shall be given. Or shall we remain idle? Woe to us if we are idle whilst they are carrying on a hard and bloody piece of work; woe to us if we only look on curiously at the great struggle! This would be Cain's spirit with the cruel words "Am I my brother's keeper?" This would be unfaithfulness toward our brave brothers who are staking their lives. Never! We will mobilize not only battalions of warriors, but also a holy force of praying men. Yes. How much there is to ask for our brothers going into the field! They are to be the strong arm which punishes assassins. They are to be the mailed fist which strikes in among them. They are to stand up with the sword in their hands for our most sacred possessions. So we shall accompany them with our prayers, out on to the heaving waves, on their marches, into the roar of the battle, and into the peacefulness of the hospitals; shall pray to God that they may stand at their posts like men, that they may fight their battles courageously and heroically, that they may bear their wounds bravely and calmly, that God may give those who die under fire a blessed end and the reward of faithfulness—in short, that He may make the warriors heroes, and the heroes victors, and then bring them home to the land of their fathers with the laurels round their puggarees and the medals on their breasts.

Or do we, perhaps, not believe in the sacred power of intercession? Well, then, what does our text say? "And it came to pass when Moses held up his hand, that Israel prevailed." The earnest prayers of a Moses made the swords of the enemy blunt. They pushed themselves like a wedge between the enemy's lines, made them waver, and brought victory to the flying banners of Israel. Should not our prayers be able to do what the prayers of Moses did? God has not taken back one syllable of His promise; heartfelt prayer can still to-day cast down the dragon banner into the dust and plant the banner of the cross on the walls. And Moses does not stand alone with his intercession. Look yonder. There on the heights of Sodom stands Abraham, interceding before his God, and with his prayers he prays Lot out of the burning city. And should not our prayers succeed in praying our fighting comrades out of the fire of the battles. Look yonder. There in Jerusalem lies the young Christian community on its knees. Their leader, their father, lies imprisoned in a dungeon, and, see, with their prayers they summon the angel of God into the prison, and he leads forth Peter unharmed. And our prayers—should not they have the power even to-day to burst the doors of the oppressed prisoners and the persecuted, and to place an angel at their side? Yes, the God of old lives still, the great Ally rules still, the Holy God who cannot let sin and acts of violence triumph, but will carry on His holy cause against an unholy people; the Almighty God, who can shatter the strongest walls as if they were spider's webs, and who can disperse the greatest crowds like heaps of sand; the merciful, faithful God, whose fatherly heart looks after the well-being of His children, who hears every sigh, and who sympathizes with every distress. Pious prayers open His fatherly hands, and they are filled with blessing. Earnest prayer opens His fatherly heart, and it is full of love. Yes, true, continuous prayer fetches the living God down from heaven and places Him among us. And if God is for us, who shall be against us?

Up in the Tavern there hang strange bells on the heights. No man's hand rings them. Still and dumb they hang in the sunshine. But when the storm winds blow, they begin to swing, and commence to ring, and deep down in the valley their song is heard. God the Lord has hung the prayer bell in every man's heart. In sunshine and happiness how often it hangs still and dumb. But when the stormy winds of distress break forth, then it begins to ring. How many a comrade who has forgotten how to pray will, out yonder, in the fight for life or death, fold his hands again! Distress teaches us to pray, and so shall it also be at home. Let the serious days which

MOSES AND AMALEK

have come upon us, let the war storm which has come on, set the bells ringing again. Let us pray for our fighting brothers. Not only now and then, in a solemn hour. No, no; let us be true in prayer. As our fathers once in war times rang the bells every evening and bared their heads at the sound and prayed, so also let us not forget intercession for a day. Moses held up his hands until the going down of the sun, and Joshua discomfited Amalek and his people with the edge of the sword. Our fight is not brought to an end in a day. But do not let the hands become tired or idle until the victory has been gained. Let our prayers be a fiery wall around the camp of our brothers. How the thought will strengthen them, make them enthusiastic, and excite them, that thousands, nay, millions, at home bear them in their praying hearts! The King of all kings calls volunteers to the fore. Who will be the praying one for the empire? Oh, if one could only say here, "The King called, and all—all came!" Not one of us must be wanting. History will one day describe the fights of these days. But man sees only what he has before him; he can say only what the wisdom of the leaders, the courage of the troops, the sharpness of the weapons, have done. But eternity will sometime reveal still more—it will show how the secret prayers of the believers were a great power in these fights, how the old promise is again fulfilled: "Then they cry unto the Lord in their trouble, and He saveth them out of their distress." And thus, keep to prayer. Amen.

Almighty God, dear Heavenly Father, Thou Lord of Hosts and Ruler of Battles, we raise, praying, our hands to Thee. On Thy heart we lay the thousands of brothers-in-arms, whom Thou thyself hast called to battle. Protect with Thy almighty protection the breasts of our sons. Lead our men to victory. On Thy heart we lay the wounded and sick. Be Thou their comfort and their strength, and heal their wounds which they receive for king and Fatherland. On Thy heart we lay all those whom Thou hast ordained to die on the field of battle. Stand by them in the last struggle, and give them everlasting peace. On Thy heart we lay our people. Preserve, sanctify, increase the enthusiasm with which we are now all imbued. Lord our God, we trust in Thee. Lead Thou us in battle. We boast, Lord, that Thou wilt help us, and in Thy name we unroll the banner. Lord, we will not leave Thee; then wilt Thou bless us. Amen.

ADDRESS TO THE GERMAN PEOPLE

SINCE the founding of the Empire, during a period of forty-three years, it has been my zealous endeavor and the endeavor of my ancestors to preserve peace to the world and in peace to promote our vigorous development. But our enemies envy us the success of our toil. All professed and secret hostility from East and West and from beyond the sea, we have till now borne in the consciousness of our responsibility and power. Now, however, our opponents desire to humble us. They demand that we look on with folded arms while our enemies girt themselves for treacherous attack. They will not tolerate that we support our ally with unshaken loyalty, who fights for its prestige as a great power, and with whose abasement our power and honor are likewise lost. Therefore the sword must decide. In the midst of peace the world attacks us. Therefore up! To arms! All hesitation, all delay were treachery to the Fatherland. It is a question of the existence or non-existence of the Empire which our fathers founded anew. It is the question of the existence or the non-existence of German might and German culture. We shall defend ourselves to the last breath of man and beast. And we shall survive this fight, even though it were against a world of enemies. Never yet was Germany conquered when she was united. Then forward march with God! He will be with us as He was with our fathers.

JEAN JAURÈS

SOCIALISTS AND THE WAR

[The two speeches by Jean Jaurès represent the struggle among the European socialists over the question of war and peace in the last days before mobilization. The first was his last address in France, delivered at Vaise near Lyons, where he spoke in support of the candidacy of a socialist colleague. From Vaise he went to Brussels to attend the great meeting of the International Socialist Bureau where he delivered the last speech of his life on July 29.

Returning from Brussels, Jaurès continued his efforts for peace but upheld the patriotic action of the Government. On the 31st of July, the day of his death, he had just come from an interview with Premier Viviani and had entered a restaurant; while he was dining he was assassinated.

Jean Jaurès was born in 1859. He became professor at Toulouse, and was elected to the French Chamber in 1885. Later, after becoming a socialist, he was returned to the French Chamber, in 1893, and became the chief of the socialist party. Selections from the great debate on socialism between Jean Jaurès and Clemenceau are given in Volume IX of this series. Jean Jaurès is universally regarded as among the greatest of modern orators.]

CITIZENS: I wish to tell you to-night that never have we, never for forty years has Europe, been in a situation more menacing or more tragic than at this moment when I have the responsibility of addressing you. Citizens, I do not wish to exaggerate the somber colors of the picture. I do not wish to say that the break in diplomatic relations between Austria and Serbia, of which we had the news half an hour ago, necessarily signifies that war will break out between them. I do not say that if war comes between Austria and Serbia the conflict will necessarily spread to the rest of Europe. But I do say that we have against us, against peace, against the life of men, at this moment, terrible chances against which the proletarians of Europe must use the efforts of supreme solidarity of which they are capable.

Citizens, the note which Austria has addressed to Serbia is full of threats, and if Austria invades Slavic territory, if the Germans—that is the Germanic people of Austria—do violence to the Serbs who are part of the Slavic world and for whom the Slavs of Russia have deep sympathy, it is to be feared that Russia will enter the conflict. And if Russia intervenes to defend Serbia against Austria, Austria having before her two adversaries, Serbia and Russia, will appeal to the treaty of alliance which unites her with Germany. And Germany makes it known through her ambassadors to all the powers that she will unite with Austria. And if the conflict does not rest between Austria and Serbia, if Russia joins in, Austria will see Germany appear on the field of battle by her side. But then it will no longer be only the treaty of alliance between Austria and Germany which will enter into play, but also the secret treaty, the essential clauses of which are nevertheless known, which binds Russia and France. Russia will say to France, "I have against me two opponents, Germany and Austria, I have the right to appeal to the treaty which unites us. France must take her place at my side." At this moment we are, perhaps, on the eve of the day when Austria will throw herself upon the Serbs, and then with Austria and Germany attacking the Serbs and the Russians, Europe will be in flames, the world ablaze.

In an hour so grave, so full of peril for all of us, for all countries, I do not wish to delay to search out responsibilities at length. We have ours, Moutet says so and I declare in the face of history that we foresaw them, that we foretold them; when we said that to enter Maroc with arms would be to open to Europe an era of ambition, of covetousness and of conflict, we were denounced as unpatriotic; and it is we who were looking out for France.

That, alas, is our part of the responsibility and it becomes definite when you consider that it is the question of Bosnia-Herzegovina that is the occasion of the struggle between Austria and Serbia, and that we French, when Austria annexed Bosnia, had neither the right nor the means to offer her the least remonstrance because we were occupied in Maroc and were forced to obtain pardon for our own sin by pardoning the sins of others.

And therefore our Minister of Foreign Affairs said to Austria, "We will allow you Bosnia on condition that you allow us Maroc." And we carried our offers of penitence from power to power, from nation to nation. We said to Italy, "You may go into Tripoli since I am in Maroc; you may rob the other end of the street since I have robbed this end."

Each nation appeared across the streets of Europe torch in hand, and now we see the flames. Citizens, we have our share of responsibility, but it does not hide the responsibility of others and it is our right and our duty to denounce the deceit and brutality of German diplomacy.

The duplicity of Russian diplomacy! The Russians who may perhaps side with the Serbs against Austria and who may say, "My heart as a great Slavic nation cannot allow the little

Slavic nation of Serbia to suffer violence!" Yes, but what struck Serbia to the heart? When Russia intervened in the Balkans in 1877, and when she created so-called independent Bulgaria, with the thought of keeping hold of her, she said to Austria, "Let me do as I please and I will intrust you with the administration of Bosnia-Herzegovina." Administration—you understand what that means among diplomats, and from the day when Austria received the order to administer Bosnia-Herzegovina, she has had but one thought—to administer Bosnia-Herzegovina to the best of her own interests.

At the interview which the Russian Minister of Foreign Affairs had with the Austrian Minister of Foreign Affairs, Russia said to Austria, "I authorize you to annex Bosnia-Herzegovina on condition that you permit me to establish an outlet on the Black Sea, near Constantinople." M. de Aehrenthal made a sign which Russia interpreted as an affirmative, and she authorized Austria to take Bosnia-Herzegovina. Then when Bosnia was in Austria's pocket Russia said to her, "It is my turn now, on the Black Sea." "What? I said nothing at all to you." And since then there has been the quarrel between Russia and Austria, between M. Iswolsky, Russian Minister of Foreign Affairs, and M. de Aehrenthal, Austrian Minister of Foreign Affairs. But Russia was Austria's accomplice in delivering the Slavs of Bosnia-Herzegovina into Austria's hands, thereby wounding the Slavs of Serbia to the heart.

That is what draws her into her present position.

If for thirty years, if since she has had the administration of Bosnia, Austria had done well by the people, there would be no difficulties in Europe to-day. But the Austrian clergy tyrannized over Bosnia-Herzegovina and roused the discontent of the people in trying to convert them to Catholicism by force, by persecuting them for their beliefs.

The colonial policy of France, the deceit of Russia, and the brutal will of Austria have contributed to create the present horrible state of affairs. Europe struggles as in a nightmare.

Citizens, in the obscurity which surrounds us, in our present deep uncertainty as to the future, I do not wish to make any rash statement. I still hope in spite of everything that because of the enormity of the disaster which threatens us, the governments will recover themselves at the last minute and that we need not tremble with horror at the thought of the disaster which a European war would bring upon mankind.

You have seen the Balkan War when almost an entire army fell either on the field of battle or in the hospitals. An army went out numbering three hundred thousand men, and left on the battlefields, in ditches along the roads or in the hospitals, infected with typhus, a hundred thousand out of the three hundred thousand.

Consider what would be the disaster for Europe. It would no longer be, as in the Balkans, an army of three hundred thousand, but four, five and six armies of two million men. What disaster, what massacre, what ruin, what barbarity! And that is why with the cloud of the storm already upon us, I still hope that the crime will not be accomplished. Citizens, if the tempest should break, we socialists would take care to save ourselves as quickly as possible from the crime committed by the authorities, and meanwhile if we still have a few hours left we shall redouble our efforts to ward off the disaster. Already in *Vorwaerts* our German socialist comrades rise in indignation against Austria's note and I believe that a meeting of our International Socialist Bureau is called.

Whatever may happen, citizens, and I say these things in a sort of despair, at this moment when we are threatened with murder and savagery, there is but one chance to preserve the peace and safety of civilization—that is for the proletariat to gather all its forces, which include a great number of brothers, and for all proletarians, French, English, German, Italian and Russian, to demand that these millions of men unite so that the unanimous beating of their hearts may ward off the nightmare.

I should be ashamed, citizens, if there were one among you who thought that I seek to turn the drama of events to the profit of an electoral victory, however precious that might be. But I have the right to tell you that it is our duty, the duty of all of you not to neglect a single occasion to show that you are with the International Socialist party which represents at this hour, in the shadow of the storm, the sole promise of a possibility of peace or of the reëstablishment of peace.

LAST SPEECH

[Speech given at Brussels on July 29, 1914, at a meeting of the International Socialist Bureau. This was the last speech of Jean Jaurès. The audience, which was composed of thousands of persons belonging to all classes of society, rose to their feet, waved their hats and applauded the speaker for more than five minutes.]

THE diplomats negotiate. It seems that they will be satisfied to take from Serbia a little of its blood. We have, therefore, a little rest to insure peace. But to what lessons is Europe submitted? After twenty centuries of Christianity, after one hundred years of the triumph of the rights of men, how is it possible that millions of persons, without knowing why, can kill each other?

And Germany? If she knew of the Austrian note it is inexcusable to have allowed such a step. And if official Germany did not know of the Austrian note what is her governmental wisdom? You have a contract which binds you and drags you into war and you don't know why you have been dragged? I ask, what people have given such an example of anarchy? [Applause.]

Nevertheless the authorities hesitate. Let us profit thereby and organize. For us, socialists, our duty is simple. We do not need to impose upon our government a policy of peace; our government is practicing it. I, who have never hesitated to bring upon my head the hatred of our patriots by my obstinate will and by my desire to bring about a Franco-German understanding, have the right to say that the French government desires peace. [Applause.]

The French government is the best ally for peace of the English government which has taken the initiative in conciliation and gives Russia advice of prudence and patience. As for us, it is our duty to insist that the government shall speak to Russia with force so that she will refrain. If unfortunately Russia pays no heed, it is our duty to say, "We know of but one treaty; the treaty which binds us to the human race." [Applause.]

This is our duty, and in expressing it we find ourselves in accord with our German comrades who demand that their government see to it that Austria moderates her acts. It is possible that the telegram of which I spoke is due partly to that desire of the German workers. One cannot go against the wish of four millions of enlightened consciences.

Do you know what the proletarians are? They are the men who have collectively an affection for peace and a horror of war. The chauvinists, the nationalists, are men who have collectively a love for war and slaughter. When, however, they feel over their heads the menace of conflicts and wars which may put an end to their capitalistic existence, then they remind themselves that they have friends who seek to reduce the storm. But for the supreme masters, the ground is mined. In the drunkenness of the first battles they will succeed in pulling along the masses. But gradually as disease completes the work of the shells, as death and misery strike, these men will turn to German, French, Russian, Austrian and Italian authorities and demand what reasons they can give for all the corpses. And then revolution let loose will say, "Go and beg grace from God and man."

SIR EDWARD (now Viscount) GREY

ENGLAND'S POSITION

[Speech in the House of Commons on August 3, 1914.

The following address by Sir Edward Grey, Secretary of State for Foreign Affairs, sets forth the circumstances and causes which led Great Britain into the World War. Sir Edward had made every effort to preserve peace with Europe and his public statement in the House of Commons was awaited with the utmost interest throughout the world. The London *Times* of the following day contained this editorial comment:

"Yesterday the House of Commons was at its best. It rose to the crisis which has been forced upon the nation and empire with a dignity and sagacity that at historic moments belong to the Mother of Parliaments. Grey rose to make his statement—destined to remain memorable in the history of the world. The cheers which greeted him showed how complete is the confidence he has won from men of all parties and opinions. The House felt as the country and empire will feel

EDWARD GREY

to-day, that when so tried and trusted an advocate of peace intimates that, at the bidding of our most vital interests no less than of our obligations to others, we may be forced to draw sword, the necessity which constrains us must indeed be inexorable. All remains of doubt and hesitation vanished as he explained, with a sincerity of pathos more effective than any eloquence, how his efforts to solve the present difference had been baffled. Papers to be laid down will prove how strenuous, how genuine, how whole-hearted have been our labors in the cause of peace."

Edward Grey, first Viscount of Fallodon, was born in 1862. He went to Winchester and then Balliol College, Oxford. From 1892-95 he was Under-Secretary for Foreign Affairs; Member of Parliament for Berwick-on-Tweed from 1885-1916; Secretary of State for Foreign Affairs 1905-16; Temporary Ambassador to the United States 1919.]

LAST week I stated that we were working for peace not only for this country, but to preserve the peace of Europe. To-day events move so rapidly that it is exceedingly difficult to state with technical accuracy the actual state of affairs, but it is clear that the peace of Europe cannot be preserved. Russia and Germany, at any rate, have declared war upon each other.

Before I proceed to state the position of His Majesty's Government, I would like to clear the ground so that, before I come to state to the House what our attitude is with regard to the present crisis, the House may know exactly under what obligations the Government is, or the House can be said to be, in coming to a decision on the matter. First of all let me say, very shortly, that we have consistently worked with a single mind, with all the earnestness in our power, to preserve peace. The House may be satisfied on that point. We have always done it. During these last years as far as His Majesty's Government are concerned, we would have no difficulty in adjusting their points of view. It took much time and labor and discussion before they could settle their differences, but peace was secured, because peace was their main object, and they were willing to give time and trouble rather than accentuate differences rapidly.

In the present crisis, it has not been possible to secure the peace of Europe; because there has been little time, and there has been a disposition—at any rate in some quarters on which I will not dwell—to force things rapidly to an issue, at any rate, to the great risk of peace, and, as we now know, the result of that is that the policy of peace, as far as the Great Powers are concerned, is in danger. I do not want to dwell on that, and to comment on it, and to say where the blame seems to lie, which Powers were most in favor of peace, which were most disposed to risk or endanger peace, because I would like the House to approach this crisis in which we are now, from the point of view of British interests, British honor, and British obligations, free from all passion as to why peace has not been preserved.

We shall publish Papers as soon as we can regarding what took place last week when we were working for peace; and when those Papers are published, I have no doubt that to every human being they will make it clear how strenuous and genuine and whole-hearted our efforts for peace were, and that they will enable people to form their own judgment as to what forces were at work which operated against peace.

I come first, now, to the question of British obligations. I have assured the House—and the Prime Minister has assured the House more than once—that if any crisis such as this arose, we should come before the House of Commons and be able to say to the House that it was free to decide what the British attitude should be, that we would have no secret engagement which we should spring upon the House, and tell the House that, because we had entered into that engagement, there was an obligation of honor upon the country. I will deal with that point to clear the ground first.

There have been in Europe two diplomatic groups, the Triple Alliance and what came to be called the "Triple Entente," for some years past. The Triple Entente was not an Alliance—it was a diplomatic group. The House will remember that in 1908 there was a crisis, also a Balkan crisis, originating in the annexation of Bosnia and Herzegovina. The Russian Minister, M. Iswolsky came to London, or happened to come to London, because his visit was planned before the crisis broke out. I told him definitely then, this being a Balkan crisis, a Balkan affair, I did not consider that public opinion in this country would justify us in promising to give anything more than diplomatic support. More was never asked from us, more was never given, and more was never promised.

In this present crisis, up till yesterday, we have also given no promise of anything more than diplomatic support—up till yesterday no promise of more than diplomatic support. Now I must make this question of obligation clear to the House. I must go back to the first Moroccan crisis of 1906. That was the time of the Algeciras Conference, and it came at a time of very great difficulty to His Majesty's Government when a General Election was in progress, and Ministers were scattered over the country, and I—spending three days a week in my constituency and three days at the Foreign Office—was asked the question whether if that crisis developed into war between France and Germany we would give armed support. I said then that I could promise nothing to any foreign Power unless it was subsequently to receive the whole-hearted support of public opinion here if the occasion arose. I said, in my opinion, if war was forced upon France then on the question of Morocco—a question which had just been the subject of agreement between this country and France, an agreement exceedingly popular on both sides—that if out of that agreement war was forced on France at that time, in my view public opinion in this contry would have rallied to the material support of France.

I gave no promise, but I expressed that opinion during the crisis, as far as I remember, almost in the same words, to the French Ambassador and the German Ambassador at the time. I made no promise, and I used no threats; but I expressed that opinion. That position was accepted by the French Government, but they said to me at the time—and I think very reasonably—"If you think it possible that the public opinion of Great Britain might, should a sudden crisis arise, justify you in giving to France the armed support which you cannot promise in advance, you will not be able to give that support, even if you wish to give it, when the time comes, unless some conversations have already taken place between naval and military experts." There was force in that. I agreed to it, and authorized those conservations to take place, but on the distinct understanding that nothing which passed between military or naval experts should bind either Government or restrict in any way their freedom to make a decision as to whether or not they would give that support when the time arose.

As I have told the House, upon that occasion a General Election was in prospect. I had to take the responsibility of doing that without the Cabinet. It could not be summoned. An answer had to be given. I consulted, I remember, Lord Haldane, who was then Secretary of State for War, and the present Prime Minister, who was then Chancellor of the Exchequer. That was the most I could do, and they authorized that on the distinct understanding that it left the hands of the Government free whenever the crisis arose. The fact that conversations between military and naval experts took place was later on—I think much later on, because that crisis passed, and the thing ceased to be of importance, but later on it was brought to the knowledge of the Cabinet.

The Agadir crisis came—another Morocco crisis—and throughout that I took precisely the same line that had been taken in 1906. But subsequently, in 1912, after discussion and consideration in the Cabinet it was decided that we ought to have a definite understanding in writing, which was to be only in the form of an unofficial letter, that these conversations which took place were not binding upon the freedom of either Government; and on the 22nd of November, 1912, I wrote to the French Ambassador the letter which I will now read to the House, and I received from him a letter in similar terms in reply. The letter which I will read to the House is this, and it will be known to the public now as the record that, whatever took place between military and naval experts, they were not binding engagements upon the Government:—

"*My dear Ambassador.*—From time to time in recent years the French and British naval and military experts have consulted together. It has always been understood that such consultation does not restrict the freedom of either Government to decide at any future time whether or not to assist the other by armed force. We have agreed that consultation between experts is not and ought not to be regarded as an engagement that commits either Government to action in a contingency that has not yet arisen and may never arise. The disposition, for instance, of the French and British Fleets respectively at the present moment is not based upon an engagement to coöperate in war.

"You have, however, pointed out that, if either Government had grave reason to expect an unprovoked attack by a third Power, or something that threatened the general peace, it should immediately discuss with the other whether both Governments should act together to prevent aggression and to preserve peace, and if so, what measures they would be prepared to take in common."

Lord Charles Beresford: What is the date of that?

Sir E. Grey: The 22nd November, 1912. That is the starting point for the Government with regard to the present crisis. I think it makes it clear that what the Prime Minister and I said to the House of Commons was perfectly justified, and that, as regards our freedom to decide in a crisis what our line should be, whether we would intervene or whether we should abstain, the Government remained perfectly free and, *a fortiori,* the House of Commons remains perfectly free. That I say to clear the ground from the point of view of obligation. I think it was due to prove our good faith to the House of Commons that I should give that full information to the House now, and say what I think is obvious from the letter I have just read, that we do not construe anything which has previously taken place in our diplomatic relations with other Powers in this matter as restricting the freedom of the Government to decide what attitude they should take now, or restrict the freedom of the House of Commons to decide what their attitude should be.

Well, Sir, I will go further, and I will say this: The situation in the present crisis is not precisely the same as it was in the Morocco question. In the Morocco question it was primarily a dispute which concerned France—a dispute which concerned France and France primarily—a dispute, as it seemed to us, affecting France, out of an agreement subsisting between us and France, and published to the whole world, in which we engaged to give France diplomatic support. No doubt we were pledged by a definite public agreement to stand with France diplomatically in that question.

The present crisis has originated differently. It has not originated with regard to Morocco. It has not originated as regards anything with which we had a special agreement with France; it has not originated with anything which primarily concerned France. It has originated in a dispute between Austria and Servia. I can say this with the most absolute confidence—no government and no country has less desire to be involved in war over a dispute between Austria and Servia than the Government and the country of France. They are involved in it because of their obligation of honor under a definite alliance with Russia. Well, it is only fair to say to the House that that obligation of honor cannot apply in the same way to us. We are not parties to the Franco-Russian Alliance. We do not even know the terms of that Alliance. So far I have, I think, faithfully and completely cleared the ground with regard to the question of obligation.

I now come to what we think the situation requires of us. For many years we have had a long-standing friendship with France. I remember well the feeling in the House—and my own feeling—for I spoke on the subject, I think, when the late Government made their agreement with France—the warm and cordial feeling resulting from the fact that these two nations, who had had perpetual differences in the past, had cleared these differences away. I remember saying, I think, that it seemed to me that some benign influence had been at work to produce the cordial atmosphere that had made that possible. But how far that friendship entails obligation—it has been a friendship between the nations and ratified by the nations. How far that entails an obligation let every man look into his own heart, and his own feelings, and construe the extent of the obligation for himself. I construe it myself as I feel it, but I do not wish to urge upon anyone else more than their feelings dictate as to what they should feel about the obligation. The House, individually and collectively may judge for itself. I speak my personal view, and I have given the House my own feeling in the matter.

The French fleet is now in the Mediterranean, and the northern and western coasts of France are absolutely undefended. The French fleet being concentrated in the Mediterranean the situation is very different from what it used to be, because the friendship which has grown up between the two countries had given them a sense of security that there was nothing to be feared from us. The French coasts are absolutely undefended. The French fleet is in the Mediterranean, and has for some years been concentrated there because of the feeling of confidence and friendship which has existed between the two countries. My own feeling is that if a foreign fleet engaged in a war which France had not sought, and in which she had not been the aggressor, came down the English Channel and bombarded and battered the undefended coasts of France, we could not stand aside and see this going on practically within sight of our eyes, with our arms folded, looking on dispassionately, doing nothing! I believe that would be the feeling of this country. There are times when one feels that if these circumstances actually did arise, it would be a feeling which would spread with irresistible force throughout the land.

But I also want to look at the matter without sentiment, and from the point of view of British interests, and it is on that that I am going to base and justify what I am presently going to say to the House. If we say nothing at this moment, what is France to do with her fleet in the Mediterranean? If she leaves it there, with no statement from us as to what we will do, she leaves her northern and western coasts absolutely undefended, at the mercy of a German fleet coming down the Channel, to do as it pleases in a war which is a war of life and death between them. If we say nothing, it may be that the French fleet is withdrawn from the Mediterranean. We are in the presence of a European conflagation; can anybody set limits to the consequences that may arise out of it? Let us assume that to-day we stand aside in an attitude of neutrality, saying, "No, we cannot undertake and engage to help either party in this conflict." Let us suppose the French fleet is withdrawn from the Mediterranean; and let us assume that the consequences—which are already tremendous in what has happened in Europe even to countries which are at peace—in fact equally whether countries are at peace or at war—let us assume that out of that come consequences unforeseen, which make it necessary at a sudden moment that, in defense of vital British interests, we should go to war: and let us assume —which is quite possible—that Italy, who is now neutral, because, as I understand, she considers that this war is an aggressive war, and the Triple Alliance being a defensive alliance her obligation did not arise—let us assume that consequences which are not yet foreseen—and which perfectly legitimately consulting her own interests—make Italy depart from her attitude of neutrality at a time when we are forced in defense of vital British interests ourselves to fight, what then will be the position in the Mediterranean? It might be that at some critical moment those consequences would be forced upon us because our trade routes in the Mediterranean might be vital to this country?

Nobody can say that in the course of the next few weeks there is any particular trade route, the keeping open of which may not be vital to this country. What will be our position then? We have not kept a fleet in the Mediterranean which is equal to dealing alone with a combination of other fleets in the Mediterranean. It would be the very moment when we could not detach more ships to the Mediterranean, and we might have exposed this country from our negative attitude at the present moment to the most appalling risk. I say that from the point of view of British interests. We feel strongly that France was entitled to know—and to know at once!—whether or not in the event of attack upon her unprotected northern and western coasts she could depend upon British support. In that emergency, and in these compelling circumstances, yesterday afternoon I gave to the French Ambassador the following statement:

"I am authorized to give an assurance that if the German Fleet comes into the Channel or through the North Sea to undertake hostile operations against the French coasts or shipping, the British Fleet will give all the protection in its power. This assurance is, of course, subject to the policy of His Majesty's Government receiving the support of Parliament, and must not be taken as binding His Majesty's Government to take any action until the above contingency of action by the German Fleet takes place."

I read that to the House, not as a declaration of war on our part, not as entailing immediate aggressive action on our part, but as binding us to take aggressive action should that contingency arise. Things move very hurriedly from hour to hour. Fresh news comes in, and I cannot give this in any very formal way; but I understand that the German Government would be prepared, if we would pledge ourselves to neutrality, to agree that its fleet would not attack the northern coast of France. I have only heard that shortly before I came to the House, but it is far too narrow an engagement for us. And, Sir, there is the more serious consideration—becoming more serious every hour—there is the question of the neutrality of Belgium.

ENGLAND'S POSITION

I shall have to put before the House at some length what is our position in regard to Belgium. The governing factor is the Treaty of 1839, but this is a Treaty with a history—a history accumulated since. In 1870, when there was war between France and Germany, the question of the neutrality of Belgium arose, and various things were said. Amongst other things, Prince Bismarck gave an assurance to Belgium that, confirming his verbal assurance, he gave in writing a declaration which he said was superfluous in reference to the Treaty in existence—that the German Confederation and its allies would respect the neutrality of Belgium, it being always understood that that neutrality would be respected by the other belligerent Powers. That is valuable as a recognition in 1870 on the part of Germany of the sacredness of these Treaty rights.

What was our own attitude? The people who laid down the attitude of the British Government were Lord Granville in the House of Lords, and Mr. Gladstone in the House of Commons. Lord Granville, on the 8th of August, 1870, used these words. He said:—

"We might have explained to the country and to foreign nations that we did not think this country was bound either morally or internationally or that its interests were concerned in the maintenance of the neutrality of Belgium. Though this course might have had some conveniences, though it might have been easy to adhere to it, though it might have saved us from some immediate danger, it is a course which Her Majesty's Government thought it impossible to adopt in the name of the country with any due regard to the country's honour or to the country's interests."

Mr. Gladstone spoke as follows two days later:—

"There is, I admit, the obligation of the Treaty. It is not necessary, nor would time permit me, to enter into the complicated question of the nature of the obligations of that Treaty; but I am not able to subscribe to the doctrine of those who have held in this House what plainly amounts to an assertion, that the simple fact of the existence of a guarantee is binding on every party to it, irrespectively altogether of the particular position in which it may find itself at the time when the occasion for acting on the guarantee arises. The great authorities upon foreign policy to whom I have been accustomed to listen, such as Lord Aberdeen and Lord Palmerston, never to my knowledge took that rigid and, if I may venture to say so, that impracticable view of the guarantee. The circumstance that there is already an existing guarantee in force is of necessity an important fact, and a weighty element in the case to which we are bound to give full and ample consideration. There is also this further consideration, the force of which we must all feel most deeply, and that is, the common interests against the unmeasured aggrandisement of any Power whatever."

The Treaty is an old Treaty—1839—and that was the view taken of it in 1870. It is one of those Treaties which are founded, not only on consideration for Belgium, which benefits under the Treaty, but in the interests of those who guarantee the neutrality of Belgium. The honor and interests are, at least, as strong to-day as in 1870, and we cannot take a more narrow view or a less serious view of our obligations, and of the importance of those obligations, than was taken by Mr. Gladstone's Government in 1870.

I will read to the House what took place last week on this subject. When mobilization was beginning, I knew that this question must be a most important element in our policy—a most important subject for the House of Commons. I telegraphed at the same time in similar terms to both Paris and Berlin to say that it was essential for us to know whether the French and German Governments respectively were prepared to undertake an engagement to respect the neutrality of Belgium. These are the replies. I got from the French Government this reply:—

"The French Government are resolved to respect the neutrality of Belgium, and it would only be in the event of some other Power violating that neutrality that France might find herself under the necessity, in order to assure the defense of her security, to act otherwise. This assurance has been given several times. The President of the Republic spoke of it to the King of the Belgians, and the French Minister at Brussels has spontaneously renewed the assurance to the Belgian Minister of Foreign Affairs to-day."

From the German Government the reply was:—

"The Secretary of State for Foreign Affairs could not possibly give an answer before consulting the Emperor and the Imperial Chancellor."

Sir Edward Goschen, to whom I had said it was important to have an answer soon, said he hoped the answer would not be too long delayed. The German Minister for Foreign Affairs then gave Sir Edward Goschen to understand that he rather doubted whether they could answer at all, as any reply they might give could not fail, in the event of war, to have the undesirable effect of disclosing, to a certain extent, part of their plan of campaign. I telegraphed at the same time to Brussels to the Belgian Government, and I got the following reply from Sir Francis Villiers:—

"The Minister for Foreign Affairs thanks me for the communication, and replies that Belgium will, to the utmost of her power, maintain neutrality, and expects and desires other Powers to observe and uphold it. He begged me to add that the relations between Belgium and the neighbouring Powers were excellent, and there was no reason to suspect their intentions, but that the Belgian Government believed, in the case of violation, they were in a position to defend the neutrality of their country."

It now appears from the news I have received to-day—which has come quite recently, and I am not yet quite sure how far it has reached me in an accurate form—that an ultimatum has been given to Belgium by Germany, the object of which was to offer Belgium friendly relations with Germany on condition that she would facilitate the passage of German troops through Belgium. Well, Sir, until one has these things absolutely definitely, up to the last moment, I do not wish to say all that one would say if one were in a position to give the House full, complete, and absolute information upon the point. We were sounded in the course of last week as to whether if a guarantee were given that, after the war, Belgian integrity would be preserved that would content us. We replied that we could not bargain away whatever interests or obligations we had in Belgian neutrality.

Shortly before I reached the House I was informed that the following telegram had been received from the King of the Belgians by our king—King George:—

"Remembering the numerous proofs of your Majesty's friendship and that of your predecessors, and the friendly attitude of England in 1870, and the proof of friendship she has just given us again, I make a supreme appeal to the diplomatic intervention of your Majesty's Government to safeguard the integrity of Belgium."

Diplomatic intervention took place last week on our part. What can diplomatic intervention do now? We have great and vital interests in the independence—and integrity is the least part—of Belgium. If Belgium is compelled to submit to allow her neutrality to be violated, of course the situation is clear. Even if by agreement she admitted the violation of her neutrality, it is clear she could only do so under duress. The smaller states in that region of Europe ask but one thing. Their one desire is that they should be left alone and independent. The one thing they fear is, I think, not so much that their integrity but that their independence should be interfered with. If in this war which is before Europe the neutrality of one of those countries is violated, if the troops of one of the combatants violate its neutrality and no action can be taken to resent it, at the end of the war, whatever the integrity may be, the independence will be gone.

I have one further quotation from Mr. Gladstone as to what he thought about the independence of Belgium. It will be found in "Hansard," Volume 203, Page 1787. I have not had time to read the whole speech and verify the context, but the things seems to me so clear that no context could make any difference to the meaning of it. Mr. Gladstone said:—

"We have an interest in the independence of Belgium which is wider than that which we may have in the literal operation of the guarantee. It is found in the answer to the question whether under the circumstances of the case this country, endowed as it is with influence and power, would quietly stand by and witness the perpetration of the direst crime that ever stained the pages of history, and thus become participators in the sin."

No, Sir, if it be the case that there has been anything in the nature of an ultimatum to Belgium, asking her to compromise or violate her neutrality, whatever may have been offered to her in return, her independence is gone if that holds. If her independence goes, the independence of Holland will follow. I ask the House from the point of view of British interests, to consider what may be at stake. If France is beaten in a struggle of life and death, beaten to her knees, loses her position as a great Power, becomes subordinate to the will and power of one greater than herself—consequences which I do not anticipate, because I am sure that France has the power to defend herself with all the energy and ability and patriotism which she has shown so often—still, if that were to happen, and if Belgium fell under the same dominating influence, and then Holland, and then Denmark, then would not Mr. Gladstone's words come true, that just opposite to us there would be a common interest against the unmeasured aggrandizement of any Power.

It may be said, I suppose, that we might stand aside, husband our strength, and whatever happened in the course of this war, at the end of it intervene with effect to put things right, and to adjust them to our own point of view. If, in a crisis like this, we run away from those obligations of honor and interest as regards the Belgian Treaty, I doubt whether, whatever material force we might have at the end, it would be of very much value in face of the respect that we should have lost. And I do not believe, whether a great Power stands outside this war or not, it is going to be in a position at the end of it to exert its superior strength. For us, with a powerful fleet, which we believe able to protect our commerce, to protect our shores, and to protect our interests, if we are engaged in war, we shall suffer but little more than we shall suffer even if we stand aside.

We are going to suffer, I am afraid, terribly in this war whether we are in it or whether we stand aside. Foreign trade is going to stop, not because the trade routes are closed, but because there is no trade at the other end. Continental nations engaged in war—all their populations, all their energies, all their wealth, engaged in a desperate struggle—they cannot carry on the trade with us that they are carrying on in times of peace, whether we are parties to the war or whether we are not. I do not believe for a moment, that at the end of this war, even if we stood aside and remained aside, we should be in a position, a material position, to use our force decisively to undo what had happened in the course of the war to prevent the whole of the West of Europe opposite to us—if that had been the result of the war—falling under the domination of a single Power, and I am quite sure that our moral position would be such as to have lost us all respect. I can only say that I have put the question of Belgium somewhat hypothetically, because I am not yet sure of all the facts, but, if the facts turn out to be as they have reached us at present, it is quite clear that there is an obligation on this country to do its utmost to prevent the consequences to which those facts will lead if they are undisputed.

I have read to the House the only engagements that we have yet taken definitely with regard to the use of force. I think it is due to the House to say that we have taken no engagement yet with regard to sending an Expeditionary armed force out of the country. Mobilization of the Fleet has taken place; mobilization of the Army is taking place; but we have as yet taken no engagement, because I do feel that in the case of a European conflagration such as this, unprecedented, with our enormous responsibilities in India and other parts of the Empire, or in countries in British occupation, with all the unknown factors, we must take very carefully into consideration the use which we make of sending an Expeditionary Force out of the country until we know how we stand.

One thing I would say, the one bright spot in the whole of this terrible situation is Ireland. The general feeling throughout Ireland—and I would like this to be clearly understood abroad—does not make the Irish question a consideration which we feel we have now to take into account. I have told the House how far we have at present gone in commitments and the conditions which influence our policy and I have put to the House and dwelt at length upon how vital is the condition of the neutrality of Belgium.

What other policy is there before the House? There is but one way in which the Government could make certain at the present moment of keeping outside this war, and that would be that it should immediately issue a proclamation of unconditional neutrality. We cannot do that. We have made the commitment to France that I have read to the House which prevents us from doing that. We have got the consideration of Belgium which prevents us also from any unconditional neutrality, and, without those conditions absolutely satisfied and satisfactory, we are bound not to shrink from proceeding to the use of all the forces in our power. If we did take that line by saying, "We will have nothing whatever to do with this matter" under any conditions—the Belgian treaty obligations, the possible position in the Mediterranean, with damage to British interests, and what may happen to France from our failure to support France—if we were to say that all those things mattered nothing, were as nothing, and to say we would stand aside, we should, I believe, sacrifice our respect and good name and reputation before the world, and should not escape the most serious and grave economic consequences.

My object has been to explain the view of the Government, and to place before the House the issue and the choice. I do not for a moment conceal, after what I have said, and after the information, incomplete as it is, that I have given to the House with regard to Belgium, that we must be prepared, and we are prepared for the consequences of having to use all the strength we have at any moment—we know not how soon—to defend ourselves and to take our part. We know, if the facts all be as I have stated them, though I have announced no intending aggressive action on our part, no final decision to resort to force at a moment's notice, until we know the whole of the case, that the use of it may be forced upon us. As far as the forces of the Crown are concerned, we are ready. I believe the Prime Minister and my right honorable friend the First Lord of the Admiralty have no doubt whatever that the readiness and the efficiency of those Forces were never at a higher mark than they are to-day, and never was there a time when confidence was more justified in the power of the Navy to protect our commerce and to protect our shores. The thought is with us always of the suffering and misery entailed from which no country in Europe will escape and from which no abdication or neutrality will save us. The amount of harm that can be done by an enemy ship to our trade is infinitesimal, compared with the amount of harm that must be done by the economic condition that is caused on the Continent.

The most awful responsibility is resting upon the Government in deciding what to advise the House of Commons to do. We have disclosed our mind to the House of Commons. We have disclosed the issue, the information which we have, and made clear to the House, I trust, that we are prepared to face that situation, and that should it develop, as probably it may develop, we will face it. We worked for peace up to the last moment, and beyond the last moment. How hard, how persistently, and how earnestly we strove for peace last week, the House will see from the Papers that will be before it.

But that is over, as far as the peace of Europe is concerned. We are now face to face with a situation and all the consequences which it may yet have to unfold. We believe we shall have the support of the House at large in proceeding to whatever the consequences may be and whatever measures may be forced upon us by the development of facts or action taken by others. I believe the country, so quickly has the situation been forced upon it, has not had time to realize the issue. It perhaps is still thinking of the quarrel between Austria and Servia, and not the complications of this matter which have grown out of the quarrel between Austria and Servia. Russia and Germany we know are at war. We do not yet know officially that Austria, the ally whom Germany is to support, is yet at war with Russia. We know that a good deal has been happening on the French frontier. We do not know that the German Ambassador has left Paris.

The situation has developed so rapidly that technically, as regards the condition of the war, it is most difficult to describe what has actually happened. I wanted to bring out the underlying issues which would affect our own conduct, and our own policy, and to put them clearly. I have put the vital facts before the House, and if, as seems not improbable, we are forced, and rapidly forced, to take our stand upon those issues, then I believe, when the country realizes what is at stake, what the real issues are, the magnitude of the impending dangers in the West of Europe, which I have endeavored to describe to the House, we shall be supported throughout, not only by the House of Commons, but by the determination, the resolution, the courage, and the endurance of the whole country.

JOHN REDMOND

IRELAND AND THE WAR

[Speech in the House of Commons on August 3, 1914.
The speech of Sir Edward Grey, explaining the causes leading to the War, was followed by speeches, pledging support, by Mr. Bonar Law, Leader of the Opposition, and by Mr. John Redmond. Mr. Bonar Law, among other things, said: "Not a single member in this House doubts that not only the right honorable gentleman himself, but also the Government he represents, have done everything in their power up to the last minute to preserve peace."
The following speech given by Mr. John Redmond made a profound impression. For some time the agitation over the question of Home Rule in Ireland had seemed to promise civil war. The leaders of both sides, however, expressed their willingness to postpone their differences in view of the national crisis. It was to this that Sir Edward Grey alluded when he said "The one bright spot in the whole of this terrible situation is Ireland."
John Redmond was born in Ireland in 1851. In 1881 he was elected to Parliament. On Parnell's death he was chosen leader of the minority group. For thirty-seven years he was a member of Parliament and devoted his life to advancing the interests of the Irish nation. Throughout the war he was loyally devoted to the government. The force and dignity of his eloquence were admired by all. He died in 1918.]

I HOPE the House will not consider it improper on my part, in the grave circumstances in which we are assembled, if I intervene for a very few moments. I was moved a great deal by that sentence in the speech of the Secretary of State for Foreign Affairs in which he said that the one bright spot in the situation was the changed feeling in Ireland. In past times when this Empire has been engaged in these terrible enterprises, it is true—it would be the utmost affectation and folly on my part to deny it—the sympathy of the Nationalists of Ireland, for reasons to be found deep down in the centuries of history, has been estranged from this country. Allow me to say that what has occurred in recent years has altered the situation completely. I must not touch, and I may be trusted not to touch, on any controversial topic. But this I may be allowed to say, that a wider knowledge of the real facts of Irish history has, I think, altered the views of the democracy of this country towards the Irish question, and today I honestly believe that the democracy of Ireland will turn with the utmost anxiety and sympathy to this country in every trial and every danger that may overtake it. There is a possibility, at any rate, of history repeating itself. The House will remember that in 1778, at the end of the disastrous American War, when it might, I think, truly be said that the military power of this country was almost at its lowest ebb, and when the shores of Ireland were threatened with foreign invasion, a body of 100,000 Irish Volunteers sprang into existence for the purpose of defending her shores. At first no Catholic—ah, how sad the reading of the history of those days is!—was allowed to be enrolled in that body of volunteers, and yet, from the very first day the Catholics of the South and West subscribed money and sent it towards the arming of their Protestant fellow-countrymen. Ideas widened as time went on, and finally the Catholics in the South were armed and enrolled as brothers in arms with their fellow-countrymen of a different creed in the North. May history repeat itself! To-day there are in Ireland two large bodies of Volunteers. One of them sprang into existence in the North. Another has sprung into existence in the South. I say to the Government that they may to-morrow withdraw every one of their troops from Ireland. I say that the coast of Ireland will be defended from foreign invasion by her armed sons, and for this purpose the Nationalist Catholics in the South will be only too glad to join arms with the armed Protestant Ulstermen in the North. Is it too much to hope that out of this situation there may spring a result which will be good not merely for the Empire, but good for the future welfare and integrity of the Irish nation? I ought to apologize for having intervened, but while Irishmen generally are in favor of peace, and would desire to save the democracy of this country from all the horrors of war, while we would make every possible sacrifice for that purpose, still if the dire necessity is forced upon this country we offer to the Government of the day that they may take their troops away, and that if it is allowed to us, in comradeship with our brethren in the North, we will ourselves defend the coasts of our country.

THEOBALD VON BETHMANN-HOLLWEG

GERMANY BEGINS THE WAR

[This speech by the German Chancellor sets forth the causes of the War from the German point of view. When the speech was made, as the Chancellor proclaims, the German troops had already entered the neutral territories of Luxemburg and Belgium. The speech contains his apology, "We are now in a position of necessity and necessity knows no law," and also his promise of reparation, "The wrong that we now do we will try to make good again as soon as our military ends have been reached."

Theobald Von Bethmann-Hollweg was born in 1856. He was educated at Bonn, where he formed the friendship with his fellow-student, Emperor William. His career as an administrator and politician reached its height on his appointment as Chancellor in 1909. He was superseded during the War in 1917 and died in 1921.]

[Speech in the Reichstag, August 4, 1914.]

A TREMENDOUS crisis threatens Europe. Since we won for ourselves the German Empire and earned the respect of the world for forty-four years we have lived in peace and have protected the peace of Europe. By peaceful labor we waxed strong and mighty and consequently aroused envy. With firm endurance we have seen how, under the pretext that Germany was eager for war, enmity was fostered in the East and West and chains were forged against us. The wind thus sown now rises in storm. We wished to live on in peaceful labor and from the Kaiser to the youngest soldier went the unexpressed vow: Only in defense of a just cause shall our sword fly from its scabbard. [Applause.] The day when we must draw it has come upon us against our will, against our honest efforts. Russia has set the torch to the house. [Stormy shouts of "Quite right!"] We are forced to war against Russia and France.

Gentlemen, a series of documents put together in the stress of events which are crowding upon one another, has been placed before you. Allow me to bring out the facts which characterize our attitude.

From the first moment of the Austro-Serbian crisis we declared that this affair must be restricted to Austria-Hungary and Serbia and we worked to that end. All the cabinets, especially that of England, represent the same point of view. Russia alone declared that she must have a word in the settlement of this dispute. With this the danger of European entanglements raised its threatening head. ["Very true!"] As soon as the first definite reports of military preparations in Russia were received, we stated to St. Petersburg in a friendly but emphatic way that warlike measures against Austria would find us on the side of our ally [Stormy applause] and that military preparations against ourselves would compel us to take counter measures [Renewed applause]; but mobilization is very near war. Russia gave us solemn assurances of her desire for peace. [Stormy cries "Hear, hear!"] And that she was making no military preparations against us. [Excitement.] In the meantime England sought to mediate between St. Petersburg and Vienna, in which she was warmly supported by us. ["Hear, hear!"] On July 28th the Kaiser besought the Czar by telegram to bear in mind that it was the right and duty of Austria-Hungary to defend herself against the Pan-Servian agitation, which threatened to undermine Austria-Hungary's existence. [Hearty assent.] The Kaiser drew the attention of the Czar to the fact that the solidarity of monarchical interests was threatened by the crime of Sarajevo. ["Hear, hear!"] He begged him to give his personal support in clearing away the differences. At about the same time, and before the receipt of this telegram, the Czar on his side begged the Kaiser for his help, and asked him to advise moderation in Vienna. The Kaiser undertook the rôle of mediator. But scarcely had the action ordered by him been started, when Russia mobilized all her forces directed against Austria-Hungary. ["Hear, hear!"] Austria-Hungary, however, had only mobilized those army corps which were directly aimed at Serbia ["Hear, hear!"]; only two army corps toward the North, far away from the Russian frontier. [Renewed cries of "Hear! Hear!"]

The Kaiser immediately called the Czar's attention to the fact that by reason of this mobilization of the Russian forces against Austria, his rôle of mediator, undertaken at the Czar's request, was rendered more difficult if not impossible. Nevertheless, we continued our work of mediation in Vienna, going to the utmost bounds—permitted by our treaty relations. ["Hear! Hear!"] During this time Russia, of her own accord, renewed her assurances that she was not taking any military measures against us. [Great excitement.]

July 31st arrived. In Vienna the decision was to be made. By our efforts up to that time we had succeeded in bringing it about that Vienna again took up the discussion with St. Petersburg through direct conversations which had ceased for some time. ["Hear, hear!"] But even before the final decision had been reached in Vienna, came the news that Russia had mobilized her entire military force against us as well. ["Hear, hear!"] The Russian government, which knew from our repeated representations what mobilization on our frontier meant, did not notify us of this mobilization, nor did it give us any explanation of it. ["Hear, hear!"] Not before the afternoon of the 31st did a telegram come from the Czar to the Kaiser, in which he guaranteed that his army would take up no provocative attitude against us. ["Hear, hear!" and laughter.] But mobilization on our frontier had been in full progress since the night between July 30th and 31st. ["Hear, hear!"] While we, at the request of Russia, were meditating in Vienna, the Russian forces drew up along our long and almost entirely open frontier; and France while not yet mobilizing nevertheless admits that she was taking military measures.

And we—up to that moment—we purposely had not called a single reserve, for the sake of European peace. [Energetic applause.] Were we still to wait patiently until perhaps the powers between whom we are wedged chose the time to strike? [Many cries of "No, no!"] To subject Germany to this danger would have been a crime! [Stormy, long-continued assent.] For that reason, still on the 31st we demanded Russian demobilization as the only measure which could still preserve the peace of Europe. ["Quite right!"] The Imperial Ambassador in St. Petersburg was furthermore instructed to declare to the Russian Government that, in case of a rejection of our demand, we should have to consider that a state of war existed.

The Imperial Ambassador carried out these instructions. How Russia has replied to our demand for demobilization, we still do not know to-day. [Cries of "Hear, hear!"] No telegraphic communications in regard to this have reached us ["Hear, hear!"] although the telegraph has delivered many less important messages. [Renewed cries of "Hear, hear!"]

Thus, when the time limit expired, the Kaiser saw himself forced on August 1st, at 5 o'clock in the afternoon, to order the mobilization of our forces. [Energetic applause.]

At the same time we had to assure ourselves as to what France's position would be. To our definite question as to whether she would remain neutral in case of a German-Russian war, France replied that she would do as her interests demanded. [Laughter.] This was an evasive reply to our question, if not a refusal. ["Quite true."]

The Kaiser nevertheless gave the order to respect the French frontier absolutely. This order was strictly carried out with a single exception. France, who mobilized at the same time that we did, declared that she would respect a zone of 10 kilometres from the frontier. ["Hear, hear!"] And what actually occurred? Aviators throwing bombs, cavalry patrols, French companies breaking into our territory! ["Hear, hear!"] In this manner France, although no state of war had yet been declared, had violated the peace, and actually attacked us. ["Quite true."]

In regard to the one exception mentioned I have the following report from the Chief of the General Staff: "Of the French complaints in regard to the violation of the frontier from our side, we admit only one. Against express command, a patrol of the 14th Army Corps, apparently led by an officer, crossed the frontier on August 2nd. This patrol was apparently shot down—only one man has returned. But long before this single case of frontier infringement, French aviators penetrated into Southern Germany and threw bombs on our railways and at the 'Schlucht Pass' French troops have attacked our frontier patrols. Up to now our troops, according to order, have confined themselves entirely to defensive action." This is the report of the General Staff.

Gentlemen, we are now in a state of necessity [Energetic assent], and necessity knows no law. [Stormy agreement]. Our troops have occupied Luxembourg [Applause]; perhaps they have already entered Belgian territory. [Renewed applause.] Gentlemen, this violates the rules of international law. The French government declared in Brussels that it was willing to respect the neutrality of Belgium as long as the enemy respected it. But we knew that France stood ready to invade. ["Hear, hear."] France could wait, we could not. A French attack on our flank on the lower Rhine might have been fatal to us. [Applause.] We were thus forced to ignore the just protests of the Luxembourg and Belgian governments. ["Quite right."] The wrong—I speak openly—the wrong that we now do, we will try to make good again, as soon as our military ends have been reached. [Applause.] Whoever is threatened as we are, and battles for all that is sacred, dares think only of how he can hack his way out! [Long, stormy applause and clapping from all sides of the house.]

Gentlemen, we stand shoulder to shoulder with Austria-Hungary.

As to England's attitude, the declarations which Sir Edward Grey made yesterday in the House of Commons make clear the standpoint adopted by the English government. We have declared to the English government that, as long as England remains neutral our fleet will not attack the north coast of France and that we will not injure the territorial integrity and independence of Belgium. This declaration I now repeat before the whole world. ["Hear, hear!"] And I may add that as long as England remains neutral we shall be ready, if equal assurances are given, to take no hostile measures against French merchant vessels. [Applause.]

Gentlemen, this is what has happened. I repeat the words of the Kaiser, "Germany enters the fight with a clear conscience!" [Applause.] We battle for the fruits of our peaceful labors, for the inheritance of a great past and for our future. The fifty years have not yet passed in which Moltke said we should have to stand armed, ready to defend our inheritance, and the conquest of 1870. Now the great hour of trial has struck for our people. But we meet it with a clear confidence. [Stormy applause.] Our army stands in the field, our fleet is ready for battle backed by the entire German people. [Long enthusiastic applause. All the members rise.] The entire German people to the last man! [Renewed applause.]

You, gentlemen, know the full extent of your duty. The bills before you need no further explanation. I beg you to pass them speedily. [Stormy applause.]

ALBERT, KING OF BELGIUM

BELGIUM READY

[The King's speech to the Belgian Parliament in extraordinary session, August 4, 1914.

This speech was made when the German army had already crossed the frontier and begun its savage attack on Liège. On August 2, Germany presented an ultimatum asking friendly neutrality of all German troops marching through Belgium. On the morning of August 3, the Belgian Minister of Foreign Affairs replied that Belgium would offer strenuous resistance to any Power, which violated its neutrality. At 6 o'clock on the morning of August 4, the German Minister handed the second ultimatum, now saying that the Germans would force a passage and later in the day German troops summoned Liège to surrender. When the King appeared in the Parliament it was generally known that War was inevitable, if it had not already begun. "We saw the King," wrote Dumont-Wilden, "in all the radiant splendor of office, who held high the sword, and his voice vibrated like a lyre quivering in the wind."]

NEVER since 1830 has a more grave moment come to Belgium: the integrity of our territory is threatened.

The strength of our just cause, the sympathy which Belgium, proud of her free institutions, and of her moral conquests, has never ceased to enjoy at the hands of other nations, the fact that our independent existence is necessary for the balance of power in Europe, these considerations give rise to hope that the events which we fear will not take place.

But if our hopes fail, if we must resist the invasion of our soil and must defend our threatened homes, this duty, hard though it be, will find us ordered and prepared for the greatest sacrifices. [Cheers and cries of "Long Live the King! Long Live Belgium!"]

From this moment, with a view to meet every contingency, the valiant youth of our nation stand ready, firmly resolved with the traditional tenacity and calmness of the Belgians to defend their fatherland at a moment of danger. [Cheers.]

To them I send a brotherly greeting in the name of the nation. [Cheers and cries of "Long Live the Army!"] Throughout Flanders and the country of Wallonie in town and country one sentiment alone fills every heart—patriotism; one vision alone fills every mind—our threatened independence. One duty alone is laid upon our wills, stubborn resistance. [Cheers.]

At this grave moment two virtues are indispensable—courage, calm [renewed cheers] but firm, and close union among all Belgians.

Striking evidence of both these virtues is already before the eyes of a nation full of enthusiasm.

The faultless mobilization of our army, the multitude of volunteers, the devotion of the civil population, the self-sacrifice of families have shown incontestably that the whole Belgian people is carried away by stimulating courage. [Applause.] The moment has come to act.

I have called you together, gentlemen, to give to the Legislative Chambers an opportunity to associate themselves with the impulses of the people in the same sentiment of sacrifice. Gentlemen, you will know how to deal urgently with all the measures which the situation requires for the war and for public order. [General assent.]

When I see this enthusiastic gathering in which there is only one party, that of the fatherland [enthusiastic cheers and cries of "Long Live Belgium!"], in which at this moment all hearts beat as one, my mind goes back to the Congress of 1830, and I ask of you gentlemen, are you determined unswervingly to maintain intact the whole patrimony of our ancestors? ["Yes, yes," from every side.]

No one in the country will fail in his duty.

The army, strong and disciplined, is fit to do this task: my Government and I have full confidence in its leader and its soldiers. ["Hear, hear!"]

The Government, firmly attached to the populace and supported by them, is conscious of its responsibilities, and will bear them to the end with the deliberate conviction that the efforts of all united in the most fervent and generous patriotism will safeguard the supreme good of the country.

If the foreigner, disregarding the neutrality whose every duty we have always scrupulously observed, should violate our territory, he will find all Belgians grouped around their sovereign who will never betray his coronation oath, and around a Government possessing the absolute confidence of the entire nation. [Cheers on all the Benches.]

I have faith in our destiny; a country which defends itself commands the respect of all; such a country shall never perish. ["Hear, hear. Long live the King! Long live Belgium!"]

God will be with us in this just cause. [Fresh applause.]

Long live independent Belgium. [Long and unanimous cheers from the Assembly and from the Galleries.]

RAYMOND POINCARÉ

DECLARATION OF WAR BY FRANCE

[Speech at the extraordinary session of Parliament August 4, 1914. This address by the President of the French Republic is the Declaration of War and an appeal to the Nation. Together with the following speech by the French Premier, M. René Viviani, it sets forth the history of the offense which led the French nation into the conflict.]

GENTLEMEN: France has just been the object of a violent and premeditated attack, which is an insolent defiance of the law of nations. Before any declaration of war had been sent to us, even before the German Ambassador had asked for his passports, our territory has been violated. The German Empire has waited till yesterday evening to give at this late stage the true name to a state of things which it had already created.

For more than forty years the French, in sincere love of peace, have buried at the bottom of their heart the desire for legitimate reparation.

They have given to the world the example of a great nation which, definitely raised from defeat by the exercise of will, patience and labor, has only used its renewed and rejuvenated strength in the interest of progress and for the good of humanity.

DECLARATION OF WAR BY FRANCE

Since the ultimatum of Austria opened a crisis which threatened the whole of Europe, France has persisted in followowing and in recommending on all sides a policy of prudence, wisdom and moderation.

To her there can be imputed no act, no movement, no word, which has not been peaceful and conciliatory.

At the hour when the struggle is beginning, she has the right, in justice to herself, of solemnly declaring that she has made, up to the last moment, supreme efforts to avert the war now about to break out, the crushing responsibility for which the German Empire will have to bear before history. [Unanimous and repeated applause.]

On the very morrow of the day when we and our allies were publicly expressing our hope of seeing negotiations which had been begun under the auspices of the London Cabinet carried to a peaceful conclusion, Germany suddenly declared war upon Russia, she has invaded the territory of Luxemburg, she has outrageously insulted the noble Belgian nation [Loud and unanimous applause], our neighbor and our friend, and attempted treacherously to fall upon us while we were in the midst of diplomatic conversation. [Fresh and repeated unanimous applause.]

But France was watching. As alert as she was peaceful, she was prepared; and our enemies will meet on their path our valiant covering troops, who are at their post and will provide the screen behind which the mobilization of our national forces will be methodically completed.

Our fine and courageous army, which France to-day accompanies with her maternal thought [Loud applause], has risen eager to defend the honor of the flag and the soil of the country. [Unanimous and repeated applause.]

The President of the Republic, interpreting the unanimous feeling of the country, expresses to our troops by land and sea the admiration and confidence of every Frenchman. [Loud and prolonged applause.]

Closely united in a common feeling, the nation will persevere with the cool self-restraint of which, since the beginning of the crisis, she has given daily proof. Now, as always, she will know how to harmonize the most noble daring and most ardent enthusiasm with that self-control which is the sign of enduring energy and is the best guarantee of victory. [Applause.]

In the war which is beginning France will have Right on her side, the eternal power of which cannot with impunity be disregarded by nations any more than by individuals. [Loud and unanimous applause.]

She will be heroically defended by all her sons; nothing will break their sacred union before the enemy; to-day they are joined together as brothers in a common indignation against the aggressor, and in a common patriotic faith. [Loud and prolonged applause and cries of "Vive la France!"]

She is faithfully helped by Russia, her ally [Loud and unanimous applause]; she is supported by the loyal friendship of England [Loud and unanimous applause].

And already from every part of the civilized world sympathy and good wishes are coming to her. For to-day once again she stands before the universe for Liberty, Justice and Reason. [Loud and repeated applause.] "Haut les cœurs et vive la France!" [Unanimous and prolonged applause.]

RENÉ RAPHAEL VIVIANI

DECLARATION OF WAR BY FRANCE

[Speech in the Chamber of Deputies August 4, 1914.
This speech by the French Premier sets forth the course of diplomatic negotiations leading to the War. The applause which frequently interrupted his recital rose at its conclusion to a frenzy of enthusiasm.

René Raphael Viviani was born in 1863. He received his degree in Law at the Faculty of Paris and was elected a member of the Chamber of Deputies in 1893. In 1906, he entered the Cabinet as Minister of Public Works. He became Premier of France in 1914 and was succeeded by Briand in 1915. In 1917 he visited the United States as Envoy of the French Government and his remarkable eloquence stirred great audiences in this country as it had so often done in France. He revisited this country in 1921.]

GENTLEMEN: The German Ambassador yesterday left Paris after notifying us of the existence of a state of war.

DECLARATION OF WAR BY FRANCE

The Government owe to Parliament a true account of the events which, in less than ten days, have unloosed a European war and compelled France, peaceful and valiant, to defend her frontier against an attack, the hateful injustice of which is emphasized by its calculated unexpectedness.

This attack, which has no excuse, and which began before we were notified of any declaration of war, is the last act of a plan, whose origin and object I propose to declare before our own democracy and before the opinion of the civilized world.

As a consequence of the abominable crime which cost the Austro-Hungarian Heir-Apparent and the Duchess of Hohenburg their lives, difficulties arose between the Cabinets of Vienna and Belgrade.

The majority of the Powers were only semi-officially informed of these difficulties up till Friday, July 24th, the date on which the Austro-Hungarian Ambassadors communicated to them a circular which the press has published.

The object of this circular was to explain and justify an ultimatum delivered the evening before to Servia by the Austro-Hungarian Minister at Belgrade.

This ultimatum, in alleging the complicity of numerous Servian subjects and associations in the Serajevo crime, hinted that the official Servian authorities themselves were no strangers to it. It demanded a reply from Servia by 6 o'clock on the evening of Saturday, July 25th.

The Austrian demands, or at any rate many of them, without doubt struck a blow at the rights of a sovereign State. Notwithstanding their excessive character, Servia, on July 25th, declared that she submitted to them almost without reserve.

This submission which constituted a success for Austro-Hungary, a guarantee for the peace of Europe, was not unconnected with the advice tendered to Belgrade from the first moment by France, Russia and Great Britain.

The value of this advice was all the greater since the Austro-Hungarian demands had been concealed from the Chanceries of the Triple Entente, to whom in the three preceding weeks the Austro-Hungarian Government had on several occasions given an assurance that their claims would be extremely moderate.

It was, therefore, with natural astonishment that the Cabinets of Paris, St. Petersburg and London learned on July 26th that the Austrian Minister at Belgrade, after a few minutes' examination, declared that the Servian reply was inacceptable, and broke off diplomatic relations.

This astonishment was increased by the fact that on Friday, the 24th, the German Ambassador came and read to the French Minister for Foreign Affairs a *note verbale* asserting that the Austro-Servian dispute must remain localized, without intervention by the great Powers, or otherwise "incalculable consequences" were to be feared. A similar *démarche* was made on Saturday, the 25th, at London and at St. Petersburg.

Need I, Gentlemen, point out to you the contrast between the threatening expressions used by the German Ambassador at Paris and the conciliatory sentiments which the Powers of the Triple Entente had just manifested by the advice which they gave to Servia to submit?

Nevertheless, in spite of the extraordinary character of the German *démarche,* we immediately, in agreement with our Allies and our friends, took a conciliatory course and invited Germany to join in it.

We have had from the first moment regretfully to recognize that our intentions and our efforts met with no response at Berlin.

Not only did Germany appear wholly unwilling to give to Austria-Hungary the friendly advice which her position gave her the right to offer, but from this moment and still more in the following days, she seemed to intervene between the Cabinet at Vienna and the compromises suggested by the other Powers.

On Tuesday, 28th July, Austria-Hungary declared war on Servia. This declaration of war, with its aggravation of the state of affairs brought about by the rupture of diplomatic relations three days before, gave ground for believing that there was a deliberate desire for war, and a systematic program for the enslavement of Servia.

Thus there was now involved in the dispute not only the independence of a brave people, but the balance of power in the Balkans, embodied in the Treaty of Bucharest of 1913, and

DECLARATION OF WAR BY FRANCE

consecrated by the moral support of all the Great Powers.

However, at the suggestion of the British Government with its constant and firm attachment to the maintenance of the peace of Europe, the negotiations were continued, or, to speak more accurately, the Powers of the Triple Entente tried to continue them.

From this common desire sprang the proposal for action by the four Powers, England, France, Germany and Italy, which was intended, by assuring to Austria all legitimate satisfaction, to bring about an equitable adjustment of the dispute.

On Wednesday, the 29th, the Russian Government, noting the persistent failure of these efforts and faced by the Austrian mobilization and declaration of war, fearing the military destruction of Servia, decided as a precautionary measure to mobilize the troops of four military districts, that is to say, the formations echeloned along the Austria-Hungarian frontier exclusively.

In taking this step, the Russian Government were careful to inform the German Government that their measures, restricted as they were and without any offensive character towards Austria, were not in any degree directed against Germany.

In a conversation with the Russian Ambassador at Berlin, the German Secretary of State for Foreign Affairs acknowledged this without demur.

On the other hand, all the efforts made by Great Britain with the adherence of Russia and the support of France, to bring Austria and Servia into touch under the moral patronage of Europe, were encountered at Berlin with a predetermined negative of which the diplomatic dispatches afford the clearest proof.

This was a disquieting situation which made it probable that there existed at Berlin intentions which had not been disclosed. Some hours afterwards this alarming suspicion was destined to become a certainty.

In fact Germany's negative attitude gave place thirty-six hours later to positive steps which were truly alarming. On the 31st July, Germany, by proclaiming "a state of danger of war," cut the communications between herself and the rest of

Europe, and obtained for herself complete freedom to pursue against France in absolute secrecy military preparations which, as you have seen, nothing could justify.

Already for some days, and in circumstances difficult to explain, Germany had prepared for the transition of her army from a peace footing to a war footing.

From the morning of the 25th July, that is to say, even before the expiration of the time limit given to Servia by Austria, she had confined to barracks the garrisons of Alsace-Lorraine. The same day she had placed the frontier-works in a complete state of defense. On the 26th, she had indicated to the railways the measures preparatory for concentration. On the 27th, she had completed requisitions and placed her covering troops in position. On the 28th, the summons of individual reservists had begun and units which were distant from the frontier had been brought up to it.

Could all these measures, pursued with implacable method, leave us in doubt of Germany's intentions?

Such was the situation when, on the evening of the 31st July, the German Government, which, since the 24th, had not participated by any active step in the conciliatory efforts of the Triple Entente, addressed an ultimatum to the Russian Government under the pretext that Russia had ordered a general mobilization of her armies, and demanded that this mobilization should be stopped within twelve hours.

This demand, which was all the more insulting in form because a few hours earlier the Emperor Nicholas II, with a movement at once confiding and spontaneous, had asked the German Emperor for his mediation, was put forward at a moment when, on the request of England and with the knowledge of Germany, the Russian Government was accepting a formula of such a nature as to lay the foundation for a friendly settlement of the Austro-Servian dispute and of the Austro-Russian difficulties by the simultaneous arrest of military operations and of military preparations.

The same day this unfriendly *démarche* towards Russia was supplemented by acts which were frankly hostile towards France; the rupture of communications by road, railway, telegraph and telephone, the seizure of French locomotives on their arrival at the frontier, the placing of machine guns in

DECLARATION OF WAR BY FRANCE

the middle of the permanent way which had been cut, and the concentration of troops on this frontier.

From this moment we were no longer justified in believing in the sincerity of the pacific declaration which the German representative continued to shower upon us. ["Hear, hear!"]

We knew that Germany was mobilizing under the shelter of the "state of danger of war."

We learned that six classes of reservists had been called up, and that transport was being collected even for those army corps which were stationed a considerable distance from the frontier.

As these events unfolded themselves, the Government, watchful and vigilant, took from day to day, and even from hour to hour, the measures of precaution which the situation required; the general mobilization of our forces on land and sea was ordered.

The same evening, at 7:30, Germany, without waiting for the acceptance by the Cabinet of St. Petersburg of the English proposal, which I have already mentioned, declared war on Russia.

The next day, Sunday, the 2nd August, without regard for the extreme moderation of France, in contradiction to the peaceful declarations of the German Ambassador at Paris, and in defiance of the rules of international law, German troops crossed our frontier at three different points.

At the same time, in violation of the Treaty of 1867, which guaranteed with the signature of Prussia the neutrality of Luxemburg, they invaded the territory of the Grand Duchy and so gave cause for a protest by the Luxemburg Government.

Finally, the neutrality of Belgium also was threatened. The German Minister, on the evening of the 2nd August, presented to the Belgian Government an ultimatum requesting facilities in Belgium for military operations against France, under the lying pretext that Belgian neutrality was threatened by us; the Belgian Government refused, and declared that they were resolved to defend with vigor their neutrality, which was respected by France and guaranteed by treaties, and in particular by the King of Prussia. [Unanimous and prolonged applause.]

Since then, Gentlemen, the German attacks have been renewed, multiplied, and accentuated. At more than fifteen points our frontier has been violated. Shots have been fired at our soldiers and Customs officers. Men have been killed and wounded. Yesterday a German military aviator dropped three bombs on Lunéville.

The German Ambassador, to whom as well as to all the great Powers, we communicated these facts, did not deny them or express his regrets for them. On the contrary, he came yesterday evening to ask me for his passports, and to notify us of the existence of a state of war, giving as his reason, in the teeth of all the facts, hostile acts committed by French aviators in German territory in the Eifel district, and even on the railway near Carlsruhe and near Nuremberg. This is the letter which he handed me on the subject:

M. le Président:
The German administrative and military authorities have established a certain number of flagrantly hostile acts committed on German territory by French military aviators. Several of these have openly violated the neutrality of Belgium by flying over the territory of that country; one has attempted to destroy buildings near Wesel; others have been seen in the district of the Eifel; one has thrown bombs on the railway near Carlsruhe and Nuremburg.
I am instructed, and I have the honour to inform your Excellency, that in the presence of these acts of aggression the German Empire considers itself in a state of war with France in consequence of the acts of this latter Power.
At the same time, I have the honour to bring to the knowledge of your Excellency that the German authorities will retain French mercantile vessels in German ports, but they will release them if, within forty-eight hours, they are assured of complete reciprocity.
My diplomatic mission having thus come to an end it only remains for me to request your Excellency to be good enough to furnish me with my passports, and to take the steps you consider suitable to assure my return to Germany, with the staff of the Embassy, as well as with the staff of the Bavarian Legation and of the German Consulate General in Paris.
Be good enough, M. le Président, to receive the assurances of my deepest respect.
(Signed) SCHOEN

Need I, Gentlemen, lay stress on the absurdities of these pretexts which they put forward as grievances? At no time has any French aviator penetrated into Belgium, nor has any

DECLARATION OF WAR BY FRANCE

French aviator committed either in Bavaria or any other part of Germany any hostile act. The opinion of Europe has already done justice to these wretched inventions. [Loud and unanimous applause.]

Against these attacks, which violate all the laws of justice and all the principles of public law, we have now taken all the necessary steps; they are being carried out strictly, regularly, and with calmness.

The mobilization of the Russian army also continues with remarkable vigor and unrestrained enthusiasm. [Unanimous and prolonged applause, all the deputies rising from their seats.] The Belgian army, mobilized with 250,000 men, prepares with a splendid passion and magnificent ardor to defend the neutrality and independence of their country. [Renewed loud and unanimous applause.]

The entire English fleet is mobilized and orders have been given to mobilize the land forces. [Loud cheers, all the deputies rising to their feet.]

Since 1912 *pourparlers* had taken place between English and French General Staffs and were concluded by an exchange of letters between Sir Edward Grey and M. Paul Cambon. The Secretary of State for Foreign Affairs yesterday evening communicated these letters to the House of Commons, and I have the honor with the consent of the British Government, to acquaint you with the contents of these two documents.

Foreign Office
November 22, 1912.

My dear Ambassador:

From time to time in recent years the French and British naval and military experts have consulted together. It has always been understood that such consultation does not restrict the freedom of either Government to decide at any future time whether or not to assist the other by armed force. We have agreed that consultation between experts is not, and ought not to be regarded as, an engagement that commits either Government to action in a contingency that has not arisen and may never arise. The disposition, for instance, of the French and British fleets respectively at the present moment is not based upon an engagement to coöperate in war.

You have, however, pointed out that, if either Government had grave reason to expect an unprovoked attack by a third Power, it might become essential to know whether it could in that event depend upon the armed assistance of the other.

I agree that, if either Government had grave reason to expect an unprovoked attack by a third Power, or something that threatened the general peace, it should immediately discuss with the other whether both Governments should act together to prevent aggression and to preserve peace, and, if so, what measures they would be prepared to take in common. If these measures involved action, the plans of the General Staffs would at once be taken into consideration, and the Governments would then decide what effect should be given to them.

Yours, &c.
E. GREY.

To this letter our Ambassador, M. Paul Cambon, replied on the 23rd November, 1912:

London, November 23, 1912.

Dear Sir Edward:

You reminded me in your letter of yesterday, 22nd November, that during the last few years the military and naval authorities of France and Great Britain had consulted with each other from time to time; that it had always been understood that these consultations should not restrict the liberty of either Government to decide in the future whether they should lend each other the support of their armed forces; that, on either side, these consultations between experts were not and should not be considered as engagements binding our Governments to take action in certain eventualities; that, however, I had remarked to you that, if one or the other of the two Governments had grave reasons to fear an unprovoked attack on the part of a third Power, it would become essential to know whether it could count on the armed support of the other.

Your letter answers that point, and I am authorised to state that, in the event of one of our two Governments having grave reasons to fear either an act of aggression from a third Power, or some event threatening the general peace, that Government would immediately examine with the other the question whether both Governments should act together in order to prevent the act of aggression or preserve peace. If so, the two Governments would deliberate as to the measures which they would be prepared to take in common; if those measures involved action, the two Governments would take into immediate consideration the plans of their general staffs and would then decide as to the effect to be given to those plans.

Yours, &c.
PAUL CAMBON.

In the House of Commons the Secretary of State for Foreign Affairs spoke of France amidst the applause of the members in a noble and warm-hearted manner and his language has already found an echo deep in the hearts of all Frenchmen. [Loud and unanimous applause.] I wish in the name of the Government of the Republic to thank the English Government from this tribune for their cordial words and the Parliament of France will associate itself in this sentiment. [Renewed, prolonged and unanimous applause.]

The Secretary of State for Foreign Affairs made in particular the following declaration:

> In case the German fleet came into the Channel or entered the North Sea in order to go round the British Isles with the object of attacking the French coasts or the French navy and of harassing French merchant shipping, the English fleet would intervene in order to give to French shipping its complete protection in such a way that from that moment England and Germany would be in a state of war.

From now onwards, the English fleet protects our northern and western coasts against a German attack. Gentlemen, these are the facts. I believe that the simple recital of them is sufficient to justify the acts of the Government of the Republic. I wish, however, to make clear the conclusion to be drawn from my story and to give its true meaning to the unheard-of attacks of which France is the victim.

The victors of 1870 have, at different times, as you know, desired to repeat the blows which they dealt us then. In 1875, the war which was intended to complete the destruction of conquered France was prevented only by the intervention of the two Powers to whom we were to become united at a later date by ties of alliance and of friendship [unanimous applause], by the intervention of Russia and of Great Britain. [Prolonged applause, all the deputies rising to their feet.]

Since then the French Republic, by the restoration of her national forces and the conclusion of diplomatic agreements unswervingly adhered to, has succeeded in liberating herself from the yoke which even in a period of profound peace Bismarck was able to impose upon Europe.

She has reëstablished the balance of power in Europe, a guarantee of the liberty and dignity of all.

Gentlemen, I do not know if I am mistaken, but it seems to me that this work of peaceful reparation, of liberation and honor finally ratified in 1904 and 1907, with the genial co-operation of King Edward VII of England and the Government of the Crown [applause], this is what the German Empire wishes to destroy to-day by one daring stroke.

Germany can reproach us with nothing.

Bearing in silence in our bosom for half a century the wound which Germany dealt us we have offered to peace an unprecedented sacrifice. [Loud and unanimous applause.]

We have offered other sacrifices in all the discussions which since 1904 German diplomacy has systematically provoked, whether in Morocco or elsewhere in 1905, in 1906, in 1908, in 1911.

Russia also has given proof of great moderation at the time of the events of 1908, as she has done in the present crisis.

She observed the same moderation, and the Triple Entente with her, when in the Eastern crisis of 1912 Austria and Germany formulated demands, whether against Servia or against Greece, which still were, as the event proved, capable of settlement by discussion.

Useless sacrifices, barren negotiations, empty efforts, since to-day in the very act of conciliation we, our allies and ourselves, are attacked by surprise. [Prolonged applause.]

No one can honestly believe that we are the aggressors. Vain is the desire to overthrow the sacred principles of right and of liberty to which nations, as well as individuals, are subject; Italy with that clarity of insight possessed by the Latin intellect, has notified us that she proposes to preserve neutrality. [Prolonged applause, all the deputies rising to their feet.]

This decision has found in all France an echo of sincerest joy. I made myself the interpreter of this feeling to the Italian Chargé d'Affaires when I told him how much I congratulated myself that the two Latin sisters, who have the same origin and the same ideal, a common and glorious past, are not now opposed to one another. [Renewed applause.]

Gentlemen, we proclaim loudly the object of their attack— it is the independence, the honor, the safety, which the Triple Entente has regained in the balance of power for the service of peace. The object of attack is the liberties of Europe, which France, her allies, and her friends, are proud to defend. [Loud applause.]

We are going to defend these liberties, for it is they that are in dispute, and all the rest is but a pretext.

France, unjustly provoked, did not desire war, she has done everything to avert it. Since it is forced upon her, she will defend herself against Germany and against every Power which has not yet declared its intentions, but joins with the latter in a conflict between the two countries. [Applause, all the deputies rising to their feet.]

A free and valiant people that sustains an eternal ideal, and is wholly united to defend its existence; a democracy which knows how to discipline its military strength, and was not afraid a year ago to increase its burden as an answer to the armaments of its neighbor; a nation armed, struggling for its own life and for the independence of Europe—here is a sight which we are proud to offer to the onlookers in this desperate struggle, that has for some days been preparing with the greatest calmness and method. We are without reproach. We shall be without fear. [Loud applause, all the deputies rising to their feet.] France has often proved in less favorable circumstances that she is a most formidable adversary when she fights, as she does to-day, for liberty and for right. [Applause.]

In submitting our actions to you, Gentlemen, who are our judges, we have, to help us in bearing the burden of our heavy responsibility, the comfort of a clear conscience and the conviction that we have done our duty. [Prolonged applause, all the deputies rising to their feet.]

HERBERT HENRY ASQUITH

ENGLAND SUPPORTS BELGIUM

[Speech by the Prime Minister, Mr. Asquith, in the House of Commons in support of the motion to vote a credit of £100,000,000—on August 6, 1914.

This speech by Prime Minister Asquith asking Commons for a credit of £100,000,000 was made the second day after War had been declared and supplements the speech of Sir Edward Grey of August 3. The *Times* in an editorial declared that in eloquence the Prime Minister touched the height which even he had rarely reached and never surpassed. It continued, "Mr. Asquith's oration was of a different type from the masterly speech of Grey on Monday. The Foreign Secretary's task was largely one of detailed explanation and quiet argument; he brought conviction by simple persuasiveness. The Prime Minister appealed to the emotions as well as to the mind. His vindication of the position of the country was impassioned but never rhetorical. The House was in a mood of confident but not assertive patriotism and all united in cheering."

Herbert Henry Asquith was born in 1852 and graduated from Balliol College, Oxford. He entered as a barrister at Lincoln's Inn in 1876 and rapidly obtained a high position at the bar. He became a member of Parliament in 1886 and was Home Secretary under the Gladstone-Rosebery Ministry of 1892-95. He was made Chancellor of the Exchequer in 1903 and Prime Minister in 1908, an office which he held at the outbreak of the World War.]

In asking the House to agree to the resolution which Mr. Speaker has just read from the Chair, I do not propose, because I do not think it is in any way necessary, to traverse the ground again which was covered by my right hon. Friend the Foreign Secretary two or three nights ago. He stated—and I do not think any of the statements he made are capable of answer and certainly have not yet been answered—the grounds upon which with the utmost reluctance and with infinite regret His Majesty's Government have been compelled to put this country in a state of war with what for many years and indeed generations past has been a friendly Power. But, Sir, the papers which have since been presented to Parliament, and which are now in the hands of hon. Members, will, I think, show how strenuous, how unremitting, how persistent, even when the last glimmer of hope seemed to have faded away, were the efforts of my right hon. Friend to secure for Europe an honorable and a lasting peace. Everyone knows in the great crisis which occurred last year in the East of Europe, it was largely, if not mainly, by the acknowledgment of all Europe due to the steps taken by my right hon. Friend that the area of the conflict was limited, and that so far as the Great Powers are concerned, peace was maintained. If his efforts upon this occasion have, unhappily, been unsuccessful, I am certain that this House and the country, and I will add posterity and history, will accord to him what is, after all, the best tribute that can be paid to any statesman: that, never derogating for an instant or by an inch from the honor and

ENGLAND SUPPORTS BELGIUM

interests of his own country, he has striven, as few men have striven, to maintain and preserve the greatest interest of all countries—universal peace. These papers which are now in the hands of hon. Members show something more than that. They show what were the terms which were offered to us in exchange for our neutrality. I trust that not merely only the Members of this House, but all our fellow-subjects everywhere will read the communications, will read, learn, and mark the communications which passed only a week ago to-day between Berlin and London in this matter. The terms by which it was sought to buy our neutrality are contained in the communication made by the German Chancellor to Sir Edward Goschen on the 29th July, No. 85 of the published Paper. I think I must refer to them for a moment. After referring to the state of things as between Austria and Russia Sir Edward Goschen goes on:—

"He then proceeded to make the following strong bid for British neutrality. He said that it was clear, so far as he was able to judge the main principle which governed British policy, that Great Britain would never stand by and allow France to be crushed in any conflict there might be. That, however, was not the object at which Germany aimed. Provided that neutrality of Great Britain were certain, every assurance would be given to the British Government that the Imperial Government"—

Let the House observe these words—

"aimed at no territorial acquisition at the expense of France should they prove victorious in any war that might ensue."

Sir Edward Goschen proceeded to put a very pertinent question:—

"I questioned His Excellency about the French Colonies"—

What are the French colonies? They mean every part of the dominions and possessions of France outside the geographical area of Europe—

"and he said that he was unable to give a similar undertaking in that respect."

Let me come to what, in my mind personally, has always

been the crucial and almost the governing consideration, namely, the position of the small states:—

"As regards Holland, however, His Excellency said that so long as Germany's adversaries respected the integrity and neutrality of the Netherlands Germany was ready to give His Majesty's Government an assurance that she would do likewise."

Then we come to Belgium:—

"It depended upon the action of France what operations Germany might be forced to enter upon in Belgium, but, when the war was over, Belgian integrity would be respected if she had not sided against Germany."

Let the House observe the distinction between these two cases. In regard to Holland it was not only independence and integrity but also neutrality; but in regard to Belgium, there was no mention of neutrality at all, nothing but an assurance that after the war came to an end the integrity of Belgium would be respected. Then His Excellency added:—

"Ever since he had been Chancellor the object of his policy had been to bring about an understanding with England. He trusted that these assurances"—

the assurances I have read out to the House—

"might form the basis of that understanding which he so much desired."

What does that amount to? Let me just ask the House. I do so, not with the object of inflaming passion, certainly not with the object of exciting feeling against Germany, but I do so to vindicate and make clear the position of the British Government in this matter. What did that proposal amount to? In the first place, it meant this: That behind the back of France—they were not made a party to these communications—we should have given, if we had assented to that, a free license to Germany to annex, in the event of a successful war, the whole of the extra European dominions and possessions of France. What did it mean as regards Belgium? When she addressed, as she addressed in these few days, her moving appeal to us to fulfill our solemn guarantee of her neutrality, what reply should we have given? What reply should we have given to that Belgian appeal? We should have been obliged to say that without her knowledge we had bartered away to the Power threatening her our obligation to keep our plighted word. The House has read, and the country has read, of course, in the last few hours, the most pathetic appeal addressed by the King of Belgium, and I do not envy the man who can read that appeal with an unmoved heart. Belgians are fighting and losing their lives. What would have been the position of Great Britain to-day in the face of that spectacle if we had assented to this infamous proposal? Yes, and what are we to get in return for the betrayal of our friends and the dishonor of our obligations? What are we to get in return? A promise—nothing more; a promise as to what Germany would do in certain eventualities; a promise, be it observed—I am sorry to have to say it, but it must be put upon record—given by a Power which was at that very moment announcing its intention to violate its own treaty and inviting us to do the same. I can only say, if we had dallied or temporized, we, as a Government, should have covered ourselves with dishonor, and we should have betrayed the interests of this country, of which we are trustees. I am glad, and I think the country will be glad, to turn to the reply which my right hon. Friend made, and of which I will read to the House two of the more salient passages. This document, No. 101 of the White Paper, puts on record a week ago the attitude of the British Government, and, as I believe, of the British people. My right hon. Friend says:—

"His Majesty's Government cannot for a moment entertain the Chancellor's proposal that they should bind themselves to neutrality on such terms. What he asks us in effect is to engage to stand by while French Colonies are taken if France is beaten, so long as Germany does not take French territory as distinct from the Colonies. From the material point of view"—

My right hon. Friend, as he always does, used very temperate language:—

"such a proposal is unacceptable, for France, without further territory in Europe being taken from her, could be so crushed as to lose her position as a Great Power, and become subordinate to German policy."

That is the material aspect. But he proceeded:—

"Altogether, apart from that, it would be a disgrace for us to make this bargain with Germany at the expense of France, a disgrace from which the good name of this country would never recover. The Chancellor also in effect asks us to bargain away whatever obligation or interest we have as regards the neutrality of Belgium. We could not entertain that bargain either."

He then says:—

"We must preserve our full freedom to act, as circumstances may seem to us to require."

And he added, I think, in sentences which the House will appreciate:—

"You should ... add most earnestly that the one way of maintaining the good relations between England and Germany is that they should continue to work together to preserve the peace of Europe. ... For that object this Government will work in that way with all sincerity and good will.

"If the peace of Europe can be preserved and the present crisis safely passed, my own endeavour will be to promote some arrangement to which Germany could be a party, by which she could be assured that no aggressive or hostile policy would be pursued against her or her allies by France, Russia, and ourselves, jointly or separately. I have desired this and worked for it"—

The statement was never more true:—

"as far as I could, through the last Balkan crisis, and Germany having a corresponding object, our relations sensibly improved. The idea has hitherto been too Utopian to form the subject of definite proposals, but if this present crisis, so much more acute than any that Europe has gone through for generations, be safely passed, I am hopeful that the relief and reaction which will follow may make possible some more definite rapprochement between the Powers than has been possible hitherto."

That document, in my opinion, states clearly, in temperate and convincing language, the attitude of this Government. Can any one who reads it fail to appreciate the tone of obvious sincerity and earnestness which underlies it? Can any one honestly doubt that the Government of this country in spite of great provocation—and I regard the proposals made to us as proposals which we might have thrown aside without consideration and almost without answer—can any one doubt that in spite of great provocation the right hon.

Gentleman, who had already earned the title—and no one ever more deserved it—of Peace Maker of Europe, persisted to the very last moment of the last hour in that beneficent but unhappily frustrated purpose? I am entitled to say, and I do so on behalf of this country—I speak not for a party, I speak for the country as a whole—that we made every effort any Government could possibly make for peace. But this war has been forced upon us. What is it we are fighting for? Every one knows, and no one knows better than the Government, the terrible, incalculable suffering, economic, social, personal, and political, which war, and especially a war between the Great Powers of the world must entail. There is no man amongst us sitting upon this bench in these trying days —more trying perhaps than any body of statesmen for a hundred years have had to pass through—there is not a man amongst us who has not, during the whole of that time, had clearly before his vision the almost unequalled suffering which war, even in a just cause, must bring about, not only to the people who are for the moment living in this country and in the other countries of the world, but to posterity and to the whole prospects of European civilization. Every step we took with that vision before our eyes, and with a sense of responsibility which it is impossible to describe. Unhappily, if in spite of all our efforts to keep the peace, and with that full and overpowering consciousness of the result if the issue were decided in favor of war, we have, nevertheless, thought it to be the duty as well as the interest of this country, to go to war, the House may be well assured it was because we believe, and I am certain the country will believe, that we are unsheathing our sword in a just cause.

If I am asked what we are fighting for I reply in two sentences. In the first place to fulfill a solemn international obligation, an obligation which, if it had been entered into between private persons in the ordinary concerns of life, would have been regarded as an obligation not only of law but of honor which no self-respecting man could possibly have repudiated. I say, secondly, we are fighting to vindicate the principle which, in these days when force, material force, sometimes seems to be the dominant influence and factor in the development of mankind, we are fighting to vindicate the principle that small nationalities are not to be crushed, in defiance of international good faith, by the arbitrary will of a strong and overmastering Power. I do not believe any nation ever entered into a great controversy—and this is one of the greatest history will ever know—with a clearer conscience and stronger conviction that it is fighting not for aggression, not for the maintenance of its own selfish interest, but that it is fighting in defense of principles, the maintenance of which is vital to the civilization of the world. With a full conviction, not only of the wisdom and justice of our cause, but of the obligations which lay upon us to challenge this great issue, we are entering into the struggle. Let us now make sure that all the resources, not only of this United Kingdom, but of the vast Empire of which it is the center, shall be thrown into the scale, and it is that this object may be adequately secured, that I am now about to ask this Committee—to make the very unusual demand upon it—to give the Government a Vote of Credit of £100,000,000. I am not going, and I am sure the Committee do not wish it, into the technical distinctions between Votes of Credit and Supplementary Estimates and all the rarities and refinements which arise in that connection. There is a much higher point of view than that. If it were necessary, I could justify, upon purely technical grounds, the course we propose to adopt, but I am not going to do so, because I think it would be foreign to the temper and disposition of the Committee. There is one thing to which I do call attention, that is, the Title and Heading of the Bill. As a rule, in the past votes of this kind have been taken simply for naval and military operations, but we have thought it right to ask the Committee to give us its confidence in the extension of the traditional area of Votes of Credit so that this money which we are asking them to allow us to expend may be applied not only for strictly naval and military operations, but to assist the food supplies, promote the continuance of trade, industry, business, and communications, whether by means of insurance or indemnity against risk or otherwise, for the relief of distress, and generally for all expenses arising out of the existence of a state of war. I believe the Committee will agree with us that it was wise to extend the area of the Vote of Credit so as to include all these various matters. It

ENGLAND SUPPORTS BELGIUM

gives the Government a free hand. Of course, the Treasury will account for it, and any expenditure that takes place will be subject to the approval of the House. I think it would be a great pity—in fact, a great disaster—if, in a crisis of this magnitude, we were not enabled to make provision—provision far more needed now than it was under the simpler conditions that prevailed in the old days—for all the various ramifications and developments of expenditure which the existence of a state of war between the Great Powers of Europe must entail on any one of them.

I am asking also in my character of Secretary of State for War—a position which I held until this morning—for a Supplementary Estimate for men for the Army. Perhaps the Committee will allow me for a moment just to say on that personal matter that I took upon myself the office of Secretary of State for War under conditions upon which I need not go back but which are fresh in the minds of every one, in the hope and with the object that the condition of things in the Army, which all of us deplored, might speedily be brought to an end and complete confidence reëstablished. I believe that is the case; in fact, I know it to be. There is no more loyal and united body, no body in which the spirit and habit of discipline are more deeply ingrained and cherished than the British Army. Glad as I should have been to continue the work of that office, and I would have done so under normal conditions, it would not be fair to the Army, it would not be just to the country, that any Minister should divide his attention between that Department and another, still less that the First Minister of the Crown, who has to look into the affairs of all departments and who is ultimately responsible for the whole policy of the Cabinet, should give, as he could only give, perfunctory attention to the affairs of our Army in a great war. I am very glad to say that a very distinguished soldier and administrator, in the person of Lord Kitchener, with that great public spirit and patriotism that every one would expect from him at my request stepped into the breach. Lord Kitchener, as every one knows, is not a politician. His association with the Government as a Member of the Cabinet for this purpose must not be taken as in any way identifying him with any set of political opinions. He has, at a great public emergency, responded to a great public call, and I am certain he will have with him, in the discharge of one of the most arduous tasks that has ever fallen upon a Minister, the complete confidence of all parties and all opinions.

I am asking on his behalf for the Army, power to increase the number of men of all ranks, in addition to the number already voted, by no less than 500,000. I am certain the Committee will not refuse its sanction, for we are encouraged to ask for it not only by our own sense of the gravity and the necessities of the case, but by the knowledge that India is prepared to send us certainly two Divisions, and that every one of our self-governing Dominions, spontaneously and unasked, has already tendered to the utmost limits of their possibilities, both in men and in money, every help they can afford to the Empire in a moment of need. Sir, the Mother Country must set the example while she responds with gratitude and affection to those filial overtures from the outlying members of her family.

Sir, I will say no more. This is not an occasion for controversial discussion. In all that I have said I believe I have not gone, either in the statement of our case or in my general description of the provision we think it necessary to make, beyond the strict bounds of truth. It is not my purpose—it is not the purpose of any patriotic man—to inflame feeling, to indulge in rhetoric, to excite international animosities. The occasion is far too grave for that. We have a great duty to perform, we have a great trust to fulfill, and confidently we believe that Parliament and the country will enable us to do it.

NICHOLAS II, CZAR OF RUSSIA

RUSSIA ENTERS THE WAR

[Speech made at the Winter Palace on August 8, 1914.
This address was made in the great Hall of the Winter Palace before the assembly to announce the opening of the War and appeals to the people for support.

In connection with the appeal of the Czar, we print the speech in the Duma made by Kerensky the leader of the Labor Party. The two speeches can now be read in the light of subsequent events—melancholy and ironical contrasts to the hopes and sentiments then expressed by the Czar.

I GREET you in these significant and troubled times which Russia is experiencing. Germany, and after her Austria, has declared war on Russia. Such an uplifting of patriotic feeling, love for our homes, and devotion to the Throne, which has swept over our land like a hurricane, serves in my eyes, and I think in yours, as a guarantee that our Great Mother Russia will by the help of our Lord God bring the war to a successful conclusion. In this united outburst of affection and readiness for all sacrifices, even that of life itself, I feel the possibility of upholding our strength, and quietly and with confidence look forward to the future.

We are not only protecting our honor and our dignity within the limits of our land, but also that of our brother Slavs, who are of one blood and faith with us. At this time I observe with joy that the feeling of unity among the Slavs has been brought into strong prominence throughout all Russia. I believe that you, each and all, in your place can sustain this Heaven-sent trial and that we all, beginning with myself, will fulfill our duty to the end. Great is the God of our Russian land! [Long cries of "Hurrah!" sounded in the Great Hall.]

ALEXANDER KERENSKY

DECLARATION OF THE LABOR PARTY

[Declaration of the Labor Party made in the Russian Duma August 8, 1914.
Kerensky's speech pledging loyalty of the Labor Party to Russia during the War was delivered with inspiring enthusiasm and drowned with enthusiastic applause.]

A HEAVY trial has fallen on the country and a great sorrow on the land. Thousands and thousands of young lives are doomed to inhuman sufferings; misery and want come to lay waste the orphaned homes of the working masses of the population. We steadfastly believe that the great primeval force of Russian democracy will join with other forces in giving decisive resistance to the enemy [applause], and in protecting the land of our birth and our civilization, created by the sweat and blood of generations. We believe that on the field of battle and amidst suffering the brotherhood of all the races of Russia will be strengthened and a common desire created to free the land from its terrible internal troubles. The responsibility of those European Governments who in the interests of the ruling classes have plunged their peoples into a fratricidal war is incalculable.

The Socialists of all these belligerent countries—France, England, Belgium, and Germany—have tried to protest against this war which has burst upon us. We, the Russian democracy, were not able, even at the last, to raise our voice freely against the impending war. But, deeply believing in the brotherhood of the workers of all lands, we send our fraternal greetings to all who protested against these preparations for this fratricidal conflict of peoples. Russian citizens, remember that we have no enemies among the working classes of these fighting countries. Protect to the end your country from attacks by Governments hostile to us, Germany and Austria, but remember that there would not have been this terrible war had the great ideals of democracy—freedom, equality, and brotherhood—been directing those who control the destinies of Russia and all other countries. As it is, our rulers even in this terrible hour show no desire to forget internal strife, give no amnesty for those who are struggling for the freedom and welfare of the land, show no desire for reconciliation with the non-Russian peoples of the Empire, who have forgiven all and are fighting by our side and for our common Fatherland, and instead of lightening the position of the working classes, the Government is laying on them the greatest weight of the military expenses, increasing the burden of indirect taxation. Peasants and workmen, all who wish for the happiness of Russia, strengthen your souls in these great trials, summon up all your strength when you have protected your country, and free it. Brotherly greetings to you and to our brothers who are shedding their blood for their country. [Wild enthusiasm and applause.]

II. THE PROGRESS OF THE WAR
SIR WILFRID LAURIER

"READY, AYE, READY"

[This speech was delivered in the Canadian House of Commons, August 19, 1914, by the veteran leader of the Liberal party, then in opposition. In his seventy-third year, Sir Wilfrid Laurier still retained the great gift of eloquence which had swayed courts and parliaments ever since he began the practice of law over fifty years before. Born in 1841, leader of the Liberal party in 1887, Prime Minister of Canada from 1896 to 1911, he was for many years the chief of Canadian orators. His tribute to Queen Victoria is printed in Volume VII of "Modern Eloquence." He died in 1919.]

THE observations which I shall have to offer to the House are few and brief. In fact, apart from the usual compliments and congratulations to the mover and seconder of the address, which, I am pleased to say, I have more than usual pleasure in extending to them, I have but one declaration to make.

The gravity of the occasion which has called us together makes it incumbent upon us even to disregard the formalities and conventionalities which in ordinary times the rules of the House, written and unwritten, enjoin as a wise safeguard against precipitate action, but which, on such occasion as this, might impede us in dealing with the momentous question before us. This session has been called for the purpose of giving the authority of Parliament and the sanction of law to such measures as have already been taken by the Government, and any further measures that may be needed, to insure the defense of Canada and to give what aid may be in our power to the Mother Country in the stupendous struggle which now confronts her. Speaking for those who sit around me, speaking for the wide constituencies which we represent, to these measures we are prepared to give immediate assent. If in what has been done or in what remains to be done there may be anything which in our judgment should not be done or should be differently done, we raise no question, we take no exception, we offer no criticism, and we shall offer no criticism so long as there is danger at the front. It is our duty, more pressing upon us than all other duties, at once, on this first day of this extraordinary session of the Canadian Parliament, to let Great Britain know, and to let friends and foes of Great Britain know, that there is in Canada but one mind and one heart, and that all Canadians stand behind the mother country, conscious and proud that she has engaged in this war, not from any selfish motive, for any purpose of aggrandizement, but to maintain untarnished the honor of her name, to fulfill her obligations to her allies, to maintain her treaty obligations, and to save civilization from the unbridled lust of conquest and domination.

We are British subjects, and to-day we are face to face with the consequences which are involved in that proud fact. Long we have enjoyed the benefits of our British citizenship; to-day it is our duty to accept its responsibilities and its sacrifices. We have long said that when Great Britain is at war we are at war; to-day we realize that Great Britain is at war and that Canada is at war also. Our territory is liable to attack and invasion. So far as invasion is concerned, I do not see that there is any cause for apprehension, for it seems to me obvious that neither Austria nor Germany, our foes in this war, can command any force able to make an attack so far from their base. But no one pretends that our maritime cities on the Pacific and the Atlantic, are free from the possibility of insult by an audacious corsair, who, descending suddenly upon our shores, might subject them to an insolent raid and decamp with his booty, before punishment could reach him. This is not an unfounded dread of danger; this is no mere illusion; it is a real and indeed a proximate danger, since it is a matter of notoriety that both on the Pacific and on the Atlantic there are German cruisers whose mission is to inflict all the injury they can upon our commerce, and even to raid our cities should they find our harbors unguarded. We are aware that the Government has already taken measures, and very appropriately, to guard against this danger. We know that one of our battleships on the Pacific has been seeking that enemy, and if she has not yet engaged him it is because the enemy has eluded her pursuit.

We have had another and more striking evidence that when Great Britain is at war we are at war, in this—that our commerce has been interrupted, and perhaps the expression would not be too strong if I were to say that it has been to some extent dislocated. From the day war was declared—nay, from the day the possibility of war was first mooted—our shipping to Great Britain and to Europe has been interrupted. Ships were lying at the docks fully loaded and ready to put to sea, but unable to do so because of the fact that when England is at war Canadian property on the high seas is liable to capture. Our ships therefore had to remain in port so long as precautions had not been taken to clear the way and to insure their safe passage across the ocean. What measures have been taken in regard to that we have not yet been told, but I have no doubt that we shall have that information in due time.

The correspondence brought down yesterday, however, has informed us that the Canadian Government has already taken steps to send a contingent of twenty thousand men or thereabouts to take their place in the firing line. Upon this occasion I owe it to the House and to myself to speak with absolute frankness and candor. This is a subject which has often been a subject of debate in this House. I have always said, and I repeat it on this occasion, that there is but one mind and one heart in Canada. At other times we may have had different views as to the methods by which we are to serve our country and our empire. More than once I have declared that if England were ever in danger—nay, not only in danger, but if she were ever engaged in such a contest as would put her strength to the test—then it would be the duty of Canada to assist the motherland to the utmost of Canada's ability. England to-day is not engaged in an ordinary contest. The war in which she is engaged will in all probability—nay, in absolute certainty—stagger the world with its magnitude and its horror. But that war is for as noble a cause as ever impelled a nation to risk her all upon the arbitrament of the sword. That question is no longer at issue; the judgment of the world has already pronounced upon it. I speak not only of those nations which are engaged in this war, but of the neutral nations. The testimony of the ablest men of these nations, without dissenting voice, is that to-day the allied nations are fighting for freedom against oppression, for democracy against autocracy, for civilization against reversion to that state of barbarism in which the supreme law is the law of might.

It is an additional source of pride to us that England did not seek this war. It is a matter of history—one of the noblest pages in the history of England—that she never drew the sword until every means had been exhausted to secure and to keep an honorable peace. For a time it was hoped that Sir Edward Grey, who on more than one occasion has saved Europe from such a calamity, would again avert the awful scourge of war. Sir, it will go down on a still nobler page of history that England could have averted this war if she had been willing to forego the position which she has maintained for many centuries at the head of European civilization;—if she had been willing to desert her allies, to sacrifice her obligation; to allow the German Emperor to bully heroic Belgium, to trample upon defenseless Luxemburg, to rush upon isolated France, and to put down his booted heel upon continental Europe. At that price England would have secured peace; but her answer to the German Emperor was: "Your proposals are infamous." And rather than accept them, England has entered into this war; and there is not to-day in the universe a British subject, there is not outside the British Empire a single man whose admiration for England is not greater by reason of this firm and noble attitude.

So to-day England is at war. Her fleets are maintaining the freedom of the ocean. Her armies have already crossed the channel towards plains made famous more than once by British valor, this time to maintain the independence of Belgium by taking a place in the fighting line beside the small and heroic Belgian army, and to help scarcely less heroic France, whose forces are concentrated in an effort to repel the invader and to maintain and to save intact that which to a proud nation makes life worth living.

I am well aware that the small contingent of some 20,000 men which we are going to send will have to show double courage and double steadiness if they are to give any account of themselves among the millions of men who are now converging towards the frontiers of France, where the battle of giants is to be decided. But, Sir, it is the opinion of the British Government, as disclosed by the correspondence which was brought to us yesterday, that the assistance of our troops, humble as it may be, will be appreciated, either for its material value or for the greater moral help which will be rendered. It will be seen by the world that Canada, a daughter of old England, intends to stand by her in this great conflict. When the call comes our answer goes at once, and it goes in the classical language of the British answer to the call to duty: "Ready, aye, ready."

If my words can be heard beyond the walls of this House in the province from which I come, among the men whose blood flows in my viens, I should like them to remember that, in taking their place to-day in the ranks of the Canadian army to fight for the cause of the allied nations, a double honor rests upon them. The very cause for which they are called upon to fight is to them doubly sacred.

In this country we are not all of the same origin; we are not all of British or of French descent. I was struck by the words of the honorable member for South Oxford [Mr. Sutherland] in reference to our fellow-citizens of German origin. They are certainly among our best citizens. This has been acknowledged on more than one occasion. They are proud of the land of their adoption, which to many of them is the land of their birth, and they have shown more than once their devotion to British institutions. But, Sir, they would not be men if they had not in their hearts a deep feeling of affection for the land of their ancestors, and nobody would blame them for that. There is nothing, perhaps, so painful as the situation in which mind and heart are driven in opposite directions. But let me tell my fellow-countrymen of German origin that we have no quarrel with the German people. We respect and admire as much as they do the proud race from which they have their descent; we acknowledge all that the world owes to the German people for their contribution to the happiness of mankind by their progress in literature, in art and in science. But perhaps our German fellow-citizens will permit me to say that, in the struggle for constitutional freedom which has been universal in Europe during the last century, the German people have not made the same advance as have some of the other nations of Europe. I am sure that they will agree with me that if the institutions of the land of their ancestors were as free as the institutions of the land of their adoption, this cruel war would never have taken place. Nothing can be truer than the words which are reported to have been uttered by a German soldier made a prisoner in Belgium that this war is not a war of the German people; and if there is a silver lining to this darkest cloud which now overhangs Europe it is that, as a result and consequence of this war, the German people will take the determination to put an end forever to this personal imperialism, and so make it impossible evermore for one man to throw millions of the human race into all the horrors of modern warfare.

We cannot forget that the issue of battles is always uncertain, as has been proven already in the present contest. In invading Belgium, some two weeks ago, the German Emperor invoked the memory of his ancestors and called upon the blessing of God. The German Emperor might have remembered that there is a treaty guaranteeing the independence, the integrity, the neutrality of Belgium, and that this treaty was signed in the last century by the most illustrious of his ancestors, Emperor William the First of Germany. He might have remembered also that there is this precept in the divine book: "Remove not the ancient landmarks which thy fathers have set up." But the German Emperor threw his legions against this landmark in the fullness of his lust of power, with the full expectation that the very weight of his army would crush every opposition and would secure their passage through Belgium. He did not expect, he could not believe, that the Belgians, few in numbers and peaceful in disposition and in occupation, would rise in his way and bar his progress; or if he harbored such a thought for one moment his next thought was that if he met such an opposition he could brush it aside by a wave of his imperial hand. Sir, he should have remembered that in the sixteenth century the ancestors of the Belgians rose against the despotism of Phillip II of Spain, and, through years of blood and fire and miseries and sufferings indescribable, they maintained an unequal contest against Spain—Spain as powerful in Europe at that time as the German Empire is to-day. Sir, if there are men who forget the teachings of their fathers, the Belgians are not of that class; they have proved equal to the teachings of their fathers; they have never surrendered; the blood of the fathers still runs in the veins of the sons; and again to-day, through blood and fire and miseries and sufferings indescribable, they hold at bay the armies of the proud Kaiser.

I repeat, Sir, that the issue of battles are always uncertain. There may be disappointments, there may be reverses, but we enter into this fight with full hope as to the ultimate result:

> For freedom's battle once begun,
> Bequeathed from bleeding sire to son,
> Tho' often lost, is ever won.

Sir, upon this occasion we too invoke the blessing of God—not the God of battles, but the God of justice and mercy; and it is with ample confidence in Providence that we appeal to the justice of our cause.

Nay, more, already England has won a single victory, a victory more precious, perhaps, than any that can be achieved by her fleets or by her armies. Only a few weeks ago the Irish problem was pending on the scales of destiny. The possibility of civil strife in Ireland already rejoiced the eyes of Britain's enemies. But to-day the specter of civil war has vanished from Ireland; all Irishmen are united, ready to fight for King and Country. The volunteers of the North and the volunteers of the South, forgetting their past differences, stand shoulder to shoulder, ready to shed their blood for the common cause. And, Sir, may I not say that the hope is not vain that in that baptism of blood may be washed away, and forever washed away, the distrust of one another which has been the curse of Ireland in ages past.

But it is not only in Ireland that you find this union of hearts. In the two other United Kingdoms the voice of faction has been silenced. Even those who on principle do not believe in war admit that this was a just war and that it had to be fought. That union of hearts which exists in the United

Kingdom exists also in Canada, in Australia, in New Zealand. Yea, even in South Africa—South Africa, rent by war less than twenty years ago, but now united under the blessing of British institutions.

With all, British and Dutch together, standing ready to shed their blood for the common cause, Sir, there is in this the inspiration and the hope that from this painful war the British Empire may emerge with a new bond of union, the pride of all its citizens, and a living light to other nations.

DAVID LLOYD GEORGE

AN APPEAL TO THE NATION

[This speech was delivered at Queen's Hall, London, on September 19, 1914. The meeting was composed mainly of the speaker's Welsh countrymen. Its primary purpose was to promote recruiting for the War, but it was awaited with interest as Lloyd George's appeal to the Nation. It was universally hailed as the greatest speech of his career. It may be noticed that unlike the speeches of Sir Edward Grey and Asquith, it was made before a large public audience. An earlier address and a biography of Lloyd George are included in Volume IX of Modern Eloquence. He was Chancellor of the Exchequer at the beginning of the war, became Commissioner of Munitions in 1914, Secretary of State for War in 1916, and Prime Minister on December 19, 1916. He led the nation to victory, and continued Prime Minister until the election of November, 1922.]

THERE is no man in this room who has always regarded the prospect of engaging in a great war with greater reluctance and with greater repugnance than I have done throughout the whole of my political life. ["Hear, hear!"] There is no man either inside or outside this room more convinced that we could not have avoided it without national dishonor. [Great applause.] I am fully alive to the fact that every nation that has ever engaged in war has always invoked the sacred name of honor. Many a crime has been committed in its name; there are some being committed now. All the same, national honor is a reality, and any nation that disregards it is doomed. ["Hear, hear!"] Why is our honor as a country involved in this war? Because, in the first instance, we are bound by honorable obligations to defend the independence, the liberty, the integrity, of a small neighbor that has always lived peaceably. [Applause.] She could not have compelled us; she was weak; but the man who declines to discharge his duty because his creditor is too poor to enforce it is a blackguard. [Loud applause.] We entered into a treaty—a solemn treaty—two treaties—to defend Belgium and her integrity. Our signatures are attached to the documents. Our signatures do not stand there alone; this country was not the only country that undertook to defend the integrity of Belgium. Russia, France, Austria, Prussia—they are all there. Why are Austria and Prussia not performing the obligations of their bond? It is suggested that when we quote this treaty it is purely an excuse on our part—it is our low craft and cunning to cloak our jealousy of a superior civilization—[Laughter]—that we are attempting to destroy.

Our answer is the action we took in 1870. ["Hear, hear!"] What was that? Mr. Gladstone was then Prime Minister. [Applause.] Lord Granville, I think, was then Foreign Secretary. I have never heard it laid to their charge that they were ever Jingoes.

What did they do in 1870? That treaty bound us then. We called upon the belligerent Powers to respect it. We called upon France, and we called upon Germany. At that time, bear in mind, the greatest danger to Belgium came from France and not from Germany. We intervened to protect Belgium against France, exactly as we are doing now to protect her against Germany. [Applause.] We proceeded in exactly the same way. We invited both the belligerent Powers to state that they had no intention of violating Belgium territory. What was the answer given by Bismarck? He said it was superfluous to ask Prussia such a question in view of the treaties in force. France gave a similar answer. We received at that time the thanks of the Belgian people for our intervention in a very remarkable document. It is a document addressed by the municipality of Brussels to Queen Victoria after that intervention, and it reads:

"The great and noble people over whose destinies you preside has just given a further proof of its benevolent sentiments towards our country. . . . The voice of the English nation has been heard above the din of arms, and it has asserted the principles of justice and right. Next to the unalterable attachment of the Belgian people to their independence, the strongest sentiment which fills their hearts is that of imperishable gratitude."

That was in 1870. Mark what followed. Three or four days after that document of thanks, a French army was wedged up against the Belgian frontier; every means of escape shut out by a ring of flame from Prussian cannon. There was one way of escape. What was that? Violating the neutrality of Belgium. What did they do? The French on that occasion preferred ruin and humiliation to the breaking of their bond. [Loud applause.] The French Emperor, the French Marshals, 100,000 gallant Frenchmen in arms, preferred to be carried captive to the strange land of their enemies, rather than dishonor the name of their country. [Applause.] It was the French army in the field. Had they violated Belgian neutrality, the whole history of that war would have been changed, and yet, when it was the interest of France to break the treaty then, she did not do it.

It is the interest of Prussia to-day to break the treaty, and she has done it. [Hisses.] She avows it with cynical contempt for every principle of justice. She says "Treaties only bind you when your interest is to keep them." [Laughter.] "What is a treaty?" says the German Chancellor; "A scrap of paper." Have you any £5 notes about you? [Laughter and applause.] I am not calling for them. [Laughter.] Have you any of those neat little Treasury £1 notes? [Laughter.] If you have, burn them; they are only scraps of paper. [Laughter and applause.] What are they made of? Rags. [Laughter.] What are they worth? The whole credit of the British Empire. [Loud applause.] Scraps of paper! I have been dealing with scraps of paper within the last month. One suddenly found the commerce of the world coming to a standstill. The machine had stopped. Why? I will tell you. We discovered—many of us for the first time, for I do not pretend that I do not know much more about the machinery of commerce to-day than I did six weeks ago, and there are many others like me—we discovered that the machinery of commerce was moved by bills of exchange. I have seen

AN APPEAL TO THE NATION

some of them—[Laughter]—wretched, crinkled, scrawled over, blotched, frowsy, and yet those wretched little scraps of paper move great ships laden with thousands of tons of precious cargo from one end of the world to the other. [Applause.] What is the motive power behind them? The honor of commercial men. [Applause.] Treaties are the currency of International statesmanship. [Applause.] Let us be fair: German merchants, German traders, have the reputation of being as upright and straightforward as any traders in the world—["Hear, hear!"]—but if the currency of German commerce is to be debased to the level of that of her statesmanship, no trader from Shanghai to Valparaiso will ever look at a German signature again. [Loud applause.] This doctrine of the scrap of paper, this doctrine which is proclaimed by Bernhardi, that treaties only bind a nation as long as it is to its interest, goes under the root of all public law. It is the straight road to barbarism. ["Hear, hear!"] It is as if you were to remove the Magnetic Pole because it was in the way of a German cruiser. [Laughter.] The whole navigation of the seas would become dangerous, difficult, and impossible; and the whole machinery of civilization will break down if this doctrine wins in this way. ["Hear, hear!"] We are fighting against barbarism [applause] and there is one way of putting it right. If there are nations that say they will only respect treaties when it is to their interest to do so, we must make it to their interest to do so for the future. [Applause.]

What is their defense? Consider the interview which took place between our Ambassador and the great German officials. When their attention was called to this treaty to which they were parties, they said "We cannot help that. Rapidity of action is the great German asset." There is a greater asset for a nation than rapidity of action and that is honest dealing. [Loud applause.] What are Germany's excuses? She says Belgium was plotting against her; Belgium was engaged in a great conspiracy with Britain and France to attack her. Not merely is it not true, but Germany knows it is not true. ["Hear, hear!"] France offered Belgium five army corps to defend her if she was attacked. Belgium said, "I do not require them; I have the word of the Kaiser. Shall Cæsar send a lie?" [Laughter and applause.] All these tales about conspiracy have been vamped up since. A great nation ought to be ashamed to behave like a fraudulent bankrupt, perjuring its way through its obligations. ["Hear, hear!"] What she says is not true. She has deliberately broken this treaty, and we are in honor bound to stand by it. [Applause.]

Belgium has been treated brutally. ["Hear, hear!"] How brutally we shall not yet know. We already know too much. What had she done? Had she sent an ultimatum to Germany? Had she challenged Germany? Was she preparing to make war on Germany? Had she inflicted any wrong upon Germany which the Kaiser was bound to redress? She was one of the most unoffending little countries in Europe. ["Hear, hear!"] There she was—peaceable, industrious, thrifty, hardworking, giving offense to no one. And her corn-fields have been trampled, her villages have been burnt, her art treasures have been destroyed, her men have been slaughtered—yea, and her women and children too. [Cries of "Shame."] Hundreds and thousands of her people, their neat comfortable little homes burnt to the dust, are wandering homeless in their own land. What was their crime? Their crime was that they trusted to the word of a Prussian King. [Applause.] I do not know what the Kaiser hopes to achieve by this war. [Derisive laughter.] I have a shrewd idea what he will get; but one thing he has made certain, and that is that no nation will ever commit that crime again.

I am not going to enter into details of outrages. Many of them are untrue, and always are in a war. War is a grim, ghastly business at best or worst ["Hear, hear!"] and I am not going to say that all that has been said in the way of outrages must necessarily be true. I will go beyond that, and I will say that if you turn two millions of men—forced, conscript, compelled, driven—into the field, you will always get amongst them a certain number who will do things that the nation to which they belong would be ashamed of. I am not depending on these tales. It is enough for me to have the story which Germans themselves avow, admit, defend, and proclaim—the burning, massacring, the shooting down of harmless people. Why? Because, according to the Germans, these people fired on German soldiers. What business had German soldiers there at all? ["Hear, hear" and applause.] Belgium was acting in pursuance of the most sacred right, the right to defend its homes. But they were not in uniform when they fired! If a burglar broke into the Kaiser's Palace at Potsdam, destroyed his furniture, killed his servants, ruined his art treasures —especially those he has made himself—[laughter and applause],—and burned the precious manuscript of his speeches, do you think he would wait until he got into uniform before he shot him down? [Laughter.] They were dealing with those who had broken into their household. ["Hear, hear!"] But the perfidy of the Germans has already failed. They entered Belgium to save time. The time has gone. [Loud and continued applause.] They have not gained time, but they have lost their good name. ["Hear, hear!"]

But Belgium is not the only little nation that has been attacked in this war, and I make no excuse for referring to the case of the other little nation, the case of Serbia. ["Hear, hear!"] The history of Serbia is not unblotted. Whose history, in the category of nations, is unblotted? ["Hear, hear!"] The first nation that is without sin, let her cast a stone at Serbia. She was a nation trained in a horrible school, but she won her freedom with a tenacious valor, and she has maintained it by the same courage. [Applause.] If the Serbians were mixed up in the assassination of the Grand Duke, they ought to be punished. ["Hear, hear!"] Serbia admits that. The Serbian Government had nothing to do with it. Not even Austria claims that. The Serbian Prime Minister is one of the most capable and honored men in Europe. ["Hear, hear!"] Serbia was willing to punish any one of her subjects who had been proved to have any complicity in that assassination. What more could you expect? What were the Austrian demands? Serbia sympathized with her fellow-countrymen in Bosnia—that was one of her crimes. She must do so no more. Her newspapers were saying nasty things about Austria: they must do so no longer. That is the German spirit; you had it in Zabern. ["Hear, hear!" and applause.] How dare you criticize a Prussian official?—[Laughter]—and if you laugh, it is a capital offense—the Colonel in Zabern threatened to shoot if it was repeated. In the same way the Serbian newspapers must not criticize Austria. I wonder what would have happened had we taken the same line about German newspapers. ["Hear, hear!"] Serbia said: "Very well, we will give orders to the newspapers that they must in future criticize neither Austria, nor Hungary, nor anything that is theirs." [Laughter.] Who can doubt the valor of Serbia, when she undertook to tackle her newspaper editors? [Laughter and applause.] She promised not to sympathize with Bosnia; she promised to write no critical articles about Austria; she would have no public meetings in which anything unkind was said about Austria.

But that was not enough. She must dismiss from her army the officers whom Austria should subsequently name. Those officers had just emerged from a war where they had added luster to the Serbian arms; they were gallant, brave, and efficient. ["Hear, hear!"] I wonder whether it was their guilt or their efficiency that prompted Austria's action! But, mark you, the officers were not named; Serbia was to undertake in advance to dismiss them from the army, the names to be sent in subsequently. Can you name a country in the world that would have stood that? [Cries of "No."] Supposing Austria or Germany had issued an ultimatum of that kind to this country, saying "You must dismiss from your Army—and from your Navy [Laughter]—all those officers whom we shall subsequently name." Well, I think I could name them now. [Laughter.] Lord Kitchener [Loud applause] would go. Sir John French [Applause] would be sent away; General Smith-Dorrien [Applause] would go, and I am sure that Sir John Jellico [Applause] would have to go. And there is another gallant old warrior who would go—Lord Roberts. [Applause.] It was a difficult situation for a small country. Here was a demand made upon her by a great military Power that could have put half a dozen men in the field for every one of Serbia's men, and that Power was supported by the greatest military Power in the world. How did Serbia behave? It is not what happens to you in life that matters. It is the way in which you face it ["Hear, hear!"] and Serbia faced the situation with dignity. She said to Austria: "If any officers of mine have been guilty, and are proved to be guilty, I will dismiss them." Austria said: "That is not good enough for me." It was not guilt she was after, but capacity. ["Hear, hear!"]

Then came Russia's turn. Russia has a special regard for

Serbia; she has a special interest in Serbia. Russians have shed their blood for Serbian independence many a time, for Serbia is a member of Russia's family, and she cannot see Serbia maltreated. Austria knew that. Germany knew it, and she turned round to Russia, and said: "I insist that you shall stand by with your arms folded whilst Austria is strangling your little brother to death." What answer did the Russian Slav give? He gave the only answer that becomes a man. ["Hear, hear!"] He turned to Austria and said: "You lay hands on that little fellow, and I will tear your ramshackle Empire—[Loud applause and laughter]—limb from limb." And he is doing it! [Loud applause.]

That is the story of the two little nations. The world owes much to little nations—and to little men! [Laughter and applause.] This theory of bigness, this theory that you must have a *big* Empire, and a *big* nation, and a *big* man—well, long legs have their advantage in a retreat. [Laughter and applause.] Frederick the First chose his warriors for their height, and that tradition has become a policy in Germany. Germany applies that ideal to nations, and will only allow 6-foot-2 nations to stand in the ranks. [Laughter.] But ah! the world owes much to the little 5-foot-5 nations. The greatest art in the world was the work of little nations; the most enduring literature of the world came from little nations; the greatest literature of England came when she was a nation of the size of Belgium fighting a great Empire. The heroic deeds that thrill humanity through generations were the deeds of little nations fighting for their freedom. Yes, and the salvation of mankind came through a little nation. God has chosen little nations as the vessels by which He carries His choicest wines to the lips of humanity, to rejoice their hearts, to exalt their vision, to stimulate and strengthen their faith; and if we stood by when two little nations were being crushed and broken by the brutal hands of barbarism, our shame would have rung down the everlasting ages. [Loud applause.]

But Germany insists that this is an attack by a lower civilization upon a higher one. [Derisive cries.] As a matter of fact, the attack was begun by the civilization which calls itself the higher one. I am no apologist for Russia: she has perpetrated deeds of which I have no doubt her best sons are ashamed. What Empire has not? But Germany is the last Empire to point the finger of reproach at Russia. ["Hear, hear!"] Russia has made sacrifices for freedom—great sacrifices. Do you remember the cry of Bulgaria when she was torn by the most insensate tyranny that Europe has ever seen? Who listened to that cry? The only answer of the higher civilization was that the liberty of the Bulgarian peasants was not worth the life of a single Pomeranian soldier. But the rude barbarians of the North sent their sons by the thousand to die for Bulgarian freedom. What about England? Go to Greece, the Netherlands, Italy, Germany, France—in all those lands I could point out places where the sons of Britain have died for the freedom of those peoples. [Loud applause.] France has made sacrifices for the freedom of other lands than her own. Can you name a single country in the world for the freedom of which modern Prussia has ever sacrificed a single life? ["No."] By the test of our faith, the highest standard of civilization is the readiness to sacrifice for others. [Applause.]

I will not say a single word in disparagement of the German people. They are a great people, and have great qualities of head and hand and heart. I believe, in spite of recent events, that there is as great a store of kindliness in the German peasant as in any peasant in the world; but he has been drilled into a false idea of civilization. It is efficient, it is capable; but it is a hard civilization; it is a selfish civilization; it is a material civilization. They cannot comprehend the action of Britain at the present moment; they say so. They say, "France we can understand; she is out for vengeance; she is out for territory—Alsace and Lorraine." [Applause.] They say they can understand Russia, she is fighting for mastery—she wants Galicia. They can understand you fighting for vengeance—they can understand you fighting for mastery—they can understand you fighting for greed of territory; but they cannot understand a great empire pledging its resources, pledging its might, pledging the lives of its children, pledging its very existence, to protect a little nation that seeks to defend herself. [Applause.] God made man in His own image, high of purpose, in the region of the spirit; German civilization would recreate him in the image of a Diesel machine

AN APPEAL TO THE NATION

—precise, accurate, powerful, but with no room for soul to operate. ["Hear, hear!"]

Have you read the Kaiser's speeches? If you have not a copy I advise you to buy one; they will soon be out of print, and you will not have many more of the same sort. [Laughter and applause.] They are full of the glitter and bluster of German militarism—"mailed fist," and "shining armor." Poor old mailed fist! Its knuckles are getting a little bruised. Poor shining armor! The shine is being knocked out of it. [Applause.] There is the same swagger and boastfulness running through the whole of the speeches. The extract which was given in the British Weekly this week is a very remarkable product as an illustration of the spirit we have to fight. It is the Kaiser's speech to his soldiers on the way to the front:

"Remember that the German people are the chosen of God. On me, the German Emperor, the Spirit of God has descended. I am His sword, His weapon, and His viceregent. Woe to the disobedient, and death to cowards and unbelievers."

Lunacy is always distressing, but sometimes it is dangerous; and when you get it manifested in the head of the State, and it has become the policy of a great Empire, it is about time that it should be ruthlessly put away. [Loud applause.] I do not believe he meant all these speeches; it was simply the martial straddle he had acquired. But there were men around him who meant every word of them. This was their religion. Treaties? They tangle the feet of Germany in her advance. Cut them with the sword. Little nations? They hinder the advance of Germany. Trample them in the mire under the German heel! The Russian Slav? He challenges the supremacy of Germany in Europe. Hurl your legions at him and massacre him! Christianity? Sickly sentimentalism about sacrifice for others! Poor pap for German digestion! We will have a new diet. We will force it upon the world. It will be made in Germany [laughter and applause]—a diet of blood and iron. What remains? Treaties have gone. The honor of nations has gone. Liberty has gone. What is left? Germany! Germany is left!—*"Deutschland uber Alles!"*

That is what we are fighting ["Hear, hear!"],—that claim to

predominancy of a material, hard civilization, which if it once rules and sways the world, liberty goes, democracy vanishes. And unless Britain and her sons come to the rescue it will be a dark day for humanity. [Applause.]

Have you followed the German Junker and his doings? We are not fighting the German people. The German people are under the heel of this military caste, and it will be a day of rejoicing for the German peasant, artisan, and trader when the military caste is broken. You know its pretensions. They give themselves the airs of demigods. They walk the pavements, and civilians and their wives are swept into the gutter; they have no right to stand in the way of the great Prussian soldier. Men, women, nations—they all have to go. He thinks all he has to say is "We are in a hurry." That is the answer he gave to Belgium—"Rapidity of action is Germany's greatest asset," which means, "I am in a hurry; clear out of my way." You know the type of motorist, the terror of the roads, with a 60-horse-power car, he thinks the roads are made for him and knocks down anybody who impedes the action of his car, by a single mile an hour. The Prussian Junker is the road-hog of Europe. [Applause.] Small nationalities in his way are hurled to the roadside, bleeding and broken. Women and children are crushed under the wheels of his cruel car, and Britain is ordered out of his road. All I can say is this: if the old British spirit is alive in British hearts, that bully will be torn from his seat. [Loud applause.] Were he to win it would be the greatest catastrophe that has befallen democracy since the day of the Holy Alliance and its ascendancy.

They think we cannot beat them. It will not be easy. It will be a long job; it will be a terrible war; but in the end we shall march through terror to triumph. [Applause.] We shall need all our qualities—every quality that Britain and its people possess—prudence in counsel, daring in action, tenacity in purpose, courage in defeat, moderation in victory; in all things faith. [Loud applause.]

It has pleased them to believe and to preach the belief that we are a decadent and a degenerate people. They proclaim to the world through their professors that we are a non-heroic nation skulking behind our mahogany counters, whilst we egg on more gallant races to their destruction. This is a description given of us in Germany—"a timorous, craven nation, trusting to its Fleet." I think they are beginning to find their mistake out already [applause]—and there are half a million young men of Britain who have already registered a vow to their King that they will cross the seas and hurl that insult to British courage against its perpetrators on the battlefields of France and Germany. We want half a million more; and we shall get them. [Loud applause.]

I envy you young people your opportunity. They have put up the age limit for the Army, but I am sorry to say I have marched a good many years even beyond that. It is a great opportunity, an opportunity that only comes once in many centuries to the children of men. For most generations sacrifice comes in drab and weariness of spirit. It comes to you to-day, and it comes to-day to us all, in the form of the glow and thrill of a great movement for liberty, that impels millions throughout Europe to the same noble end. [Applause.] It is a great war for the emancipation of Europe from the thraldom of a military caste which has thrown its shadows upon two generations of men, and is now plunging the world into a welter of bloodshed and death. Some have already given their lives. There are some who have given more than their own lives: they have given the lives of those who are dear to them. I honor their courage, and may God be their comfort and their strength. But their reward is at hand; those who have fallen have died consecrated deaths. They have taken their part in the making of a new Europe—a new world. I can see signs of its coming in the glare of the battlefield.

The people will gain more by this struggle in all lands than they comprehend at the present moment. ["Hear, hear!"] It is true they will be free of the greatest menace to their freedom. That is not all. There is something infinitely greater and more enduring which is emerging already out of this great conflict—a new patriotism, richer, nobler, and more exalted than the old. [Applause.] I see amongst all classes, high and low, shedding themselves of selfishness, a new recognition that the honor of the country does not depend merely on the maintenance of its glory in the stricken field, but also in protecting its homes from distress. ["Hear, hear!"] It is bringing a new outlook for all classes. The great flood of luxury and sloth which had submerged the land is receding and a new Britain is appearing. We can see for the first time the fundamental things that matter in life, and that have been obscured from our vision by the tropical growth of prosperity. ["Hear, hear!"]

May I tell you in a simple parable what I think this war is doing for us? I know a valley in North Wales, between the mountains and the sea. It is a beautiful valley, snug, comfortable, sheltered by the mountains from all the bitter blasts. But it is very enervating, and I remember how the boys were in the habit of climbing the hill above the village to have a glimpse of the great mountains in the distance, and to be stimulated and freshened by the breezes which came from the hilltops, and by the great spectacle of their grandeur. We have been living in a sheltered valley for generations. We have been too comfortable and too indulgent, many, perhaps, too selfish, and the stern hand of fate has scourged us to an elevation where we can see the great everlasting things that matter for a nation—the great peaks we had forgotten, of Honor, of Duty, Patriotism, and, clad in glittering white, the great pinnacle of sacrifice pointing like a rugged finger to Heaven. We shall descend into the valleys again; but as long as the men and women of this generation last, they will carry in their hearts the image of those great mountain peaks whose foundations are not shaken, though Europe rock and sway in the convulsions of a great war. [Enthusiastic and continued applause.]

RENÉ RAPHAEL VIVIANI

THE SPIRIT OF FRANCE

[At the first meeting of the Chambers since the memorable sitting of August 4, M. Viviani, Premier of France, defined the policy of his government in what the *Times* described as "eloquence of the highest order which springs at great moments from the heart." "It embodies in language that stirs men's blood, a train of serried appeals to reason and to conscience. It is all that France could wish her Prime Minister to say and all that the Allies could wish to hear from his lips. It reaffirms in strongest and plainest words what's their common policy and becomes therefore a diplomatic and political event."

The session was an impressive demonstration of national unity and determination and the voice of the whole nation was heard in the thunders of applause which marked the calm and defiant passages in which M. Viviani stated the unfaltering resolve of the whole of France to fight to the end. The speech was given in the Chamber of Deputies on December 22, 1914.]

THIS communication is not the customary declaration in which a Government, presenting itself to Parliament for the first time, defines its policy. For the moment there is but one policy—a relentless fight until Europe attains definite liberation guaranteed by a completely victorious peace. That was the cry uttered by all when, in the sitting of August 4, a sacred union arose, as the President of the Republic has so well said, which will throughout history remain an honor to the country. It is the cry which all Frenchmen repeat after having put an end to the disagreements which have so often embittered our hearts and which a blind enemy took for irremediable division. It is the cry that rises from the glorious trenches into which France has thrown all her youth, all her manhood.

Before this unexpected uprising of national feeling, Germany has been troubled in the intoxication of her dream of victory. On the first day of the conflict she denied right, appealed to force, flouted history, and in order to violate the neutrality of Belgium and to invade France, invoked the law of self-interest alone. Since then her Government, learning that it had to reckon with the opinion of the world, has recently attempted to put her conduct in a better light by trying to throw the responsibility for the war upon the Allies. But through all the gross falsehoods, which fail to deceive even the most credulous, the truth has become apparent. All the documents published by the nations interested and the remarkable speech made the other day at Rome by one of the most illustrious representatives of the noble Italian nation, demonstrate that for a long time our enemy has intended a *coup de force*. If it were necessary, a single one of these documents would suffice to enlighten the world. When, at the suggestion of the English Government, all the nations concerned were asked to suspend their military preparations and enter into negotiations in London, France and Russia on July 31, 1914, adhered to this proposal. Peace would have been saved even at this last moment, if Germany had conformed to this proposal. But Germany precipitated matters. She declared war on Russia on August 1 and made an appeal to arms inevitable. And if Germany, by her diplomacy, killed the germ of peace, it is because for more than forty years she had untiringly pursued her aim, which was to crush France in order to achieve the enslavement of the world.

Since, in spite of their attachment to peace, France and her Allies have been obliged to endure war, they will wage it to the end. Faithful to the signature which she set to the treaty of September 4 last, in which she engaged her honor—that is to say, her life—France, in accord with her Allies, will not lay down her arms until she has avenged outraged right, regained for ever the provinces torn from her by force, restored to heroic Belgium the fullness of her material prosperity and her political independence, and broken Prussian militarism, so that on the basis of justice she may rebuild a regenerated Europe.

This plan of war and this plan of peace are not inspired by any presumptuous hope. We have the certainty of success. We owe this certainty to the whole army, to the navy which, in conjunction with the English Navy, gives us the mastery of the sea, to the troops which have repulsed in Morocco attacks that will not be repeated. We owe it to the soldiers who are defending our flag in those distant colonies of France, who, on the first day that war broke out, turned with patriotic affection towards the mother country; we owe it to our army, whose heroism in numerous combats has been guided by their incomparable chiefs, from the victory on the Marne to the victory in Flanders; we owe it to the nation, which has equalled that heroism with union in silence and quiet trust in critical hours.

Thus we have shown to the world that an organized democracy can serve by its vigorous action the ideal of liberty and equality which constitutes its greatness. Thus we have shown to the world, to use the words of our Commander-in-Chief, who is both a great soldier and a noble citizen—that "the Republic may well be proud of the army that she has prepared." And thus this impious war has brought out all the virtues of our race, both those with which we were credited, of initiative, *élan,* bravery and fearlessness, and those which we were not supposed to possess—endurance, patience, and stoicism. Let us do honor to all these heroes. Glory to those who have fallen before the victory, and to those also who through it will avenge them to-morrow! A nation which can arouse such enthusiasm can never perish.

Everything serves to demonstrate the vitality of France, the security of her credit, the confidence which she inspires in all, despite the war which is shaking and impoverishing the world. The state of her finances is such that she can continue the war until the day when the necessary reparation has been obtained.

We should honor also those innocent civilian victims who hitherto had been safe from the ravages of war, and whom the enemy, in the effort to terrify the nation which remains and will continue immovable, has captured or massacred. The Government hereby takes a solemn engagement, which it has already partly discharged, in asking you to open a credit of three hundred million francs ($60,000,000). France will rebuild the ruins, anticipating the indemnities that we shall exact and the help of a contribution which the entire nation will pay, proud to fulfill its duty of national solidarity, in the hour of distress for a portion of its sons.

Gentlemen, the day of final victory has not yet come. Till that day our task will be a severe one, and it may be long drawn out. Let us stiffen our will and our courage for that task. Destined to uphold the heaviest burden of glory that a people can carry, this country is prepared beforehand for every sacrifice.

Our Allies know it. Those nations who have no immediate interest in the fight know it too, and it is in vain that an unbridled campaign of false news has attempted to rouse in them the sympathy which has been won by us. If Germany, at the beginning of the war, made pretense to doubt it, she doubts no longer. Let her recognize once more that on this day the French Parliament, after more than four months of battle, has renewed before the world the spectacle that it gave on the day on which our nation took up the challenge.

In order to conquer, heroism on the frontier does not suffice. There must be union within. Let us continue to preserve this sacred union intact from every attempt made upon it. To-day, as it was yesterday, and as it will be to-morrow, let us have only one cry—Victory; only one vision before our eyes—"La Patrie"; only one ideal—Right. It is for Right that we are striving, for which Belgium has poured out her blood, for which unshakable England, faithful Russia, intrepid Serbia, and the gallant Japanese Navy are still striving.

If this is the most gigantic war that history has ever known, it is not because nations are in arms to conquer new lands, to obtain material advantage or political and economic rights; it is because they are fighting to settle the fate of the world. Nothing more grand has ever appeared before the eyes of men. Against barbarism and despotism, against a system of provocation and methodical menace which Germany called peace, against the system of murder and universal pillage which Germany calls war, against the insolent hegemony of a military caste which has unchained this scourge, France, the liberator and avenger, with her Allies, has raised herself at one bound.

The stakes are more than our own lives. Let us continue, then, to work with a single mind, and to-morrow, in the peace of victory, when politics have been freed from the restraints which we have voluntarily placed upon them, we shall recall with pride these tragic days, for they will have made us more valiant and better.

KITCHENER OF KHARTUM

MORE MEN

[On July 8th a bill was passed in the House of Commons, providing for State registration of all persons between the ages of 15 and 65. At the Guild Hall on July 9th, Mr. Walter Long, the introducer of the bill, replied to the critics who saw in the bill the first steps toward compulsory service, that the government was absolutely free to take any measures which they believed to be right and necessary to

MORE MEN

bring the war to an end. Other speakers supported Mr. Long, and Earl Kitchener opened a recruiting campaign.

The meeting was an impressive tribute to Lord Kitchener whose services in raising the armies of the first great needs will never be overestimated. Though he was a man of action who made few public addresses, his spoken words always commanded attention.

Horatio Herbert Kitchener, First Earl of Khartum and of Broome, was born in 1850. He rose rapidly to high command in the army and achieved the reconquest of the Sudan in 1898. For this achievement he was made a peer and voted £30,000 by Parliament. He went to South Africa as Chief of Staff for Lord Roberts in 1900, took command in the same year, and brought the Boer war to a conclusion in 1902. He was raised to a viscountcy, voted £50,000 by Parliament, and appointed Commander-in-Chief in India. Upon the outbreak of the World War, Lord Kitchener was made Secretary of State for War, with the universal approval of the nation. On June 5, 1916, he embarked on the cruiser *Hampshire* sailing for Russia on an important mission. The ship struck a mine, and Lord Kitchener with all his staff perished.]

HITHERTO the remarks that I have found it necessary to make on the subject of recruiting have been mainly addressed to the House of Lords; but I have felt that the time has now come when I may with advantage avail myself of the courteous invitation of the Lord Mayor to appear among you, and in this historic Guildhall make another and a larger demand on the resources of British manhood. Enjoying, as I do, the privilege of a Freeman of this great city, I can be sure that words uttered in the heart of London will be spread broadcast throughout the Empire.

Our thoughts naturally turn to the splendid efforts of the Oversea Dominions and India, who from the earliest days of the war, have ranged themselves side by side with the Mother Country. The prepared armed forces of India were the first to take the field, closely followed by the gallant Canadians who are now fighting alongside their British and French comrades in Flanders, and there presenting a solid and impenetrable front against the enemy.

In the Dardanelles the Australians and New Zealanders, combined with the same elements, have already accomplished a feat of almost unexampled brilliancy. In each of these great Dominions new and large contingents are being prepared, while South Africa, not content with the conclusion of the arduous campaign in South-West Africa, is now offering large forces to engage the enemy in the main theater of war.

Strengthened by the unflinching support of our fellow-citizens across the seas, we seek to develop our own military resources to their utmost limits, and this is the purpose which brings us together to-day. Napoleon, when asked what were the three things necessary for a successful war, replied: "Money, money, money." To-day we vary that phrase, and say: "Men, Material, and Money." As regards the supply of money for the war, the governments are negotiating a new loan, the marked success of which is greatly due to the very favorable response made by the city. To meet the need of material, the energetic manner in which the new Minister of Munitions is coping with the many difficulties which confront the production of our great requirements, affords abundant proof that this very important work is being dealt with in a highly satisfactory manner.

There still remains the vital need for men to fill the ranks of our armies, and it is to emphasize this point and bring it home to the people of this country that I have come here this afternoon. When I took up the office that I hold, I did so as a soldier, not as a politician, and I warned my fellow-countrymen that the war would be not only arduous, but long. In one of my earliest statements, made after the beginning of the war, I said that I should require "Men, men, and still more, until the enemy is crushed." I repeat that statement to-day with even greater insistence. All the reasons which led me to think in August, 1914, that this war would be a prolonged one hold good at the present time. It is true we are in an immeasurably better situation now than ten months ago, but the position to-day is at least as serious as it was then.

The thorough preparedness of Germany, due to her strenuous efforts, sustained at high pressure for some 40 years, has issued in a military organization as complex in character as it is perfect in machinery. Never before has any nation been so elaborately organized for imposing her will upon the other nations of the world; and her vast resources of military strength are wielded by an autocracy which is peculiarly adapted for the conduct of war. It is true that Germany's long preparation has enabled her to utilize her whole resources from the very commencement of the war, while our policy is one of gradually increasing our effective forces. It might be said with truth that she *must* decrease, while we *must* increase.

Our voluntary system, which as you well know has been the deliberate choice of the English people, has rendered it necessary that our forces in peace should be of relatively slender dimensions, with a capacity for potential expansion; and we have habitually relied on time being allowed us to increase our armed forces during the progress of hostilities.

The time has now come when something more is required to ensure the demands of our forces overseas being fully met, and to enable the large reserve of men imperatively required for the proper conduct of the war to be formed and trained. The public has watched with eager interest the growth and the rapidly acquired efficiency of the new armies, whose dimensions have already reached a figure which only a short while ago would have been considered utterly unthinkable. But there is a tendency perhaps to overlook the fact that these large armies require still larger reserves, to make good the wastage at the front. And one cannot ignore the certainty that our requirements in this respect will be large, continuous, and persistent; for one feels that our gallant soldiers in the fighting line are beckoning with an urgency at once imperious and pathetic, to those who remain at home to come and play their part, too.

Recruiting meetings, recruiting marches, and the unwearied labors of the recruiting officers, committees, and individuals have borne good fruit, and I look forward with confidence to such labors being continued as energetically as hitherto.

What the numbers required are likely to be it is clearly inexpedient to shout abroad. Our constant refusal to publish either these or any other figures likely to prove useful to the enemy needs neither explanation nor apology. It is often urged that if more information were given as to the work and whereabouts of various units recruiting would be strongly stimulated. But this is the precise information which would be of the greatest value to the enemy, and it is agreeable to note that a German Prince in high command ruefully recorded the other day his complete ignorance as to our new armies.

But one set of figures, available for everybody, and indicating with sufficient particularity the needs of our forces in the field, is supplied by the casualty lists. With regard to these lists, however, serious and sad as they necessarily are, let two points be borne in mind. First, that a very large percentage of the casualties represents comparatively slight hurts, the sufferers from which in time return to the front; and, secondly, that if the figures seem to run very high, the magnitude of the operations is thereby suggested.

Indeed, these casualty lists, whose great length may now and again induce undue depression of spirits, are an instructive indication of the huge extent of the operations undertaken now reached by the British forces in the field.

There are two classes of men to whom my appeal must be addressed:

(1) Those for whom it is claimed that they are indispensable, whether for work directly associated with our military forces, or for other purposes, public or private; and

(2) Those to whom has been applied the ugly name of "shirkers."

As regards the former the question must be searchingly driven home whether their duties, however responsible and however technical, cannot in this time of stress be adequately carried out by men unfit for active military service or by women—and here I cannot refrain from a tribute of grateful recognition to the large number of women, drawn from every class and phase of life, who have come forward and placed their services unreservedly at their country's disposal. The harvest, of course, is looming large in many minds. It is possible that many men engaged in agriculture have so far not come forward owing to their harvest duties.

This may be a good reason at the moment, but can only be accepted if they notify their names at once as certain recruits on the very day after the harvest has been carried. Also the question of the private employment of recruitable men for any sort of domestic service is an acute one, which must be gravely and unselfishly considered by master and man alike.

There has been much said about "slackers"—people, that is to say, who are doing nothing literally to help the country. Let us by all means avoid over-statement in this matter. Let us make every allowance for the very considerable number of men, over and above those who are directly rendering their country genuine service, who are engaged directly in patriotic work, or are occupied in really good and necessary work at home. Probably the residuum of absolute "do-nothings" is relatively smaller than is commonly supposed. At any rate it is not of those that I am speaking for the moment. I am anxious especially to address myself to the large class drawn from the category of those who devote themselves to more or less patriotic objects or to quite good and useful work of one kind or another. I want each one of those to put this question to himself seriously and candidly. "Have I a real reason for not joining the army, or is that which I put before myself as a reason, after all only an excuse?"

Excuses are often very plausible and very arguable, and seem quite good until we examine them in the light of duty before the tribunal of our conscience. To take only a single instance. Are there not many special constables who, being of recruitable age, are really qualified to undertake the higher service which is open to them? Perhaps the favorite excuse for neglecting to join the colors is one which appears in various forms—"I am ready to go when I am fetched." "I suppose they will let me know when they want me." "I don't see why I should join when so many others remain behind." "To be fair, let us all be asked to join together." "After all, if the country only entreats and does not command us to enlist, does not that prove that it is not a duty to go, that only those need go who choose?"

Granted that legally you need only go if you choose, is it not morally "up to you" to choose to go? If you are only ready to go when you are fetched, where is the merit of that? Where is the patriotism of it? Are you only going to do your duty when the law says you must? Does the call to duty find no response in you until reinforced, let us rather say superseded, by the call of compulsion?

It is not for me to tell you your duty; that is a matter for your conscience. But make up your minds and do so quickly. Don't delay to take your decision, and, having taken it, to act upon it at once. Be honest with yourself. Be certain that your so-called reason is not a selfish excuse. Be sure that hereafter, when you look back upon to-day and its call to duty, you do not have cause, perhaps bitter cause, to confess to your conscience that you shirked your duty to your country and sheltered yourself under a mere excuse.

It has been well said that in every man's life there is one supreme hour towards which all earlier experience moves and from which all future results may be reckoned. For every individual Briton, as well as for our national existence, that solemn hour is now striking. Let us take heed to the great opportunity it offers and which most assuredly we must grasp *now and at once—or never.* Let each man of us see that we spare nothing, if only we may lend our full weight to the impetus which shall carry to victory the cause of our honor and of our freedom.

SIR ROBERT LAIRD BORDEN

THE VOICE OF THE EMPIRE

[From the opening of the War Great Britain received the enthusiastic support of the Over-Seas Dominions. The troops from Canada, Australia and New Zealand played a large part in winning the War. In this speech the Premier of Canada gives some description of the service and the loyalty rendered by the Dominions. The speech was made in seconding the resolution of Mr. Balfour, at a great patriotic meeting held in the London Opera House, August 4th, 1915, the first anniversary of the outbreak of the War.

The Right Honorable Sir Robert Laird Borden was born at Grand Pré in 1854; was called to the bar in 1878, and became Queen's Council in 1891. He was elected leader of the Conservative party in the Canadian House of Commons in 1901 and became Premier of Canada in 1911, a position which he held throughout the World War.]

I BELIEVE that in Japan the Constitution recognizes great men, men with distinguished services to the State, men of great experience, men of high ability, men of acknowledged unwavering patriotism, to whom the title of Elder Statesmen is given. You have not in these islands any Constitutional

THE VOICE OF THE EMPIRE

recognition of such men, but there are those among you who have that status, and among those stands prominent the great statesman to whose inspiring words we have listened to-night. We of the Overseas Dominions may perhaps be allowed to term ourselves the younger statesmen, and as one of those I have the honor and privilege of seconding the resolution which Mr. Balfour has just moved.

Considering all the events of the year, there are indeed some matters on which we have the right and privilege to-night of congratulating ourselves to the full. Was the unity of this Empire ever so strikingly made manifest before? Was it ever more clearly demonstrated that the race which inhabits these islands and the Overseas Dominions is not a decadent race? What has been the result of the call of duty to this Empire? You in these islands debated years ago, and not so long ago for that matter, as to whether in case of necessity you could send abroad an Expeditionary Force of 80,000 or 120,000 or 160,000 men, and if I am not mistaken the most optimistic among you believed that 160,000 men was the limit. What has been the result of the call? You have in part organized, and you are now organizing, armies from ten to twenty times greater than those which were the limit you set for yourselves in the past. That is not an indication of a decadent race, and I am glad indeed to know that we in the Overseas Dominions as well are doing our part as best we can. Indeed in Canada, and I believe the same is true in all the Overseas Dominions, the difficulty has been with armament and equipment, all that is necessary for the organization of a great modern army, and not with the provision of men, for the men came faster than we were able to organize the armor to equip them. And so it has been in India as well. I remember having in the early months of the war the privilege of reading a debate which took place in the Council of India, a great debate which was worthy of the Mother of Parliaments herelf; a debate couched in language of the most intense patriotism; and in that debate the demand of India was that she should be permitted to do her part in this war. The same is true of Egypt and all the Crown Colonies. From East to West, from North to South, throughout the Empire, the response on all hands has been more than we could have ventured to anticipate.

Mr. Balfour has referred in the most eloquent and appropriate terms to the work of the great Navy which is under his direction, and which has accomplished its task so wonderfully ever since the war broke out. We of the Overseas Dominions realize as much as you realize that the pathways of the seas are the veins and arteries of this Empire through which its life blood must flow. If these are once stopped or interfered with in any way the Empire cannot continue to exist. We are as conscious as you are conscious of the wonderful vigil in the North Sea and of the patience, endurance, and fortitude of officers and men. We are grateful as you are grateful, with the most intense appreciation of all they have done for us, and, more than all, the fact that they have rid the seas of the marauders by which our commerce was troubled has enabled us to keep in close contact with you and keep up that intercourse which is so absolutely necessary for you and for us, not only in war but in peace as well.

I have no military knowledge nor experience—I am going to say a word with regard to military affairs in a moment—but before doing that I would like to express my own appreciation, and I think of all the people in the Dominion which I have the honor to represent, of the splendid work which has been done by the Royal Flying Corps in this war. Knowing the great efforts that have been made by other nations in this particular branch of the military and naval services, we were rather inclined to anticipate and expect that it might not be up to the highest standard of the great nations of the world. I have good reason to know, because I have had some intimate accounts of what has transpired at the front—I have good reason to know that the work of our aëroplane service has been equal to the best, and that in initiative, courage, resourcefulness, and fortitude our men have held their place with the best ever since the outbreak of this war.

It was not necessary to dwell on the valor of our troops, to which eloquent reference has been made by Lord Crewe and Mr. Balfour. I do not believe, that in all the splendid traditions of the British Army for centuries past a more splendid record can be shown than that displayed in the retreat from Mons. I believe that no retirement was ever conducted successfully under greater difficulties and against more overwhelming odds, and the conduct of officers and men adds glory to the British Army that will not be forgotten as long as our race endures. I may, perhaps, be permitted to say that those who were sent across the sea to France and to the Dardanelles from Australia, from New Zealand, from Canada have proved that the old traditions of our race are not forgotten overseas and that the men there are prepared in any danger, in any peril to stand side by side with their comrades of these islands. A splendid force has been raised in South Africa, and I associate myself with what has been so well said as to the valor of the troops from India who have fought by the side of our men in France and Belgium.

Mr. Balfour has spoken of our Allies, and with what he has said I may be permitted to associate myself. One cannot forget the courage, the patience, the fortitude of France. We know that the soul of Russia is unconquered and unconquerable. The devotion and heroism of Belgium and Serbia have moved the admiration of the world. The fine valor of Italy is now in the fighting line with the Allies, and she is doing her appointed task as we expected she would do it. She stands ready, I imagine, for further services in case the emergencies of this war should demand them. I have said before that this is not like the wars of a hundred or two hundred years ago. This is a war of nations, and not of armies alone. But it is more than that. It is a war of material resources to an extreme degree. The industrial resources of the nations are being organized; all that the knowledge and science of the nations can devise is being brought into play. The command of the forces of nature which in the past centuries, and especially in the past one hundred years, we have learned has been brought to bear, and for that reason as well as for the reasons which Mr. Balfour has given I have every confidence in the outcome of this struggle because we have within this Empire resources almost limitless—resources infinitely greater than those of Germany and Austria-Hungary combined, and it merely depends upon our self-denial, and organized capacity and patriotism, as to whether we can and shall organize those resources to the end that our cause shall triumph.

I do not believe that we shall fail in that. Our race has

never failed in time of crisis. Why should it fail now? To fail in doing that would be accounted to us in the years to come as dishonor. We will not fail. All that men can do our men have done at the front, and they will continue to do in the future.

In Canada we began as early as possible to organize our industrial resources for the production of munitions of war. We made our first effort as far back as August 21. Munitions of war have been the great and growing need of our men at the front. Because it is apparent to us that so far as it is in the power of this Empire to strain every effort for the purposes of the war we must not attempt to do with men alone what our enemies are doing with munitions and guns.

As to what we have done in the past, whether in Canada or in these islands or elsewhere, let the dead past bury its dead. This is not the time to speak of the past, but to look at the future. What concerns us, whether in these islands or in any of the Overseas Dominions, is to see that, so far as the future is concerned, there shall be no failure, and I believe there will be no failure.

It may be said that in some respects the twelve months' war has not been all that we anticipated. I believe I am entirely within the bounds of truth, when I state that if there is any disappointment with us the disappointment of Germany is tenfold greater, and if there has been any disappointment, or if there should be any reverse in the future, that should merely inspire us with a higher resolve and a more inflexible determination to do our duty and to see that that which concerns the cause of civilization and humanity shall be carried to the issue which we all desire.

For a hundred years we have not had any wars which threatened the existence of our Empire, and for more than fifty years we have not been involved in any war which might perhaps be called a great one. Under the conditions of modern democracies here and elsewhere in the Empire considerations of material prosperity have been urged, and this is especially a danger in a new country like Australia or Canada. The call of the market-place has been sometimes clamorous and insistent, and in days such as these the soul of a nation is more truly tried than it is in war days, for the highest character of an Empire is sometimes formed then and not in the days of stress and trial, through the consequences of duty and self-sacrifice.

I rejoice greatly that in these islands and in the Overseas Dominions men have realized most fully that there is something greater than material prosperity, something greater than life itself. This war cannot fail to influence most profoundly the whole future of the world and of civilization. It has already most profoundly influenced the people of this Empire. There were great strivings for wealth everywhere, but no one could deny that the material advancement and prosperity of the Empire has not in itself been a good thing. The standards of life for the people have been raised and comfort increased. It is not the wealth we should rail at. Rome fell, I know, at a time of wealth, but it was because she made wealth her god.

In the early days of the war we were much comforted by the fact that men and women were ready to make sacrifices for this, the greatest cause of all. In Canada, and I am sure elsewhere throughout the Empire, there has been manifest a spirit of coöperation, of mutual helpfulness, of a desire to assist, of self-sacrifice which is most comforting to those who have at heart the welfare of our Empire in years to come. So I am sure it will be in the future. The influence of a spirit of helpfulness and self-sacrifice which we see everywhere throughout the world and within our Empire is one for which I give thanks and am most grateful.

I have come far across this ocean to see our men within these islands and at the front, and our men in hospital who are wounded. To see them, whether at the front, where they stand almost within the valley of the shadow of death, or wounded in the hospitals, is an inspiration in itself. I am glad to say that in visiting the hospitals I have had the opportunity of speaking to many soldiers, officers and men, from these islands, and with them I have found, as among our Canadians, just one spirit, a wonderful spirit of heroism and of patience, a spirit of consecration to the cause we all have at heart. We who come from overseas are touched by all this, perhaps more than you can imagine.

Last night I walked down the Embankment. At my right was the great Abbey, at my left the great Cathedral. The historic river was at my feet. Here came in bygone centuries the Celt, the Saxon, the Dane, the Norman, each in turn, finally all in coöperation, lending their influence to our national life. And how splendid a structure they built; what an influence for good it has carried throughout the world!

Standing thus on what seems to us hallowed ground, we of the Overseas Dominions meditate perhaps more than you do on the wonderful memories of the past and the great events to which the life of our Empire has moved. Let us never for one moment forget that of all the mighty events in our history none are greater than those through which we are passing to-day. Is an Empire like ours worth living for? Yes, and worth dying for, too. And it is something greater than it was a year ago. Indeed, it can never be quite the same again. The old order has in some measure passed away. Once for all it has been borne in upon the minds and souls of all of us that the great policies which touch and control the issues of peace and war concern more than the peoples of these islands.

And more than that, we shall so bear ourselves in this war and in the mighty events to which it must lead, that whether in these islands or in the Overseas Dominions citizenship of this Empire shall be a still greater and more noble possession in the years to come than it has been even in the glorious past. I have spoken to you frankly on some matters of great moment. If I had not done so I should have been unworthy of my position. And now before I close let me bring to you this latest message from Canada:

For those who have fallen in this struggle we shall not cease to strive. We are supremely confident that that cause will assuredly triumph and for that great purpose we are inspired with an inflexible determination to do our part.

THEODORE ROOSEVELT

NATIONAL DUTY AND INTERNATIONAL IDEALS

[Before America entered the War, Colonel Roosevelt continually advocated national preparedness. After the sinking of the *Lusitania* he was strongly in favor of the entry of the United States into the War. The following speech before the Illinois Bar Association at Chicago, April 29, 1916, sets forth his policies in view of the approaching presidential campaign.]

A YEAR and three-quarters have passed since the opening of the great war. At the outset our people were stunned by the vastness and terror of the crisis. We had been assured by many complacent persons that the day of great wars had ended, that the reign of violence was over, that the enlightened public opinion of the world would prevent the oppression of weak nations. To be sure, there was ample proof that none of these assurances were true, and far-seeing men did not believe them. But there was good excuse for the mass of the people being misled. Now, however, there is none. War has been waged on a more colossal scale than ever before in the world's history; and cynical indifference to international morality and willingness to trample on inoffensive peace-loving peoples who are also helpless or timid have been shown on a greater scale than since the close of the Napoleonic wars over a century ago. Alone of the great powers, we have not been drawn into this struggle.

A twofold duty was imposed upon us by the fact of our prosperity and by the fact of our momentary immunity from danger. This twofold duty was, first, to make our voice felt for the weak who had been wronged by the strong, and for international humanity and honor, and for peace on terms of justice for all concerned; and, second, immediately and in thorough-going fashion to prepare ourselves so that there might not befall us on an even greater scale such a disaster as befell Belgium. We have signally failed in both duties. Incredible to relate, we are not in any substantial respect stronger at this moment in soldiers or rifles, in seamen or ships, because of any Governmental action taken in consequence of this war; and moreover we have seen every device and provision designed by humanitarians to protect international right against international wrongdoing torn into shreds, and have not so much as ventured to speak effectively one word of protest.

The result is that every nation in the world now realizes our weakness, and that no nation in the world believes in either our disinterestedness or our manliness. The effort to placate outside nations by being neutral between right and wrong, and to gain good-will along professional pacifist lines by remaining helpless for self-defense, has resulted, after two fatuous years, in so shaping affairs that the nations either already feel, or are rapidly growing to feel for us, not only dislike but contempt.

This is not a pleasant truth; but it is the truth; and as a people we will do well to remember Emerson's saying that in the long run the most unpleasant truth is a safer traveling companion than the pleasantest falsehood. Our duty is to face the facts and then to take the thorough-going actions necessary in order to meet the situation that these facts disclose.

Our prime duty, infinitely our most important duty, is the duty of preparedness. Unless we prepare in advance we cannot when the crisis comes be true to ourselves. If we cannot be true to ourselves, it is absolutely certain that we shall be false to every one else. If we are not able to safeguard our own national honor and interest, we shall make ourselves an object of scorn and derision if we try to stand up for the rights of others. We have been sinking into the position of the China of the Occident; and we will do well to remember that China—pacificist China—has not only been helpless to keep its own territory from spoliation and its own people from subjugation but has also been helpless to exert even the most minute degree of influence on behalf of right dealing among other nations.

There are persons in this country who openly advocate our taking the position that China holds, the position from which the best and wisest Chinamen are now painfully trying to raise their land. Nothing that I can say will influence the men and women who take this view. The holding of such a view is entirely incompatible with the right to exercise the privileges of self-government in a democracy, for self-government cannot permanently exist among people incapable of self-defense.

But I believe that the great majority of my fellow-countrymen, when they finally take the trouble to think on the problem at all, will refuse to consent to or acquiesce in the Chinafication of this country. I believe that they will refuse to follow those who would make right helpless before might, who would put a pigtail on Uncle Sam, and turn the Goddess of Liberty into a pacificist female huckster, clutching a bag of dollars which she has not the courage to guard against aggression. It is to these men and women that I speak. I speak to the mass of my fellow-countrymen. I speak to all men and women who are loyal to the principles of those who in the Revolutionary War made us a nation, and who have in their souls the high qualities possessed by the men who in the iron days of the Civil War followed the banners of Grant and of Lee, and of the mothers and wives of these men. My appeal may not be heeded; if so, then either our people will pay heed in time to the appeal of some other man, able to speak more strongly and more convincingly, or else they will when it is too late learn the lesson from some terrible gospel in which it is written by an alien conqueror in letters of steel and of flame.

The first necessity is that we shall in good faith and without reservation undertake to be a nation, and not merely to call ourselves a nation. I make my especial appeal to the national spirit here in Chicago, here in the great Middle West, here in the territory stretching from the Alleghanies to the Rockies. The prophets of gloom have said that the West, prosperous and indifferent, secure in her fancied safety because she is in the middle of the continent, cares nothing for the dangers that might befall the cities on the Atlantic or the Pacific Coast, cares nothing for what has befallen the dwellers along the Mexican boundary, and is as indifferent to what befalls elsewhere as Peking once was to what befell its outlying Chinese provinces—to the ultimate ruin of Peking, by the way.

This I do not for one moment believe. If I did, I should despair of the republic. This is to a peculiar degree the democratic, the intensely and characteristically American, section of our land. The West produced for the service of the whole nation Abraham Lincoln and Andrew Jackson; and I know that their spirit is still the spirit of her sons.

I appeal to the men of the West to take the lead in the movement for the genuine nationalization of our people. If the republic founded by Washington and saved by Lincoln is to be turned into a mere polyglot boarding-house, where dollar-hunters of twenty different nationalities scramble for gain. each nationality bearing no real allegiance except to the land from which it originally came, then we may as well make up our minds that the great experiment of democratic government on this continent will have failed. No less will it have failed if each section thinks only of the welfare of that section, and with crass blindness believes that disaster to some other section will not affect it. And the failure will be the greatest of all if foolish men are pursuaded by wicked men that one caste or class is the prime enemy of some other class or caste. I appeal to the men of the East to prepare so that the men of the Pacific Slope shall be free from all menace of danger. I appeal to the men of the West to prepare so that the men of the Atlantic Coast shall be free from all danger. I appeal to the North, South, West and East alike, to hold the life of every man and the honor of every woman on the most remote ranch on the Mexican border as a sacred trust to be guaranteed by the might of our entire nation—and the life of every man, woman and child who should be protected by the United States on the high seas likewise. I appeal to every good American, whether farmer or merchant, business man or professional man, whether he works with brain or hand. Anything of disgrace or dishonor that befalls our people anywhere is of vital moment to all of us wherever we live; and any deed that reflects credit on the American name is a subject of congratulation for every American of every section of this country.

I speak of the United States as a whole. Surely it ought to be unnecessary to say that it spells as absolute ruin to permit divisions among our people along the lines of creed or of national origin as it does to permit division by geographical section. We must not stand merely for America first. We must stand for America first and last; and for no other nation second—except as we stand for fair play for all nations. There can be no divided loyalty in this country. The man who tries to be loyal to this country and also to some other country is certain in the end to put his loyalty to the other country ahead of his loyalty to this. The politico-racial hyphen is the breeder of moral treason. We are a new nation, by blood akin to but different from all the nations of Europe. In the veins of our people runs the blood of German, Englishman, and Irishman, of Scandinavian, Slav and Latin. Any one of these people can bring something of value to our common national life. Each can contribute social and cultural traditions and customs of value; and all must join in cordial mutuality of respect for whatever is valuable that each brings; but each must put the contribution at the service of our common and unified citizenship, and by utilizing all that is thus contributed, and by adapting and developing it so that it shall meet and express our common needs, we shall build our own distinctive national culture.

There is no room in this country for German-Americans or English-Americans, Irish-Americans or French-Americans; just as there is no room in this country for a political party based upon fealty or opposition to any particular creed, whether Protestant, Catholic or Jew. There is just one way to be a good citizen of the United States, and that is to be an American and nothing else. This is not a question of birthplace or national origin or creed. Any big group of loyal and patriotic Americans will include men of many creeds and many different race strains and birthplaces. But they will not be loyal and patriotic Americans at all unless they are Americans and nothing else. The first step in preparedness is dependent upon our common and exclusive American nationality.

Preparedness must be both of the soul and of the body. It must be not only military but industrial and social. There can be no efficient preparedness against war unless there is in time of peace, economic and spiritual preparedness in the things of peace. Well-meaning men continually forget this interdependence. Well-meaning men continually speak as if efficient military preparedness could be achieved out of industrial and social chaos, whereas such military preparedness would represent merely a muscular arm on a withered body. Other well-meaning people speak as if industrial preparedness, social preparedness, would by itself solve the problem. This is worse folly than the first.

Let these men look at Belgium and compare her fate with that of Switzerland. Belgium was one of the countries in Europe in which the greatest advance had been made in industrial efficiency, and as regards social justice she was at least well ahead of us. But there had been no corresponding military preparedness. There had been great success along lines of business materialism, great success along the lines of humanitarianism, but no development of military efficiency. The result is that both the materialist and the humanitarian have been ground into the dust together, simply because the men so successful in peace had not in peace trained themselves so as to be able to defend themselves in war, and to make other nations realize in advance that they were able to do so.

If our people are not willing to study the lessons of history, let them look at what has gone on before their eyes in China. For centuries China has looked down on the military caste, and has discouraged the development of the fighting spirit. The vagaries and dreams and blindness of her pacificist leaders and pacificist statesmen have paralleled those of our own. Her people have been peaceful and industrious; they have put peace above honor, above justice, above national self-respect. As a consequence, China, the most populous empire on the earth, sees half her territory under the control of alien powers, and in the remainder holds what precarious independence remains at the mercy of whichever one of these alien powers is for the time being able to nullify the influence of the others. If the short-sighted pacificist and the short-sighted materialist have their way, the same fate will overtake us; and it would be hastened, not averted, by business prosperity and efficiency and harmlessness. To mobilize our resources, and introduce efficiency everywhere in business, would merely make us a more attractive and a more helpless prey unless we in similar fashion develop our power and purpose for self-defense. I stand heartily for protection. By that I mean not only protection to American industries and to the material interests of American workingmen, farmers and business men. I also mean, and with even greater emphasis, protection for the whole American nation, protection for American honor, protection for America's self-respect, protection for America's position among the nations, protection for her when she strives, as she ought to strive, to bring peace to the rest of the world. And there can be no such protection without thorough-going preparation—military, social and industrial.

AMERICA STILL UNPREPARED AFTER 21 MONTHS OF WAR

I have before used the effect of non-preparedness on China as an argument for preparedness. Really the events of the last twenty-one months, including especially the events of the last month, show that no argument is needed save our own history during these past twenty-one months. On August 1st, 1914, the great war began; and it had already become clear that the already dreadful situation in Mexico was going steadily from bad to worse. It should have been perceptible to any nation—and it is not to our credit as a nation that it was not evident to us—that there was the gravest danger of our being involved at some point with the European belligerents and the almost certainty that we would have to take action sooner or later as regards Mexico.

Even the first few weeks of the great war made it evident that the prime factor in success in war was preparedness in advance, and that is was impossible adequately to prepare after war had begun. Yet our well-meaning, foolish, peace-at-any-price people clamored so loudly that we must not prepare because preparedness would increase the chances of war, that we followed their advice. Six months went by without one particle of preparation by us. Our army and navy remained as weak as ever. Nothing of any sort was done to help put our industries in shape to help us in the event of war. The professional pacificist hailed this refusal to exercise precaution in the face of the hurricane as an evidence of virtue on our part. It was merely an evidence of blind and timid weakness. Then, after six months, Germany announced that she would conduct a submarine blockade of England under circumstances which rendered inevitable the loss of American lives. We sent her an ultimatum announcing that in such case we would hold her to strict accountability. I use the word "ultimatum" for it is the only word to describe the document containing the words "strict accountability," if these words mean anything. When we took that action we placed ourselves in a position where it became a crime against ourselves not immediately to prepare. Fourteen months have passed since. Germany has again and again done what we said she should not do. We have protested, sometimes strongly, sometimes weakly, against what has been done; but we never took a single step in the way of preparation to enforce our words if unhappily it should become necessary to do so. At present we have sent another ultimatum to Germany no stronger than the one sent fourteen months ago; but the circumstances of its delivery are such as seem to indicate that more weight must be attached to it.

Yet we are still not preparing in any way. The Lower House of Congress has taken what measures it could to interfere with the organizations on which we should have to rely in any belated and hurried efforts to meet our needs should we have to act in support of our note, and has passed legislation excellently designed to prevent all efficiency from the military standpoint. Substantially we are not in the smallest degree better prepared in the army or the navy than we were twenty-one months ago, and instead of endeavoring to secure industrial preparedness Congress has done everything it could to interfere with it. At this moment after nearly six weeks of effort we have been unable to scrape together an army sufficient to capture the bandit Villa. We have not an efficient body of troops of a size that would make it a tangible asset in the huge death-wrestle that is going on around Verdun. We have not in these twenty-one months prepared in any shape or way to make good on any field of action any demand we might make for our own rights or the rights of humanity. Our words have been like a check issued by a man on a bank in which he has no funds but expects that somehow or other he will get them by the time the check comes around. Rarely indeed does such a man have the funds there in time, and desperately humiliating indeed are his experiences meanwhile.

If we meant what we said in our strict-accountability note fourteen months ago, then we have followed a policy both wicked and cruel in its neglect of the lives of our men, women and children by deliberately refusing to follow up any program of preparedness, whether with our army, our navy or our industries. Now, if under these circumstances war does come, all the men who think as I do will stand promptly by the country. We will go to the war but we shall expect to pay a heavy penalty with our blood and the blood of those dearest to us for the failure to prepare during the past twenty-one months. And what I ask now of our professional peace-at-any-price friends, of the professional pacificists, is that they get clearly in mind the fact that the preparedness I, whom they call a militarist, have unceasingly advocated for so many years and above all the preparedness that I have advocated with all my strength since this great war began, would in all probability have averted all need of sending the strict-accountability note fourteen months ago.

If now there is no war, it will be proof positive that if fourteen months ago we had made it evident that we meant what we said Germany would have abandoned her submarine policy and the lives of thousands of non-combatants, including many hundreds of women and children, would have been saved, so that their blood is at our doors because we failed, when we sent that note, to show that we meant what we said. If on the other hand, war does come, it will be a cruel and a dreadful thing that, having had the amplest opportunity and time to prepare for it on the largest scale, we drifted into it stern foremost, having shown ourselves helplessly unable to provide in the smallest degree to make our vast strength effective.

A FIRST CLASS NAVY NEEDED

We need beyond everything else a first-class navy. We cannot possibly get it unless the naval program is handled with steady wisdom from the standpoint of a nation that accepts the upbuilding and upkeep of such a navy as cardinal points of continuous policy. There should be no party division along these lines. A party which whatever its views are on other subjects, stops the upbuilding of the navy or lets it be impaired in efficiency, should be accepted as false to the vital interests of the American people. The navy should be trained in deep water, in salt water; and it should be trained always with one end in view, to increase its fighting efficiency. It is not an educational institution. It is Uncle Sam's right arm of defense; and that arm is meant to hold the sword and not the pen. The minute the effort is made to turn a battleship into an ambulatory schoolhouse, we spoil the battleship without getting the schoolhouse. The minute we fail to treat the navy as the one most vitally important international asset of the Nation, which it is imperatively necessary to keep to the highest standard of efficiency, disregarding all other matters in connection therewith, that very minute we lay the seeds for the conditions which result in submarines that cannot go under water and aëroplanes that do not fly. The navy is by no means all-sufficient; but the special part it plays is of more importance even than the very important parts played by other arms.

It is a prime necessity for any great nation which expects to be taken seriously always to correlate policy and armament. There never should be a treaty made or a policy announced save after careful consideration whether our prepared strength is sufficient to make that treaty respected or that policy observed. The Monroe Doctrine will never be one particle stronger than the navy. Our hold on the Canal, our power of protecting our own citizens abroad and defending our own coasts, all these depend upon other considerations also; but among the various vital factors, none of which can be neglected, the navy stands foremost.

The navy stands foremost. But to rely only on the navy would be as foolish as in a battle to rely upon infantry or only upon artillery or only upon trench digging. Back of the navy must stand the regular army; and back of the regular army must stand the trained strength of the nation.

THE REGULAR ARMY INDISPENSABLE

The regular army is indispensable. Here again, gentlemen, let me ask you to do your part in seeing that our people understand the utter folly of embarking on a policy unless we have the means to enforce that policy. A treaty has recently been proposed by the Governmental authorities in Washington under which we would guarantee the territorial integrity of all the South American republics, with, as a *quid pro quo,* the assurance of these republics (Honduras, Nicaragua and Ecuador, for instance) that they will guarantee our territorial integrity. Translate this into terms of fact. If the treaty does not mean what it purports to mean, it is insincere, and worse. If it does mean what it purports to mean, then we are to guarantee that we will go to war to defend, say, Terra del Fuego on behalf of somebody else. Yet the upholders of this proposal in the same breath announce that we are not to go to war for our own rights or our citizens. It is possible to defend either proposition with sincerity (although not with wisdom) but it is not possible to defend both propositions with either sincerity or wisdom. Well-meaning people propose that we shall enter into an International League to Enforce Peace by making treaties under which we would pledge ourselves, if for instance Belgium were invaded, to back Belgium in war by the two or three million men without whom our unsupported backing would amount to little. Before going into any more grandiose promises, let us keep the moderate promises we made in the Hague Conventions; and before we promise action on behalf of others which might necessitate an army of two or three million men being sent abroad to fight in a quarrel in which interest was purely altruistic, let us ponder the fact that in order to send an army after a Mexican bandit, although this army was operating in company with the forces of the *de facto* government of Mexico, we had to strip our country of regular soldiers until we did not have enough left to patrol the border.

The Mexican affair, by the way, offers the best possible example of the need that this country should deal with things and not merely with words. For some years Mexico has stood to us much as the Balkan Peninsula with its weak and turbulent states once stood to Europe. Success or failure in our Mexican policy is no mere local matter; if in this place our foreign policy fails, it means general failure. The problem is not a military one, although now unfortunately our failure to grapple with it intelligently and in terms of fact may well mean that there may have to be a military prelude to the real settlement. The settlement itself will come only when we make up our minds to render constructive and disinterested service on a common-sense basis, as we so successfully did in Cuba.

NO REAL VALUE IN HALF-PREPAREDNESS

Remember always that there is no real value to half-preparedness. To prepare a little but not very much is just like trying to put out a fire a little but not a great deal. If you want to build a bridge across a river, you build it for the whole distance. If you build it only halfway, you might as well leave it unbuilt. To increase the armed forces of the nation a little, but not much, leaves the situation, from the standpoint of national defense, practically unchanged. The advocates of half-preparedness are no more loyal to the interests of this country than are the advocates of unpreparedness. As for the statement that preparedness incites war, it ranks on a par with that hoary falsehood which says that it takes two to make a quarrel. With the fate of Belgium before our eyes no man, not willfully blind to the truth, can question that absolutely good conduct, absolute peacefulness, absolute devotion to industry, and the possession of a good government and the doing of justice at home and abroad, all put together, do not by one moment delay or in the smallest degree work to prevent an attack from a powerful militaristic nation outside, if there has been failure of military preparedness on the part of the attacked nation and if the militaristic nation thinks it advantageous to make the attack. Preparedness is like fire insurance. There are individuals so wicked that they insure their houses for the purpose of setting fire to them. Likewise there are nations which prepare in order to commit aggressions on other nations. But the first fact does not alter the desirability of fire insurance for honest men, nor does the second fact alter the desirability of preparedness for self-defense on the part of peaceful and well-behaved nations.

The preparedness of a big, highly efficient navy and a small, highly efficient regular army will meet our immediate needs and can be immediately undertaken. But ultimately and to meet our permanent needs I believe with all my heart in universal training and universal service on some modification of the Swiss and Australian systems adapted to the needs of our American life. Such training would not merely, indeed perhaps not primarily be of benefit from the military standpoint, although the good from this standpoint would be inestimable; it would not take our young men away from their life-work; it would, on the contrary, help to fit them for their life-work, make them more valuable socially and industrially, train them to order, discipline, the power to enjoy and make use of self-respecting liberty, the power to coöperate with their fellows. It would be an antiseptic to militarism; for Switzerland and Australia are the least militaristic and most democratic of commonwealths. It would be done in the schools and then by four to six months' work in the field when they leave the schools. It would mean only extending the system already admirably applied in Wyoming. With such a system we should be guaranteed forever against the kind of conflict which is known as a rich man's war and a poor man's fight. We should never have a war unless the people who were to fight it deliberately determined upon it. It would be a war waged by the people for the people.

As I have said again and again, and as I cannot too often repeat, I advocate this preparedness as a means to secure peace and to avoid war. A good mother wrote me the other day that she feared preparedness because she did not wish her boys "to go up against the cannon." Now, the one perfectly certain method of insuring that her boys and all the other boys in this country shall "go up against the cannon" is to persuade foreign powers that they can attack us with impunity, because our mothers have refused to let their boys be trained efficiently. I abhor unjust and wanton war. More than that, if there were a great war my sons would go, and probably all my young kinsfolk would go. If the war became serious enough I would have to go. It would be the bitterest grief to me to see my sons go, as every father here will understand. All that I honorably could do would be done to help keep this country out of war, so that my sons would not have to go. But I would far rather have them go than have them stay at home under conditions which would make their children ashamed of them and ashamed of being Americans.

Our foreign policy should be managed on the basis of showing courteous regard for the rights and the feelings of others and a refusal to be irritated over or take offense at trifles; but at the same time an equally courteous but resolute insistence upon our own rights. Insolence and disregard of the rights and feelings of others may embroil us in war; but weakness, and conveying the impression that we fear others, are even more certain to do so in the long run. Strength, courage and the courteous doing of justice tend to avert war; weakness, and above all weakness combined with bluster, tend in the long run to make it inevitable. We stand for the peace which comes as a matter of right to the just man armed, and not for the peace which is purchased by the coward at the cost of abject submission to wrong. The peace of cowardice ultimately leads to war as the end of a record of shame.

INDUSTRIAL PREPARATION

Industrial service is essential. There can be no full preparation for military service unless there is industrial preparation. Few of our people have even the slightest idea of the enormous amount of supplies of every kind necessary to carry on modern war; its quantities of food, clothing, rifles, cannon, shells, cartridges, medical supplies, automobiles, railway cars, high explosives. If the supply of raw materials gives out, if skilled laborers fitted for manufacture are not to be found, if the deliveries of goods are not made with the promptness and certainty only to be obtained through perfectly organized industrial machinery, the result is that the loss would have to be made good by an incalculable wastage of life among our soldiers. Unless our industries are highly efficient, and moreover are trained for this particular work in advance, the penalty will inevitably be paid in the shape of dreadful loss of life among our soldiers. Such a need cannot be met by government-owned and managed plants, although there should be some such to serve as checks and regulators.

The need is to train, to educate many business firms by means of giving them small orders in time of peace for the various things which the Government would need in enormous quantities in time of war. There should be a survey of the producing resources of the country and the development and practical working-out in time of peace of plans for minimum annual educational orders to be placed by the Army and the Navy with thousands of firms widely distributed geographically, and the enrollment in time of peace of the skilled labor which it

DUTY AND IDEALS

is necessary to keep on the job in time of war. We shall need organized business in time of war just as in time of peace. Our duty is to encourage it, but also to see that its activities are for the benefit of the whole country. The government should provide against excessive profit making in time of war; and it can only do this as a sequence to reasonable encouragement of the many private plants which in the event of war could be trusted to do public business. These plants, through some such system as the annual educational orders above referred to, could be made ready for efficient munitions work in time of war. The government encouragement could be also used to secure as one of its features those things for labor which it is most necessary to secure; proper working and living conditions, and provision for insurance compensation against sickness, accident and old age.

Not one step has been taken by Congress to help secure these industrial conditions. Not one step has been taken to secure the nationalization of industry in time of war. The railroad business in particular, in so far as interstate commerce and everything directly and indirectly connected with it is concerned, should be made a national matter, with a national incorporation law, and the whole power of regulation (which should itself be part of a process of encouragement) lodged in the Federal Commission, the purpose being to encourage the business in every legitimate way, while also seeing that it is managed in the interest of the public, no less than of the investors, managers and wage-workers. We can have no national economic program until we make ourselves really a nation. National needs cannot be met by conflicting locality actions. This is the age of coöperation. Surely if we really are a business people this means that there should be coöperation and not hostility between the Government and the mighty agencies through which alone modern business, especially international business, can be managed. Let the Government regulate the corporations; but let this regulation be an incident of hearty coöperation with them, to secure their well-being and also the well-being of those who work for them and of those for whom they work. Capital must be organized on a large scale just as labor must be organized on a large scale; but, both forms of organization must justify themselves by showing that they are not only beneficial to themselves but to the people as a whole.

No form of government will survive unless it can justify its existence. Boasting about democracy won't make democracy succeed. We are the greatest democratic republic and we are false not only to our own country but to democracy everywhere if we do not seriously endeavor to show, by our actions and success, that with us the many men can make a nation as efficient as elsewhere nations have been made efficient by a few men. We must make America efficient within its own borders, efficient to repel attack from beyond its own borders, and yet a friend and not a menace to other peoples. We must make ourselves serviceable to democracy, to the cause of popular rights and popular duties in national and also in international matters. A happy-go-lucky belief that we can become serviceable by combining sentimental speeches with selfish actions will bring us to futility. Serviceableness comes only through preparedness; and both the training and the service—through economic, social and military efficiency—imply courage, sustained effort, clear vision, and the power for self-sacrifice.

I speak for military preparedness. I speak for industrial preparedness. I speak for the performance of international duty, which can only come when we fit ourselves to do our duty to ourselves, and when we have made up our minds never to make a promise to any other nation which cannot be kept, which ought not to be kept, and which will not be kept. I speak of all this in the interest of national unity and manhood, of international peace, and of the service of our country and of the world at large. It is our duty to secure justice and well-being at home; but we live in a fool's paradise if we think that we shall be permitted to secure such justice and well-being, as the world now is, unless we are prepared to hold our own against all alien enemies. I appeal to the men of the West; I appeal to Americans everywhere, to stand against the crass materialism which can show itself just as much in peace as in war. I appeal to our people to prepare in advance so that there shall be no hideous emergency which renders it necessary to submit to inordinate profit-making by the few simply because, when the emergency comes, we must improvise at whatever cost the things that for our sins we have failed to provide beforehand. We cannot afford to leave this democracy of ours inefficient. If we do it will assuredly some day go down in ruin. We cannot afford to tolerate with cynical indifference the pork-barrel theories of government so dear to the hearts of politicians of the baser sort. With a wealth of billions of dollars, and a population of one hundred million we cannot afford to be in a condition of utterly unstable social and industrial equilibrium, nor to see our sons grow up steeped in a spirit of mere selfish individualism, without self-control or discipline or sense of coöperation, or firmness of purpose. We have great individual capacity. This we must keep. But we must train it so that we shall have great collective capacity, so that there may be that collective democratic power and discipline without which no great modern democracy can permanently subsist.

We must not only do away with sectionalism but we must see that our land really is a melting-pot of citizenship and that all peoples who come here become Americans and nothing else. We have equally to dread the sleek, well-fed materialist whose be-all and end-all in life are ease and comfort; and the base, selfish man who thinks only of his individual aggrandizement; and the foolish, boastful, wordy sentimentalist who with amazing ignorance fancies that Americans armed only with words can successfully oppose strong and brutal men with rifles.

THE PEACE OF RIGHTEOUSNESS AND JUSTICE

Our national character is in the balance. Americanism is on trial. If we produce merely the self-seeking, ease-loving, duty-shirking man, whether he be a mere materialist or a mere silly sentimentalist; if we produce only the Americanism of the grafter and the mollycoddle and the safety-first, get-rich-quick, peace-at-any-price man, we will have produced an American faithful only to the spirit of the Tories of 1776 and the Copperheads of 1861 and fit only to vanish from the earth. Love of ease, shirking of effort and duty, unwillingness to face facts, the desire to comfort ourselves by words that mean nothing—all these spell worthlessness while our civilization lasts, and spell also a speedy and an ignoble end of that civilization. In this tremendous crisis of the world, if we think we can sit apart, do nothing, utter lofty platitudes, and devote ourselves only to money-making we shall surely go down with a crash. I ask you of the West to take the lead in the effort for a robust and virile nationalism, fit and ready to cope with all possible dangers at home and abroad. I appeal to the spirit of sane common sense which faces things as they practically are, and I appeal also to that spirit of idealism which sees a great goal and struggles toward that goal. I ask for military preparedness as an arm to help the soul of the nation. I ask for it to quicken the national conscience, to help the national discipline.

I ask that we prepare ourselves within; and we cannot prepare ourselves within unless we also prepare against danger from without. You hate the waste and blood-spilling of war. So do I. You cannot hate such waste and such blood-spilling more than I do. The most lamentable of all the tragedies connected with blood-spilling is the spilling of the blood of brave men too late to secure the end for which the blood is spilt. Under such conditions there is no chance of triumph; the dreadful choice is between dying hopelessly for the right and yielding abjectly to triumphant iniquity. May we so act in the present that neither we ourselves nor our children's children shall ever in the future have to face so evil an alternative. We wish to secure peace both for ourselves and for others. To do so we must be both strong and just; for weakness invites injustice at its own expense and is powerless to ward off injustice from others. I ask you to prepare so that we may secure peace for ourselves and for others, not the peace of cowardice nor the peace of selfishness, but the peace of righteousness and of justice, the peace of brave men pledged to the service of this mighty democratic republic, and through that service pledged also to the service of the world at large.

JAMES MONTGOMERY BECK

AMERICA AND THE ALLIES

[James M. Beck is now Solicitor General of the United States and has been for a long time one of our eminent lawyers and public speakers. During the early years of the War he was distinguished by his ardent advocacy of the cause of the Allies. The *Daily Telegraph* declared, "There is no man who has done more than he—and many Americans have done much—to place before the people of the United States the fundamental truths which are the foundation of the Allies' attitude in this War." The following speech was given in London, on July 5, 1916, at a luncheon of the Pilgrims Club. Lord Bryce presided and proposed Mr. Beck's health which was received with the singing of "For He's a Jolly Good Fellow."]

MY LORDS AND GENTLMEN, I fear I am not at the present moment the "jolly good fellow" chanted in your song. I am a very serious fellow at this minute, because I have a task of unusual delicacy and difficulty.

Let me say in the first place to Lord Bryce that I shall carry back the message with which he has done me the honor to entrust me, and it will receive a very ready response among the thoughtful people of my country, for I am persuaded that the best thought of America is that it would be a worldwide calamity if this war did not end with a conclusive victory for the principles so nobly defended by the Allies. [Cheers.] I will also carry back the possibly unnecessary message that this war is not going to be a draw. I was in this country in the first month of the war, and then England reminded me of a great St. Bernard dog which, in a spirit of *noblesse oblige,* complacently wagged its tail when attacked by a powerful adversary. To-day England seems to me like a bull-dog with the business end of his jaws firmly set in his assailant's throat.

What I appreciate more than I can express in words, is the magnificent compliment of this luncheon, and yet I know full well that the distinction of this gathering of notable men in a busy hour is due in great part to the dynamic energy and thoughtful kindness of Mr. Harry Brittain, the Chairman of the Pilgrims, of whose good work for Anglo-American fraternity for many years past on both sides of the Atlantic we have a grateful appreciation in the United States. In America we generally know your Empire as England. There are some Americans who are not quite sure as to the exact political significance of the other name, Great Britain. I shall carry back another message to my countrymen as to the exact meaning of that term. [Laughter and applause.] Great Britain is an individual, not a nation. [Laughter.]

Let me further say, by way of introduction, that I also take with a great deal of hesitation the magnificent compliment which the author of the "American Commonwealth" has been pleased to pay me. I know full well that in the generous appreciation, which you have shown me, and which he has confirmed by his gracious reference to the little I have done, that you have greatly exaggerated any service that I was privileged to render, and yet I shall not blunt the fine edge of the compliment by too vigorous a disclaimer. [Laughter.] You know that Lord Bryce's name in my country carries immense weight, possibly more so than any other publicist of any nation. [Cheers.] When Lord Bryce speaks, whether in printed page or oral speech, we are accustomed to accept it as almost *ex cathedra,* and I therefore feel, in view of what he has said about my modest contribution to the controversial history of the war, very much as Dr. Johnson did when he visited King George III and His Majesty was pleased to make some very complimentary remarks about the Fleet Street philosopher's dictionary. When Dr. Johnson returned to the ever faithful Boswell, and told him with natural gratification what His Majesty had said, Boswell said, "What did you say when the King praised your dictionary?" Dr. Johnson replied: "Am I a man to bandy words with my Sovereign? If His Majesty says that my dictionary is the best in the English language, it must be so." [Laughter.] Similarly I shall accept, not because I believe it, or without great misgivings, Lord Bryce's gracious introduction and the generous references which he has made to the "Evidence in the Case."

I have come here to bring a message of good will from the American Pilgrims, and because you are all busy men I wish to speak as briefly and rapidly as possible. I have not any prepared speech. This is not the time for didactic essays or ornate orations. In these dreadful days—to use the fine phrase of Tom Paine, "the times that try men's souls"—the only thing that is valuable in speech is sincerity, and it is in that spirit I want to speak to you about the only topic of which you may wish to hear me; namely, the relations of the United States to this war and to the Allies.

There is one obvious limitation upon any discussion of the subject at my hands. Whatever may be my views at home, I cannot discuss here the political policies of the party of the day of the United States. I have very strong convictions with respect to many of these policies, and I have not hesitated to express them with great freedom to audiences of my own countrymen, but if I shall ever be tempted to criticize in a public gathering in a foreign land either the President of the United States or the Government of the day, may my tongue cleave to the roof of my mouth!

Be the acts of a political Government what they may, the vital importance for the great future is what has been the spirit of the people, because in the long run that is more significant than the temporary policy of any party of the day. [Cheers.] I have only gratifying news to bring to this distinguished audience as to the attitude of our people.

I was in England, as I have said, in the first month of the war. I remember with what interest, perhaps I might almost say solicitude, thoughtful Englishmen asked, when the war came as a bolt out of the blue, what will be the verdict of America? It was not merely the sentimental side of that verdict which interested you, although I think some of you attached great importance to what your kinsmen across the Atlantic would say as to the ethical aspects of the great controversy. But there were obvious practical aspects with respect to your great Empire which made the question of some importance. It was important to know how America would view a great world crisis, as to which all its past political traditions gave it no preliminary prepossessions.

The verdict that came to you across the Atlantic was spontaneous and overwhelming. We have in our history viewed with varied feelings and a lack of clearly preponderating views the previous wars of Europe in the Nineteenth century, as we considered them in their ethical and practical aspects. But in this case the overwhelming sentiment of the people, whether expressed by press or pulpit, by university or college, by bankers, merchants, or the masses toiling in the factories and the fields, was overwhelmingly in favor of the Allies. Excluding one or two elements of our population, which by reason of ties of blood to some extent ran counter to that general opinion, the preponderating judgment of the American people was then and after eighteen months remains to-day, without diminution or shadow of turning, heart and soul with the Allies. [Cheers.]

While that verdict needs no further statement, for it is a commonplace of our current political history, yet it has certain features which may not have received full recognition in this country.

In the first place, it was a *dispassionate* verdict. I mean by that it was little affected by racial kinship. I believe that the American people, if they had thought that England was in the wrong in unsheathing its sword on behalf of Belgium, or in entering upon this great world quarrel, would have reached that conclusion uninfluenced by racial kinship or the ties of blood. The verdict was as clearly dispassionate as one could expect in a verdict of human beings.

In the second place it was not an *academic* verdict, reached after coffee at the breakfast table and forgotten before the shadows of evening fell. It was a verdict rendered after one of the greatest intellectual controversies that my country ever knew. For eighteen months its people day and night discussed this question; it was a commonplace of conversation to say that whenever a group of intelligent men and women were gathered together all subjects inevitably led to the war. Moreover, Germany, appreciating the value of the American verdict, did not hesitate to appoint its *advocatus diaboli* in the person of Dr. Dernburg, who, financed by millions, and aided by thousands of German volunteers, attempted at every crossroad and in the centers of our cities, to reverse that verdict by a very torrent of controversial argument and by appeals to every idea or emotion which they thought might impress the American. They appealed to our supposed cupidity, our fears, our prejudices, our interests, to every consideration which might affect the spontaneous verdict that was first pronounced.

Yet they were finally obliged to admit that this judgment of the American people was a settled, matured, deliberate and irrevocable judgment—in no respects academic, but such a judgment as a court of law would pronounce upon a consideration of all the facts. [Cheers.]

Again, this verdict was a *militant* verdict. I mean that the American people did not in a spirit of moral dilettantism simply express an opinion about this war, and then resume their normal activities. To an extent far greater than perhaps some of you appreciate, American men, women and children have been for eighteen months working in their several capacities, either to alleviate the sufferings of the war or to stem the German propaganda, by building up a strong militant public opinion for the Allies. So that if the war is a war primarily of ideas and ideals, we have been participants to some extent, and our part has not been only that of a cold, callous, selfish outsider, as some have thought.

Finally, this verdict was in a sense a *disinterested* verdict, by which I mean that it was little affected by our own interests. We did not ask whether it was to our interests that this or that group of nations should triumph. Indeed, our sense of detachment made it seem to us that the fate neither of Belgium nor Servia affected us directly in a purely practical sense, and it was therefore the ethical aspects of the issue which powerfully appealed to our emotions and made us willing and enthusiastic adherents of the Allies' cause.

You will however ask, that if the verdict were thus overwhelming, why did it not find a greater reflex in the action of the Government as a political entity?

I have said that I cannot discuss the political policies of the party of the day of my country. While I am not of that party, still it speaks for my nation, and while I reserve the right to criticize it in my own land, yet with me and every true American, politics stop at the margin of the ocean, and therefore I cannot criticize the present Administration in Washington in another country.

But I can give you the reason why in the very nature of things the United States as a political entity could not take any other part than that of neutrality in this world crisis.

England and the United States are both conservative nations, certainly the two most conservative democracies of the world. We love settled institutions. We cling to the old; we dread the new. We believe that that which has in the past been tried, has a violent presumption in its favor.

Never was a nation more dominated by a tradition than our nation was by the tradition of its political isolation. It has its roots in the very beginnings of the American Commonwealth. In nine generations no political party and few public men have ever questioned its continued efficacy.

The pioneers, who came in 1620 across the Atlantic to Plymouth Rock and founded the American Commonwealth, desired, like the intrepid Kent in "King Lear," to "shape their old course in a country new," so that the spirit of detachment from Europe was implanted in the very souls of the pioneers who conquered the virgin forests of America.

Our Colonial history was a constant struggle between this spirit of detachment on the part of the pioneers and the centralizing demands of the Mother Country. Our revolt was not merely about a 2d. stamp on tea. We proclaimed independence from the same instinct of separation and detachment.

When Washington in the Napoleonic wars proclaimed a policy of neutrality, he again expressed the instinctive feeling of his countrymen that America should not be the shuttlecock of European politics. We had had long experience of this. As Macaulay said, the rape of Silesia had made the whites and the Indians fight upon the shores of the Hudson and the Great Lakes.

When Washington gave in his great Farewell Address his last testament to his countrymen, he defined the foreign policy of the United States better than it has been defined before or since. He said that Europe has a "set of primary interests which to us have none or a very remote relation," and therefore he advised that we should not by *"artificial* ties implicate ourselves in the *ordinary* vicissitudes of her politics or the *ordinary* combinations and collisions of her friendships and enmities."

My countrymen for many generations have accepted this counsel of our Founder as infallible, but they have not always appreciated the weight that Washington meant to give to the expression "artificial ties," and "ordinary vicissitudes," and "ordinary combinations and collisions of her friendships and enmities." Washington recognised that there might, as is now the case, be an extraordinary vicissitude in which a conflict, while originating primarily on the Continent of Europe and primarily affecting its internal policies, might yet affect the very bases of civilization, and impose upon the United States, as upon every civilized nation, the fullest responsibility to aid in maintaining the peace of the world by establishing international justice. [Cheers.] By "artificial ties" Washington meant, I think, hard and fast alliances of an entangling nature. He did not intend to ignore the natural ties, which spring from racial kinship or common ideals.

The Monroe Doctrine illustrates the same policy of isolation, for it was founded upon an express disclaimer of any interest by the United States "in the internal affairs of Europe."

I appeal to you, men of England—as many of you here present stand high in the public life of this country of settled traditions—if a tradition had existed in England for three centuries, and had persisted among nine generations of men who, although they differed upon every other question, yet never differed with respect to such policy—could you reasonably expect that in a day or a week or a year England, even in a great crisis of humanity, would throw aside a great settled tradition, the value and justice of which all its political parties had accepted for three centuries? If such a policy had had in successive generations the unquestioning support of the elder and the younger Pitt, of Fox, Camden, Burke, Sheridan, of Peel, Palmerston and Russell, of Gladstone, Disraeli and Salisbury, of Balfour, Bonar Law, Asquith and Sir Edward Grey, and then a quarrel arose in another country three thousand miles away, would England in a day, or a month, or a year have disregarded a tradition of such exceptional authority? *Mutatis mutandis,* and that was the position of the United States on August 1, 1914.

Were this all, the attitude of the United States as a political entity would be easily understood. But we have another tradition, which in this crisis has conflicted with our tradition of isolation. In every true American soul in the last eighteen months there has been a conflict of ideals. One was this ideal of detachment from European politics and our isolation; the other was the ideal which we derived from the French Revolution, namely, that of cosmopolitanism, which taught us that humanity was greater than any nation; that the interests of civilization were above those of any country; that above all there was a conscience of mankind, by which the actions of any nation must be judged.

When, therefore, the rape of Belgium affronted our conscience the question inevitably arose, "Shall we abandon the great tradition of political isolation, under which we have grown great, or shall we fail by inaction to do a duty, where the spirit of international justice imperiously calls upon us and every nation to play its part?"

The practical genius of our people tried to solve the problem as best it could in so short a time, and our government was permitted by public opinion to follow an official policy of neutrality, which I think it is no exaggeration to call one of benevolent neutrality to the Allies, while the people of the United States, as individuals and collectively, were permitted to ignore the policy of neutrality by helping the Allies in every practicable way in their noble struggle for the best interests of civilization.

I believe that this war, among other surpassing benefits, will bring nearer to realisation than ever before a sympathetic understanding between Great Britain and the United States. [Cheers.] We appreciate the greatness of your Empire more than we ever appreciated it before. Our views in the past have been somewhat affected by our earlier history, and to a greater extent than you may imagine by the Napoleonic wars, because every American boy, at least in the exuberance of youthful imagination, ranks the great Napoleon as his hero next to Washington. This has always affected the attitude with which the American in the past has viewed the policies of your Empire. But now we have seen your Empire rise, in this great crisis of civilization, to defend the rights of a little nation, and reveal itself—to use Milton's noble imagery—as "a noble and puissant nation, rousing itself like a strong man after his sleep and shaking its invincible locks."

With deep admiration we have seen Great Britain follow the noblest policy in all its long and glorious history in staking its whole existence to save Belgium and aid France. [Hear,

hear!] The immortal valor of Tommy Atkins has also powerfully impressed us. We saw you, within three days, send that little army—little in this war—of over one hundred thousand men across the Channel, and offer them as a sacrifice to save your great and heroic neighbor on the south of the English Channel. We saw the thin red line at Ypres, suffocated by gases, rained upon by shrapnel, opposed by forces greater than their own and yet standing like a stone wall against the red tide of Prussian invasion. We saw Tommy Atkins realizing that song that I heard in London twenty years ago:

> To keep the flag a'flying,
> He's a'doing and a'dying
> *Every inch of him a soldier and a man.*

[Cheers.]

That has been the great benefit of the war to us, that it has brought us into a profound understanding and more sympathetic appreciation of your great Empire. If I were asked to say who was *unwittingly* the most beneficent statesman of modern times, I should undoubtedly say the Kaiser [laughter], for he has consolidated the British Empire, reinvigorated France, reorganized Russia, and has brought the United States and Great Britain nearer to a realization of that complete sympathetic understanding, upon which an *Entente Cordiale* may ultimately rest, than any other individual in the world. [Cheers.]

An *Entente Cordiale* must rest not merely upon a sympathetic understanding, but, as long as men are human, to some extent upon common interests. We are entering upon the most portentous half century the world has ever seen. You will end this war, and you may end it speedily or within six months, or a year, or two years. But what lies beyond? Over ravaged homes, desolated fields, and new-made graves, men will gaze at each other for possibly fifty years with irreconcilable hatred. This world will be a seething caldron of international hatred in my judgment for the next half-a-century.

In this portentous and critical time to come, the United

States will need you, and England will need the United States.

May this possible interdependence in vital interests lead us to a practical recognition that these two great divisions of our race form a spiritual Empire of the English-speaking peoples, not made by constitutions, written documents or formal alliances, but constituting, as Proudhon said in 1845 of Society in general, a "living being, endowed with an intelligence and activity of its own, and as such, a (spiritual) organic unit." This great Empire of the English-speaking race must stand united in spirit, though not organically, for unless it stands together, there is little hope that in these dreadful years to come there will be the maintenance of any permanent peace in the only way that peace can be maintained, namely, through the vindication of justice. [Cheers.]

I have taken far too long [cries of "No! No!"], but I may add that in order to develop this sympathetic understanding we must fully appreciate the difficulties of each nation and "bear and forbear."

For example, we have learned to appreciate that which your Empire has done. But, if you will pardon me, I do not think you quite appreciate the great difficulty of the United States in this crisis, a difficulty which would have been great if we had only to contend with our heterogeneous population. Has it ever occurred to you that we have in the United States of teutonic origin, counting birth or immediate parentage, a population equal to one-third of all the men, women and children of Great Britain? Then we have, as I have explained, the great difficulty of a persistent tradition, which in all generations has powerfully influenced the American mind and has been hitherto vindicated by its results. Can you not see that you must not misinterpret a nation which cannot in a day abandon a cherished tradition, even if it be conceded that the interests of civilization required it?

Then there is a disposition on this side among some men to misinterpret what we have tried to do as a people to help you. Some of the very things for which we have been most criticized are those that seem to me to redound to our credit.

Take for example the sale of munitions. It is believed by many here that we have in a sordid and mercenary way deliberately profited by this world tragedy; that while civilization was bleeding on the Cross we have been, as the Roman soldiers, parting the raiment of the crucified.

Only an infinitesimal portion of the American people directly profited by this traffic. Indirectly it is true Americans generally have profited by the immense prosperity thereby stimulated, but have you thought of the other side?

In thus serving you, we have abandoned not only an unbroken friendship with the first military power of the world to give you munitions; but we have incurred an obligation that will weigh heavily upon us in future years far beyond any possible economic profits that our industries may temporarily gain by furnishing the Allies with munitions. To have placed an embargo on the export of these munitions to safeguard our internal peace and outward safety would not have violated neutrality in a legal sense. Sweden and Holland have forbidden many exports to protect their vital interests. We refused to do so because the American people believed that in the earlier stages of the war, you needed our aid and were determined that at any cost you should have it.

We fully realized that in doing so we exposed ourselves to a great and continuing peril. Why did 145,000 men recently parade the streets of New York from early dawn to night? Why did 130,000 men parade in Chicago? Why did 60,000 men parade in Boston?

Was it Mexico? We care no more about a possible war with Mexico than a St. Bernard dog cares for a black and tan terrier.

What was the meaning of this outpouring of all classes? We know that we have incurred the undying enmity of Germany by doing you a service. We know that if she wins this war or even makes it a draw, as sure as political events can ever be prognosticated, Germany will settle its accounts with the United States, for there is no country in the world next to the British Empire that Germany to-day hates as she does the United States. To avoid this very danger, which will burden us for generations to come cautious politicians attempted to put an embargo on the export of munitions, but public opinion said "No," and our President made our Congressmen stand up and be counted, and thereafter there was no threatened interruption to the flow of munitions of war to the Allies. [Cheers.] As a result, we are now doubling our army and largely increasing our navy, and future generations will bear the burden.

Do you realize that not only have we contributed by the sacrificing labors of men, women and children, at least 10 millions of pounds to relieve suffering in this war [Cheers]; but that over 4,000 of our boys are fighting under the Maple Leaf for the Union Jack [Cheers]; and 10,000 more are serving under the tricolor of France? [Cheers.]

The best blood of our youth from our Colleges and Universities are serving with the Ambulances, and doing the arduous and often dangerous work of taking the wounded from the trenches. If the bones of your sons are now buried in France there are the bones of many a brave American boy who, without the protection of his flag, and with only the impulse of race patriotism, with the sympathy which the majority of the American people feel for the cause of the Allies in this crisis, has gone and given his young life as a willing sacrifice.

Therefore, I say to you, men of England, if there are pin-pricks, do not misjudge the American people, who have done what they did under the most trying and delicate circumstances, and whose loyalty to the Empire of the English-speaking race has been demonstrated in this crisis of history.

I am reminded of a scene I once saw in Switzerland, in Lauterbrunnen, that most beautiful valley in all the world. There are the three crowning peaks of the Bernese Oberland, the Eiger, the Monch, and the Jungfrau. They are apparently separate, and yet all three are based upon the common granite foundation of the same range of the eternal Alps. So I like to think of the three great democracies of civilization—Great Britain, France and the United States—that while they are separate peaks in a purely political sense, yet they too stand upon a common foundation of justice and liberty.

Our affection and admiration for France passes description. We think of France in this crisis as brave as Hector and yet like Andromache "smiling through her tears" and offering up the sacrifice of her noble youth for the principles of liberty and justice, to which Great Britain and the United States have always been dedicated.

I remember once when I was in this Valley of Lauterbrunnen that the Swiss guide asked me if he could sound for me the echo of an Alpine horn. He played the four notes of the common chord, and as they reverberated back across the valley they were merged into the most gracious and beautiful harmonies that the mind of man could conceive. It sounded in that Cathedral of Nature as a divinely majestic organ. May not these four notes thus mingled typify the common traditions of these three great democracies and create a lasting harmony, which will contribute to the symphony of universal progress?

The Swiss guide also asked me to hear the echo of a little brass cannon, and as he fired it the effect was almost bewildering. It seemed to me as if the very mountains had toppled from their bases. The smoke of the cannon drifted across my eyes, and for a moment obliterated the majestic range of the Bernese Alps. Finally the smoke cleared from my eyes, and the Eiger, the Monch, and the Jungfrau were again revealed in their undiminished beauty. May not that little cannon well typify Prussian militarism?

When the smoke of this Titanic conflict passes from our eyes and the echoes of this portentous war shall die away into the terrible past, we shall—please God—see outlined against the infinite blue of His future the three great democracies of civilization—Great Britain, France, and the United States. [Cheers.]

CARDINAL MERCIER

CORONATION DAY SERMON

[Address given by His Eminence Cardinal Mercier on the day of the National Fête, July 21, 1916 at Sainte Gudule, Brussels.

This sermon was given under extraordinary circumstances. The German Governor of Brussels had forbidden, under a penalty of fine and imprisonment, any demonstration on the Belgian National Day, July 21. The result of this prohibition was to stimulate the inhabitants of Brussels to efforts for the manifestation of their patriotism. In most churches a dirge was substituted for the customary Te Deum. Cardinal Mercier appeared at the church of Sainte Gudule which was crowded by an audience that overflowed into the adjoining square. In spite of the German prohibition, the Cardinal found a way in his opening words to stir the patriotism of the people to the highest.

At the close of the service, the organ played the national hymn. Up to this time the audience had heeded the recommendation of the Cardinal to restrain their emotions, but now broke forth into cries of "Long live Belgium," "Long live the King." The crowd pressed upon the Cardinal as he left the church, crying "Long live the Cardinal," "Long live Liberty." In the evening the Cardinal's motor car was recognized in the streets and he was acclaimed with great enthusiasm. As a result of this demonstration, the German Governor of Brussels inflicted a fine of 1,000,000 marks upon the City. The Cardinal's sermon also brought a sharp protest from the Governor General.

Cardinal Mercier was born in 1851 and was created Cardinal in 1907. His great services for Belgium during the War may perhaps be best stated in the words of the German Officials. Just before the Germans evacuated Belgium, Baron Von der Lancken called at the Archbishop's house and presented him with a note beginning "You are in our estimation the incarnation of occupied Belgium, of which you are the venerated and trusted pastor. For this reason, it is to you that the Governor General and my Government also have commissioned me to come and to announce that when we evacuate your soil, we wish to hand over to you, unasked and of our own free will, the political prisoners serving their time either in Belgium or in Germany."]

> "Jerusalem was made an habitation of strangers;
> Her festival days were turned into mourning."
> 1st Book of Maccabees,
> Chapter 1, verses 40, 41.

BELOVED BRETHREN: We ought to have met together here to celebrate the 86th anniversary of our national independence.

To-day, in fourteen years' time, our restored cathedrals and our rebuilt churches will be thrown widely open; the crowds will surge in; our King Albert, standing on his throne, will bow his unconquered head before the King of Kings; the Queen and the Royal Princes will surround him; we shall hear again the joyous peals of our bells, and throughout the whole country, under the vaulted arches of our churches, the Belgians, hand in hand, will renew their vows to their God, their Sovereign, and their liberty, while the bishops and the priests, interpreters of the soul of the nation, will intone a triumphant Te Deum in a common transport of joyous thanksgiving.

To-day the hymn of joy dies on our lips.

The Jewish people in captivity at Babylon, sitting in tears on the banks of the Euphrates, watched the waters of the river flow by. Their dumb harps were hung on the willows by the bank. Who amongst them would have the courage to sing the song of Jehovah in a strange land? "O Jerusalem," cried the Psalmist, "if ever I forget thee, let my right hand wither, let my tongue cleave to the roof of my mouth if I do not remember thee; if thou art no longer the beginning of my joys."

The Psalm ends in imprecations: but we do not allow ourselves to repeat them: we are not of the Old Testament, tolerating the laws of retaliation: "An eye for an eye, and a tooth for a tooth." Our lips, purified by the fire of Christian charity, utter no words of hate. To hate is to make it one's object to do harm to others and to delight in so doing. Whatever may be our sufferings, we must not wish to show hatred towards those who have inflicted them. Our national unity is joined with a feeling of universal brotherhood. But even this feeling of universal brotherhood is dominated by our respect for the unconditional justice, without which no relationship is possible, either between individuals or between nations.

And that is why, with St. Thomas Aquinas, the most authoritative teacher of Christian Theology, we proclaim that public retribution is commendable.

Crimes, violation of justice, outrage on the public peace whether enacted by an individual or by a group must be repressed. Men's minds are stirred up, tortured, uneasy, as long as the guilty one is not put back in his place, as the strong, healthy, colloquial expression has it. To put men and things back in their places is to reëstablish order, readjust the balance and restore peace on a just basis.

Public retribution in this sense may distress the affected sentimentality of a weak nature; all the same, it is, says St. Thomas, the expression and the decree of the highest, the purest form of charity, and of the zeal which is its flame. It does not make a target of suffering, but a weapon wherewith to avenge outraged justice.

How can one love order without hating disorder; intelligently wish for peace without expelling that which is destroying it; love a brother, that is to say wish him well, without desiring that willingly, or by force, his will shall bend before the unalterable edicts of justice and truth?

It is from these heights that one must view the war in order to understand the greatness of its extent.

Once more, perhaps, you will find yourself face to face with effeminate natures for whom the war means nothing beyond explosions of mines, bursting of shells, massacres of men, spilling of blood, piling up of corpses. You will meet politicians of narrow vision who see no further stake in a battle beyond the interest of one day, the taking of so much ground, of a stretch of country, or of a province.

But no! If, in spite of its horrors, war, I mean a just war, has so much austere beauty, it is because war brings out the disinterested enthusiasm of a whole people, which gives, or is prepared to give, its most precious possession, even life itself, for the defense and the vindication of things which cannot be weighed, which cannot be calculated, but which can never be swallowed up: Justice, Honor, Peace, Liberty!

Do you not feel that, in these two years, the war, the ardent unflagging interest which you give to it, purifies you, separates your higher nature from the dross, draws you away to uplift you towards something nobler and better than yourselves?

You are rising towards the ideals of justice and honor. They support you and draw you upwards.

And, because this ideal, if it is not a vain abstraction, which evaporates like the phantasies of a dream, must have its foundation in a living subject, I am never tired of maintaining this truth, which holds us all under its yoke. God reveals Himself as the Master, the Director of events, and of our wills, the holy Master of the universal conscience.

Ah, if we could clasp in our arms our heroes who are fighting for us over there, or are awaiting anxiously in the trenches their turn to go under fire; if we could take them by surprise, and feel the beating of their hearts, would not each one of them say to us: I am doing my duty, I am sacrificing myself on the altar of justice?

And you, wives and mothers, tell us in your turn of the beauty of these tragic years; wives, whose every thought goes, sad, but resigned, towards the absent one, bringing him your hopes, your long expectation, your prayers. Mothers, whose divided existence is consumed in unceasing anguish, you have given your sons, and you will not take them back; we stand breathless with unceasing admiration before you.

The head of one of our noblest families wrote to me: "Our son in the 7th Line Regiment has fallen; my wife and I are broken-hearted; and yet, if it had to be, we would give him again."

One of the curates of the capital has been condemned to twelve years penal servitude. I was allowed to go into his cell to embrace and to bless him. "I have three brothers at the front," he said, "and I think I am here chiefly because I helped the youngest, he is only seventeen—to rejoin the elder ones; one of my sisters is in a neighboring cell, but, thank God, my mother is not left alone; indeed she has sent us a message to say so; she does not weep."

Is it not true that our mothers make us think of the mother of the Maccabees?

What lessons of moral greatness there are to be learnt here around us, and in exile and in the prisons, and in the concentration camps, in Holland and in Germany!

Do we think enough of what those brave men must be suffering, who since the beginning of the war, from the morrow of the defense of Liège and Namur, or the retreat from Antwerp, saw their military career shattered, and now chafe and fret under their inability to bear arms; these guardians of our rights, and of our communal liberties, whose valor has reduced them to inaction?

It needs courage to throw oneself forward, but it needs no less to hold oneself back. Sometimes it is more noble to suffer in silence than to act.

And what of these two years of calm submission by the Belgian people before the inevitable; this unshakable tenacity, which moved a humble woman, before whom the possibilities of an approaching conclusion of peace were being discussed, to say: "Oh, as for us, we must not worry; we can go on waiting." How beautiful is all this, and how full of instruction for the generations to come.

This is what you must look at, my brothers, the greatness of the nation in her sacrifice; our universal and enduring brotherhood in anguish and in mourning, and in the same unconquerable hope; this is what you must look at to appraise your Belgian fatherland at its true value.

Now the first exponents of this moral greatness are our soldiers.

Until that day when they return to us, and when grateful Belgium acclaims the living, and places a halo of glory about the memory of her dead, let us build up for them in our hearts a permanent monument of sacred gratitude.

Let us pray for those who are no more. Let us exclude no one from our commiseration; the blood of Christ was shed for all. Some of them are atoning in Purgatory for the last remnants of their human weakness. It is for you to hasten their entry into Paradise. Succor the poor in distress, both the poor who are known to you and those who are ashamed to beg. Give of your abundance to those who are in need of the necessities of life. Be present at the Mass, which is celebrated every week in your parish churches for our dead soldiers; take your children with you, encourage them to communicate, and communicate with them.

Let us also pray for those who are still holding the firing line on the field of battle. Remember that, even at this moment, while I am speaking to you, some of them are in the agony of death. The prospect of eternity stretches out before them. Let us think of them, let us mortify ourselves for them, resign ourselves to God for them, and obtain for them a holy death.

"Our soldiers are our masters," wrote a French Academician yesterday; "they are our leaders, our teachers, our judges, our supporters, our true friends; let us be worthy of them, let us imitate them, so that we may not do less than our duty; they are always ready to do more than their own."

The hour of deliverance approaches, but it has not yet struck. Let us be patient. Let us not suffer our courage to waver. Let us surrender to Divine Providence the work of making perfect our national probation.

Young women, young girls, let me ask if you are thinking seriously enough about the gravity of this present time? I entreat you not to turn aside from the mourning of your country. There are attitudes, there are ways of behaving which are an insult to grief.

For your modesty is at all times a virtue and a halo of glory; but to-day it is in addition a patriotic duty.

You, also, must think of the privations and of the endurance of our soldiers.

Let us all try to adopt the great principle of austerity in our lives.

"How much," continues the patriot whom I have just quoted, "how much ought we, in the relatively easy conditions and the less exposed districts, which are ours, and which do not deserve the name of fire zones, to endeavor to reduce and simplify our needs, and like the soldiers, though in our own sphere, to show more concentrated energy. Let us not allow ourselves a moment's distraction or relaxation. Let us devote every minute in our lives to the magnificent cause for which our brothers are so devotedly sacrificing theirs.

"And, just as our heroes at the front show us a wonderful and consoling spectacle of indissoluble unity, of a brotherhood in arms which nothing can destroy, even so, in our ranks, less compact and well-disciplined though they may be, we shall earnestly strive to maintain the same patriotic sense of union. We will respect the truce imposed on our quarrels by the one great Cause which alone ought to use and absorb all our powers of attack and combat; and if there are any godless or unfortunate people, who fail to understand the urgency and the beauty of this national precept, and insist, in spite of all, on keeping alive and fomenting the passions which divide us when other matters are concerned, we will turn aside our heads, and continue without answering them, to remain faithful to the pact of fellowship, of friendship, of loyal and true confidence which we have concluded with them, even in spite of themselves, under the great inspiration of the war."

The approaching date of the first centenary of our independence ought to find us stronger, more intrepid, more united than ever. Let us prepare ourselves for it with work, with patience and in true brotherhood.

When, in 1930, we recall the dark years of 1915-1916, they will appear to us as the brightest, the most majestic and, if, from to-day we resolve that they shall be so, the happiest and the most fruitful in our national history. *Per crucem ad lucem* —from the sacrifice flashes forth the light!

ARISTIDE BRIAND

THE GERMAN PEACE PROPOSAL

[Throughout the world in Allied and neutral countries public opinion pronounced judgment against Germany's proposals of peace after the French victory at Verdun. The recent victory and the formation of a new War Cabinet were a clear declaration of France's determination to continue the war. Premier Briand, head of the new cabinet warned the French people against being duped by the German offers, in a speech in the Chamber of Deputies on December 13, 1916.]

GENTLEMEN: At the very moment when she is proclaiming victory on every front, Germany, feeling in the bottom of her heart that she cannot win this war, sends us a message which I feel it is impossible to let pass without comment.

You have read the speech of von Bethmann-Hollweg, Chancellor of the German Empire.

Regarding this address, of which I have not the authentic text, it is impossible for me to speak definitely. I cannot give you an official opinion. No government, moreover, has up to this time been impressed by these so-called offers, and it is doubtful whether those who have been asked to intervene would, at the present time and under existing conditions, accept a task which is so delicate and which might easily trouble their conscience.

In the last analysis, as in every instance, I could not bring you an official opinion until the subject had been carefully studied, debated, and a conclusion reached in full accord and in complete unanimity with our allies.

But I consider it my right and my duty forthwith to do what I can to prevent the possibility of poisoning the public opinion in my country.

When I see Germany arming herself to the teeth, mobilizing her entire civil population at the risk of ruining her commerce and her industry and of disorganizing the homes of which she is so proud; when I see her furnaces blazing to produce munitions of war; when I see her seizing men everywhere, in violation of the laws of nations, and forcing them to work for her —when I see these things, I would be very guilty if I did not cry out to my country: "Look out! Take care!"

THE GERMAN PEACE PROPOSAL 137

Gentlemen, note that what comes to us from across the frontier is an invitation to negotiate for peace. It is made under conditions with which you are familiar: Belgium invaded; Serbia invaded; Rumania invaded; ten of our departments invaded.

This invitation is made in a vague and indefinite manner, expressed in solemn words, destined to confuse the minds, to upset the consciences and to trouble the hearts of peoples bearing so grievous a burden of bereavement. Gentlemen, I would call your attention to the fact that this is a moment full of danger.

I discern in these declarations the same complaint which has always sought to deceive neutral nations and is trying perhaps to delude the clear-headed elements among the German people also. "This horrible war," they announce, "is not of our unchaining."

This cry is ever upon the lips of the German people: "We have been attacked, we are defending ourselves, we are the victims of this war."

To this cry, first of all, I wish to reply for the hundredth time: "No! It is you who are the aggressors. Whatever you may say, the facts are there and they accuse you. The blood is on your heads and not on ours."

Furthermore, considering the conditions under which these propositions are made, I am justified in denouncing them as a manoeuver, as a crude trap; when, after reading such words as these: "We wish to give to our people all the liberties which they need, to offer them every means of subsistence and every opportunity for success which they can desire," I find that, in the same document, our enemies generously offer to the other nations, as a form of charity, a willingness to spare them from being crushed, annihilated, I cry out: "Is it true? Do they dare, after the Marne, after the Yser, after Verdun, to make such an offer to France, erect and glorious?"

One must stop and consider such a document; one must see what it means at the time when it is sent out to the different nations of the world; one must ascertain its purpose.

I am expressing my personal feelings to this body; I should not have brought forward my impressions if it had not been my duty to put my country on her guard against the possibility of demoralization.

It is not that I doubt its clarity nor its perspicacity. I am very sure that it will not be duped.

But, nevertheless, from this place, before the proposals are presented in official form, I feel it is my duty to say that there is in this offer a ruse. There is an attempt to weaken our alliance, to confuse our minds and to lower the *morale* of the allied nations.

In closing—and you will not criticize me, I think, for having discussed this question—let me say that the French Republic of to-day will play her part as formerly, under similar circumstances, did the Convention.

ELEUTHERIOS VENISELOS

GREECE ENTERS THE WAR

[From the beginning of the War Mr. Veniselos was convinced that Greece must join the Allies, but he was continually thwarted in all his efforts by the German agents of the King. Under his inspiring leadership Greece finally emerged reunited and fighting on the side of the Allies. During the session of the Greek Chamber in August in 1917, M. Veniselos, who had returned triumphantly to power after the abdication of Constantine, denounced the methods of the German agents and explained his reasons for setting up a Provisional Government at Salonica and his actions since his return to Athens.

Eleutherios Veniselos was born in Crete in 1864. He became a leader in Cretan politics and in 1909 was invited to Athens to aid in the efforts for constitutional reform. Gifted with great power and persuasiveness as a speaker Veniselos was soon chosen as Prime Minister. Through his efforts Greece played a part in the Balkan Wars and finally joined the Allies in the Great War.

The earlier part of the speech had traced the struggle of the party of the Allies resulting finally in the revolution and the overthrow of King Constantine and the pro-German ministry.]

NOT long afterwards, when it became possible for us to mobilize, New Greece produced a military force of which I said at the time that the whole of Greece had never seen a finer body of troops. [Applause.] When I said this, Gentlemen, I never imagined that it could give rise to feelings of bitterness and sorrow in any Greek heart. I thought that all Greeks, whatever their political opinions, would have been proud to know that, even after being cut in two and after being poisoned by the German propaganda, the nation succeeded in assembling an army of 60,000 men as fine, I repeat, as any army that had ever been seen in Greece. One of the "Saviors," however, the deputy from Attica, who spoke yesterday from this tribune, attempted in a mean partisan spirit to make use of that assurance of mine in order to produce if he could a new rift between the armies of Old and New Greece, which constitute to-day the one army of a united country. Of course, so long as the army of Old Greece had momentarily forgotten its national character and allowed itself to be reduced to the position of a dynastic weapon, the division between the two armies was inevitable. But even then there was no question of two armies levied in different districts, since the army of the New Greece included a large proportion of volunteers from the Old. Consequently, there was no question of a geographical division, but only of a difference of opinion, and that transitory, between the two sections of the National Army. Nobody ever thought of denying, of undervaluing the honors and the laurels which the army of Old Greece culled on the battlefield in our glorious wars of 1912 and 1913. It was just because that I was convinced that as soon as the pernicious influence, exercised on the army from above, was removed, just because I believe that the Greek nation in arms is capable of going to war again at the side of the great military Powers with full confidence in its army, that I became a rebel and organized a new army; and I am already hoping to reassemble the other army of veterans, confident that once it is released from those evil influences they will achieve once more, as they did in our recent wars, great and noble works; they will write new pages of glory, and will perform deeds by means of which we will succeed through all disasters in saving what can still be saved and in establishing Greece once again as a worthy member of the family of European Powers. [Prolonged applause from Chamber and galleries.]

THE ABOLITION OF AUTOCRACY

So we got our army together, and we tried and succeeded in extending our authority over the remaining islands. But in spite of the intervention of the Powers, and in spite of the release of our friends who have been persecuted and thrown into gaol as conspirators against the established order, we knew that every day throughout the whole of Greece our friends were suffering real martyrdoms of persecution. Nobody could possibly suppose that we were capable, conscious as we were of having on our side the strength, not only moral, but material and military as well, no one of us could endure the idea of leaving our friends throughout Greece a prey to the persecution of the established autocracy, a prey to the actions of that Government of political scum, without seeking to hasten to their assistance. We saw besides that the lack of national unity, for all the admirable efforts of the Army of National Defense, would not permit us, unfortunately, to champion the interests of the nation all along the line and to the full extent of our national requirements. We therefore asked the Powers to suspend, if possible, the neutral zone and allow us to come to a trial of strength with the State organization in Old Greece, so as to bring the division of the country to an end and restore in time the national unity. In the second place we asked them, if this did not meet their wishes, to allow us at least to suspend the neutral zone temporarily, so as to settle the question of Thessaly. For on the one hand we did not want to leave the Thessalian crops at the disposal of the Athens Government, and we knew on the other hand that our advance into Thessaly and arrival at Œta would bring into further disrepute the established Government, the Ministry, as I have said, of offscourings, and that this loss of prestige would bring about, without any great effort, the extension of our authority to the rest of Greece. The Powers accepted neither proposal—neither the suspension, that is to say, of the neutral zone nor the extension of our authority to Thessaly. They only undertook to move into Thessaly themselves. But it was owing to our request, I imagine, that they took occasion to review their decisions on the Greek question, and knowing as they did that the New Greece, that

GREECE ENTERS THE WAR

was fighting with them and had constituted itself into an organized State at Salonica, could no longer tolerate King Constantine, they arrived at the decision they did, to intervene, that is, on the ground of the treaties and of the guarantee they had given to the Greek State as constitutional, and to demand the removal of King Constantine. Thus came about our return to Athens, the reunion of all Greece, and the assumption of authority by the Salonica Government.

One of the speakers complained from this tribune of the intervention of the Powers, and allowed it to be believed that if it had not been for that intervention the Athenian State would have been capable of resisting that of Salonica, even if the neutral zone had been removed and the two organizations had been confronted. At the period in which our return took place the Salonica Government had an army of 60,000 men, well organized in three divisions, with a fourth division, that of the Kyklades and Ionian Islands, ready for immediate organization, 60,000 men ready to face any sacrifice in order to attain the high aims which they had in view, whereas at that period the force at the disposal of the Athenian State was not even distantly comparable. The Athenian State had succeeded by its own faults in breaking up the army. But above all it had succeeded in infusing most of the soldiers with the idea that there is no greater misfortune for a citizen than the sacrifice of his own individuality for the sake of the more general interests of his country. Whoever therefore wishes to judge the matter openly will observe that the utter defeat of the Athenian régime, with its Ministry of offscourings, would have been the task of an ordinary route march for the established Government of Salonica.

THE TRIUMPH OF THE NATIONAL MOVEMENT

I have said this much, because I do not want it to be believed here, even for a moment, that if I were not deeply conscious of this I should be able to remain in Athens after allowing a foreign Power, however friendly, however protecting, however guaranteeing, to lead me by the hand. We came to Athens, and the Revolution triumphed; and this even our opponents have been compelled to recognize. But now they say: "Why did you bring back the Chamber of 31 May [13

June, 1915]? Why don't you govern without any Chamber?" They are really at a loss to know why, if the Government of the Scum was capable of ruling without a Chamber, we refuse to govern under the same conditions. I could not possibly undertake to govern the country without any popular representation, yet at the same time it was impossible to think of carrying out elections immediately and under present conditions; no one, for that matter, even thought of suggesting the possibility of a General Election under present conditions. In such circumstances to summon the Chamber of 31 May [13 June] was the only solution indicated of the problem of government. If the present Ministry is rightly seated on this bench to-day then the present House, from which that Ministry derives, is rightly seated on these benches. I must also remind you that never for a moment have the Liberal Party qualified or suspended their refusal to recognize the King's illegal dissolution of the Chamber of 31 May [13 June]. We took no part in the Elections of 6 December [19], and when later on we thought fit to take part in by-elections, we expressly informed our constituents that our participation did not imply any obligation to take our seats in that counterfeit Chamber, which we refused to recognize. It was therefore impossible to misunderstand our claim to consider the King's dissolution of the Chamber of 31 May [13 June] as an illegal and unconstitutional action, an action by means of which King Constantine intended to set aside the sovereignty of the people and concentrate all power in his own hands, so that he might become a Monarch by the Grace of God. The summoning of the Chamber of 31 May [June 13] will not be judged as cases are decided in the Law Courts. There will be no judicial decision; it will be judged as a political measure. The Chamber was summoned because the two established Governments (of Athens and Salonica) when they decided to reconstitute the State, expressly agreed that these should be the conditions of its reunion.

Nevertheless, it is my duty to inform the House that even if I had thought it possible to hold a General Election immediately, I should still have refused to take office without this condition: I should still have insisted that the Chamber of 31 May [13 June] must be recalled, in order to continue its labors, in order to continue, I should have said, the sitting of 31 October [13 November], 1915. [Applause.] I should have insisted on the recall of this House to work for some time at least; if only to furnish the political history of Greece with one clear precedent, which may serve as a lesson to future generations. [Applause.]

A WARNING TO TYRANTS—THE TWO POLICIES

Those of you, Gentlemen, who have visited the Palace of Westminster, where the two English Chambers sit, will remember that on the left just after you have crossed the threshold of the great entrance, there is a tablet, on which is engraved in clear letters this inscription—I cannot remember the exact words, but this is their meaning—"Here was beheaded Charles, King of England, because he had plotted and usurped the liberties of the English people." ["Hear, hear!" and prolonged applause.] Whenever the King of England visits the Palace of Westminster, to proclaim the opening and the closing of Parliament, he goes exactly by the place where this tablet is fixed, and as he passes by he sees what is written there. And this has been happening since that date for two centuries and a half, because it is just the peoples who are worthy of liberty, as the English people is, who do not mean to forget the lessons of their history, and make use of them for the coming generations. For my part, I intend to propose to the National Assembly, which will in due time be summoned, that on a tablet, to be placed perhaps there, opposite the President's chair—or wherever else a competent committee might think suitable, so that it would be in front of the King when he comes to this place, to proclaim the opening of the Chamber —should be written some such words as these: "King Constantine having dissolved for the second time the Chamber of 1915, in order to impose a personal policy, himself fell from the throne, while the Chamber which had been dissolved was called together again and continued its work according to the Constitution."

Gentlemen, those who embraced a German policy in Greece tried to persuade the people that the difference between the Liberal Party and themselves consisted in the fact that the Liberals wanted to pursue a radical policy which aimed at realizing our national desires, but entailed certain dangers; while themselves, we are to suppose, wanted to pursue a conservative policy by which the realization of our national desires was certainly to be relinquished for the present, but our present possessions were secured and war was avoided.

No, Gentlemen, it was not this that divided one policy from the other. I have already shown at the beginning of my statement how little radical was the policy of the Liberal Government; how little conservative was the German policy which prevailed, events themselves have proved. By that policy of theirs nothing, as a matter of fact, was "conserved." We saved neither Eastern Macedonia and Northern Epirus, nor the balance of power in the Balkans, which was overthrown at our expense and in favor of our hereditary enemy, nor did we escape the atrocities of war.

THE CONSEQUENCES OF SERVING GERMANY

The German policy, aiming simply at serving German interests, accepted the loss of Eastern Macedonia and of Northern Epirus. But it did not even succeed in averting from us the disasters of war. They knew that by permitting the landing of the English and French at Salonica without at the same time hastening themselves to the assistance of the Serbians, they would transfer the theater of the war on to Macedonian territory; and they accepted the fact without even attempting to avert it because the attempt would have hurt German interests.

If this policy had not been pursued, and our own had been followed instead, not only would our territory never have been invaded by our enemies, even if we had failed to defeat the Bulgarians, but we should still have been in occupation of Eastern Macedonia and Northern Epirus, and also of Cyprus, which was offered us; and even on the impossible supposition of the victory of the Central Empires Greece would have come to the Peace Congress, with her national territory inviolate, and, indeed, increased by the addition of Cyprus, and five or six Great Powers at her side to defend her.

The opposite policy, Gentlemen, has no right to be called

conservative; it was simply a policy of deserting and betraying every political interest and every national ideal.

It might, after all, have been called a conservative policy if, for all its betrayal of the treaty of alliance with Serbia, it had taken care, while observing a very benevolent neutrality by every means towards Serbia, to secure at least all that I have more than once indicated, namely, the inviolability of the national territory, checking of the undue expansion of Bulgaria, exchange of populations, preservation of Hellenism in Asia Minor, Thrace, and Macedonia, immunity of our mercantile fleet, and guarantee of our integrity for a period of ten years after the war. And nobody, Gentlemen, can maintain that all this was not attainable, for Greece at the beginning had a general mobilization on her hands, which might at least have been made use of for attaining it. For my part, even if such a policy as this had been pursued, I should have been one of its most bitter opponents, because I should have been stirred by the idea that Greece had dishonored herself by disowning her obligations, and because it would have created for Greece a position of subservience in every way to Bulgaria. But, I should, at all events, have recognized that it was a conservative policy I had to deal with. But let me repeat, Gentlemen, to return to the point at issue, this so-called conservative policy, what did it conserve, and what did it not betray? The ten months' mobilization, the Bulgarian invasion of Eastern Macedonia, the laying waste of Greek Macedonia, the imprisonment of an Army Corps—are all these not equivalent to an unsuccessful war? The annihilation of Hellenism in Asia Minor and in Eastern Macedonia, are they not equivalent in themselves to another unsuccessful war? The suppression of every noble sentiment, the instillation of fear and cowardice, the insinuation of the idea that not only any further expansion of the realm was dangerous and unnecessary, but that even the expansion that had resulted from the Balkan wars was injurious, and that the loss of it might be viewed without concern if only the work of the hated adversary could be proved to be short-lived—are not all these again equivalent to another unsuccessful war? Was it then a conservative and a peaceful policy that was pursued by the "Saviors," when they brought upon us the disasters of three unsuccessful wars, and left a final war still hanging over us, the war to be waged against a greater Bulgaria, the war in which Greece was to have been crushed once for all?

I assert once more, then, that they did not pursue a conservative, but only a German, policy, and they got from it nothing but the contempt of the men to whom they ministered. They lost Eastern Macedonia and Northern Epirus, they refused Cyprus, they remained without friends and without allies, and so would have remained on the morrow outside the door of the Congress of Peace, where all the other peoples in the Balkans would have been represented, and where Serbia, invoking our repudiation of the treaty as one of the reasons of her downfall, might well have obtained compensations at our expense. Their so-called conservative policy reduced us to a military, a moral, and a political wreck, so that on the morrow we might more certainly succumb to the blow which would certainly be aimed at us by an unduly aggrandized Bulgaria.

Such were the results, Gentlemen, of the policy of the "Saviors." Such consequences as these the Liberal Party and its leaders could not endure. This is the cause that made us rebels; and this it was that led us to create a second State and to gather round us a new and national army, and by these means we have succeeded in abolishing tyranny, in setting up once more our free Constitution, and in imposing the policy which has repeatedly received the assent of the people, not only directly by their verdict of 31 May [13 June], but by the votes of their legally elected representatives.

But some one will ask: Are we to suppose that it is still possible to apply this [Liberal] policy under the conditions in which it was originally conceived?

I am not blind, Gentlemen, to the picture which is presented before me.

That which I feared, when I left office in September, 1915, has unfortunately come to pass. The Greece of 1917 does not even distantly resemble the Greece of 1915 which we then handed over to their keeping. The men who pursued a German policy can boast of the truly alarming success that has attended their efforts.

I see our ally Serbia overthrown, even though her overthrow is only temporary, and will be followed, as I feel assured, by the restoration of her full national unity. [Prolonged applause]. I see Bulgaria overwhelmingly aggrandized, and ready to fall on us to-morrow to crush and subjugate us. I see the régime of internal corruption risen from the dead with a fresh impetus and fresh vigor. I see the economic wreck, I see the Royal Army almost in a state of dissolution.

The Greece of 1917 does not resemble the Greece of 1915 in either a territorial, a moral, a financial, a military, or a political sense.

Nevertheless, with all these disadvantageous conditions, my optimism does not desert me. [Applause.]

A nation which for no less than three thousand years has passed through such great trials without disappearing, a nation which only yesterday recorded the victories of 1912 and 1913, a nation which, although betrayed by its rulers, succeeded in finding within itself sufficient moral strength to create a new State, and raise a new army, and write, as I have often said, some of the brightest pages of our military history, I am unshakably convinced that such a nation still conceals within itself enough vitality, even at this last moment, to achieve its own salvation. [Applause.]

Gentlemen, the nation is aware that I have never promised it anything that was not attainable. The nation knows that I have never fallen short of the undertakings I have given.

In taking part in this world-wide war, at the side of the democratic nations, which have been brought together in a common cause, in a truly holy alliance, by Germany's claims to the empire of the world, whose clients are our two hereditary enemies, we shall not only regain the national territories we have lost, we shall not only reëstablish our honor as a nation, we shall not only effectively defend our national interests at the Congress of Peace and secure our national future, but we will also be a worthy member of the family of free nations which that Congress will organize, and we will hand on to our children such a Greece as generations past have dreamed of, whom we must show ourselves not unworthy to succeed, such a Greece as we ourselves foreshadowed in our recent victories of 1912 and 1913. [Tumultuous cheers and applause.]

GABRIELE D'ANNUNZIO

TO THE OFFICERS ON THE PIAVE [1]

[It was after the great Italian retreat from October to December 1917 in the face of the new offensive by which Germany hoped to destroy Italy, as she had Serbia and Bulgaria before, that D' Annunzio addressed a gathering of officers of all branches on the Piave, the point to which the Italians had fallen back fighting valiantly. This was only one of many speeches by which D'Annunzio aroused his countrymen to new exertions. In this speech as in others D' Annunzio's fervent emotion finds expression in extraordinary figures of speech.

Gabriele D' Annunzio, born in 1863, is the most famous living Italian poet. His poems, novels and dramas had won him a world-wide reputation before the War. During the War his ardent patriotism was manifested in deeds as well as speeches. He was an officer in the army and after the peace treaty was prominent in the occupation of Fiume. D'Annunzio seized this city and organized a separate government, hoping to restore it eventually to Italy.]

COMPANIONS AT ARMS: Is there one among you who does not know that I held the bitterest of silences between my clenched teeth in the days of our sudden anguish, when the country demanded neither lamentation nor imprecation nor chorus of exhortation, but only the unanimous act of turning face to the enemy never to yield again? Nor would I speak to-day, were not these words, for you and me, as the drawing of breath in the midst of the fight, a pause in the battle, a way of looking into one another's eyes, recognizing, summing up one another, and taking our oath together once more as in the caverns and stone dunes of the Carso which is still ours and will be for ever ours by that same grace which gives possession of the Holy Sepulcher to all the faithful.

I see in your eyes the quiver of a love which is pain.

I cannot remember without a shudder those fraternal leave-takings on the edge of Fate. The little flags, not much larger than a man's heart, were like sparks of a greater flag. Divinity was present, as at the distribution of the eucharistic specie.

[1] Translated by Magda Sindici.

TO OFFICERS ON THE PIAVE

All hands were outstretched to grasp one. Some there were who, on the lip of a foiba or on the teeth of a ridge, held it in a passionate grip, bearing it almost stamped on his palm as the mark of his country, in the sublime sacrament of death. You know their names. They still cling to those places, as their bodies have clung to them. We shall find them again, we shall name them again.

We shall find again the love that bound us to those stones, that tamed their harshness and made the waste places fertile: a love that had hell and damnation in it, but that was not without hope and not without melody. For us of the Third Army, the love of the Carso is beautiful as the love of Fate. It cannot be deceived nor wiped out nor lessened.

I recognize some of those lovers amongst you. The dearest of them are left behind, become one with the rock now, forsaken by battle as a corpse is forsaken by heat. And I regret now that I did not leave the best beloved of these dearest ones at Monfalcone in his naked grave—the best beloved who went further than any other and had me with him, and shines with falcon-like glory between Faiti salient and the salient of the old Trieste road beyond the Timavo. He would lie burning and whole in his tomb. But he is fire for certain to-day, wherever he may be.

That sacrifice was all of love. In order to fight, one had to love and believe. One had to divine the features of Italy at each leap, beneath the alien crust. The jet of one vein was enough, sometimes, to alter the countenance of a place that had been fashioned by many causes in the slowness of time. We shed this mystic blood in a full tide, along stony valleys, up steep slopes, down squalid craters, in blackened woods, on heaps of ruined houses. We found once more the flint and the fever of Rome in the shimmer of the deadly marshes. Obstinately, we carved out our country anew on the saddest of Calvaries.

And now, what shall we do?

Some of you have grown pale, unless the little sight I have left be failing me.

Behold, all that love is overcome by an infinite wave of blood, is carried away by a flood that seems to be without source and without end like the flow of eternity.

If that was love, what can this be which tortures and multiplies us? If that was sacrifice, what test is being asked of us to-day? What are we about to give?

Dying is not enough.

If dying means to desist from fighting, then we cannot die. We must rise up again. The country gives constant birth to her strong sons: raises them up and hurls them forward. She gives back a living man for each dead man, a soldier for each one that falls. No place may stay empty to-day. Wherever there is room for a man, there a man must be—standing or kneeling, creeping or crawling, but ever with a rifle in his hand, ever at the service of some new weapon.

And if weapons fail, anything else will do. On the Carso, we rooted up and hurled stones. At the Cenghio, one night, fists and kicks did their work, teeth and nails. And here, shall not the stones rise themselves? Shall not two arms avail to drag down an enemy once he has been seized?

To-day, we can conquer pain and fury with but one intent, with but one sort of attention: to aim straight, not to miss one's blow. It fills one with amazement that our common life should continue to flow, that any should find relief except in action, that it be possible to smile and banter, that any should stop to rest.

The wounded, if their wound hurt, know no peace. If neck or shoulder ache, the whole body takes part in that torment and cannot sleep. Italy is one nation, a mother-country, one same living substance; and can the whole not suffer for the one part that suffers? Can she be other than unceasingly anxious for the one part that is under torture? Can she help being in travail at every instant because of this evil which has fastened to her and threatens her to her heartstrings?

This river where we now stand is not the Frigido, nor the Timavo—nor even the Isonzo. Beyond it there is not merely some land to be reconquered from the usurper who withholds it from us. This is the Piave, a sheer Venetian river, and not the first on this side of the old frontier—not the first. Beyond, there is no desert of stone, no hollow or rock dune or mountain Calvary or wreck of villages and farms, but the pure flower of Italy, the truest early figure of her soul, the straight furrow of our plows and our history, the antique grace of our little cities, worthy to be carried by our Saints on their open palms.

Now the foul maul of the invader is upon them. The nauseous beast befouls and contaminates our garden. What shall we do?

We have fought so hard for the Carso desert; what shall we do for this paradise?

Let me tell you again that shedding our blood is not enough, that no gift is enough, that dying is not enough. We must live and fight, live and resist, live and conquer.

Multiply yourselves, and multiply your men. Let one be as ten, let ten be as a thousand. Thus our Latin war has done away with the limitations of glory. Let this our Latin war do away with personal terms and with conditions of number.

Some Italian mothers, of those who are blessed by the God of Armies, complain when they have but one son, or two or three—and not more—to give up. That regret is an act of spiritual fruitfulness, it spurs on the effort of the flesh and doubles the value of giving.

Miserable indeed is she who saw her son return all of a sudden, disarmed, distorted, beside himself—unrecognizable at first, and cried out: "What has happened?"

Needless to ask what had happened: it is not worth knowing. In that first hour, some of us longed rather to lose all consciousness than stand condemned to know the horror of the thing which had happened. Better the darkness of despair than that sinister light. Better a desperate death than that weight of abomination.

Behind true courage there is, as in deep suffering, a firm power of understanding. Our suffering has become a rock, a diamond. Has not the diamond a property of indomitable clearness? This property is also present in our courage and our pain. O new men—men who have made a compact with truth.

If there has been shame it shall be washed away. If there has been infamy, it shall be avenged. The spirit is blowing on the unhappy mass, quickening it.

That mother, on the appearance of her mud-bespattered fugitive, stammered in her dismay: "Is this my son?"

The blood which was upon him was not his own—not that

blood which, even clotted, has a certain splendor; it was the mud of the loathsome road, the filth of sewers and holes. There was no wound upon him, but something more terrible: a brand. Not the brand of the slave or the criminal on his shoulder or between his brows, but one single brand upon his whole body, as if his vile flesh had been sent back to a new womb and marked there to his greater shame.

The mother looked upon his unknown features and a cry rose from her very entrails: "I have not borne you!"

These are the most awful words a mother can say, the most terrible of human denials. They lacerate and torture anew, far more than the spasms of difficult childbirth.

We have heard this cry rise from the earth itself, like a voice from within, vibrate along the hills, along shores and banks, heard it in the splendor of landscapes, when the sad, helpless mothers passed by with bent heads, as if goaded already by an invisible lash.

Who has said that there is no abysmal horror equal to the horror of some human faces? It is true. Those disfigured men had lost the imprint of their race and all manliness of expression. They looked like the enemy: an odious resemblance that seemed to have passed through from their spines to stamp itself on their docile muzzles. They reminded one of these mixed herds of prisoners of all races that we used to see dragging themselves down to Vallone, at fall of day after a battle. They all had the same earthly color, as of some excrement, and their flaccid belly was the only thing they lived by.

They did not look round; they looked neither back nor forward. Shame had put blinkers to their unconscious bestiality. Each had the back of his accomplice for his sole horizon. Strangers on their own soil, enemies on their own roads, of no land in their own land!

One knew not, seeing them, whether one's heart misgave one for indignation, contempt, abomination or pity. Throughout the country, we suffered through them; in every clod of earth, in every shadow, in every color, in every fair and innocent thing steeped in a beauty that had never seemed so poignant. For the wiser and more passionate among us this land of greenswards and waters, of slopes and smooth roads, of blue hills and melancholy had never possessed so deep a grace. It was our own creature, as we were its creatures. It came close to us and spoke to us, its breath upon our breath; it pressed up against us and embraced us in an almost human way, trembled on our breast, became flesh of our flesh, as when a great misfortune gathers together those of the same blood; as when one suffers and remembers and fears and hopes and despairs together.

Ah, truly, comrades, of all the regions of Italy this Veneto seems the most human, the fairest to those who love it, the most sensitive to those who touch it. It has come from man, as man has come from it. Man has sought it out and saved it from the conflict of sea and rivers; has raised it up to the sun's heat and warmed it with his own self, has fashioned and refashioned it; made it fruitful and enriched and refined it throughout years without number. It seems to have emerged not from the gray Paduan marsh, but from the ardor of man's faith.

Thus, you will understand why I speak like this to-day, in this divine autumn passion. None can watch the slight grass of a flexible river-bank, the purple and the oblivion of a patrician park, an old hulk rotting in a lazy canal, a misty furrow in a quiet field, a strip of sunshine across a meadow hemmed in by willows, a heap of dead leaves at the foot of a trophy of worn stones, and not feel each of these things becoming within us a love that cannot be endured without suffering. And the centuries suffer within us as the morrow will suffer. And our distant forbears suffer within us as do our children that are to come.

But those dark herds without countenance and without name looked upon all these things recognizing nothing, understanding nothing. There were hours in which the beauty of the earth became so violent that it seemed as if it must burst open the brow of the very oxen under their yokes. But the cry of that denying mother did not reach their dehumanized, isolated hearts: "I have not borne you!"

And yet, to-day, our ever renewed faith tells us that even for the dullest there shall be light; that the most evil shall be saved.

There is no other escape for them. There is no escape for whosoever yields or seeks refuge in flight. There is no salvation except in fighting with all one's strength and with all one's weapons.

Our country's order is not "Foot by foot." Nor is it "Inch by inch." Our country's order to-day is: "Do not yield the space of a nail's breadth!"

If there be cowards who hope for forgiveness or condonation or indulgence from the enemy, they deceive themselves ignominiously. This war is without pity; this world war is without mercy. This compact has been imposed on us by the enemy, observed by the enemy, hourly confirmed by the enemy.

It is a war waged for the abolition of one great civilization for the benefit of another that is unworthy; of a great history in honor of another that does not equal it; of one great state of conscience in favor of another that daily proves itself inferior.

It is unfair to recall the Goths and the Herules and the Huns in the face of this rage. The cruelty of those barbarians was unconscious; the cruelty of these is meditated, disciplined, coordinated like the laws of an explosive. Its frenzy itself is like a chemical product. It happens that one stops to laugh in the midst of horror, when one considers certain antics and postures of this massive, mechanical beast.

It must be dismembered.

Let us persevere.

What was the cry of the victor to the vanquished, a thousand and a thousand years ago, under the flash of the two-edged sword?

"You are not men, you are things possessed by us, of less value than our clothes and our vessels and our beds. Of your entrails, we will make catgut for our bows and slings, and keep them for the day when we might need them to tame the madness of slaves, should a chip grow again on the block we have felled. But we will leave no roots."

Some of you already know the text of the war-song found, among stolen things, in the pocket of a soldier taken prisoner in the invaded Friuli. It is the renewed injunction to the invader on the threshold of Italy, to the plunderers of churches and schools and hospitals, to the torturers of women and children and old people. "On, children of Germany in arms! This is the hour of glory and merry-making!"

TO OFFICERS ON THE PIAVE

The old hymn had nobler, more agile numbers, measured by the step of the light sandal, not of the shapeless boot. "Your gentle maidens shall be smothered in our clasp. We will shatter your children like puppies on the marble of your hearths. We will search the womb of your mothers, and no germ shall remain in their smoking wounds."

The hoarse Teutonic sequence would persuade the fool that our unwarlike flesh is fit only to manure the fields that shall belong to him and his children's children. He teaches him that the life of the vanquished is taken on by the victor, the life of his victim transfused in the one who kills and that the whole life of the world must be garnered up in the bosom of his own country.

"Be not effeminate in your pity for women and children. The son of the conquered has often been the conqueror of the morrow. What is victory worth if the morrow holds its revenge? And what manner of father would you be if you were to cut down your enemy and leave life to your sons' enemy?

"Children of Germany in arms, forward! Blast, break through, cut down, pierce, plunder, set on fire, and kill, and kill, and kill!

"The path of glory is open to you!"

This is the ferocious and foolish song gurgling through the ogre's jaws on the threshold of Italy the Beautiful. Can we ever believe that on the mournful night of Caporetto, a chorus of peace should have answered it? It is a thought to make one recall the lightning-like punishments of the miraculous ages. One imagines a mouth suddenly grown cancerous, a tongue dried up like tinder, a heart suddenly become ashes choking an infamous throat.

Comrades it is not true, it cannot be true.

Behold, the new-made heroes of our rally are answering with a soul's measure of steel, as it is fine to answer, as it is Roman and Italian to answer, springing up from the earth between Brenta and Piave, between the pastures of Asiago and the rocks of the Val Gadena, down the spurs of the Grappa to the shores of the lagoons, from our Alps to our sea.

And the Italian who kills most to-day shall be the best beloved son of Italy in arms.

DAVID LLOYD GEORGE

VICTORY OR DEFEAT: NO HALF-WAY HOUSE

[The following speech by Mr. Lloyd George was made at a dinner given by Sir Frederick Smith at Gray's Inn, December 14, 1917. The London *Times* of the next day declared in an editorial that "No living statesman can appeal so directly to the masses of the nation as Mr. Lloyd George. The chief merit of the speech made last night—and it has many merits—is the clearness and directness with which it keeps the things that really matter before the people. Sonorous words and unctuous phrases are useless to wage war or secure peace. Deeds only can do either, and the whole speech is a fervid exhortation not to be weary of well-doing."]

LET me express how honored I feel to be invited to this historic building to meet representatives of the most romantic service in this war. In the House of Commons I gave what I fear must be regarded as an inadequate expression to the gratitude and admiration which the nation feels for this gallant service. I have sometimes felt that the operations of the Air Service will, probably, have greater effect in determining the nations that this must be the last war than any other weapons, however terrible their effect. They bring home to the people, who in former wars dwelt in security, something of the perils and the horrors of the battlefield; and, as the war goes on, these will spread and increase and intensify. These winged messengers of death, therefore, may well be angels of peace. But we must also remember that, while all that is true, they also give a greater significance and permanence to either victory or defeat. For, however unjust or oppressive might be the peace imposed on us, the new terror added to war by this new weapon of dismay will create an increased reluctance on the part of the world to challenge the issue anew. It is, therefore, more important than ever that the peace we secure should be a just, an honorable, and a beneficent peace.

Recently a highly respected nobleman, who has rendered distinguished service to the State in many spheres, startled the nation by a letter which gave rise to very considerable apprehension on the part of those whose main anxiety is that

VICTORY OR DEFEAT

this war should terminate in an upright and enduring peace and not in a humiliating surrender. I now understand that all our anxieties as to this epistle were groundless, that Lord Lansdowne had not intended in the least to convey the meaning which his words might reasonably bear; that all the time he was in complete agreement with President Wilson, and only meant to say exactly the same thing as the American President said in his recent great speech to Congress. Now the Government are in full agreement with that speech. Mr. Asquith, I am not surprised to see, is also in agreement with it. The British nation is undoubtedly in agreement with it, and as Lord Lansdowne has also declared that he agrees with it, things which agree with the same thing agree with one another. I, therefore, take it that the interpretation placed on Lord Lansdowne's letter, not merely by strong supporters of the Allied cause, but also by its opponents, in this country, in America, and in France, and now also, I observe in Germany and in Austria, was not in the least that which Lord Lansdowne desired to give it. I do not desire to force a controversy if none exists, for national unity is essential to success. But I might be forgiven for saying that if Lord Lansdowne simply meant to say exactly the same thing as President Wilson, it is a great misfortune that he did not carry out that intention. I was attending the Allied Conference in Paris at the time that this letter appeared. It was received there with painful amazement. However, it is satisfactory to know that Lord Lansdowne was misunderstood, both by his friends and by his critics, and that the whole weight of his authority and influence may be reckoned on the side of the enforcement of what I call the Wilson policy.

I shall, therefore, pass on from this letter to the view which it was supposed to advocate, but did not, to the opinions which are held and expressed by a number of people in this country. It is true they are in a minority, but they are a very active minority, and they busy themselves insidiously, persistently, skillfully, impressing these views on the people. The Lansdowne letter brought them out into the open. They thought that at last they had discovered a leader, and there is no doubt that they were prepared to take action wih a view to forcing this country into a premature and vanquished peace.

The danger is not the extreme pacifist. I am not afraid of him. But I warn the nation to watch the man who thinks that there is a half-way house between victory and defeat. There is no half-way house between victory and defeat. These are the men who think that you can end the war now by some sort of what they call pact of peace, by the setting up of a League of Nations with conditions as to arbitration in the event of disputes, with provision for disarmament, and with a solemn covenant on the part of all nations to sign a treaty on those lines, and not merely to abide by it themselves, but to help to enforce it against any nation that dares to break it.

That is the right policy after victory. Without victory it would be a farce. Why, we are engaged in a war because an equally solemn treaty was treated as a scrap of paper. Who would sign the new treaty? I presume, among others, the people who have so far successfully broken the last. Who would enforce the new treaty? I presume that they would be the nations that have so far quite succeeded in enforcing the last. To end the war entered on, to enforce a treaty without reparation for the infringement of that treaty, merely by entering into a new, a more sweeping and a more comprehensive treaty, would be, indeed, a farce in the setting of a tragedy. We must take care not to be misled by mere words—"league of nations," "disarmament," "arbitration," "security." They are all great and blessed phrases. But without the vitalizing force of victory they are nothing but words. You cannot wage war with words. You cannot secure peace with words. You cannot long cover defeat with words. Unless there are deeds behind them, they are but dead leaves which the first storm will scatter and reveal your strangled and abandoned purpose to the world.

We ought never to have started unless we meant, at all hazards, to complete our task. There is nothing so fatal to character as half-finished tasks. I can understand, although I cannot respect, the attitude of the man—and there are a few —who said from the first, "Do not interfere, whatever happens." When you said to them, "Supposing the Prussians overrun Belgium?" their answer was, "Let them overrun Belgium!" If you said, "We promised solemnly to protect Belgium against all invaders, and we ought to stand by our word," they replied, "We ought never to have given our word." If you said to them, "What if the Germans trample in the mire our friends and neighbors, the free Republic of France?" they answered, "That is not our business." If you asked, "What if they murder innocent people, old and young, male and female, burn cities and ravage and outrage before your eyes?" in effect they said, "Let them perpetrate every crime in the calendar so long as it is not done in our land. What concern is it of ours? Are we our brothers' keepers? Let us not meddle and provoke anger which might disturb our serenity and our comfort." In fact, as one leading journalist put it with shameless candor, "Let us rather profit by manufacturing goods for both sides; for the assassins as well as for the survivors among our friends."

That is not an exalted line to take, but it is a definite and clear line of action, intelligible in consciences of a certain quality. "Ourselves first, ourselves last, ourselves all the time, and ouselves alone." It is pretty mean, but there are in every country men built that way, and you must reckon with them in the world. But the man I cannot comprehend is the sort of man who, when he first saw these outrages, called out, his generous soul aflame with righteous wrath, "In the name of Heaven let us leap in and arrest this infamy, and, if we fail, then at least let us punish the perpetrators so as to make it impossible for it to happen again." And, having said all this and having helped to commit the nation to that career of honor, now, before the task is nearly accomplished, he suddenly turns round and says: "I have had enough of this. It is time it should come to an end. Let us shake hands with the malefactor. Let us trade with him to our mutual advantage."

He is not to be asked for reparation for damage done. He need not even apologize. He is simply invited to enter into a bargain to join with you in punching the head of the next man who dares to imitate his villainies. And we are told that we can have peace now on these terms. Germany has said so, Austria has said so, the Pope has said so. It must, therefore, be true. Of course, it is true. Why should they refuse peace on such terms? Especially as it would leave them with some of the richest provinces and fairest cities of Russia in their pockets. There are distinguished judges present.

They are often called on to administer justice for offenses not unlike those committed by Prussia. It is true that rarely have they had before them a criminal who, in his own person, has committed all these offenses—murder, arson, rape, burglary, fraud, piracy. Supposing next time they try such a case and are tired out by the insistence of the prisoners' advocate they were to turn to the offender and say, "This is profitless business. We are wasting a good deal of money and valuable time. I am weary of it. I want to get back to more useful work. If I let you off now without any punishment beyond that which is necessarily entailed in the expenses to which you have been put in defending your honor, will you promise me to help the police to catch the next burglar? If you agree to these terms I propose to enroll you now as a special constable. I will now formally put on your armlet, and, by the way, if you leave me your address I will promise to cement the good feeling which I wish to prevail in future between us, to deal at your store without further inquiry as to where, or how, you got the goods. I might add that you need not worry to return the stuff you stole from your next-door neighbor on your right, as I understood he has withdrawn his claim to restoration."

Now, what do you think would be the effect on crime? It is idle to talk of security to be won by such feeble means. There is no security in any land without certainty of punishment. There is no protection for life, property, or money in a State where the criminal is more powerful than the law. The law of nations is no exception, and, until it has been vindicated, the peace of the world will always be at the mercy of any nation whose professors have assiduously taught it to believe that no crime is wrong so long as it leads to the aggrandizement and enrichment of the country to which they owe allegiance. There have been many times in the history of the world criminal States. We are dealing with one of them now. And there will always be criminal States until the reward of international crime becomes too precarious to make it profitable, and the punishment of international crime become too sure to make it attractive.

Let there be no doubt as to the alternatives with which we are confronted. One of them is to make easy terms with the triumphant outlaw, as men are driven to in order to buy immunity in lands where there is no authority to enforce law. That is one course. It means, ultimately, a world intimidated by successful bandits. The other is to go through with our divine task of vindicating justice, so as to establish a righteous and everlasting peace for ourselves and for our children. Surely, no nation with any regard for its interests, for its self-respect, for its honor, can hesitate a moment in its choice. Victory is an essential condition for the security of a free world. All the same, intensely as I realize that, if I thought things would get no better the longer you fought, not merely would there be no object in prolonging the war, to do so would be infamous. Wantonly to sacrifice brave lives, nay to force brave men to endure for one profitless hour the terrible condition of this war merely because statesmen had not the courage to face the obloquy which would be involved in agreeing to an unsatisfactory peace, would be a black crime when we remember what we owe to these gallant men. It is because I am firmly convinced that, despite some untoward events, despite discouraging appearances, we are making steady progress towards the goal we set in front of us in 1914, that I would regard peace overtures to Prussia, at the very moment when the Prussian military spirit is drunk with boastfulness, as a betrayal of the great trust with which my colleagues and I have been charged.

Much of the progress we are making may not be visible except to those whose business it is to search out the facts. The victories of Germany are all blazoned forth to the world. Her troubles appear in no Press *communiqués* or wireless messages, but we know something of these. The deadly grip of the British Navy is having its effect, and the valor of our troops is making an impression which in the end will tell. We are laying, surely, the foundation of the bridge which, when it is complete, will carry us into the new world. The river is, for the moment, in spate, and some of the scaffolding has been carried away, and much of the progress we had made seems submerged and hidden, and there are men who say, "Let us abandon the enterprise altogether. It is too costly. It is impracticable of achievement. Let us rather build a pontoon bridge of new treaties, league of nations, understandings." It might last you some time. It would always be shaky and uncertain. It would not bear much strain. It would not carry heavy traffic, and the first flood would sweep it away. Let us get along with the pile-driving, and make a real, solid, permanent structure.

Meanwhile, let us maintain our steadiness and sanity of outlook. There are people who are too apt at one moment to get unduly elated at victories which are but incidents in the great march of events, and the same people get unwholesomely depressed by defeats which, again, are nothing more than incidents. The very persons who within the last fortnight have been organizing a nervous breakdown in the nation some weeks ago were organizing a hysterical shout over our victories in Flanders and at Cambrai. We were breaking through the enemy's barrier. We were rolling up the German armies and clearing them out of Belgium and the North of France. They remind me of a clock I used to pass at one time in my life almost every day. It worried me a great deal, for whatever the time of the day the finger always pointed at 12 o'clock. If you trusted that clock you would have believed it was either noon or midnight. There are people of that type in this war, who, one moment, point to the high noon of triumph and the next to the black midnight of defeat or despair. There is no twilight. There is no morning. They can claim a certain consistency, for they are always at 12, but you will find that their mainspring in this war is out of repair. We must go through all the hours, minute by minute, second by second, with a steady swing, and the hour of the dawn will, in due time, strike.

This is not the most propitious hour. Russia threatens to retire out of the war and leave the French democracy, whose loyalty to the word they passed to Russia brought on them the horrors of this war, to shift for themselves. I do not wish to minimize in the least the gravity of this decision. Had Russia been in a condition to exert her strength this year we might now be in a position to impose fair and rational terms of peace. By her retirement she strengthens Hohenzollernism and weakens the forces of democracy. Her action will not lead, as she imagines, to universal peace. It will simply prolong the agony of the world, and it will inevitably put her in bondage to the military dominance of Prussia. But, if Russia persists in her present policy, then the withdrawal from the Eastern flank of the enemy forces which have hitherto absorbed over a third of his strength must release hundreds of thousands of his troops and masses of material to attack Britain, France, and Italy. It is a serious addition to our task, which was already formidable enough. It would be folly to underrate the danger. It would be equally folly, on the other hand, to exaggerate it, The greatest folly of all would be not to face it.

If the Russian democracy have decided to abandon the struggle against military autocracy, the American democracy are taking it up. This is the most momentous fact of the year. It has transposed the whole situation. The Russians are a great-hearted people, and valiantly have they fought in this war, but they have always been—certainly throughout this war—the worst organized State in Europe, and Britain, with but a third of the population of Russia, has been, for the last two years, a more formidable military obstacle to Germany. And had you asked Germany, not now, but even a year ago, which country she would prefer to see out of the war, I do not think that there would have been any doubt about her answer. But what about America? There is no more powerful country in the world than the United States of America, with their gigantic resources and their indomitable people. And, if Russia is out, America is coming in with both arms. If this is the worst moment, it is because Russia has stepped out and America is only preparing to come in. Her Army is not ready. Her equipment is not complete, her tonnage has not been built. Every hour that passes, the gap formed by the retirement of the Russians will be filled by the valiant sons of the great American Republic. Soon it will be more than filled. Germany knows it. Austria knows it. Hence the desperate efforts which they are making to force the issue before America is ready. They will not succeed. All the same, these two unfortunate circumstances—the collapse of Russia and the temporary defeat of Italy—undoubtedly cast on us a heavier share of the burden until the strength of America is ready to come underneath to share it. We must, therefore, be prepared for greater efforts, for greater sacrifices. It is not the time to cower, to falter, or to hesitate. It is the time for the nation to plant its feet more firmly than ever on the ground and to square its shoulders to bear the increased weight cast on it by events.

When I talk of the nation I do not mean the nation in the abstract, but the millions of individuals who constitute the nation. If we are to win the security which it is the common purpose of all sections to attain, every man and every woman must be prepared for greater endeavors and greater sacrifices. A friend of mine, speaking the other day, said that there was not the enthusiasm observable which characterized the early days of the war. That may be so. If a man undertakes a long, arduous, and perilous journey you do not expect him in the fatiguing hours of the afternoon to exhibit the same ardor as when he started in the freshness of the morning. But, although he may not display the same keenness in his demeanor, if he is a man of any purpose, his ardor may be less but his resolution is greater. There is a hot zeal and a cold zeal and the greatest things of the world have been accomplished by the latter. The will of Britain is as tempered steel. There is no sign of a break in it and, although the pressure may increase and will increase, I have never doubted that it will bear it all right to the end.

We shall have to call on the nation for further effort, for further sacrifice, but we shall only do so because it is absolutely necessary now. Premature sacrifice is waste of *moral*. There must be a further drain on our man power to sustain, until the American Army arrives, the additional burden cast on us by the defection of Russia and the reverses in Italy. We must have enough men to defend the lines which we have held against fierce onsets for three years, and to defend them against all comers from any quarter of the enemy front. We must also have an army of manœuvre which will enable us to appear with the least delay at any point of emergency in any part of the colossal battlefield. There is no ground for panic. Even now, after we have sent troops to the assistance of Italy, the Allies have a marked superiority of numbers in France and Flanders, and we have considerable reserves at home. Much greater progress has been made in man power, especially during the last few months, than either friends or foes realize, but it is not enough to enable us to face new contingencies without anxiety unless we take further steps to increase our reserves of trained men.

Before I leave this branch of the subject I must, however,

add another important consideration. While the Cabinet are prepared with recommendations for raising more men, they are conducting a searching investigation, with the assistance of our military advisers, into the best methods of husbanding the man power already existing in our Armies, so as to reduce the terrible wastage of war.

But the problem of man power does not end with the provision of men for the Armies. It is not even the most urgent part of the problem. We need more men, not merely for the battle line across the seas, but for the battle line in this country. We, especially, need men to help us to solve the problems associated with tonnage. You can increase tonnage in two ways—by building tonnage and by saving tonnage. Victory is now a question of tonnage, and tonnage is victory. Nothing else can defeat us now but shortage of tonnage. The advent of the United States into the war has increased the demand enormously. Tonnage must be provided for the transportation of that gigantic new army with its equipment across thousands of miles of sea. It is no use raising ten million men and equipping them unless you get them somewhere in the vicinity of the foe. Germany has gambled on America's failure to transport her army to Europe, and that is why she is still laughing at the colossal figures of soldiers in training and aëroplanes in course of construction. We know that the Prussian war lords have promised their own people, have promised their allies that these formidable masses will never find their way into the battle line, and that President Wilson's speeches, M. Clemenceau's speeches, and my speeches will thus be added to the vast collection of unredeemed rhetoric with which, according to them, democracies have always deluded themselves.

The Prussian claim is that autocracy alone can do things, and that democracies can only talk of doing things. The honor of democracy is at stake. I have no doubt that here, as in many other respects, those who trust the Prussian will be disillusioned; but both America and ourselves will have to strain our resources to the utmost to increase the tonnage available. The fact that American tonnage will be absorbed in the transport of their own armies makes it necessary that we should increase our responsibilities in the matter of assisting our French and our Italian Allies to transport essential commodities to their shores. We must, therefore, increase our tonnage. In spite of the fact that we have had less labor available in this, the fourth, year of the war than we have ever had before, we have increased the shipbuilding of war and merchant vessels beyond the record of any other war years; and, as Sir Eric Geddes stated in the House of Commons, we are now turning out ships at a rate which is above that of the record year of shipbuilding in the days of peace.

But we must do more. As the whole future of this country and of the world depends on the efforts Britain and America make this next year to increase the output of ships, we are resolved that it must, and shall, be done. But we must have men; and to have men we must interfere, even to a greater extent than we have done already, with the industries which are not absolutely essential for the prosecution of the war or to the maintenance of the life of the nation. And, however great the hardships that may be inflicted by this interference on the particular trades involved, we must ask the nation to support us. And I feel certain that the trades themselves will show that patriotism which has characterized every section of the community in this great national endeavor.

I would only add one further word about shipping. As I have already pointed out, you can increase tonnage in two ways —by building tonnage and by saving tonnage. I have dealt with the first. I will say a word about the second. You save tonnage by economizing—economizing in food, economizing in dress. You save tonnage by increasing the production in this country of material formerly imported from abroad—food, timber, minerals. All this involves additional labor. As to food, this year we increased the home production by two or three million tons. We are the only belligerents who have succeeded in increasing our food output during the war, and great credit is due to those who, by a superb feat of organization and inspiration, have achieved this result. But it is essential that we should still further increase the home supplies. We must save another three million tons in our food imports next year. This means that all those who have land, either as owners or cultivators, must help us, must without delay show their readiness to fall in with plans for increasing the produce of the land. We shall do our best to provide the necessary labor and machinery, and I am confident that we shall succeed. But all prejudices, all predilections must be swept aside. The nation must be saved. Victory must come first. Two or three million tons more food raised in this country means two or three million tons of shipping made available for strengthening the armies in the field. Every ton of food which you produce or save in this country is an increased weight hurled against the Prussian barrier.

The nation can help by giving up the things which are not essential to victory. We must strip even barer for the fight. The nation can help in another way—by discouraging "grousers." "Grousing" undermines *moral,* and when it is a question of holding out, the national *moral* is vital. You cannot expect things to go on smoothly in war as they do in peace. You can realize how much the ordinary life of the nation has been disturbed by the simple transposition of the figures of our War Budget into terms of the amount of national energy which its huge sums are intended to purchase. You cannot take millions of men away from the tasks of supplying the peace needs of the community without seriously interfering with the comforts and amenities of the life of that community. The wonder is that the disturbance has not been greater, and I feel that we owe much gratitude to the experienced and able business men who, in various directions, have undertaken to organize the resources of the State for war, for the services which they have rendered not merely in increasing our efficiency for war, but in minimizing the evils and inconveniences of war.

It is a remarkable fact that, although our imports have enormously diminished, there is less hunger in the land to-day than in August, 1914. I ask you to help these men and not to "rattle" them. The strain on them is enormous. Make their task easier. There are some people engaged in a constant and systematic grumble. The peace propaganda is fed with grumbles. These people are anxious to break down the national nerve and then to rush us into a premature and disastrous peace. Let us beware of playing their game. We have challenged a sinister power which is menacing the world with enslavement. It would have been better never to have issued the challenge unless we meant to carry it through. A challenged power which is not overthrown always becomes stronger for the challenge. The people who think that they can begin a new era of peace while the Prussian military power is unbeaten are laboring under a strange delusion. We have all been dreaming of a new world to appear when the deluge of war has subsided. Unless we achieve victory for the great cause for which we entered this war the new world will simply be the old world with the heart out of it.

The old world, at least, believed in ideals. It believed that justice, fair play, liberty, righteousness, must triumph in the end; that is, however you interpret the phrase, the old world believed in God, and it staked its existence on that belief. Millions of gallant young men volunteered to die for that divine faith. But, if wrong emerged triumphant out of this conflict, the new world would feel in its soul that brute force alone counted in the government of man; and the hopelessness of the dark ages would once more fall on the earth like a cloud. To redeem Britain, to redeem Europe, to redeem the world, from this doom must be the settled purpose of every man and woman who places duty above ease. This is the fateful hour of mankind. If we are worthy of the destiny with which it is charged, untold generations of men will thank God for the strength which He gave us to endure to the end.

GEORGES CLEMENCEAU
ONE AIM: VICTORY

[After the German offensive in the spring of 1918 an attempt was made by the militant socialists of France to embarrass the government by demanding information about military matters which it was considered unwise to reveal. On June 4th Clemenceau, the Premier of France, made a victorious speech defying his critics. He was subjected to constant and annoying interruptions, but his eloquence and power once more conquered and he received an overwhelming vote of confidence.

Georges Clemenceau was born in 1841. He was for many years a prominent member of the Chamber of Deputies and a leading journalist. He became Premier in 1906 and again in 1917. His famous debate with Jaurès on socialism is given in Volume IX.]

WHEN I accepted the premiership offered to me by the President of the Republic I could not ignore the fact that we were at the most critical period of the War. I remember that I told you we should pass together through difficult and exacting times; I remember I spoke of "cruel hours." No one protested when I announced that they would come. They are coming and the only question is whether we can stand them. [Applause and interruption.]

When Russia's desertion occurred, when men who believed that it was only necessary to will a democratic peace to obtain it from William II, had given up their country, unwittingly I prefer to think, to the army of the invader, what one of you here could believe that the million German soldiers who were thus liberated would not be turned against us? This and more is what happened. For four years our forces have been wearing themselves out. Our front was guarded by a line of soldiers which was becoming thinner and thinner, with our allies who had themselves suffered enormous losses. And at that moment you saw arrive against you a fresh mass of German divisions in good condition when you were far from your best strength.

Is there any one of you who did not realize that under the shock of this enormous mass our lines had to give way at some points? Certainly not, for in all the conversations which I had with members of this assembly, the question asked me was, how much we had to give way.

The recoil was very serious for the English army, which had suffered formidable losses. It was grave and dangerous for the French army. I said dangerous, serious, but nothing more, and there is nothing in that to shake the confidence we should have in our soldiers. [Applause and interruptions.]

Our men are engaged in the battle, a terrible one. They fought one against five without sleep for three and four days together. [Applause and interruptions.] These soldiers, these great soldiers, have good and great leaders: worthy of them in every way. [Applause and interruptions.] I have seen these leaders at work and some of them against whom I will not deny that I was prejudiced, struck me with admiration. [Applause.]

Is that saying that there are nowhere mistakes? I cannot maintain that. I know it too well; my duty is to discover these mistakes and correct them. In this I am supported by two great soldiers,—General Foch and General Petain. [Applause.] General Foch enjoys the confidence of our allies to such a degree that yesterday at the conference of Versailles they wished to have their unanimous confidence in him expressed in the communiqué given to the press. [Applause and interruptions.]

These men are at this moment fighting the hardest battle of the war, fighting it with a heroism which I can find no phrase worthy to express. [Applause.] And it is we who for a mistake made in such and such a place, or which may not even have been made, demand explanations, on the field of battle of a man worn with fatigue. It is of this man that we demand to know whether on such and such a day he did such and such a thing! Drive me from this place if that is what you ask, for I will not do it. [Applause.]

I came here with the desire to find simple, brief and measured words to express the sentiment of the French people at the front and at the rear, to show the world a state of mind which cannot be analyzed, but which at this moment is the admiration of all civilized people. [Applause.]

I accuse no one. I am the leader of these men and it is my

duty to punish them if I consider it of general benefit to do so; but it is also my greater duty to protect them if they have been unjustly attacked. [Applause.]

The army is better than we could ever have expected and when I say "the army" I mean men of all ranks who are under fire. That is one of the elements of our confidence, the main element. Although faith in a cause is an admirable thing, it will not bring victory; men must die for their faith to assure victory and our men are dying. We have an army made up of our children and our brothers—what can we say against it? Their leaders too have come from among us; they too are our brothers, they too are good soldiers. They come back covered with wounds when they are not left on the field of battle. What can you say against them? [Applause.]

We have yielded ground, much more ground than either you or I should have wished. There are men without number who have paid for this with their blood, without reproach. I know of the deeds of a group of lost men, Bretons, surrounded in a wood all night. The next day, still resisting, they sent a carrier pigeon to their corps to say "We are here. We have promised not to yield. We shall fight to the end. If you can come to find us, come; we can hold out half a day longer." [Applause.] Those men make and safeguard the country of which you are so proud. They die for the greatest and most noble ideal—to continue a history which shall be the foremost among all the histories of civilized peoples.

Our own duty is very simple, very tame. We run no danger. We are at our posts, you here, I with my cabinet—posts which are not dangerous as are those of the soldiers, but which are nevertheless where the capital interests of the country are decided.

As long as you remain calm, confident in yourselves, determined to hold out to the end of this hard struggle, victory is yours. It is yours because our enemies, who are not as intelligent as they are said to be, have only one method—to throw their whole force into the venture and risk everything. They tried it at Verdun and on the Yser, at Dunkirk and at Calais. They were checked—by whom? First by the English and then by the French. After that they appeared in Champagne; they advanced. Do you think it possible to make a war in which you never have to retreat? There is only one thing that matters, the victorious issue, the final success. Our men can only give their lives; but you through patience, firmness and determination can give them what they deserve—victory. [Applause.]

You have before you a government, which, as it told you at the very beginning, never conceived of the possibility of negotiating without victory. [Applause.] You know what you are doing. You can keep us in power or send us away; but as long as you keep us, whatever may happen, you can be sure that the country will be defended to the death and that no force will be spared to obtain success. [Applause.] We will never consent to anything but peace with victory. That is the watchword of our government. [Applause and interruptions.]

The Germans are once more staking all. The "coup" which they are attempting is to terrorize you, to frighten you so that you will abandon the struggle. [Applause.] One must be ignorant of German tactics to doubt this. Why did they suddenly throw all their forces on the Yser? It was to gain Calais, to separate us from England and force us to surrender. For what was the dreadful march on Paris? To take Paris and through terror force us to surrender. Why are they beginning again to-day? To secure this effect of terror which they have never yet achieved.

The decision is in your hands for the simple reason that it is not a matter of mere reasoning but a question of action. The Americans are coming. The forces of the English and the French, as well as of our enemies, are worn out; but we have allies who are coming as a decisive factor. I have said from the beginning that American coöperation would decide the issue of the war. The point is this: events in Russia have allowed a million of the enemy's men to appear on the Franco-British front. We have allies, whom we did not have in 1870, when we yielded because we were alone. We have Allies, who represent the foremost nations of the world, who have pledged themselves to continue the war to the end, to the success which we hold in our grasp, which we are on the point of achieving if we have the necessary tenacity. [Applause.]

I declare, and it must be my last word, that victory depends upon us. The civil forces must rise to the height of their duty; it is not necessary to make this demand of the soldiers. Send me away if I have been an unworthy servant; drive me out, condemn me, but at least take the trouble to formulate criticisms. As for me, I assert that the French people have in all ways done their full duty. Those who have fallen have not fallen in vain, for they have made French history great. It remains for the living to complete the magnificent work of the dead. [Applause.]

III. THE RUSSIAN REVOLUTION
ALEXANDER KERENSKY
ADDRESSES TO WORKINGMEN AND SOLDIERS

[Kerensky was an inspired orator and won great enthusiasm and support through the force of his eloquence. As leader of the workingmen and soldiers, the strongest part of the revolutionary forces who overthrew the Czar, he became the foremost member of the provisional government set up by the revolution. The first speech given below, calling on the people to support him, was made in March, 1917, before an enthusiastic labor assembly.

Russia's part in the war was complicated by the disorganization at the front, and Kerensky made strenuous efforts to prevent the total collapse of the army. In May he made the second speech below, to a deputation of delegates from the front.

Alexander Kerensky was born about 1882. He became a lawyer and a defender of the peasants. He was a member of the fourth Duma. In an earlier part of this volume is given his speech supporting the government as leader of the Labor party at the opening of the War. After his office of Minister of Justice under the provisional government, he later became Premier, Dictator, and for a short time President of the Russian republic set up by the revolution, until he was overthrown by Trotsky and Lenine.]

Reprinted by permission from the War Volumes published by the New York Times Company.

I

COMRADES! In entering the Provisional Government I remain a republican. In my work I must depend for help on the will of the people. I must have in the people my powerful support. May I trust you as I trust myself? [Tremendous cheers.]

I cannot live without the people, and if ever you begin to doubt me, kill me! I declare to the Provisional Government that I am a representative of democracy and that the government must take especially into account the views I shall uphold as a representative of the people, by whose efforts the old government was overthrown.

Comrades! Time does not wait, I call you to organization and discipline. I ask you to support us, your representatives, who are prepared to die for the people and have given the people their whole life.

Comrades! In my jurisdiction are all the premiers and ministers of the old régime. They will answer before the law for all crimes against the people. [Cries of "No mercy for them."]

Comrades! Regenerated Russia will not resort to the shameful means utilized by the old régime, without trial nobody will be condemned. All prisoners will be tried in the open court of the people.

Comrades, soldiers and citizens! All measures taken by the new government will be published.

Soldiers! I ask your coöperation. Free Russia is born and none will succeed in wresting liberty from the hands of the people. Do not listen to the promptings of the agents of the old régime. Listen to your officers. Long live free Russia!

II

I came to you because my strength is at an end. I no longer feel my former courage nor have my former conviction that we are conscientious citizens, not slaves in revolt. I am sorry I did not die two months ago when the dream of a new life was growing in the hearts of the Russian people, when I was sure the country could govern itself without the whip.

As affairs are going now, it will be impossible to save the country. Perhaps the time is near when we will have to tell you that we can no longer give you the amount of bread you expect or other supplies upon which you have a right to count. The process of the change from slavery to freedom is not going on properly. We have tasted freedom and are slightly intoxicated. What we need is sobriety and discipline.

You could suffer and be silent for ten years and obey the orders of a hated government. You could even fire upon your own people when commanded to do so. Can you now suffer no longer?

We hear it said that we no longer need the front because they are fraternizing there. But are they fraternizing on all the fronts? Are they fraternizing on the French front? No, comrades, if you are going to fraternize, then fraternize everywhere. Are not enemy forces being thrown over on to the Anglo-French front and is not the Anglo-French advance already stopped? There is no such thing as a "Russian front," there is only one general allied front. [Tremendous applause.]

We are marching toward peace and I should not be in the ranks of the Provisional Government if the ending of the war were not the aim of the whole Provisional government. But if we are going to propose new war aims we must see that we are respected by friend as well as by foe. If the tragedy and desperateness of the situation are not realized by all in our state, if our organization does not work like a machine, then all our dreams of liberty, all our ideals will be thrown back for decades and perhaps will be drowned in blood.

Beware! The time has now come when every one in the depth of his conscience must reflect where he is going and where he is leading others who were held in ignorance by the old régime and still regard every printed word as law. The fate of the country is in your hands, and it is in most extreme danger. History must be able to say of us, "They died but they were never slaves."

GENERAL KORNILOFF

APPEAL TO HIS SOLDIERS

[In spite of Kerensky's efforts the morale of the troops was shattered and the Russian retreat followed. Over the discussion of reorganization arose the conflict between Kerensky and Korniloff, Commander-in-Chief under the Provisional Government. Korniloff refused to resign. On September 10, 1917, he made the following eloquent appeal to his troops to march with him against Kerensky.

APPEAL TO HIS SOLDIERS

Korniloff, born in 1870, was a self-made man who came up from the ranks to the position of general. He fought valiantly during the early part of the war and became world famous for his fighting in Galicia after his escape from the Austrians.
Reprinted by permission from the War Volumes published by the New York Times Company.

COSSACKS, brothers, beloved companions! Was it not over the graves of your forefathers that the Russian Empire expanded and enlarged its boundaries? Was it not through your strong courage, your high deeds, your sacrifices and heroism, that Great Russia was strong?

You, free and independent sons of the quiet River Don, of the beautiful Kuban, of the impetuous Terek, puissant eagles migrating from the plains and mountains of the Ural, of Orenburg, of Astrakhan of Semiretchensk, and from Siberia and the far Transbaikal, from the Amur and the Ussur—to you belongs the glory of having always guarded the honor of your flag, filling the Russian land with the fame of your own and your fathers' deeds.

To-day the hour has struck when you must come to the aid of your native land!

I accuse the Provisional Government of indecision in action, of ignorance and incapacity, and of admitting the Germans into the administration, into the interior of our country, in proof of which I cite the explosion at Kasan, where nearly 1,000,000 shells and 12,000 howitzers were destroyed. Moreover, I accuse certain members of the Government of actual treason, and I bring the proofs. When I attended a session of the Provisional Government in the Winter Palace on August 3 Ministers Kerensky and Savinkoff told me that "one could not talk about everything, because there were among the ministers men of whom one could not be sure." It is clear that such a Government is leading our country to destruction, that under it there can be no safety for unhappy Russia.

Therefore, when the Provisional Government, to please our enemies, yesterday [September 9, 1917] demanded my resignation as Commander-in-Chief, I as a Cossack, through duty of conscience and honor, was obliged to refuse the demand, preferring death on the battlefield to opprobrium and treason against my country.

Cossacks! Knights of the Russian land, you promised to rise with me for the safety of the Fatherland when I should judge it necessary. The hour has struck, the Fatherland is on the eve of death! I will not submit to the orders of the Provisional Government, and for the safety of free Russia I will march against it and against those of its counselors who are selling our native land.

LEON TROTSKY

TO THE RED ARMY

[In October, 1917, the strength of the Bolsheviki had greatly increased and it was clear that Kerensky's government had lost the confidence of the radicals throughout Russia. On November 7th, led by Lenine, the Bolsheviki overthrew the government and Lenine and Trotsky became the leaders in Kerensky's place and made peace with Germany at Brest-Livotsk.

The address by Trotsky, in characteristic manner, was made in April, 1919, encouraging the Reds against the White Guardist bands of the Kolchak. Leon Trotsky was born about 1877. He was at one time exiled in Siberia for his revolutionary ideas. He was prominent among radical circles on the East Side in New York City and edited a revolutionary newspaper. After the Czar's overthrow he returned to Russia and joined Lenine.]

THE decisive weeks in the history of mankind have arrived. The wave of enthusiasm over the establishment of a Soviet Republic in Hungary had hardly passed when the proletariat of Bavaria got possession of power and extended the hand of brotherly union to the Russian and Hungarian Republics. The workmen of Germany and Austria are hurrying in hundreds of thousands to Budapest where they enter the ranks of the Red Army. The movement of the German proletariat, temporarily interrupted, again burst forth with ever-increasing strength. Coal-miners, metal workers, and textile workers, are sending brotherly greetings to the victorious Hungarian Republic and demand of the German Soviets a complete change of front, that is, a break with imperialists—their own, the English, French and American—and the forming of a close union with Russia and Hungary. There is no doubt that this movement will be given a still more powerful swing by the victory of the proletariat in Bavaria, the Soviet Government of which has broken all ties with the oppressors of Berlin and Weimar, with Ebert and Scheidemann, the servants of German imperialism, the murderers of Liebknecht and Rosa Luxemburg.

In Warsaw, which the allied imperialists tried to make the center for the attack on Soviet Russia, the Polish proletariat rises in its full stature and through the Warsaw Soviet of Workmen's Deputies sends greetings to the Hungarian Soviet Republic.

The French minister of foreign affairs, Pichon, the sworn enemy of the Russian Revolution, reports in Parliament on the sad state of affairs: "Odessa is being evacuated" (this was before the occupation of Odessa by Soviet troops); "the Bolsheviks are penetrating the Crimean Peninsula, the situation in the north is not favorable." Things are not going well. The Greek soldiers landed on the shores of Crimea, according to the reports of allied diplomats and newspaper men, were mounted on Crimean donkeys, but the donkeys were not able to arrive in time at the Perekop Isthmus. Things are not going well. Evidently even donkeys have begun to shake off the imperialistic harness.

Foreign consuls do not wish to leave the Ukraine and urge their governments to recognize the Ukrainian Republic. Wilson sent to Budapest not troops of occupation, to overthrow the Soviet Republic, but the honey-tongued General Smuts to negotiate with the Hungarian Council of People's Commissaries.

Wilson has definitely changed front and evidently has forced France to give up all hope of an armed crusade against Soviet Russia. War with Soviet Russia, which was demanded by the senseless French General, Foch, would take ten years in the opinion of the American statesman.

Less than six months have passed since the decisive victory of the Allies over the central empires; six months ago it seemed that the power of the Anglo-French and American imperialism was without limits.

At that time all the Russian counter-revolutionists had no

doubt that the days of the Soviet Republic were numbered; but events now move steadfastly along the Soviet road. The working masses of the whole world are joining the flag of the Soviet authority, and the world robbers of Imperialism are being betrayed even by the Crimean donkeys. At the present moment one awaits from day to day the victory of the Soviet Republic in Austria and in Germany. It is not impossible that the proletariat of Italy, Poland, or France will violate the logical order and outstrip the working class of other countries. These spring months become the decisive months in the history of Europe. At the same time this spring will decide definitely the fate of the bourgeois and rich peasant, anti-Soviet Russia.

In the east, Kolchak has mobilized all his forces, has thrown in all his reserves, for he knows definitely that if he does not win immediately then he will never win. Spring has come, the spring that decides. Of course the partial victories of Kolchak are insignificant in comparison with the general conquests of Soviet authority in Russia and in the whole world. What does the temporary loss of Ufa mean in the face of the occupation of Odessa, the movement into the Crimea and especially the establishment of the Bavarian Soviet Republic? What does the evacuation of Belebey, caused by military considerations, mean in the face of the powerful growth of the proletarian revolution in Poland and in Italy? Nevertheless, it would be criminal frivolity on our part to disregard the danger represented by the White Guardist bands of Kolchak on the east. Only stubbornness, steadfastness, watchfulness, and courage in the military struggle have guaranteed till now to the Russian Soviet Republic its international success. The victorious struggle of the Red Army on all fronts aroused the spirit of the European working class, and has made possible the establishment and strengthening first of the Hungarian and then of the Bavarian Republic. Our work has not yet been completed. The bands of Denikin have not been definitely defeated. The bands of Kolchak continue to move toward the Volga.

Spring has come; the spring that decides; our strength is increased tenfold by the consciousness of the fact that the wireless stations of Moscow, Kiev, Budapest, and Munich not only exchange brotherly greetings but business agreements respecting common defensive struggle. But at home, on our own territory, we must direct the main portion of our increased strength against the most dangerous enemy—against the Kolchak bands. Our comrades of the Volga district are well aware of this. In the province of Samara all Soviet institutions have been put on a war footing, and the best forces have been diverted to support the army, to form reserve regiments to carry on agitation of an educational character in the ranks of the Red Army. Party, Soviet, and trade union organizations in Syzran have unanimously responded to the appeal of the central authority to support the eastern front. A special shock regiment is being organized from the workmen and popular elements, which only recently were groaning under the heel of the White Guardist. The Volga district is becoming the center of attention of all Soviet Russia. To carry out our international duty we must first of all break up the bands of Kolchak in order to support the victorious workmen of Hungary and Bavaria. In order to assist the uprising of workmen in Poland, Germany, and all Europe, we must establish definitely and irrefutably the Soviet authority over the whole extent of Russia.

To the Urals: This is the slogan of the Red Army and of the whole Soviet country.

The Urals will be the last stage in this bitter struggle. Victory in the Urals not only will give grain to the famished country and cotton to the textile industries, but will secure finally the well-earned rest of our heroic Red Army.

NIKOLAI LENINE

A DICTATORSHIP OF THE PROLETARIAT

[Lenin was born about 1870 and by the early nineties had become known as a leader among the most radical socialists. After the failure of the revolution of 1905 he escaped from Russia and lived for a time in the United States. On the outbreak of the revolution in 1917 he returned to Russia, and on November 7th led in the overthrow of the Kerensky government. From that time until his death he was head of the Bolshevik party and virtually dictator of Russia.

The two speeches that follow deal with two important aspects of the Bolshevik despotism. The first is a defense of the dictatorship on the grounds of necessity as a transition stage between the bourgeois and the communistic state. The second deals with the difficult problem of extending communism to the peasants.

Both speeches were made before the Communist International Congress; the first is taken from the *Petrograd Pravda,* March 8, 1919; the second from the issue of April 9, 1919.]

The growth of the revolutionary movement of the proletariat in all countries has called forth convulsive efforts of the bourgeoisie and its agents in workmen's organizations, to find ideal political arguments in defense of the rule of the exploiters. Among these arguments stands out particularly condemnation of dictatorship and defense of democracy. The falseness and hypocrisy of such an argument, which has been repeated in thousands of forms in the capitalist press and at the conference of the yellow International in February, 1919, Berne, are evident to all who have not wished to betray the fundamental principle of socialism.

First of all, this argument is used with certain interpretations of "democracy in general" and "dictatorship in general" without raising the point as to which class one has in mind. Such a statement of the question, leaving out of consideration the question of class as though it were a general national matter, is direct mockery of the fundamental doctrine of socialism, namely, the doctrine of class struggle, which the socialists who have gone over to the side of the bourgeoisie recognize when they talk, but forget when they act. For in no civilized capitalist country does there exist "democracy in general," but there exists only bourgeois democracy, and one is speaking not of "dictatorship in general" but of dictatorship of the oppressed classes, that is, of the proletariat with respect to the oppressors and exploiters, that is, the bourgeoisie, in order to overcome the resistance which the exploiters make in their struggle to preserve their rule.

History teaches that no oppressed class has ever come into power and cannot come into power, without passing through a period of dictatorship, that is, the conquest of power and the forcible suppression of the most desperate and mad resistance which does not hesitate to resort to any crimes, such has always been shown by the exploiters. The bourgeoisie, whose

A DICTATORSHIP OF THE PROLETARIAT

rule is now defended by the socialists who speak against "dictatorship in general" and who espouse the cause of "democracy in general," has won power in the progressive countries at the price of a series of uprisings, civil wars, forcible suppression of kings, feudal lords, and slave owners, and of their attempts at restoration. The socialists of all countries, in their books and pamphlets, in the resolutions of their congresses, in their propaganda speeches, have explained to the people thousands and millions of times the class character of these bourgeois revolutions, and of this bourgeois dictatorship. Therefore the present defense of bourgeois democracy in the form of speeches about "democracy in general," and the present wails and shouts against the dictatorship of the proletariat in the form of wails about "dictatorship in general," are a direct mockery of socialism, and represent in fact going over to the bourgeoisie and denying the right of the proletariat to its own proletariat revolution, and a defense of bourgeois reformism, precisely at the historic moment when bourgeois reformism is collapsing the world over, and when the war has created a revolutionary situation.

All socialists who explain the class character of bourgeois civilization, of bourgeois democracy, of bourgeois parliamentarism, express the thought which Marx and Engels expressed with the most scientific exactness when they said that the most democratic bourgeois republic is nothing more than a machine for the suppression of the working class by the bourgeoisie, for the suppression of the mass of the toilers by a handful of capitalists. There is not a single revolutionist, not a single Marxist of all those who are now shouting against dictatorship and for democracy, who would not have sworn before the workmen that he recognizes this fundamental truth of socialism. And now, when the revolutionary proletariat begins to act and move for the destruction of this machinery of oppression, and to win the proletarian dictatorship, these traitors to socialism report the situation as though the bourgeoisie were giving the laborers pure democracy, as though the bourgeoisie were abandoning resistance and were ready to submit to the majority of the toilers, as though there were no state machinery for the suppression of labor by capital in a democratic republic.

The Paris Commune, which all who wish to be considered socialists celebrate in words, for they know that the working masses sympathize with the Paris Commune keenly and sincerely, showed with particular clearness the historically conditional character and the limited worth of bourgeois parliamentarism and bourgeois democracy—institutions in a high degree progressive as compared with the Middle Ages, but inevitably requiring radical changes in the epoch of proletarian revolution. It was Marx who best showed in his analysis the exploiting character of bourgeois democracy and of bourgeois parliamentarism, under which the oppressed classes received the right to decide once every few years which representatives of the propertied classes are to "represent and suppress" the people in parliament. Precisely at the present moment when the Soviet movement, covering the whole world, continues the work of the Commune before the eyes of the whole world, the traitors to socialism forget concrete experiences and the concrete lessons of the Paris Commune, repeating the old bourgeois rubbish about "democracy in general." The Commune was not a parliamentary institution.

Further, the significance of the Commune lies in the fact that it attempted to break up and destroy completely the bourgeois state machinery of officials, of judges, of military officials, of police, setting up instead self-administrative mass organizations of workmen, which did not recognize the division into legislative and executive authorities. All present-day bourgeois democratic republics, including the German, which the traitors of socialism, scoffing at truth, call proletarian, preserve this governmental apparatus. Therefore it is proven once more, and quite clearly, that the shouts in defense of "democracy in general" are in fact defense of the bourgeoisie and its exploiting privileges.

"Freedom of meeting" may be taken as an example of the demands for "pure democracy." Any conscious workman who has not broken with his own class will understand immediately that it would be stupid to permit freedom of meetings to exploiters at this period, and under the present circumstances, when the exploiters are resisting their overthrow, and are fighting for their privileges. When the bourgeoisie was revolutionary, in England in 1649, and in France in 1793, it did not give "freedom of meetings" to monarchists and nobles who were calling in foreign troops and who were "meeting" to organize attempts at restoration. If the present bourgeoisie, which has been reactionary for a long time now, demands of the proletariat that the latter guarantee in advance freedom of meetings for exploiters no matter what resistance the capitalists may show to the measures of expropriation directed against them, the workmen will only laugh at the hypocrisy of the bourgeoisie.

On the other hand the workmen know very well that "freedom of meetings," even in the most democratic bourgeois republic is an empty phrase, for the rich have all the best public and private buildings at their disposal, and also sufficient leisure time for meetings and for protection of these meetings by the bourgeois apparatus of authority. The proletarians of the city and of the village, and the poor peasants, that is, the overwhelming majority of the population, have none of these three things. So long as the situation is such, "equality," that is, "pure democracy" is sheer fraud. In order to secure genuine equality, in order to realize in fact democracy for the toilers, one must first take away from the exploiters all public and luxurious private dwellings, one must give leisure time to the toilers, one must protect the freedom of their meetings by armed workmen, and not by noble or capitalist officers with brow-beaten soldiers.

Only after such a change can one speak of freedom of meetings and of equality, without scoffing at workmen, toilers, and the poor. And no one can bring about this change except the advance guard of the toilers, that is, the proletariat, by overthrowing the exploiters, the bourgeoisie.

"Freedom of press" is also one of the main arguments of "pure democracy," but again the workmen know that the socialists of all countries have asserted millions of times that this freedom is a fraud so long as the best printing machinery and the largest supplies of paper have been seized by the capitalists, and so long as the power of capital over the press continues, which power in the whole world is clearly more harsh and more cynical in proportion to the development of democratism and the republican principle, as, for example, in America. In order to secure actual equality and actual democracy for the toilers, for workmen and peasants, one must first take from capitalists the possibility of hiring writers, of buying up publishing houses, of buying up newspapers, and to this end one must overthrow the yoke of capital, overthrow the exploiters, and put down all resistance on their part. The capitalists have always called "freedom" the freedom to make money for the rich, and the freedom to die of hunger for workmen. The capitalists call "freedom" the freedom of the rich, freedom to buy up the press, to use wealth, to manufacture and support so-called public opinion. The defenders of "pure democracy" again in actual fact turn out to be the defenders of the most dirty and corrupt system of the rule of the rich over the means of education of the masses. They deceive the people by attractive, fine-sounding, beautiful but absolutely false phrases, trying to dissuade the masses from the concrete historic task of freeing the press from the capitalists who have gotten control of it. Actual freedom and equality will exist only in the order established by the Communists, in which it will be impossible to become rich at the expense of another, where it will be impossible either directly or indirectly to subject the press to the power of money, where there will be no obstacle to prevent any toiler (or any large group of such) from enjoying and actually realizing the equal right to the use of public printing presses and of the public fund of paper. . . .

Dictatorship of the proletariat resembles dictatorship of other classes in that it was called forth by the need to suppress the forcible resistance of a class that was losing its political rulership. But that which definitely distinguishes a dictatorship of the proletariat from a dictatorship of other classes, from a dictatorship of the bourgeoisie in all the civilized capitalist countries, is that the dictatorship of the landlords and of the bourgeoisie was the forcible suppression of the resistance of the overwhelming majority of the population, namely, the toilers. On the other hand, the dictatorship of the proletariat is the forcible suppression of the resistance of the exploiters, that is, of an insignificant minority of the population—of landlords and capitalists.

It therefore follows that a dictatorship of the proletariat must necessarily carry with it not only changes in the form and institutions of democracy, speaking in general terms, but specifically such a change as would secure an extension such as has never been seen in the history of the world of the actual use of democratism by the toiling classes.

The essence of the Soviet authority consists in this, that the permanent and sole basis of all State authority, of the entire apparatus of government, is the mass organization precisely of those classes which were oppressed by capitalism, that is, of the workmen and of the half-proletarians (peasants who did not exploit the labor of others and constantly had to sell at least a portion of their labor strength). Precisely those masses which even in the most democratic bourgeois republics had equal rights before the law but in fact were deprived of participation in the political life of the country, and by thousands of tricks and traps of the use of democratic rights and liberties, are now brought into constant and actual, and, in addition, decisive participation in the democratic administration of the State.

THE PEASANTS

We have solved so far only the first fundamental task of the socialist revolution, the task of victory over the bourgeoisie. We have solved this task in a fundamental manner although now begins a dangerously difficult half year, during which the imperialists of the whole world are making the last efforts to suppress us. We can say now without exaggeration that they themselves have understood that after this next half year their cause will be absolutely suppressed. Either they must now take advantage of our exhaustion and conquer one country, namely Russia, or we will be the victors, and not only with reference to our own country. During this half year, when the food supply and transportation crisis have become more acute and the imperialistic powers are trying to attack on several fronts, our position is extremely difficult, but this is the last difficult half year. One must as before concentrate all efforts on the struggle with the foreign enemy who is attacking us.

When we speak of the tasks in connection with work in the villages, in spite of all difficulties, in spite of the fact that our knowledge has been directed to the immediate suppression of exploiters, we must nevertheless remember and not forget, that in the villages with relation to the middle peasantry the task is of a different nature. All conscious workmen, of Petrograd, Ivanovo-Voznesensk and Moscow, who have been in the villages, tell us of instances of many misunderstandings, of misunderstandings that could not be solved it seemed, and of conflicts of the most serious nature, all of which were, however, solved by sensible workmen who did not speak according to the book but in language which the people could understand, and not like an officer allowing himself to issue orders though unacquainted with village life, but like a comrade explaining the situation and appealing to their feelings as toilers. And by such explanation one attained what could not be attained by thousands who conducted themselves like commanders or superiors.

The resolution which we now present for your attention is drawn up in this spirit. I have tried in this report to emphasize the main principles behind this resolution, and its general political significance. I have tried to show, and I trust I have succeeded, that from the point of view of the interests of the revolution as a whole, we have not made any changes. We have not altered our line of action. The White Guardists and their assistants shout and will continue to shout that we have changed. Let them shout. That does not disturb us. We are developing our aims in an absolutely logical manner. From the task of suppressing the bourgeoisie we must now transfer our attention to the task of building up the life of the middle peasantry. We must live with the middle peasantry in peace. The middle peasantry in a communistic society will be on our side only if we lighten and improve its economic conditions. If we to-morrow could furnish a hundred thousand first-class tractors supplied with gasoline and machinists (you know of course that for the moment this is dreaming) then the middle peasant would say: "I am for the Commune." But in order to do this we must first defeat the international bourgeoisie, we must force them to give us these tractors, or we must increase our own production so that we can ourselves produce them. Only thus is the question stated correctly.

The peasant needs the industries of the cities and cannot live without them and the industries are in our hands. If we approach the situation correctly then the peasant will thank us because we will bring him the products from the cities, implements and culture. It will not be exploiters who will bring him these things, not landlords, but his own comrades, workers whom he values very deeply. The middle peasant is very practical and values only actual assistance, quite carelessly thrusting aside all commands and instructions from above.

First help him and then you will secure his confidence. If this matter is handled correctly, if each step taken by our group in the village, in the canton, in the food-supply detachment, or in any organization, is carefully made, is carefully verified from this point of view, then we shall win the confidence of the peasant, and only then shall we be able to move forward. Now we must give him assistance. We must give him advice and this must not be the order of a commanding officer, but the advice of a comrade. The peasant then will be absolutely for us.

And this is what our resolution contains, and this is what it seems to me should be the decision of the congress. If we accept this resolution and it defines all the activity of our party organizations, then we shall solve the second great task that is before us. We learned how to overthrow the bourgeoisie and suppress it and we are very proud of what we have done. We have not yet learned how to regulate our relations with the millions of middle peasants and how to win their confidence. We must say this frankly; but we have understood the task and we have undertaken it and we say to ourselves with full hope, complete knowledge and entire decision: We shall solve this task and then socialism will be absolute, invincible.

IV. THE UNITED STATES IN THE WAR

WOODROW WILSON

DECLARATION OF WAR BY THE UNITED STATES

[President Wilson's address to Congress on April 2, 1917, followed immediately by the action of Congress in declaring war, created a profound sensation throughout the world. It was received by the nations of the Entente Alliance with unbounded enthusiasm, as the turning point in the Great War. Messages of congratulation and appreciation poured in from all countries.

President Poincaré of France said, "In never to be forgotten language you have made yourself before the universe the eloquent interpreter of outraged laws and of a menaced civilization."

Lloyd George, Prime Minister of England, declared that "The glowing phrases of President Wilson's noble deliverance illumine the horizon and make clearer the goal we strive to reach. Three phrases will stand out forever in the history of this crusade: 'The world must be made safe for democracy,' and second 'The menace to peace and freedom lies in the existence of autocratic governments backed by organized force which is controlled wholly by their will and not by the will of their people' and the crowning phrase is that in which he declares that, 'A steadfast concert for peace can never be maintained except by the partnership of democratic nations.'"]

GENTLEMEN OF THE CONGRESS: I have called the Congress into extraordinary session because there are serious, very serious, choices of policy to be made, and made immediately, which it was neither right nor constitutionally permissible that I should assume the responsibility of making.

On the third of February last I officially laid before you the extraordinary announcement of the Imperial German Government that on and after the first day of February it was its purpose to put aside all restraints of law or of humanity and use its submarines to sink every vessel that sought to approach either the ports of Great Britain and Ireland or the western coasts of Europe or any of the ports controlled by the enemies

WOODROW WILSON

of Germany within the Mediterranean. That had seemed to be the object of the German submarine warfare earlier in the war, but since April of last year the Imperial Government had somewhat restrained the commanders of its undersea craft in conformity with its promise then given to us that passenger boats should not be sunk and that due warning would be given to all other vessels which its submarines might seek to destroy, when no resistance was offered or escape attempted, and care taken that their crews were given at least a fair chance to save their lives in their open boats. The precautions taken were meager and haphazard enough, as was proved in distressing instance after instance in the progress of the cruel and unmanly business, but a certain degree of restraint was observed. The new policy has swept every restriction aside. Vessels of every kind, whatever their flag, their character, their cargo, their destination, their errand, have been ruthlessly sent to the bottom without warning and without thought of help or mercy for those on board, the vessels of friendly neutrals along with those of belligerents. Even hospital ships and ships carrying relief to the sorely bereaved and stricken people of Belgium, though the latter were provided with safe conduct through the proscribed areas by the German Government itself and were distinguished by unmistakable marks of identity, have been sunk with the same reckless lack of compassion or of principle.

I was for a little while unable to believe that such things would in fact be done by any government that had hitherto subscribed to humane practices of civilized nations. International law had its origin in the attempt to set up some law which would be respected and observed upon the seas, where no nation had right of dominion and where lay the free highways of the world. By painful stage after stage has that law been built up, with meager enough results, indeed, after all was accomplished that could be accomplished, but always with a clear view, at least, of what the heart and conscience of mankind demanded. This minimum of right the German Government has swept aside, under the plea of retaliation and necessity and because it had no weapons which it could use at sea except these which it is impossible to employ as it is employing them without throwing to the wind all scruples of humanity or of respect for the understandings that were supposed to underlie the intercourse of the world. I am not now thinking of the loss of property involved, immense and serious as that is, but only of the wanton and wholesale destruction of the lives of non-combatants, men, women, and children, engaged in pursuits which have always, even in the darkest periods of modern history, been deemed innocent and legitimate. Property can be paid for; the lives of peaceful and innocent people cannot be. The present German submarine warfare against commerce is a warfare against mankind.

It is a war against all nations. American ships have been sunk, American lives taken, in ways which it has stirred us very deeply to learn of, but the ships and people of other neutral and friendly nations have been sunk and overwhelmed in the waters in the same way. There has been no discrimination. The challenge is to all mankind. Each nation must decide for itself how it will meet it. The choice we make for ourselves must be made with a moderation of counsel and a temperateness of judgment befitting our character and our motives as a nation. We must put excited feeling away. Our motive will not be revenge or the victorious assertion of the physical might of the nation, but only the vindication of right, of human right, of which we are only a single champion.

When I addressed the Congress on the twenty-sixth of February last I thought that it would suffice to assert our neutral rights with arms, our right to use the seas against unlawful interference, our right to keep our people safe against unlawful violence. But armed neutrality, it now appears, is impracticable. Because submarines are in effect outlaws when used as the German submarines have been used against merchant shipping, it is impossible to defend ships against their attacks as the law of nations has assumed that merchantmen would defend themselves against privateers or cruisers, visible craft giving chase upon the open sea. It is common prudence in such circumstances, grim necessity indeed, to endeavor to destroy them before they have shown their own intention. They must be dealt with upon sight, if dealt with at all. The German Government denies the right of neutrals to use arms at all within the areas of the sea which it has proscribed, even in the defense of rights which no modern publicist has ever before questioned their right to defend. The intimation is conveyed that the armed guards which we have placed on our merchant ships will be treated as beyond the pale of law and subject to be dealt with as pirates would be. Armed neutrality is ineffectual enough at best; in such circumstances and in the face of such pretensions it is worse than ineffectual; it is likely only to produce what it was meant to prevent; it is practically certain to draw us into the war without either the rights or the effectiveness of belligerents. There is one choice we cannot make, we are incapable of making; we will not choose the path of submission and suffer the most sacred rights of our nation and our people to be ignored or violated. The wrongs against which we now array ourselves are no common wrongs; they cut to the very roots of human life.

With a profound sense of the solemn and even tragical character of the step I am taking and of the grave responsibilities which it involves, but in unhesitating obedience to what I deem my constitutional duty, I advise that the Congress declare the recent course of the Imperial German Government to be in fact nothing less than war against the government and people of the United States; that it formally accept the status of belligerent which has thus been thrust upon it; and that it take immediate steps not only to put the country in a more thorough state of defense, but also to exert all its power and employ all its resources to bring the Government of the German Empire to terms and end the war.

What this will involve is clear. It will involve the utmost practicable coöperation in counsel and action with the governments now at war with Germany, and, as incident to that, the extension to those governments of the most liberal financial credits, in order that our resources may so far as possible be added to theirs. It will involve the organization and mobilization of all the material resources of the country to supply the materials of war and serve the incidental needs of the nation in the most abundant and yet the most economical and efficient way possible. It will involve the immediate full equipment of the navy in all respects but particularly in supplying it with the best means of dealing with the enemy's submarines. It will involve the immediate addition to the armed forces of the United States already provided for by law in case of war of at least five hundred thousand men, who should, in my opinion, be chosen upon the principle of universal liability to service, and also the authorization of subsequent additional increments of equal force so soon as they may be needed and can be handled in training. It will involve also, of course, the granting of adequate credits to the Government, sustained, I hope, so far as they can equitably be sustained by the present generation, by well-conceived taxation.

I say sustained so far as may be equitable by taxation because it seems to me that it would be most unwise to base the credits which will now be necessary entirely on money borrowed. It is our duty, I most respectfully urge, to protect our people so far as we may against the very serious hardships and evils which would be likely to arise out of the inflation which would be produced by vast loans.

In carrying out the measures by which these things are to be accomplished we should keep constantly in mind the wisdom of interfering as little as possible in our own preparation and in the equipment of our own military forces with the duty— for it will be a very practical duty—of supplying the nations already at war with Germany with the materials which they can obtain only from us or by our assistance. They are in the field and we should help them in every way to be effective there.

I shall take the liberty of suggesting, through the several executive departments of the Government, for the consideration of your committees, measures for the accomplishment of the several objects I have mentioned. I hope that it will be your pleasure to deal with them as having been framed after very careful thought by the branch of the Government upon whom the responsibility of conducting the war and safeguarding the nation will most directly fall.

While we do these things, these deeply momentous things, let us be very clear, and make very clear to all the world, what our motives and our objects are. My own thought has not been driven from its habitual and normal course by the unhappy events of the last two months, and I do not believe that the thought of the nation has been altered or clouded by them. I have exactly the same things in mind now that I had in mind when I addressed the Senate on the twenty-second of

January last; the same that I had in mind when I addressed the Congress on the third of February and on the twenty-sixth of February. Our object now, as then, is to vindicate the principles of peace and justice in the life of the world as against selfish and autocratic power, and to set up among the really free and self-governed peoples of the world such a concert of purpose and of action as will henceforth ensure the observance of those principles. Neutrality is no longer feasible or desirable where the peace of the world is involved and the freedom of its peoples, and the menace to that peace and freedom lies in the existence of autocratic governments, backed by organized force which is controlled wholly by their will, not by the will of their people. We have seen the last of neutrality in such circumstances. We are at the beginning of an age in which it will be insisted that the same standards of conduct and of responsibility for wrong done shall be observed among nations and their governments that are observed among the individual citizens of civilized States.

We have no quarrel with the German people. We have no feeling towards them but one of sympathy and friendship. It was not upon their impulse that their government acted in entering this war. It was not with their previous knowledge or approval. It was a war determined upon as wars used to be determined upon in the old, unhappy days when peoples were nowhere consulted by their rulers and wars were provoked and waged in the interest of dynasties or of little groups of ambitious men who were accustomed to use their fellow-men as pawns and tools. Self-governed nations do not fill their neighbor states with spies or set the course of intrigue to bring about some critical posture of affairs which will give them an opportunity to strike and make conquest. Such designs can be successfully worked out only under cover and where no one has the right to ask questions. Cunningly contrived plans of deception or aggression, carried, it may be, from generation to generation, can be worked out and kept from the light only within the privacy of courts or behind the carefully guarded confidences of a narrow and privileged class. They are happily impossible where public opinion commands and insists upon full information concerning all the nation's affairs.

A steadfast concert for peace can never be maintained except by a partnership of democratic nations. No autocratic government could be trusted to keep faith within it or observe its covenants. It must be a league of honor, a partnership of opinion. Intrigue would eat its vitals away; the plottings of inner circles who could plan what they would and render account to no one would be a corruption seated at its very heart. Only free peoples can hold their purpose and their honor steady to a common end and prefer the interests of mankind to any narrow interest of their own.

Does not every American feel that assurance has been added to our hope for the future peace of the world by the wonderful and heartening things that have been happening within the last few weeks in Russia? Russia was known by those who knew her best to have been always in fact democratic at heart in all the vital habits of her thought, in all the intimate relationships of her people that spoke their natural instinct, their habitual attitude towards life. The autocracy that crowned the summit of her political structure, long as it had stood and terrible as was the reality of its power, was not in fact Russian in origin, character, or purpose; and now it has been shaken off and the great, generous Russian people have been added, in all their naïve majesty and might, to the forces that are fighting for freedom in the world, for justice, and for peace. Here is a fit partner for a League of Honor.

One of the things that has served to convince us that the Prussian autocracy was not and could never be our friend is that from the very outset of the present war it has filled our unsuspecting communities, and even our offices of government, with spies and set criminal intrigues everywhere afoot against our national unity of counsel, our peace within and without, our industries and our commerce. Indeed, it is now evident that its spies were here even before the war began; and it is unhappily not a matter of conjecture but a fact proved in our courts of justice that the intrigues which have more than once come perilously near to disturbing the peace and dislocating the industries of the country have been carried on at the instigation, with the support, and even under the personal direction of official agents of the Imperial Government accredited to the Government of the United States. Even in checking these things and trying to extirpate them we have sought to put the most generous interpretation possible upon them because we knew that their source lay, not in any hostile feeling of the German people toward us (who were, no doubt, as ignorant of them as we ourselves were), but only in the selfish designs of a government that did what it pleased and told its people nothing. But they have played their part in serving to convince us at last that that government entertains no real friendship for us, and means to act against our peace and security at its convenience. That it means to stir up enemies against us at our very doors the intercepted note to the German Minister at Mexico City is eloquent evidence.

We are accepting this challenge of hostile purpose because we know that in such a government, following such methods, we can never have a friend; and that in the presence of its organized power, always lying in wait to accomplish we know not what purpose, there can be no assured security for the democratic governments of the world. We are now about to accept the gauge of battle with this natural foe to liberty and shall, if necessary, spend the whole force of the nation to check and nullify its pretensions and its power. We are glad, now that we see the facts with no veil of false pretense about them, to fight thus for the ultimate peace of the world and for the liberation of its peoples, the German peoples included; for the rights of nations, great and small, and the privilege of men everywhere to choose their way of life and of obedience. The world must be made safe for democracy. Its peace must be planted upon the tested foundations of political liberty. We have no selfish ends to serve. We desire no conquest, no dominion. We seek no indemnities for ourselves, no material compensation for the sacrifices we shall freely make. We are but one of the champions of the rights of mankind. We shall be satisfied when those rights have been made as secure as the faith and the freedom of nations can make them.

Just because we fight without rancor and without selfish object, seeking nothing for ourselves but what we shall wish to share with all free peoples, we shall, I feel confident, conduct our operations as belligerents without passion and ourselves observe with proud punctilio the principles of right and of fair play we profess to be fighting for.

I have said nothing of the government allied with the Imperial Government of Germany because they have not made war upon us or challenged us to defend our right and our honor. The Austro-Hungarian Government has, indeed, avowed its unqualified endorsement and acceptance of the reckless and lawless submarine warfare adopted now without disguise by the Imperial German Government, and it has therefore not been possible for this Government to receive Count Tarnowski, the Ambassador recently accredited to this Government by the Imperial and Royal Government of Austria-Hungary; but that Government has not actually engaged in warfare against citizens of the United States on the seas, and I take the liberty, for the present at least, of postponing a discussion of our relations with the authorities at Vienna. We enter this war only where we are clearly forced into it because there are no other means of defending our rights.

It will be all the easier for us to conduct ourselves as belligerents in a high spirit of right and fairness because we act without animus, not with enmity toward a people or with the desire to bring any injury or disadvantage upon them, but only in armed opposition to an irresponsible government which has thrown aside all considerations of humanity and of right and is running amuck. We are, let me say again, the sincere friends of the German people, and shall desire nothing so much as the early reëstablishment of intimate relations of mutual advantage between us,—however hard it may be for them, for the time being, to believe that this is spoken from our hearts. We have borne with their present government through all these bitter months because of that friendship, exercising a patience and forbearance which would otherwise have been impossible. We shall, happily, still have an opportunity to prove that friendship in our daily attitude and actions toward the millions of men and women of German birth and native sympathy who live among us and share our life, and we shall be proud to prove it towards all who are in fact loyal to their neighbors and to the Government in the hour of test. They are, most of them, as true and loyal Americans as if they had never known any other fealty or allegiance. They will be prompt to stand with us in rebuking and restraining the few who may be of a different mind and purpose. If there should be disloyalty, it will be dealt with a firm hand of stern repression; but, if it lifts its head at all, it will lift it only here and there and without countenance except from a lawless and malignant few.

It is a distressing and oppressive duty, Gentlemen of the Congress, which I have performed in thus addressing you. There are, it may be, many months of fiery trial and sacrifice ahead of us. It is a fearful thing to lead this great peaceful people into war, into the most terrible and disastrous of all wars, civilization itself seeming to be in the balance. But the right is more precious than peace, and we shall fight for the things which we have always carried nearest our hearts—for democracy, for the right of those who submit to authority to have a voice in their own governments, for the rights and liberties of small nations, for a universal dominion of right by such a concert of free peoples as shall bring peace and safety to all nations and make the world itself at last free. To such a task we can dedicate our lives and our fortunes, everything that we are and everything that we have, with the pride of those who know that the day has come when America is privileged to spend her blood and her might for the principles that gave her birth and happiness and the peace which she has treasured. God helping her, she can do no other.

DAVID LLOYD GEORGE

TO AMERICAN COMRADES IN ARMS

[The meeting of the American Luncheon Club on April 12, 1917, at which Ambassador Page and Mr. Lloyd George spoke, was the first celebration of America's entry into the Great War. Speaking before Mr. Lloyd George, Ambassador Page said that "The clear, solemn call of the President and the voice of Congress, which is the voice of the people, are to us a high call of duty. We come for nothing but to succor democracy, the ideal that is the republic."

The London *Times* declares that "The speeches of Mr. Page and Mr. Lloyd George are instinct with the light of the new dawn rising on earth, of the new brotherhood of freedom and peace through which Mr. Lloyd George prophesies the great democracies and their allies will march into the full glory of a perfect day. The prophecy may be too bold, the goal for which the noblest of mankind have yearned for generations may be still remote; but these speeches show how fast and how surely the light is gathering since Mr. Wilson spoke. For the first time a British Prime Minister yesterday was able to 'salute the American nation as comrades in arms.'"]

I WAS invited to attend a small family luncheon—[Laughter] —but when I entered this room I found that was another American legend—dispelled when I saw this great and impressive gathering. I am in the happy position, I think, of being the first British Minister of the Crown who, speaking on behalf of the people of this country, can salute the American nation as comrades in arms. [Cheers.] I am glad. I am proud. I am glad not merely because of the stupendous resources which this great nation can bring to the succor of the Alliance, but I rejoice as a Democrat [cheers] that the advent of the United States into this war gives the final stamp and seal to the character of the conflict [cheers] as a struggle against military autocracy throughout the world.

That was the note that rang through the great deliverance of President Wilson. It was echoed in your resounding words to-day, sir. The United States of America have a noble tradition, never broken, of having never engaged in a war except for liberty [cheers] and this is the greatest struggle for liberty they have ever embarked upon. [Cheers.] I am not at all surprised, when one recollects the wars of the past, that America took its time to make up its mind about the character of this struggle. In Europe most of the great wars of the past were waged for dynastic aggrandizements and for conquest. No wonder that when this great war started there were some elements of suspicion still lurking in the minds of the people of the United States of America. There were many who thought, perhaps, that kings were at their old tricks [laughter], and although they saw the gallant Republic of France, fighting, they, some of them perhaps, regarded France as the poor victim of conspiracy and of monarchical swashbucklers.

The fact that the United States of America has made up its mind finally makes it abundantly clear to the world that this is no struggle of that character, but a great fight for human liberty. [Cheers.] They naturally did not know at first what we had endured in Europe for years from this military caste in Prussia. It never reached as far as the United States of America. Prussia is not a democracy [laughter], but the Kaiser promises it will be a democracy after the war. I think he is right. [Laughter and cheers.] But Prussia not merely was not a democracy; Prussia was not a state. Prussia was an army. It had great industries, highly developed. It had a great educational system. It had its universities. It developed its sciences. But all these were subordinate to the one great predominant purpose of an all-conquering army which was to intimidate the world. The army was the spear-point of Prussia; the rest was merely the gilded shaft.

That is what we had to deal with in these old countries. It got on the nerves of Europe. They knew what it all meant. The Prussian army in recent times had waged three wars—all for conquest. And the incessant tramping of its legions through the streets of Prussia and on the parade grounds of Prussia had got into the Prussian head. The Kaiser, when he witnessed it on a grand scale in his reviews, got drunk with the sound of it. He delivered the law to the world, as though Potsdam were a new Sinai and he were uttering the law from the thunder-cloud. But make no mistake; Europe was uneasy. Europe was half intimidated; Europe was anxious; Europe was apprehensive. We knew the whole time what it meant. What we did not know was the moment it would come. This is the menace, this is the oppression, from which Europe has suffered for fifty years. It paralyzed the beneficent activities of all States, which ought to have been devoted to, and concentrated upon, the well-being of their people. They had to think about this menace, which was there constantly as a cloud, ready to burst over the land.

Take France. No one can tell except the Frenchman what they endured from this tyranny [cheers], patiently, gallantly, with dignity, until the hour of deliverance came. The best energies in democratic France have been devoted to defense against the impending terror. France was like a nation which had put up its right arm to ward off a blow, and it could not use the whole of its strength for the great things France was capable of. That great, bold, imaginative, fertile mind, which would otherwise have been cleaving new paths of progress, was paralyzed. This was the state of things we had to encounter.

The most characteristic of all Prussian institutions is the Hindenburg line. What is the Hindenburg line? The Hindenburg line is a line drawn in the territories of other people with a warning that the inhabitants of those territories shall not cross it at the peril of their lives. That line has been drawn in Europe for fifty years in many lands. You recollect what happened some years ago in France when the Foreign Minister, the French Foreign Minister, was practically driven out of office by Prussian interference. Why? What had he done? He had done nothing that the Minister of an independent State had not the most absolute right to do. He crossed that imaginary line drawn in French territory by Prussian despotism, and he had to leave.

Europe, after enduring this for generations, made up its mind at last that the Hindenburg line must be drawn along the legitimate frontiers of Germany herself. [Cheers.] It has been an undoubted fight for the emancipation of Europe and the emancipation of the world. It was hard at first for the people of America quite to appreciate that. Germany had not interfered to the same extent with their freedom, if at all. But at last she has endured the same experience to which Europe has been subjected. Americans were told they were not to be allowed to cross and recross the Atlantic except at their peril. American ships were sunk without warning. American subjects were drowned with hardly an apology, in fact as a matter of German right. At first America could hardly believe it. They could not think it possible that any sane people could behave in that manner. And they tolerated it once, they tolerated it twice, until at last it became clear that the Germans really meant it. Then America acted and acted promptly. The Hindenburg line was drawn along the shores of America and Americans were told they must not cross it. America said, "What is this?" and was told that this was a line beyond which they must not go. Then America said, "The place for that line is not the Atlantic, but on the Rhine, and we mean to help you to roll it up." And they have started. [Cheers.]

There are two great facts which clinch the argument that this is a great struggle for freedom. The first is the fact that America has come in. She could not have done otherwise. The second is the Russian Revolution. When France in the eighteenth century sent her soldiers to America to fight for the freedom and independence of that land France also was an autocracy. But when the Frenchmen were in America their aim was freedom. They acquired a taste for freedom and they took it home, and France became free. That is the story of Russia. Russia engaged in this great war for the freedom of Serbia, of Montenegro, and Bulgaria. Russians have fought for the freedom of Europe, and they wanted to make their own country free. They have done it. The Russian Revolution is not merely the outcome of the struggle for freedom. It is a proof of its character as a struggle for liberty. And if the Russian people realize, as there is evidence they are doing, that national discipline is not incompatible with national freedom, and know that national discipline is essential to the security of national freedom, they will indeed become a free people. [Cheers.]

I have been asking myself the question why is it that Germany deliberately in the third year of the war provoked America to this declaration, and to this action? Deliberately! Yes; resolutely! It has been suggested that the reason was that there were certain elements in American life which Germany was under the impression would make it impossible for the United States to declare war. That I can hardly believe; but the answer has been afforded by General Hindenburg himself in the very remarkable interview which appears, I think, this morning in the Press. He depended clearly on one of two things—that the submarine campaign would have destroyed international shipping to such an extent that England would have been put out of business before America was ready. According to his computation, America would not be ready for twelve months. He does not know America. [Cheers.] Then alternatively, and when America was ready at the end of twelve months with her army, she would have no ships to transport that army to the field of battle. In Hindenburg's words, "America carries no weight." [Laughter.] I suppose he means that she has no ships to carry on. [Laughter.] That is undoubtedly their reckoning.

Well, it is not wise always to assume, even when the German General Staff has miscalculated, that they have had no ground for their calculation; and therefore it behooves the whole of the Allies—Britain and America in particular—to see that that reckoning of von Hindenburg is as false as the one he made about the famous line which we have broken already. [Cheers.] The road to victory, the guarantee of victory, the absolute assurance of victory, is to be found in one word—ships. [Cheers.] In a second word—ships [cheers]; in a third word—ships. [Renewed cheers.] I see that America, with that quickness of comprehension which characterizes your nation, fully realizes that, and to-day I observe that they have already made an arrangement to build—is it 1000? ("yes")—3000-tonners for the Atlantic. [Cheers.] I think that the German military advisers must already begin to realize that this is another of the tragic miscalculations which is going to lead them to disaster and to ruin. [Cheers.]

But, Mr. Chairman, you will pardon me for just emphasizing that we are a slow people in these islands. [Laughter.] Yes, but sure! [Cheers.] Slowly, blunderingly; but we get there. [Cheers.] You get there sooner, and that is why I am glad to see you in. But may I say we have been in this business for three years? We have made blunders; we generally do; we have tried every blunder. [Laughter.] In

TO AMERICAN COMRADES IN ARMS   205

golfing phraseology, we have gone through every bunker; but we have a good niblick stroke [laughter and cheers]—and we are now right out on the course. May I respectfully suggest that it is worth America's while to study our blunders so as to begin just where we are now—not where we were three years ago? [Cheers.] In war, time is everything, time has a tragic significance. A step taken to-day may lead to assured victory, but taken to-morrow may barely avert disaster. All the Allies have discovered that. It was a new country for us all. It was trackless, mapless; we had to go by instinct, but we found the way, and I am so glad that you are sending your great naval and military experts here just to exchange experiences with men who have been through all the dreary, anxious course of the last three years. [Cheers.]

America has helped us even to win the battle of Arras—this great battle. Those guns which destroyed the German trenches and shattered the barbed wire—I remember with some friends of mine I see here discussing the matter and arranging to order from America the machines to make those guns. [Cheers.] Not all. [Laughter.] You got your share; it was only a share, but it is a glorious one. America has been making guns, making munitions, making machinery to prepare both, supplying us with steel, and she has got all that organization, that wonderful facility, adaptability, and resourcefulness of the great people who inhabit that great continent. Ah! it was a bad day for military autocracy in Prussia when she challenged the great Republic of the West. [Cheers.] We know what America can do; and we also know that now she is in it she will do it. [Cheers.] She will wage an effective and successful war.

There is something more important. She will ensure a beneficent peace. [Cheers.] I am the last man in the world—knowing for three years what our difficulties have been, what our anxieties have been, what our fears have been—to deny that the succor which is given us from America is something to rejoice in, and rejoice greatly in; but I do not mind telling you that I rejoice even more in the knowledge that America is going to win her right to be at the conference table when the terms of peace are being discussed. [Cheers.] That conference will settle the destiny of nations, the course of human life, for God knows how many ages. It would have been a tragedy for mankind if America had not been there, and there with all the influence, and the power, and the right, which she has now won by flinging herself into this great struggle. [Cheers.]

I can see peace coming now, not a peace which would be a beginning of war, not a peace which would be an endless preparation for strife and bloodshed; but a real peace. The world is an old world which has never had peace. It has been rocking, swaying like the ocean, and Europe—poor Europe—has always lived under the menace of the sword. When this war began two-thirds of Europe was under autocratic rule. It is the other way about now, and democracy means peace. [Cheers.] The democracy of France did not want war. The democracy of Italy hesitated long before entering the war. The democracy of this country shrank from it and shuddered, and would never have entered that cauldron if it had not been for the invasion of Belgium. Democracy sought peace, strove for peace, and if Prussia had been a democracy there would have been no war. [Cheers.]

But strange things have happened in this war, and stranger things are to come—and they are coming rapidly. There are times in history when the world spins so leisurely along its destined course that it seems for centuries to be at a standstill. There are also times when it rushes along at a giddy pace covering the track of centuries in a year. These are the times we are living in now. Six weeks ago Russia was an autocracy. She is now one of the most advanced democracies in the world. [Cheers.] To-day we are waging the most devastating war that the world has ever seen. To-morrow—not perhaps a distant to-morrow—war may be abolished forever from the categories of human crimes. [Cheers.] This may be something like that fierce outburst of winter which we are now witnessing before the complete triumph of spring.

It was written of those gallant men who won that victory on Monday [cheers]—men from Canada, from Australia, and from this old country [cheers]—which has proved that in spite of its age it is not decrepit [cheers]—it was written of those gallant men that they attacked with the dawn. Fitting work for the dawn to drive out of forty miles of French soil those miscreants who had defiled it for nearly three years. They attacked with the dawn. It is a significant phrase. The breaking up of the dark rule of the Turk, which for centuries has clouded the sunniest lands in the world, the freeing of Russia from the oppression which has covered it like a cloud for so long, the great declaration of President Wilson [cheers], coming with the might of the great nation he represents in the struggle for liberty are heralds of dawn. "They attacked with the dawn," and those men are marching forward in the full radiance of that dawn, and soon Frenchmen and Americans, British, Italians, and Russians, yea, Serbians, Belgians, Montenegrins, and Rumanians will march into the full light of perfect day. [Loud cheers.]

RENÉ VIVIANI

ADDRESSES IN AMERICA

[The entrance of the United States into the great conflict was followed by the decision of the English and French governments to send a high commission to convey the greetings and the appreciation of those governments to this country, and to discuss ways and means of securing the most effective coöperation of the United States.

Emile Hovélaque states that "M. Viviani's speeches were in every case improvised; for the ceaseless stress of hurried work imposed on the mission by the brevity of its stay in this country, and its innumerable duties, allowed neither preparation nor revision nor even careful translation. The burning words so eloquently spoken, with impassioned gesture and all the moving inflections of a thrilling voice, stand here cold and motionless, stripped of the glow and glory of quick life. But their force, their superiority and their message remain."

Of the two addresses given here by M. Viviani, the first was made April 29, 1917, at an impressive ceremony at Mt. Vernon, where he paid glowing tribute to Washington and America, and the second on May 4th, before a large audience in the Chicago Auditorium. Reprinted from "Addresses in the United States by M. René Viviani and Marshal Joffre," copyright, 1917, by Doubleday Page and Co.]

AT MOUNT VERNON

GENTLEMEN: We could not remain any longer in Washington without accomplishing this pious pilgrimage. In this spot lies all that is mortal of a great hero. Close by this spot stands the modest abode where Washington rested after the tremendous labor of achieving the emancipation of a nation. In this spot meet the admiration of the whole world and the veneration of the American people. In this spot rise before us the glorious memories left by the soldiers of France led by Rochambeau and Lafayette; a descendant of the latter, my friend M. de Chambrun, accompanies us. And I esteem it a supreme honor as well as a satisfaction for my conscience

RENE R. VIVIANI

to be entitled to render this homage to our ancestors in the presence of my colleague and friend, Mr. Balfour, who so nobly represents his great nation. By thus coming to lay here the respectful tribute of every English mind, he shows, in the historic moment of communion which France has willed, what nations that live for liberty can do. When we contemplate in the distant past the luminous presence of Washington, in nearer times the majestic figure of Abraham Lincoln; when we respectfully salute President Wilson, the worthy heir of these great memories, we at one glance measure the vast career of the American people. It is because the American people proclaimed and won for the nation the right to govern itself, it is because it proclaimed and won the equality of all men, that the free American people at the hour marked by fate has been enabled with commanding force to carry its action beyond the seas; it is because it was resolved to extend its action still further that Congress was enabled to obtain within the space of a few days the vote of conscription and to proclaim in the full splendor of civil peace the necessity for a National Army. In the name of France I salute the young army which will share in our common glory.

While paying this supreme tribute to the memory of Washington, I do not dimish the effect of my words when I turn my thoughts to the memory of so many unnamed heroes. I ask you by this tomb to bow in earnest meditation and all the fervor of piety before all the soldiers of the allied nations who for nearly three years have been fighting under different flags for the same ideal. I beg you to address the homage of your hearts and souls to all the heroes, born to live in happiness, in the tranquil pursuit of their labors, in the enjoyment of all human affections, who went into battle with virile cheerfulness and gave themselves up, not to death alone, but to the eternal silence that closes over those whose sacrifice remains nameless, in the full knowledge that, save for those who loved them, their very names would disappear with their bodies. Their monument is in our hearts. Not the living alone greet us here; the ranks of the dead themselves rise to surround the soldiers of liberty.

At this solemn hour in the history of our world, while heralding from this sacred mound the final victory of justice,

I extend to the Republic of the United States the greetings of the French Republic.

AT THE AUDITORIUM, CHICAGO

As I came in, to the burning strains of the Marseillaise, which was the war song of our forefathers that bore them on to victory after victory, and also to the strains of the American National Hymn which carries echoes of past and future victories; as I came into this vast hall in which the grace of the women gathered together here and the virility of the men give us an image of the greatness and beauty of the American people; as I came in, I saw and heard your acclamations rising toward us as we heard them rise on our arrival in this seething city, this magnificent capital of the Middle West, it was impossible for us to suppress the pride and emotion that swelled up in our hearts.

And when a few moments ago we heard your orators, Mr. Bancroft; the Mayor of Chicago, whom I thank for the splendid welcome we received this morning; and the Governor of Illinois, who spoke in the name of the State, I said to myself (and I think you will not accuse our just pride of sinking to the level of base vanity) that you were indeed right in loving, in admiring France, for no country more than she deserves all praise. What constitutes her greatness in the world is that she has not only labored and suffered for herself, but that throughout her long history her eyes have been fixed on all mankind; it is to all mankind her thoughts have ever gone. She it was that accomplished the French Revolution and who, through that Revolution, has enlightened the whole world; she it is who in the nineteenth century educated the other peoples in her ideals, and held in her grasp the banner of emancipation toward which from all the corners of the earth the oppressed look longingly. And if, in 1871, by a decree of fate, her glory seemed to suffer eclipse, if she has known defeat, after defeat she has sought and found fresh vigor in the labors of peace. She has forgotten nothing; she gazed with broken heart and streaming eyes at her violated frontier, at Alsace-Lorraine, which shall be ours once more to-morrow, not by conquest, but by right, because it is ours, and shall be by right restored to us.

And meanwhile she gathered fresh strength; she rose once more in the esteem of all nations; she was so profoundly attached to peace that she sent the children who might have defended her away to colonize other lands. And yet for ten years she has been systematically browbeaten and blackmailed. First came Tangier, then Casablanca, then Agadir: by turns she was hectored and insulted; and yet remained pacific and unmoved, until in 1914 she was summoned to break her written treaties, bow her head, humiliate her national honor. But as Mr. Bancroft so truly said, no country can be asked to despise itself. The supreme end of life is not peace; it is honor for men, and for nations their independence.

And then what a spectacle did France offer the world! Oh, doubtless German slanders have represented her as corrupt and dissolute: it was a mere jest to march against so frivolous a nation which would capitulate at the first shock of battle: Germany dreamt that in a few hours, a few days at the most, the souls of Frenchmen and the power of France would be beaten to the ground. And because they had come to study France in certain haunts of amusement where Frenchmen were never seen; because they knew not the real France, the France of our factories, the France of our soil, the France of intellectual labor; because, even through this transparent veil, the true France was hidden from them, they wantonly entered into this war with the full assurance conquest would be a matter of a few months, and victory secured.

And then what did you see? However far removed you may be distant from our land, it is not possible that so admirable a spectacle, the greatest France has ever given, should not have been revealed to all your eyes. Frenchmen, divided into hostile groups, and political sets forever at war, Frenchmen who were said never to be able to agree, to a man rose under the Flag of France; and as children who have quarreled erstwhile at once answer the call of their mother, all the children of France answered the call of their country.

From you we have nothing to conceal. The first shock was a fearful one. I do not think that in all history a single people ever remained more resolute and dauntless under the tempest of steel and fire that was unchained against us. We stood undaunted: but our hearts felt the impact of an avalanche of two millions of men. The German machine was well organized: for forty years no cog was lacking in it; and in that machine that knew not the rule of an individual, in which a man counted for nothing, in which the machine was all, in that machine all was ready. And you know what happened. Serbia trampled under foot, murdered, simply because it was weak; Belgium summoned to throw open her frontiers to her invader and refusing, hurling herself in spite of her material weakness, in the full splendor of moral greatness and strength, because she would leave no stain on the pages of her history, offering up the blood of her children to save her honor. And England, unshakable as we were, because her signature was on a treaty and she would not betray her faith, she also rose with us. But in the early days of the campaign we, the children of France almost alone bore the onset of the avalanche. We do not pretend not to have yielded physically for a short space— Yes, ever fighting, struggling against overwhelming odds, scattering the corpses of our sons on the roads we retreated along, we retreated tactically until the day when, under my premiership, the Marshal, who was then a general only, warned us, as early as the 23rd of August, that his battle plan was fixed, and that he had communicated it to his generals: until the 4th of September (and by one of those happy coincidences of history that date was the birthday of the Third Republic) when our troops received the order to march forward, to march forward against the enemy, the invaders of our territory. And then our poor soldiers, worn out by twenty consecutive days and nights of fighting, exhausted, without sleep, without proper food, after fighting day and night for all that period, answered the call of their chief; they rallied to his call and with smiling lips and radiant eyes along the fighting line, to the sound of the drum and clarion, marched against the enemy; and in the space of a few days fifty kilometers of French territory were freed.

Perhaps the details of that great historic battle are not familiar to you; they were concealed from you; the Germans kept them to themselves, so long as it was possible to conceal them from the rest of the world. But the power of truth is too great; it is impossible that that glorious battle, the greatest France ever fought, should be all unknown to you. In that battle we remained faithful to the mission of France. And do you know why the soldiers of the Marne fought as they did? It is because they were the soldiers of the democratic army, in which the most capable man can climb to the top of the hierarchy, in which the highest officers are the friends and comrades of their soldiers. And if they fought thus it was, let me tell you, because all the history of France was behind them, and was familiar to them, because they were the descendants of the soldiers of Valmy who under the French Revolution had already saved France and the liberty of the world; because they were also the descendants of Charles Martel's soldiers who in the plains of Poitiers stayed the avalanche of the Barbarians, and thus fulfilled the historic mission of France.

And they vanquished. And then you came to us; you came to us from the first. And I seek in vain words to tell our infinite gratitude for the moral support you gave us. You came to us with full hearts, smiling. I still see in my mind's eye, in the Paris ambulances, and in the ambulances on the front, those American women who bent over the beds of our dying and wounded men and calmed the anguish of their livid brows by the sweetness of their beauty. I see your doctors hastening at the call of our doctors to shower their benefits, without reward, on the sufferings of our wounded. I yet hear the orphans of France appealing to the Government of the Republic to thank the Americans who showered kindness on their poor, fair, young heads, their innocent heads. And I thank you, citizens of Chicago, men and women, for what from the first hour on you have never ceased to do. We know of your admirable Bazaar, which through your devotion brought in an enormous sum. I thank those who subscribed to the fifty-four ambulances which we have received and who to-morrow, at the call of their friends, will subscribe yet more to increase the number. I thank the Press of Chicago which, by helping us to make the truth known, has fought disinterestedly for the cause of truth and justice and rendered the greatest service to France and her allies. But that was not enough to content you. Not only by material benefits have you shown your good will: you have shown it in ways more moving yet. And I cannot do better than repeat the words which just now rose in my heart and were said by the orators of your nation— We have been received in the name of the State like brothers, in the name of the City like brothers, in the name of your organizing committee like brothers. You came to us! Why? In the first place why did you come with full hands to bring all these benefits to our country? Moved by your kind hearts, undoubtedly. But let me say that however glowing were your hearts, that was not the only reason. It was not possible even when you were chained down to the duties of neutrality, that your reason should not speak, and that your approval of France's cause should not arise from your outraged consciences. It was not possible you should not recognize the justice of our cause, not see that France was not only fighting to defend its rights, but to defend those of all peoples, the liberty of man. And all this was clearly manifest when under the guidance of your illustrious President you entered this war.

Just now, Mr. Bancroft was enumerating the causes of the war and, in flaming words, he said what were its deeper causes, and that it was sufficient to question your own history to discover them. Doubtless, like ourselves, you entered this war under the sting of German insults, in order that the honor of the nation formed by Washington should suffer no humiliation, in order to avenge your dead and dying, the children and the women murdered on the desolate, bleak, high seas, at night, in winter, by the criminal hands of those which we are fighting against together. You went into this war for that. But not for that alone. Was it possible for you to see, through the immense distances that separate us, the frightful spectacle which unchained Europe shows? Possible to see all the blood spilt; so many martyrs falling in a sacred cause: possible to count the thousands of dead, wounded, and sick: possible to count the mourning women whose pride and sorrow are hidden under their black veils: possible to count one by one all our orphans: possible to contemplate such sights without deep emotion and a revolt of your souls: possible to see the Marne, the Yser, the Somme, Verdun, where a fraction of the French Army held back a million men: and see, from far away, the lightnings of the tremendous battle rise above the immortal city to form the luminous beacon-light which illuminates the whole world; was it possible, I say, to see all this and not feel your hearts thrill and burn? No; it was not possible. And for months past I have been saying to myself that it was not possible. When French democracy, which made the French Revolution, which gave directing thoughts to all Europe, which long ago sent its flags, its generals and its soldiers to fight for independence; when that demcracy was struggling for its life, could you stand aloof? No; that was the one thing impossible.

No: You understand the deeper meanings of this war. The allied peoples are not fighting for territories; they are not fighting to satisfy some morbid ambition! No. The stake is a greater one; it is the fate of the whole world we now bear in our hands. In them are the fate of free men, of democracy. And it is because you felt that this contest between democracy and autocracy must be fought to its bitter end: it is because you felt that so long as the peoples do not possess, as you and we do, governing assemblies, responsible governments, war might again be let loose: because you felt that, so long as there are forces of aggression in the world, no democracy can live in peace, that you rallied to our side at the call of your President and the call of democracy all the world over.

Come to us then: come as brothers to the fight we are fighting for right and truth and justice. But remember well that out of this war must come the great lesson it holds. I have already said it is an empty and deadly dream for democracies to imagine they can live under purely ideal conditions and that they are threatened by no evil or perverse powers. If the democracies do not arm themselves for their defense; if they do not possess free men ready to seize the sword, not for conquest, but for the defense of their native land; sooner or later the imperial eagle will swoop down on them at an hour when it will be too late to organize resistance.

Consider our example. We are a people of forty millions of men. What are forty millions in comparison with the one hundred millions of the American people? But we were organized; but we had a national force; but we had officers, generals; but we had a chief; all was ready, so far at least as any democracy can be ready; and notwithstanding, by a fatality, for some days it seemed as if we might be annihilated. Therefore, let democracies arm in their own defense so long as in the wide world there remains a threatening autocracy. But it shall not long threaten. It is not to be believed that with all our coalized forces we cannot crush an autocracy at which we have in these last years struck such powerful blows: it is not possible that the absolute monarchs who, in the Central Empires, by their bloody whims dispose of the destinies of the world, should be allowed to continue. We will reach them: we will carry to their ears the cries of oppressed peoples: we shall declare that it is unthinkable that the strong should forever oppress the weak: we shall exact peace for all, liberty for all, equality for all. And when we have won the victory of Democracy, when as a free people we have brought our labors to full consummation, then all our thoughts will turn to the victims of this war. Together we will go to lay the palms of justice on the tombs of our children; and you in your pilgrimage will repair to Mount Vernon to ask the great soul of Washington: Founder of the Republic, Father of your country, have we done well in doing this? Are you well pleased with your children? Have they rightly understood the glorious tradition you inscribed on our flag?

And, rest assured, his great shade will arise to thank you, and to bless you.

WOODROW WILSON

FLAG DAY ADDRESS

[The New York *Times* in an editorial comment on the President's Flag Day address of June 14, 1917, says, "It is hard to believe there is any American who is in doubt as to why we are at war with Germany, but if there be such, the force and lucidity of the President's explanation must at once dispel that doubt. Every American should read it, the vast majority for refreshment of memory and firmer resolution, the hypothetical few to whom we have alluded, for information or for the ending of their fake pretenses. In this address the President uses language of unwonted severity. He no longer deplores, protests and remonstrates, he delivers against Germany shafts of downright denunciation barbed with just anger. It was in every way appropriate that on the National Flag Day the President of the United States should speak these words to the people exhorting them to an unflinching performance of their duty in an undertaking which will bring new luster to the Flag."]

MY FELLOW CITIZENS: We meet to celebrate Flag Day because this flag which we honor and under which we serve is the emblem of our unity, our power, our thought and purpose as a nation. It has no other character than that which we give it from generation to generation. The choices are ours. It floats in majestic silence above the hosts that execute those choices, whether in peace or in war. And yet, though silent, it speaks to us,—speaks to us of the past, of the men and women who went before us and of the records they wrote upon it. We celebrate the day of its birth; and from its birth until now it has witnessed a great history, has floated on high the symbol of great events, of a great plan of life worked out by a great people. We are about to carry it into battle, to lift it where it will draw the fire of our enemies. We are about to bid thousands, hundreds of thousands, it may be millions, of our men, the young, the strong, the capable men of the nation, to go forth and die beneath it on fields of blood far away,—for what? For some unaccustomed thing? For something for which it has never sought the fire before? American armies were never before sent across the seas. Why are they sent now? For some new purpose, for which this great flag has never been carried before, or for some old, familiar, heroic purpose for which it has seen men, its own men, die on every battlefield upon which Americans have borne arms since the Revolution?

These are questions which must be answered. We are Americans. We in our turn serve America, and can serve her with no private purpose. We must use her flag as she has always used it. We are accountable at the bar of history and must plead in utter frankness what purpose it is we seek to serve.

It is plain enough how we were forced into the war. The extraordinary insults and aggressions of the Imperial German Government left us no self-respecting choice but to take up arms in defense of our rights as a free people and of our honor as a sovereign government. The military masters of Germany denied us the right to be neutral. They filled our unsuspecting communities with vicious spies and conspirators and sought to corrupt the opinion of our people in their own behalf. When they found that they could not do that, their agents diligently spread sedition amongst us and sought to draw our own citizens from their allegiance,—and some of those agents were men connected with the official Embassy of the German Government itself here in our own capital. They sought by violence to destroy our industries and arrest our commerce. They tried to incite Mexico to take up arms against us and to draw Japan into a hostile alliance with her,—and that, not by indirection, but by direct suggestion from the Foreign Office in Berlin. They impudently denied us the use of the high seas and repeatedly executed their threat that they would send to their death any of our people who ventured to approach the coasts of Europe. And many of our own people were corrupted. Men began to look upon their own neighbors with suspicion and to wonder in their hot resentment and surprise whether there was any community in which hostile intrigue did not lurk. What great nation in such circumstances would not have taken up arms? Much as we had desired peace, it was denied us, and not of our own choice. This flag under which we serve would have been dishonored had we withheld our hand.

But that is only part of the story. We know now as clearly as we knew before we were ourselves engaged that we are not the enemies of the German people and that they are not our enemies. They did not originate or desire this hideous war or wish that we should be drawn into it, and we are vaguely conscious that we are fighting their cause, as they will some day see it, as well as our own. They are themselves in the grip of the same sinister power that has now at last stretched its ugly talons out and drawn blood from us. The whole world is at war because the whole world is in the grip of that power and is trying out the great battle which shall determine whether it is to be brought under its mastery or fling itself free.

The war was begun by the military masters of Germany, who proved to be also the masters of Austria-Hungary. These men have never regarded nations as peoples, men, women, and children of like blood and frame as themselves, for whom governments enlisted and in whom governments had their life. They have regarded them merely as serviceable organizations which they could by force or intrigue bend or corrupt to their own purpose. They have regarded the smaller states, in particular, and the peoples who could be overwhelmed by force, as their natural tools and instruments of domination. Their purpose has long been avowed. The statesmen of other nations, to whom that purpose was incredible, paid little attention; regarded what German professors expounded in their classrooms and German writers set forth to the world as the goal of German policy as rather the dream of minds detached from practical affairs, as preposterous private conceptions of German destiny, than as the actual plans of responsible rulers; but the rulers of Germany themselves knew all the while what concrete plans, what well advanced intrigues lay back of what the professors and the writers were saying, and were glad to go forward unmolested, filling the thrones of Balkan states with German princes, putting German officers at the service of Turkey to drill her armies and make interest with her government, developing plans of sedition and rebellion in India and Egypt, setting their fires in Persia. The demands made by Austria upon Servia were a mere single step in a plan which compassed Europe and Asia, from Berlin to Bagdad. They hoped those demands might not arouse Europe, but they meant to press them whether they did or not, for they thought themselves ready for the final issue of arms.

Their plan was to throw a broad belt of German military power and political control across the very center of Europe and beyond the Mediterranean into the heart of Asia; and Austria-Hungary was to be as much their tool and pawn as Servia or Bulgaria or Turkey or the ponderous states of the East. Austria-Hungary, indeed, was to become part of the central German Empire, absorbed and dominated by the same forces and influences that had originally cemented the German states themselves. The dream had its heart at Berlin. It could have had a heart nowhere else! It rejected the idea of solidarity of race entirely. The choice of peoples played no part in it at all. It contemplated binding together racial and political units which could be kept together only by force,—Czechs, Magyars, Croats, Serbs, Roumanians, Turks, Armenians,—the proud states of Bohemia and Hungary, the stout little commonwealths of the Balkans, the indomitable Turks, the subtile people of the East. These peoples did not wish to be united. They ardently desired to direct their own affairs, would be satisfied only by undisputed independence. They could be kept quiet only by the presence of the constant threat of armed men. They would live under a common power only by sheer compulsion and await the day of revolution. But the German military statesmen had reckoned with all that and were ready to deal with it in their own way.

And they have actually carried the greater part of that amazing plan into execution! Look how things stand. Austria is at their mercy. It has acted, not upon its own initiative or upon the choice of its own people, but at Berlin's dictation ever since the war began. Its people now desire peace, but cannot have it until leave is granted from Berlin. The so-called Central Powers are in fact but a single Power. Servia is at its mercy, should its hands be but for a moment freed. Bulgaria has consented to its will, and Roumania is overrun. The Turkish armies, which Germans trained, are serving Germany, certainly not themselves, and the guns of German warships lying in the harbor at Constantinople remind Turkish statesmen every day that they have no choice but to take their orders from Berlin. From Hamburg to the Persian Gulf the net is spread.

Is it not easy to understand the eagerness for peace that has been manifested from Berlin ever since the snare was set and sprung? Peace, peace, peace has been the talk of her Foreign Office for now a year and more; not peace upon her own initiative, but upon the initiative of the nations over which she now deems herself to hold the advantage. A little of the talk has been public, but most of it has been private. Through all sorts of channels it has come to me, and in all sorts of guises, but never with the terms disclosed which the German Government would be willing to accept. That government has other valuable pawns in its hands besides those I have mentioned. It still holds a valuable part of France, though slowly relaxing grasp, and practically the whole of Belgium; its armies press close upon Russia and overrun Poland at their will. It cannot go further; it dare not go back. It wishes to close its bargain before it is too late and it has little left to offer for the pound of flesh it will demand.

The military masters under whom Germany is bleeding see very clearly to what point Fate has brought them. If they fall back or are forced back an inch, their power both abroad and at home will fall to pieces like a house of cards. It is their power at home they are thinking about now more than their power abroad. It is that power which is trembling under their very feet; and deep fear has entered their hearts. They have but one chance to perpetuate their military power or even their controlling political influence. If they can secure peace now with the immense advantages still in their hands which they have up to this point apparently gained, they will have justified themselves before the German people: they will have gained by force what they promise to gain by it: an immense expansion of German power, an immense enlargement of German industrial and commercial opportunities. Their prestige will be secure, and with their prestige their political power. If they fail, their people will thrust them aside, a government accountable to the people themselves will be set up in Germany as it has been in England, in the United States, in France, and in all the great countries of the modern time except Germany. If they succeed they are safe and Germany and the world are undone; if they fail Germany is saved and the world will be at peace. If they succeed, America will fall within the menace. We and all the rest of the world must remain armed, as they will remain, and must make ready for the next step in their aggression; if they fail, the world may unite for peace and Germany may be of the union.

Do you not now understand the new intrigue, the intrigue for peace, and why the masters of Germany do not hesitate to use any agency that promises to effect their purpose, the deceit of the nations? Their present particular aim is to deceive all those who throughout the world stand for the rights of peoples and the self-government of nations; for they see what immense strength the forces of justice and of liberalism are gathering out of this war. They are employing liberals in their enterprise. They are using men, in Germany and without, as their spokemen whom they have hitherto despised and oppressed, using them for their own destruction,—socialists, the leaders of labor, the thinkers they have hitherto sought to silence. Let them once succeed and these men, now their tools, will be ground to powder beneath the weight of the great military empire they will have set up; the revolutionists in Russia will be cut off from all succor or coöperation in western Europe and a counter revolution fostered and supported; Germany herself will lose her chance of freedom; and all Europe will arm for the next, the final struggle.

The sinister intrigue is being no less actively conducted in this country than in Russia and in every country in Europe to which the agents and dupes of the Imperial German Government can get access. That government has many spokesmen here, in places high and low. They have learned discretion. They keep within the law. It is opinion they utter now, not sedition. They proclaim the liberal purposes of their masters; declare this a foreign war which can touch America with no danger to either her lands or her institutions; set England at the center of the stage and talk of her ambition to assert economic dominion throughout the world; appeal to our ancient tradition of isolation in the politics of the nations; and seek to undermine the government with false professions of loyalty to its principles.

But they will make no headway. The false betray themselves always in every accent. It is only friends and partisans of the German Government whom we have already identified who utter these thinly disguised disloyalties. The facts are patent to all the world, and nowhere are they more plainly seen than in the United States, where we are accustomed to deal with facts and not with sophistries; and the great fact that stands out above all the rest is that this is a Peoples' War, a war for freedom and justice and self-government amongst all the nations of the world, a war to make the world safe for the peoples who live upon it and have made it their own, the German people themselves included; and that with us rests the choice to break through all these hypocrisies and patent cheats and masks of brute force and help set the world free, or else stand aside and let it be dominated a long age through by sheer weight of arms and the arbitrary choices of self-constituted masters, by the nation which can maintain the biggest armies and the most irresistible armaments,—a power to which the world has afforded no parallel and in the face of which political freedom must wither and perish.

For us there is but one choice. We have made it. Woe be to the man or group of men that seeks to stand in our way in this day of high resolution when every principle we hold dearest is to be vindicated and made secure for the salvation of the nations. We are ready to plead at the bar of history, and our flag shall wear a new luster. Once more we shall make good with our lives and fortunes the great faith to which we were born, and a new glory shall shine in the face of our people.

BRAND WHITLOCK

LAFAYETTE, APOSTLE OF LIBERTY

["Lafayette, we are here." This single sentence spoken by General Pershing as he placed a wreath on the tomb of the great Frenchman became one of the most famous speeches of the War. It might have served as the text of the following address by Brand Whitlock, distinguished American author, United States Minister to Belgium during the War, and Ambassador to Belgium since 1919. It was delivered at the tomb of Lafayette in Picpus Cemetery, on July 4, 1917. Reprinted from "The World War," copyright, 1919, by The American Academy of Arts and Letters.]

At long intervals in the progress of our race, once or twice in a century perhaps, there is born into the world one of those rare and lofty souls whose passion for humanity makes them worthy to be intrusted with the cause of human liberty. They are born with a vision, a courage and a faith that lift them high above their fellows and yet their love and sympathy and pity keep them close to the heart of mankind. By their sacrifices and their toils they work new emancipations and they come somehow to sum up, and to express in their great personalities, their peoples and their times. The story of their lives is the history of the nations—as with Washington and Lincoln, as with him at whose tomb we are assembled to-day.

It was the distinction of Lafayette, indeed, to sum up the history of two nations in his time. For, as he used to say, he had two countries, France and America, and he seemed to find it difficult to say which he loved the more. With his keen perception he discerned that in essential, spiritual ways the two nations, inspired by the same motives and devoted to the same ideals, were but a part of that larger nation of the mind, where all who love liberty and mankind are citizens by right.

There are few stories more romantic than his. As an ardent youth, not yet twenty years of age, without the consent of his father or his King, he sets forth across the seas on that matchless adventure, the old yet ever new alluring quest of human liberty.

We see him before that first Congress in the old Liberty Hall at Philadelphia; then by the side of Washington, who comes so to love him that when he is wounded at Brandywine Washington tells the surgeon to treat him as his son. He has an honored place in the councils of war and he "shudders to think that the voice of a twenty-year-old youth might decide the fate of two worlds." Then the long winter at Valley Forge, where the snows are reddened by bleeding feet, and, with the sword that Congress gave him, he comes back to France for succor and returns with the army corps that went with Rochambeau. Finally, he is at Yorktown, and four years later is once more in America at Mount Vernon, the guest of Washington. He is elected a citizen of the Republic and adopted into the very heart of the nation. Every one refers to him affectionately as "The Marquis," while the Indians call him "Kayewla." All over the land, towns are named for him; there is not a city in America that has not an avenue bearing his name, and, as children in our schools, we are taught to revere him.

We see him then engage in the struggle for liberty in his own land; he is at the assembly of the Notables and drafts the Declaration of the Rights of Man. And ever after, whether at Paris, at Olmutz or at Lagrange, down to the memorable days of July, 1830, it is for liberty that he strives, it is of liberty that he writes and dreams; "la liberté américaine," he used to call it.

To us his correspondence with his friends in America must ever have a peculiar personal interest. He was always writing to them, to Washington, to Jefferson, to Adams, to Monroe, to J. Fenimore Cooper, Jefferson, when President, after the purchase of Louisiana, offered him the governorship of the new province, if he would come back, and Hamilton, the great rival of Jefferson, wrote him that there was only one subject on which the various parties in America could agree and that was in their love for him.

The thought of returning to America continually fascinated him; he was always referring to it. And it must have been a moment big in its implications when in his old age he made that last visit and there, under the stately portico of Monticello, he and Jefferson clasped each other in a long embrace. When he died, and old Andrew Jackson in an order of the day announced that the last Major-General of the armies of the Revolution was no more, the same military honors that had been paid to Washington were rendered to him, guns were fired until the sun went down, flags were at half mast, the army wore mourning for six months, and in the Senate, in the presence of the President, the two houses and the diplomatic corps, John Quincy Adams pronounced an oration in his memory.

We assemble then at his tomb at this solemn moment in the history of the world, on this day that meant so much to him and means so much to us, to pay our tribute to his memory and to render homage to the nation whose various virtues were so nobly exemplified in his character and career. We come to reverence the memory not only of our sons who fell in other wars for liberty, but to salute those who have fallen in this great and, as we would fain believe, this final war for liberty, those noble dead who fell heroically at the Marne, on the Yser, at Verdun, on the Somme, giving their lives that freedom might not perish from the earth, those boys, your own and ours, French, English, Belgian, who went forward with smiles upon their beardless lips, and in John Hay's fine figure are triumphant now in the beautiful immortality of youth.

The ground whereon we stand to-day is not foreign soil, for when France came to bury her hero, America claimed a privilege of affection and sent her earth from our own land that it might be mingled with the soil of France, as a last resting place for him who was the son of both. Even were it otherwise, it would not be foreign soil, for the soil of liberty is always home to him who loves liberty.

This day meant much to Lafayette all his life, he never forgot it, and he celebrated it always by writing to one or other of his American friends. Once writing to Jefferson he referred to it as that day of which the expression was worthy of the event. He was addressing the author of the classic Declaration of human liberty, written, to employ one of the fine phrases in its opening passages, in "a decent respect to the opinions of mankind." "We hold these truths to be self-evident: that all men are created equal; that they are endowed by their Creator with certain inalienable rights; that among these are life, liberty, and the pursuit of happiness; that, to secure these rights, governments are instituted among men, deriving their just powers from the consent of the governed."

How these old truths blaze out to-day with a new and vivid meaning! We were so accustomed to hear them that familiarity had dulled our appreciation; we were so accustomed to live them that their repetition brought only a superior smile to the face of sophistication. And now, even as we stand here, the world is in the agony of a war that is to determine, in Lincoln's words, whether nations conceived in these liberties, and dedicated to these propositions are to endure. The right to life, the right to liberty, the right to happiness! These three phrases are the synthesis of the ideals of the western world; they resume in themselves all that culture, all that imagination, all that taste, all that honor, all that art and beauty have revealed to the human mind.

Considered in relation to its time and construed with the Constitution and the Bill of Rights, that sought to apply its ideals to the practical affairs of life and government, the Declaration marked the highest point that the human ideal at that day had attained. It was the logical conclusion of the old struggle for English liberty, bearing a direct relation to the revolution of 1649 and forming one of the great series of charters of human liberty that began with Magna Charta. Its stately and sonorous cadences are not the rigid impossibilities of doctrinaires, nor the vague dreams of idealists and mystics, but the practical statement of the terms on which human beings can live together in political equality with a chance for self-expression and development. Every one of its concepts recalls the bitter lesson of some tragic experience in human history; those lines were written one after the other with the blood and sweat and tears of generations that had resisted tyrants for the right to live. In highly concentrated thought they represent the conclusions that intelligent mankind had reached during the eighteen centuries of struggle upward out of savagery. Well might Lafayette write to his old friend Jefferson that the expression was worthy of the event!

It was by such means, and on the solid bases of such principles, that over the ugly ruins of feudalism there had arisen a new structure of human society. Slowly, with infinite toil and pain, in spite of many blunders and mistakes, Man has reared the edifice of modern civilization. It was imperfect as yet, but it was being built according to certain fundamental conceptions of liberty, of honor, of justice, words whose connotation were common to all intelligent and refined persons. At each step in its progress he paused to consolidate the victory of mind over matter, of reason over force, of the spiritual over the material, of the ideal over the low and base. He had witten down the results of these various victories in declarations and constitutions and laws that embodied one by one the triumphs of Italian genius, the visions of Russian prophecy, the clear conceptions of French intelligence, and the solid achievements of English thought. They become the memoranda of the means by which liberty has been kept alive, that the best in man might be given expression, that culture might dwell in the earth, that there might be sweetness and light in life, that Man, the Individual, might stand up in the world and realize the aspirations of the poets and saviors of the race.

And then suddenly, as though it had stepped out of the Middle Ages, autocracy, reincarnated in a military despotism with a camouflage of culture, made its apparition in the modern world, ready to tear up all the charters of human liberty, to destroy the work of the centuries. It challenged the validity of the principles on which democratic nations rest, and with them the noblest and most exalted conceptions of the human mind. It impugned justice, it sneered at liberty, it scorned compassion, it flouted honor, and in the name of the amazing theory that any deed is right if one has the brute force to commit it, it would take away what Lincoln called the last, best hope of man.

It precipitated anew the old conflict between freedom and slavery, the old battle between the prince of the powers of the air and the prince of the powers of darkness. But thereby it decreed its own destruction, for the world has grown too small for autocracy and democracy to live in it together. The urge of democracy is irresistible; it is the destiny of men to be free; peoples developed in the light of free institutions do not turn backward to the dark. The history of the liberal nations of the earth all tends one way, toward liberty, upward toward the light. Read the story of valiant France, read the story of Belgium, ah, Belgium! Three years ago this summer day it was a smiling land of happy people whose every scene evoked the memory of some joyous canvas of Jordæns or Teniers. To-day it is the land of sorrow, lightened only by the heroism of an indomitable people. They have not only endured all the cruelties and the woes of war, but they have been subjected to the ignominies of a military occupation; they live in the presence of the great injustice, in the shadow of a mighty wrong. Yet those brave spirits back there behind that tragic veil come of a line of men who, ages since, learned what liberty is, and in their communal form of government have stubbornly, through successive alien dominations, clung to the right to rule themselves. And undaunted and undismayed as she stood her ground at Liège, and along the Yser, so Belgium stands her ground to-day in every commune and at every hearthstone in the land.

What was it that led Lafayette to go forth to a new land in the midst of war? He had a place at the most brilliant court of his time; he had youth, and wealth and a noble name; he had a bride, and he was in Paris. And yet, when he heard of the struggle across the sea, he said:

"My heart was enrolled and I had no other idea than to join my colors."

My colors! The colors of liberty, whose radiant vision beckoned the loving and the daring in all times. He knew that wherever the flag of freedom was unfurled there was his post. *Noblesse oblige!* And the noblest, like Lafayette and Washington, are not content with liberty for themselves alone; they must have it for all men on equal terms, for they know that character can be developed only in liberty, where the human soul has the right not only to live but the exceedingly more important right to live a beautiful life.

To-day, as we stand here by the tomb of him who in his youth went forth alone to join his colors across the seas, we hear the tread of a million youths of America, sons of his spirit, marching to the ships that bear them hither to join their colors on this new front of Liberty.

They come with the same unselfish motive that led him forth, not for conquest but for freedom, to help, as our President said, to make the world safe for democracy. They come as the brothers of their English blood, with the grim determination of their race, vowing that autocracy shall not tear up Magna Charta and the Bill of Rights, the Declaration of Independence and the Declaration of the Rights of Man. They come in the name of those great principles of which Lincoln, for us, is the incarnation, resolved that the dead on all the battlefields of liberty shall not have died in vain, that each nation under God shall have a new birth of freedom, and that government of the people, by the people, for the people shall not perish from the earth. They come singing the "Battle Hymn of the Republic," to the blowing of the bugles that shall never sound retreat. They come bearing the hopes and the resolutions and the faith of a whole free people, a mighty continent aroused, whose genius salutes the sister republic in the strophes of Walt Whitman, the poet and prophet of democracy:

> O Star! O ship of France, beat back and baffled long!
> Bear up, O smitten orb! O ship, continue on!

WALTER HINES PAGE

THE FOURTH OF JULY IN LONDON

[The Fourth of July, 1917, was a memorable celebration in both France and England. In London by the King's wish the Stars and Stripes flew from the Houses of Parliament, and the Welsh Guards played American airs at the changing of the guard at St. James' Palace. Many distinguished Englishmen attended Mr. Page's reception, paying honor to the American Ambassador not less than to the American nation.

Mr. Balfour and Sir William Robertson, then Chief of Staff, were the guests of the evening at the dinner of the American Society. The British Foreign Secretary, having recently returned from his successful visit to the United States, was a most fitting speaker on the occasion. The speeches of both Mr. Page and Mr. Balfour were full of the spirit of the crisis to which America so proudly rose.

Walter Hines Page was born in Cary, North Carolina, in 1855. He was a student at Randolph-Macon College and a fellow at Johns Hopkins. From 1890-1895 he was editor of the *Forum;* literary adviser to Houghton Mifflin & Co., 1895-1899; editor of the *Atlantic Monthly* 1896-1899, and of the *World's Work* 1900-1913. In 1913 he went to London as Ambassador Extraordinary and Plenipotentiary to Great Britain. He died in 1918.]

FOR one hundred forty years American citizens celebrated the birthday of the Republic reminding one another of their political, social and religious freedom, and during that period their liberties had been extended and fortified by their keeping in mind that the remedy for the shortcomings of democracy was the application of more democracy. Thus that anniversary has become the most sacred day in our calendar. Every American present can picture to himself that august spectacle of the millions of their fellow-citizens assembled to-day in every State to celebrate with reverence, if with noise, the immortal structure of government and of society which our fathers fashioned out of their ideal.

We have now begun a new era in the history of the world. Hitherto we have been concerned chiefly with the development and the extension of liberty at home. We have now entered upon a larger crusade to help in an extension of liberty in this Old World, since the foundations of liberty throughout the whole world have been assailed. We have committed ourselves to this crusade because otherwise we could not keep our future birthdays worthily. And whither does this commitment lead us? It leads us first to victory and then it leads to our making sure that this victory shall be permanent. And then whither does it lead us? It must lead us inevitably and joyfully to a definite and a permanent understanding with all other steadfast friends of freedom.

This kingdom is the steadfast friend of freedom. In the celebration of this birthday we therefore dedicate ourselves not only to our own ideals but likewise to the additional task of strengthening our close friendship with this other great branch of the English-speaking world. I call on every American who hears my voice thus solemnly to dedicate himself to this most important task in the whole world. It is the earnest wish, I might say the dearest wish, of every American here to dedicate himself to this task. More than that, it is the earnest wish of every true American everywhere. Let us now, remember that during our residence here we have enjoyed the hospitality of this land and made lifelong friends here, give ourselves to making a closer understanding, that the unity of these two peoples and these two Governments shall become the immutable basis of sympathetic relations forever.

ARTHUR JAMES BALFOUR

THE FOURTH OF JULY IN LONDON

[Arthur James Balfour was born in Scotland in 1848, and was educated at Eton and Trinity College, Cambridge. He entered Parliament in 1874. He was Secretary for Scotland 1886-1887, Chief Secretary for Ireland 1887-1891. He was First Lord of the Treasury in Lord Salisbury's Cabinet 1871-1892 and in 1895. He became Prime Minister 1902-1905. He is a distinguished British statesman, a scholar and a brilliant debater. He was raised to the peerage in 1921.]

On this anniversary in every part of the world American citizens meet together and renew, as it were, their vows of devotion to the great ideals which have animated them. All the world admires, all the world sympathizes with the vast work of the great American Republic. All the world looks back upon the one hundred forty-one years which have elapsed since the Declaration of Independence and sees in that one hundred forty-one years an expansion in the way of population, in the way of wealth and of power, material and spiritual, which is unexampled in that period, and, as far as I know, in the history of the world.

We of the British race, who do not fall short of the rest of the world in our admiration in this mighty work, look at it in some respects in a different way, and must look at it in a different way, from that of other people. From one point of view we have surely a right to look at it with a special satisfaction, a satisfaction born of the fact that, after all, the thirteen colonies were British colonies; that the thirteen colonies, in spite of small controversies, grew up broadly speaking, under the protection of England; that it was our wars, the English wars with Spain in the 16th century, with Holland in the 17th century, and with France in the 18th century, which gave that security from external European attack which enabled those thirteen colonies to develop into the nucleus of the great community of which they were the origin.

We British may also surely, without undue vanity, pride ourselves on the fact that the men who founded the great American Republic, the men whose genius contrived its constitution, their forefathers who, struggling in the wilderness, gradually developed the basis of all that has happened since, were men speaking the English language, obeying and believing in English laws, and nourished upon English literature; and although we may say that the originality and power and endurance were theirs, they were men of our own race, born of the same stock, and to that extent at least we may feel that we have some small and not insignificant part in the great development which the world owes to their genius, courage, and love of liberty.

In that sense we may well look with peculiar pride and satisfaction upon this great anniversary. There is, of course, another side to the question. The Fourth of July is the anniversary of the separation, the final political separation—not, thank God, the final separation in sentiment, in emotion, or in ideal—but the final separation between the thirteen colonies and the Mother Country. We of the Mother Country cannot look back on that event as representing one of our successes. No doubt there was something to be said, though perhaps it is not often said, for those on this side of the Atlantic who fought for unity, who desired to preserve the unity of the Empire. Unity is a cause for which the American people have sacrificed rivers of blood and infinite treasure.

I am not going into ancient history, but the mistake we made, an almost inevitable mistake at that particular period of the development of the history of the world, was in supposing that unity was possible so long as one part of the Empire which you tried to unite, speaking the same language, having the same traditions and laws, having the same love of liberty and the same ideals, would consent to remain a part of the Empire except on absolutely equal terms. That was a profound mistake, a mistake which produced a great schism and produced all the collateral, though I am glad to think subordinate, evils which followed on that great schism.

All I can say in excuse for my forefathers is that, utterly defective as the colonial policy of Great Britain in the middle of the 18th century undoubtedly was, it was far better than the colonial policy of any other country. Imperfectly as we conceived the kind of relations that might, or could, bind the colonies to their Mother Country, thoroughly as we misconceived them, we misconceived them less than most of our neighbors.

I went on Monday last to the ceremonial at Westminster Abbey in which the 50th anniversary of the Constitution of Canada was celebrated. There is a great difference between 50 years and 141 years. It took us a long time to learn the lesson that if you want to make an Empire of different widely separated communities of the British race you must do it on terms of absolute equality. We have learnt the lesson and in our own way we are now carrying out a task as great, as momentous as—even more difficult than—fell to the great and illustrious framers of the American Constitution. We are endeavoring to carry out by slow degress an Imperial Constitution which shall combine this absolute equality of different communities with the machinery for the perpetual attainment of common Imperial ends.

But that great experiment was begun in its fullness only 50 years ago, within my lifetime. It will take the lifetime of many generations of statesmen all over the world in this great and scattered Empire to bring it to a full and successful fruition. It is impossible not to speculate as to how many ills would have been spared us if in 1776 those who preceded us could have foreseen the future and understood wherein the true path of political wisdom lay. Many people have plunged in endless speculations as to what would have happened if there had been no violent division between the two great sections of our people. I do not follow them in those speculations. No man can do so. No man can say what would have happened if a country which has now 100 millions of population, with infinite resources and admirable organization, had never formally been separated from these small islands. But this at all events would have happened. The separation, if and when it had occurred, would have been a friendly separation.

There would never have been a memory of the smallest kind dividing the feelings of those, every one of whose emotions moved in the same key to be directed towards the same end. That would have been a great gain. It is a loss to us in this country. I almost venture to say it might have been in some respects a loss to those of you, the great mass of my audience, who own a different allegiance. It would have been an infinite gain if there had been no memory in either of the two nations which pointed to sharp divisions, to battles lost and won, with all the evils of war, with all the evils of defeat, with all the evils, almost as great, of victory, if any sting or soreness remained behind.

If I rightly read the signs of the times, a truer perspective and a more charitable perspective is now recognized and felt by all the heirs of these sad and ancient glories. Heaven knows I do not grudge the glories of Washington and his brother soldiers. I do not shed tears over the British defeat which ended in the triumphant establishment of the American Republic. I do not express any regrets on that subject. My only regrets are that the memories of it should carry with them the smallest trace of bitterness on our side. I do not know why there should be. I think it may properly carry memories of triumph on your side, but it should be a triumph seen in its true perspective, and by this true perspective seen in such a way that it does not interfere with the continuity of history in the development of free institutions, with the consciousness of common kinship and common ideals, and the considerations which ought to bind us together, and which have bound us together, and which day by day and year by year, generation by generation, and century by century are going to bind us still closer together in the future.

Therefore I rejoice to find myself joining with my American friends in celebrating this great anniversary. Hitherto, from the necessities of history, battles that have been waged on American soil have been battles waged between peoples of the same speech and of the same traditions. In the future the ideas which, even in the moment of struggle, were always fundamentally and essentially the same, will find a sphere of action outside even the ample limits of the United States, and bind us together in a world task. That is the great thought. We are not brought together in this colossal struggle: we are not working together at this identical moment—this great and unsurpassed moment in the history of the world—aiming at narrow or selfish objects, or bound together partly by antiquated traditions. We are working together in all the freedom of great hopes and with great ideals. Those hopes and those ideals we have not learned from each other. We have them in common from a common history and from a common ancestry. We have not learnt freedom from you, nor you from us. We both spring from the same root. We both cultivate the same great aims. We both have the same hopes as regards the future of Western civilization, and now we find ourselves united in this great struggle against a Power which if it be allowed to prevail is going to destroy the very roots of that Western civilization from which we all draw our strength. We are bound together in that.

Are we not bound together forever? Will not our descendants, when they come to look back upon this unique episode in the history of the world, say that among the incalculable circumstances which it produces the most beneficent and the most permanent is, perhaps, that we are brought together and united for one common purpose in one common understanding —the two great branches of the English-speaking race? That was the theme on which the Ambassador dwelt. That is the theme which I have endeavored to develop. It is a theme which absorbs my thoughts day and night. It is a theme which moves me more, I think, than anything connected with public affairs in all my long experience. It is a theme which I hope you will dwell upon; a theme which I hope and trust you will do your best to spread abroad in all parts of the world, so that from this date onwards for all time, we who speak the common language and have these common ideals may feel that we are working not merely for ourselves individually, nor even for our joint interests, but that we are working together for the best interests of the whole of mankind and for the civilization not only of the Old World but of the New.

VISCOUNT ISHII

TO THE UNITED STATES SENATE

[Viscount Ishii visited the United States as Ambassador Extraordinary at the head of the Imperial Japanese Mission. This mission was received in the United States Senate and Viscount Ishii made the following address on August 30, 1917.]

MR. PRESIDENT AND GENTLEMEN OF THE SENATE OF THE UNITED STATES: No words at my command can give adequate expression to the profound appreciation I have of this honor you confer upon us. We know full well the exalted dignity and the proud traditions of this illustrious branch of the great Legislature of the United States; and in the name of my country, my mission, and myself, I thank you most sincerely. To accept your courteous invitation and to occupy even the smallest fraction of the time allowed for the momentous deliberation of this august body is a great responsibility—a responsibility I do not underestimate, but from which I may not shrink.

I shall not, however, abuse this rare privilege by attempting to address at length in a language of which I have but little command, trained leaders of thought and masters of argument and oratory. But I grasp this occasion to say to you that the whole people of Japan heartily welcome and profoundly appreciate the entrance of this mighty Nation of yours into the struggle against the insane despoiler of our civilization. [Applause.] We all know that you did not undertake this solemn task on the impulse of the moment, but that you threw your mighty weight into the struggle only after exercising a most admirable patience, with a firm determination that this world shall be made free from the threat of aggression, from the black shadow of a military despotism wielded by a nation taught with the mother's milk that human right must yield to brutal might. [Applause.] To us the fact that you are now on the side of the Allies in this titanic struggle constitutes already a great moral victory for our common cause, which we believe to be the cause of right and justice, for the strong as for the weak, for the great as for the small.

We of Japan believe we understand something of the American ideal of life, and we pay our most profound respects to it. Jefferson, your great democratic President, conceived the ideal of an American Commonwealth to be not a rule imposed on the people by force of arms but as a free expression of the individual sentiments of that people. Jefferson saw Americans not as a set of people huddled together under the muzzles of machine guns, but he saw them as a myriad of independent and free men, as individuals only relying on a combined military force for protection against aggression from abroad or treachery from within. He saw a community of people guided by a community of good thought and pure patriotism, using their own special talents in their own special way under their own sacred rooftrees; not a machine-made Nation, but a living, growing organism, animated by one passion—the passion of liberty. [Applause.]

I assure you, gentlemen, that the Japanese ideal of national life is, in its final analysis, not so very far removed from yours. We conceive of our nation as a vast family, held together not by the arbitrary force of armed men but by the force of a natural development. We shall call the common force that animates us a passion of loyalty to our Emperor and to our homes, as we shall call that of Americans a passion for liberty and of loyalty to their flag. [Applause.]

Blind loyalty without rational consciousness of the responsibility of self is but another name for slavery, while a right of liberty ill-conceived, ignoring the mutual human affection and respect for the rights of every man, which forms the essence of true loyalty, must be tantamount to anarchy. These two passions—passion of loyalty and passion for liberty—are they not really one? Is not the same control working in both cases—the intense desire to be true to our innermost selves and to the highest and best that has been revealed to us? You must be free to be Americans, and we must be free to be Japanese. But our common enemy is not content with this freedom for the nation or for the individual; he must force all the world to be German, too! You had hoped against hope that this was not so; but that noble hope fled and your admirable patience was exhausted. You did not then hesitate to face the issue and the foe, as you are facing it, with that great American spirit which has loved and still loves liberty, which loves the right more than peace and honor, more than life. [Applause.]

We of Japan took up arms against Germany because a solemn treaty was not to us "a scrap of paper." [Great applause.] We did not enter into this war because we had any selfish interest to promote or any ill-conceived ambition to gratify. We are in the war, we insist on being in it, and we shall stay in it, because earnestly, as a nation and as individuals, we believe in the righteousness of the cause for which we stand; because we believe that only by a complete victory for that cause can there be made a righteous, honorable, and permanent peace, so that this world may be made safe for all men to live in and so that all nations may work out their destinies untrammeled by fear. [Applause.]

Mr. President and gentlemen, whatever the critic half-informed or the hired slanderer may say against us, in forming your judgment of Japan we ask you only to use those splendid abilities that guide this great Nation. The criminal plotter against our good neighborhood takes advantage of the fact that at this time of the world's crisis many things must of necessity remain untold and unrecorded in the daily newspapers; but we are satisfied that we are doing our best. In this tremendous work, as we move together shoulder to shoulder, to a certain victory, America and Japan must have many things in which the one can help the other. We have much in common and much to do in concert. That is the reason I have been sent, and that is the reason you have received me here to-day.

I have an earnest and abiding faith that this association of ours, this proving of ourselves in the highest, most sacred, and most trying of human activities—the armed vindication of right and justice—must bring us to a still closer concord and a deeper confidence one in the other, sealing for all time the bonds of cordial friendship between our two nations.

Again I thank you. [Great applause.]

ELIHU ROOT

THE WAR AND DISCUSSION

[Address at a War Mass Meeting in the Coliseum, Chicago, September 14, 1917. Reprinted from collected addresses of Elihu Root, copyright, 1918, by Harvard University Press.]

THE declaration of war between the United States and Germany completely changed the relations of all the inhabitants of this country to the subject of peace and war.

Before the declaration everybody had a right to discuss in private and in public the question whether the United States should carry on war against Germany. Everybody had a right to argue that there was no sufficient cause for war, that the consequences of war would be worse than the consequences of continued peace, that it would be wiser to submit to the aggressions of Germany against American rights, that it would be better to have Germany succeed than to have the Allies succeed in the great conflict. Everybody holding these views had a right by expressing them to seek to influence public opinion and to affect the action of the President and the Congress, to whom the people of the country by their Constitution have entrusted the power to determine whether the United States shall or shall not make war. But the question of peace or war has now been decided by the President and Congress, the sole authorities which had the right to decide, the lawful authorities who rested under the duty to decide. The question no longer remains open. It has been determined, and the United States is at war with Germany.

The power to make such a decision is the most essential, vital, and momentous of all the powers of government. No nation can maintain its independence or protect its citizens against oppression or continue to be free, which does not vest the power to make that decision in some designated authority, or which does not recognize the special and imperative duties of citizenship in time of war following upon such a decision lawfully made. One of the cardinal objects of the union which formed this nation was to create a lawful authority whose decision and action upon this momentous question should bind all the states and all the people of every state.

The Constitution under which we have lived for a hundred and thirty years declares: "We, the people of the United States, in order to . . . provide for the common defense, promote the general welfare, and secure the blessings of liberty to ourselves and our posterity, do ordain and establish this Constitution." The Constitution so ordained vests in Congress the power to declare war, to raise and support armies, to provide and maintain a navy, and it vests in the President the power to command the army and navy. The power in this instance was exercised not suddenly or rashly, but advisedly, after a long delay and discussion, and patience under provocation, after repeated diplomatic warnings to Germany known to the whole country, after clear notice by breach of diplomatic relations with Germany that the question was imminent, after long opportunity for reflection and discussion following that notice, and after a formal and deliberate presentation by the President to Congress of the reason for action, in an address which compelled the attention not of Congress alone, but of all Americans and of all the world, and which must forever stand as one of the great state papers of modern times. The decision was made by overwhelming majorities of both houses of Congress. When such a decision has been made, the duties—and therefore the rights—of all the people of the country immediately change. It becomes their duty to stop discussion upon the question decided, and to act, to proceed immediately to do everything in their power to enable the government of their country to succeed in the war upon which the country has entered.

It is a fundamental necessity of government that it shall have the power to decide great questions of policy, and to act upon its decision. In order that there shall be action following a decision once made, the decision must be accepted. Discussion upon the question must be deemed closed. A nation which declares war and goes on discussing whether it ought to have declared war or not is impotent, paralyzed, imbecile, and earns the contempt of mankind, and the certainty of humiliating defeat and subjection to foreign control. A democracy which cannot accept its own decisions made in accordance with its own laws, but must keep on endlessly discussing the questions already decided, has failed in the fundamental requirements of self-government; and, if the decision is to make war, the failure to exhibit capacity for self-government by action will inevitably result in the loss of the right of self-government. Before the decision of a proposal to make war, men may range themselves upon one side or the other of the question; but, after the decision in favor of war, the country has ranged itself, and the only issue left for the individual citizen to decide is whether he is for or against his country. From that time on, arguments against the war in which the country is engaged are enemy arguments. Their spirit is the spirit of rebellion against the government and laws of the United States. Their effect is to hinder and lessen that popular support of the government in carrying on the war which is necessary to success. Their manifest purpose is to prevent action by continuing discussion. They encourage the enemy. They tend to introduce delay and irresolution into our own councils. The men who are to-day speaking and writing and printing arguments against the war, and against everything which is being done to carry on the war, are rendering more effective service to Germany than they ever could render in the field with arms in their hands. The purpose and effect of what they are doing are so plain that it is impossible to resist the conclusion that the greater part of them are at heart traitors to the United States, and are willfully seeking to bring about the triumph of Germany and the humiliation and defeat of their own country.

The same principles apply to the decision of numerous questions which arise in carrying on the war. Somebody must decide such questions before there can be action, and, when they are decided, the action can be only in accordance with the decision. You may be opposed to raising an army in one way, and I may be opposed to raising it in another way; and so long as the question is undecided, we are entitled to try to get our own views about it adopted; but we do not have the decision. The whole of the American people have elected a President and Congress to listen to your views and to mine, and then to decide the question. When they have decided, and a law has been passed which provides for raising part of the army by voluntary enlistment and part of the army by conscription, it is plain that the only way in which we can raise an army and go on with the war is by accepting that decision, and following that law; and any attempt to discourage volunteering or to oppose conscription is an attempt to hinder and embarrass the Government of the United States in the conduct of the war, and to help Germany by preventing our Government from raising armies to fight against her.

Somebody has to decide where armies are to fight, whether our territory is to be defended by waiting here until we are attacked, or by going out and attacking the enemy before they get here. The power to make that decision and the duty to make it rest, under the Constitution of this country, with the President as Commander-in-Chief. When the President has decided that the best way to beat Germany is to send our troops to France and Belgium, that is the way the war must be carried on, if at all. I think the decision was wise. Others may think it unwise. But when the decision has been made, what we think is immaterial. The Commander-in-Chief, with all the advice and all the wisdom he can command, has decided when and where the American army is to move. The army must obey, and all loyal citizens of the country will do their utmost to make that movement a success. Anybody who seeks by argument or otherwise to stop the execution of the order sending troops to France and Belgium is simply trying to prevent the American Government from carrying on the war successfully. He is aiding the enemies of his country; and, if he understands what he is really doing, he is a traitor at heart.

It is beyond doubt that many of the professed pacifists, the opponents of the war after the war has been entered upon, the men who are trying to stir up resistance to the draft, the men who are inciting strikes in the particular branches of production which are necessary for the supply of arms and munitions of war, are intentionally seeking to aid Germany and to defeat the United States. As time goes on, and the character of these acts becomes more and more clearly manifest, all who continue to associate with them must come under the same condemnation as traitors to their country.

There are doubtless some who do not understand what this struggle really is. Some who were born here resent interference with their comfort and prosperity, and the demands for sacrifice which seem to them unnecesary, and they fail to see that the time has come when, if Americans are to keep the independence and liberty which their fathers won by suffering and sacrifice, they in turn must fight again for the preservation of that independence and that liberty. There are some born abroad who have come to this land for a greater freedom and broader opportunities, and have sought and received the privilege of American citizenship, who are swayed by dislike for some ally or by the sympathies of German kinship, and fail to see that the time has come for them to make good the obligations of their sworn oaths of naturalization. This is the oath that the applicant for citizenship makes:

That he will support the Constitution of the United States, and that he absolutely and entirely renounces and abjures all allegiance and fidelity to any foreign prince, potentate, state, or sovereignty; . . . that he will support and defend the Constitution and laws of the United States against all enemies, foreign and domestic, and bear true faith and allegiance to the same.

All these naturalized citizens who are taking part in this obstruction to our Government in the conduct of the war are false to their oaths, are forfeiting their rights of citizenship, are repudiating their honorable obligations, are requiting by evil the good that has been done them in the generous and unstinted hospitality with which the people of the United States have welcomed them to the liberty and the opportunities of this free land. We must believe that in many cases this is done because of a failure to understand what this war really is.

This is a war of defense. It is perfectly described in the words of the Constitution which established this nation: "To provide for the common defense," and "To secure the blessings of liberty to ourselves and our posterity." The national defense demands not merely force, but intelligence. It requires foresight, consideration of the policies and purposes of other nations, understanding of the inevitable or probable consequences of the acts of other nations, judgment as to the time when successful defense may be made, and when it will be too late, and prompt action before it is too late. By entering this war in April, the United States availed itself of the very last opportunity to defend itself against subjection to German power before it was too late to defend itself successfully.

[Mr. Root discussed further German aggression and methods and then concluded as follows:]

The history, the character, the avowed principles of action, the manifest and undisguised purposes of the German autocracy, made it clear and certain that if America stayed out of the great war, and Germany won, America would forthwith be required to defend herself, and would be unable to defend herself against the same lust for conquest, the same will to dominate the world, which has made Europe a bloody shambles.

When Germany did actually apply her principles of action to us; when by invasion of Belgium she had violated the solemn covenant she had made with us to observe the law of neutrality established for the protection of peaceful states; when she had arrogantly demanded that American commerce should surrender its lawful right of passage upon the high seas under penalty of destruction; when she had sunk American ships and sent to their death hundreds of American citizens, peaceful men, women, and children, when the *Gulflight* and the *Falaba* and the *Persia* and the *Arabic* and the *Sussex* and the *Lusitania* had been torpedoed without warning in contempt of law and of humanity; when the German Embassy at Washington had been found to be the headquarters of a vast conspiracy of corruption within our country, inciting sedition and concealing infernal machines in the cargoes of ships, and blowing up our factories with the workmen laboring in them; and when the Government of Germany had been discovered attempting to incite Mexico and Japan to form a league with her to attack us, and to bring about a dismemberment of our territory; then the question presented to the American people was not what shall be done regarding each of these specific aggressions taken by itself, but what shall be done by America to defend her commerce, her territory, her citizens, her independence, her liberty, her life as a nation, against the continuance of assaults already begun by that mighty and conscienceless power which has swept aside every restraint and every principle of Christian civilization, and is seeking to force upon a subjugated world the dark and cruel rule of a barbarous past. The question was, how shall peaceful and unprepared and liberty-loving America save herself from subjection to the military power of Germany?

There was but one possible answer. There was but one chance for rescue, and that was to act at once, while the other democracies of the world were still maintaining their liberty against the oppressor; to prepare at once while the armies and the navies of England and France and Italy and Russia and Rumania were holding down Germany so that she could not attack us while our preparation was but half accomplished, to strike while there were allies loving freedom like ourselves to strike with us, to do our share to prevent the German Kaiser from acquiring that domination over the world which would have left us without friends to aid us, without preparation, and without the possibility of successful defense.

The instinct of the American democracy which led it to act when it did arose from a long-delayed and reluctant consciousness still vague and half-expressed, that this is no ordinary war which the world is waging. It is no contest for petty policies and profits. It is a mighty and all-embracing struggle between two conflicting principles of human right and human duty. It is a conflict between the divine right of kings to govern mankind through armies and nobles, and the right of the peoples of the earth who toil and endure and aspire, to govern themselves by law and justice, and in the freedom of individual manhood. It is the climax of the supreme struggle between autocracy and democracy. No nation can stand aside and be free from its effects. The two systems cannot endure together in the same world. If autocracy triumphs, military power, lustful of dominion, supreme in strength, intolerant of human rights, holding itself above the reach of law, superior to morals, to faith, to compassion, will crush out the free democracies of the world. If autocracy is defeated and nations are compelled to recognize the rule of law and of morals, then and then only will democracy be safe.

To this great conflict for human rights and human liberty,

America has committed herself. There can be no backward step. There must be either humiliating and degrading submission, or terrible defeat, or glorious victory. It was no human will that brought us to this pass. It was not the President. It was not Congress. It was not the press. It was not any political party. It was not any section or part of our people. It was the fact that in the providence of God the mighty forces that determine the destinies of mankind beyond the control of human purpose have brought to us the time, the occasion, the necessity, that this peaceful people so long enjoying the blessings of liberty and justice for which their fathers fought and sacrificed, shall again gird themselves for conflict, and with all the forces of manhood nurtured and strengthened by liberty, offer again the sacrifice of possessions and of life itself, that this nation may still be free, that the mission of American democracy shall not have failed, that the world shall be free.

NEWTON DIEHL BAKER
THE MARCH TOWARD LIBERTY

[On October 8, 1917, Secretary Baker made the following address before a Liberty Loan Meeting at Keith's Theater in Washington. Mr. Baker says of his addresses, "They were delivered extemporaneously and without any other preparation than constant occupation on the subjects with which they deal. They are the spontaneous reflections of the Secretary of War upon the social, economic and personal aspects of the War waged by democracy." Reprinted from "Frontiers of Freedom" by Newton D. Baker, copyright, 1918, by George H. Doran Company.]

Newton Diehl Baker was born at Martinsburg, West Virginia, in 1871. He graduated from Johns Hopkins in 1894. He was Mayor of Cleveland, Ohio, from 1912-14 and 1914-16. In 1916 he was appointed Secretary of War by President Wilson and served until 1921.]

IN this center of the nation's activity; in this city, which since we went into this war has perhaps doubled in population; in this city where the once peaceful beauty of a quiet capital has given place to almost feverish preparation and activity, there seems to be obvious lessons on every street and in every house, of the character of the task which the nation has assumed; and yet it is not inappropriate that a few words should be said that will give some comprehension, perhaps, of the size of that task and bring home its patriotic lesson to the people who are privileged to live thus close to the center of the nation's life.

For a thousand years, children will read in their books of history and the literature of the world will be enriched with the poetry and romance growing out of this age in which we live. The stories which will then be told are the history which is now being made, and I delight, in moments of idleness, to try to project myself into that remote and distant future and see the bent figure of some school-boy as he pores over the history of this period; I think I can detect even in a boy so remote from the action of this time, the surge of enthusiasm in the things that the world is now doing.

I shall not undertake in the very brief time allotted for this address, to recount the history of the European War prior to our entrance into it nor the occasion for our entrance. But if there be anything certain about a contemporaneous estimate of the historical facts, the verdict of history will be that this, the first great free nation of the world—in this age the greatest nation in the world, in material resources, and in the progress she has made—was also the greatest nation on the face of the earth at this time in her moral quality and in the superb patience with which she endeavored to avert this catastrophe.

For long and weary months, with our minds daily harrowed and our hearts nightly torn with the stories of destruction, devastation, cruelty and despoliation of peoples everywhere, we still hoped against hope that the war could be brought to a conclusion, just to mankind and promising for future progress, without the unsheathing of our sword.

When, finally, after one bitter evidence had accumulated upon another, and we realized that this was really the final war of two great philosophies; and when we as Americans realized that the nations fighting on what we now call our side were really children of our spirit and baptized with the notion of liberty which we had fostered in this country for over a hundred years; and when we realized that England, France, Italy and Russia were fighting the battle not for selfish aggrandizement, but for liberty and opportunity, and for the philosophy of democracy on the part of the whole world, it became necessary for us to join with them in order to vindicate that philosophy.

On the bottom of the pathless ocean lie now the bones and the bodies of American men, women and children slain while we were still neutral, in defiance of every law that man ever ordained for the limitation of the horrors of war. Our special grievance was only the occasion, and now that we are entered in this great conflict, we realize, with an inspiration that I think must fire every man, that this is merely the second stage in the march of the human race toward liberty. It began in 1776. In 1917 we pass the next milestone, and when it is passed, men and women everywhere will realize that no return of the Darker

Age is possible; that victory has been won in this contest, autocracy having been demonstrated as too wasteful and too regardless of human life and human treasure to be tolerated, and democracy having been demonstrated to be not only the source of fruitful happiness and opportunity in time of peace, but to contain in itself the strength to survive. Having thus demonstrated the feebleness and viciousness of the principle of autocracy and the virility and salvation of the principle of democracy, we will start from a fresh platform with a new idea of its possibilities and a new hold upon permanent liberty and democratic institutions.

As a result, this country presents a strange but inspiring spectacle. I have had some opportunity at Washington to participate in the formulation of plans, and out of Washington, I have had some opportunity to see the fruition of those plans. In sixteen places in this country cities have been built, as it seems, over night, housing great multitudes of peoples—thirty and forty thousand young men selected out of the body of our men; not in response to a sudden impulse of the military power, but selected by the civilian agencies of our people and presented to our government to be trained as a great army to participate in this reconquest of the world's liberty. Thus great cities have been built.

Where we used to spend five, ten or fifteen millions of dollars, we are now spending money that counts up in the billions. We are financing to some extent those associated with us in this war who have been long bearing the drain and strain of continuous warfare. We are spending money for munitions of war and for supplies, and our factories are responding with extraordinary energy. In workshops, factories, stores, the people of America have associated themselves in this great enterprise until our nation, our peaceful and peace-loving nation, is to-day knit together in spirit, more harmonious in its aspirations, more effective in its occupations. We are more of a nation to-day than we have been at any time in the whole hundred years and more of our glorious history.

I have stood at those camps and watched the boys who are preparing to be soldiers. I have seen them stream past by tens of thousands; some of them fresh-called to the colors from homes in remote places, far from the great rush of the world's events, some of them students from colleges; some of them engineers, men of occupations, professions, science; and as I have seen those youthful faces I have had a new realization of the springs of national action. As I saw those men I could not persuade myself that all of them were deeply read in the history of the world; I could not persuade myself that they knew the ultimate nature of this conflict of freedom with autocracy in the world; but there they marched with the sun shining on their faces, with flushed health in their cheeks, determination and a heroic quality about them that simply pervaded the atmosphere. And I realized that it is not necessary for a man to be a philosopher or a scholar to be a patriot, that there is something subtle in the very character of our soil that goes into the system of those born on it, and that this great army of young men reaching from the Pacific to the Atlantic, and now streaming across the Atlantic are men who possess that subtle quality and are filled with the spirit of patriotism, and that when our forces actually join with those on the other side the great battle will be won.

And that schoolboy a thousand years from now who reads the history of this age will read with admiration and throbbing heart of France—leader in the world's civilization, that country through which Guizot said every great idea had to pass in order that it might be familiarized to the world—he will read of that France, not prepared for this sort of struggle, devoting herself to the redemption of her freedom and protection of her soul. When he comes to her glorious victory at the Marne, he will experience such a thrill as we used to feel as we read the story of Thermopylæ and Marathon. And when he comes to read of England he will have a realization of the English people which I think is slowly being brought home to us all. The English people speak of themselves as "muddling through"; but that schoolboy a thousand years from now will promptly see that that nation, with its terrible patience, was able to wait and coördinate its military and industrial strength until it arrived at a point, when it could and did, with the clocklike regularity, beat back the foe.

Then he will come to our entrance into the war, and coupling it up with what he has been reading before, he will go back to the origin of our liberty and see the people of this continent, having wrought out their own civilization, having elevated the individual man to a new dignity in world affairs, join the others, and he will realize that the victory will belong to the heroic quality of these united races.

He will ask whether all the war, all the victory was won at the front. He will find that war had become of such a quality that the fighting men are but part of a nation's army, that there is required to be at home in the field the grower of food and in the factory the maker of products, in order that the men at the front may fight; and that underlying the whole structure is the financial stability and the financial willingness of the people to fight the fight.

And so, with this opportunity to subscribe to Liberty Bonds, we are appealing now to the very foundation of the nation's strength and the indispensable thing upon which its activities must rest, and we ask the people of the United States to sacrifice. I have had, since I have been Secretary of War, thousands of letters from high-spirited men and women all over the United States, from children nine and ten years old to men eighty and ninety, asking me "Where can I do my bit? What sacrifice can I make to advance this cause?" Some are too young and some are too old to fight, but none are too old or too young to sacrifice in this great financial effort, which is the basis upon which all must rest.

I can see victory ahead of us; a victory in arms, it is true, but a higher victory than that. I can see the American spirit, the unselfish, uncorrupted, untainted spirit of America with which we have gone into this struggle, dominant in the world as the result of that victory. I can see the peace that is to be made as the result of this great struggle; and it is a peace which brings us no selfish advantage, no national monopoly of the goods of the world, the possession of nobody else's goods and fortunes as the outcome, but an enkindling of a new spirit of justice; a peace after which the nations of the earth will join hands in harmonious coöperation rather than in selfish, deadly preparation for mutual destruction. And in order that there may be a war fought to a victorious conclusion, a peace so high and beneficent as that, those who are carrying forward this campaign ask you to pour out your money, not at the feet of the God of War, but into the lap of the Goddess of Liberty.

FRANKLIN K. LANE

THE MESSAGE OF THE WEST

[Franklin K. Lane (born in 1864, died in 1921) was Secretary of the Interior during the Wilson Administration. He has already been represented in "Modern Eloquence" by two speeches in Volume VII. The address which follows was made in Philadelphia, Oct. 18, 1917. Reprinted by permission from "The American Spirit" by Franklin K. Lane. Copyright, 1918, by Frederick A. Stokes Company.]

I HAVE just returned from a three weeks' trip throughout the West. I went from Louisiana through Oklahoma, Kansas, Colorado, Wyoming, Utah, Idaho, to Oregon. My journey was one of curiosity. I had been told that somewhere in far distant reaches of the continent the men and women of our country were disloyal to their flag, or at least that they did not think enough of to it to fight for it. Washington, as some of you know, is a strange place. It is a cup, a valley surrounded by a horseshoe of mountains into which, by some strange law, the miasmic vapors of the country drop and set up strange states of mind. I was told in Washington that the only section of this country which was enlightened and patriotic enough to understand the deep significance of this war and to be willing to sacrifice for it was that fortunate section which borders on the Atlantic Ocean; that out beyond the hills to the westward were to be found limitless plains upon which lived those who, like some Buddhist monks of whom I have read, sat throughout the days in silent and solemn contemplation, their eyes centered on the pits of their stomachs, never looking up at the sky nor out upon the fields, and never hearing the voice of the world as it passed by—self-centered, flabby, spiritless. And so I went out beyond these western hills to find these strange creatures at this time. There are many hills between the Atlantic and the Pacific, and as I crossed one range after another I was told " If there are any such people they are beyond the other range," until I came to the sea that looks out upon China. And I did not find those for whom I sought. I came back with the feeling that it was a good thing to leave Washington once in a while. This is a very great country that we live in. To know how great it is and to know its spirit one must not rest long in any one spot.

I went to Oklahoma. There I had been told that I would find the very seat and center of hostility to the Government. I found there a few misled tenant farmers had objected to the draft. When I asked what reason they gave they said New York had brought on the war, and New York should make the fight. But that was not the spirit of Oklahoma, not nearly so much the spirit of Oklahoma as the draft riots were the spirit of New York in '63. There is one town of 5,000 people in Oklahoma who bought $275,000 worth of Liberty Bonds, more than one fifty-dollar bond for each inhabitant, man, woman and child, and who raised $18,000 for the Red Cross, more than three dollars and a half for each inhabitant of the town. That does not look like slacking. After a meeting in Tusla a man came to me, dressed in a blue jumper and overalls, and said: "Mr. Lane, I am doing my bit. I have six children, four boys and two girls. The four boys are in the Army and the two girls are Red Cross nurses, and I am saving to buy a Liberty Bond." That does not look like slacking either. In Salt Lake City I reviewed the newly organized troops, and the grandson of Brigham Young, who is a colonel of one of the regiments, pointed with justifiable pride to one of the companies that passed and said: "Every boy in that company has bought a Liberty Bond. They are not only willing to fight but they are willing to pay for their own support while they are fighting." In Idaho, ex-Governor Hawley took me into his library, and showed me the picture of four boys upon the wall, his sons, and said: "I am left all alone. All those boys have gone into the war." In Portland, Oregon, they told me that not one man had been drafted from that county, because the full quota of the county had been filled by men who volunteered for the regular army or militia. That is the spirit of the West. Kipling says that "East is East and West is West," but I say to you that there is neither East nor West to this country. It is one, bound by a common determination to win this war.

Another thing I found was that the people of the United States have entire confidence in President Woodrow Wilson, the Commander-in-Chief of the Army and the Navy. They believe that the President knows how to make war and when to make peace. They know that he is honest and that their money will not be wasted. They know that in the conduct of the war he has arisen above partisanship, above politics, into the high, clear air of patriotic statesmanship. The men that he asks for and the money that he asks for they will give. They may not know the intricacies of international law or the fine points of national pride, and may not even realize the significance to themselves and to the world of this momentous contest, but they know that President Wilson endured with patience, and came to his judgment solemnly and slowly. And they will follow wherever he leads and at the pace he wishes to go. They have seen moving pictures of the President marching at the head of the parade when the men from Washington marched to Fort Myer, and they like his stride.

We are an impatient people. There are some who cannot understand why we do not have a million men in France at this moment. And when we ask them: "How would you get them there? Where are the ships to carry them? Where are the ships to munition them? Where are the ships to support them?" they have no answer. "We should have the ships," they say. I remember that Secretary McAdoo three years ago, within a month after the war broke out in Europe, advocated the construction of a great fleet of merchant ships by the Government or under Government guaranty. And if there was a voice raised in this city in favor of that program I failed to hear it. But we are going to have those ships. By next spring we will have one million tons of new shipping. By then we are promised the equivalent of two 5,000-ton steamships per day, to continue indefinitely. And after the war we will restore the American flag to the seven seas of the world and enter into a generous rivalry with all Europe to sell our goods stamped "Made in America."

We are a critical people. Each one of us knows best how a thing should be done. Now I have no doubt that we have made mistakes and will make mistakes in preparation for and in the conduct of the war. There never yet was a railroad laid in the United States that did not have to have its lines changed after construction. Let me say this bluntly to you, that if this huge and unparalleled job cannot be done it will be because there are not men in the United States who can do it, for we have not hesitated to call upon those men who have proved themselves in the conduct of the greatest enterprises on this continent,—railroad presidents, engineers, chemists, contractors, manufacturers, inventors. The brains of the United states are involved in the conduct of this war. We have asked no man whether he is a Republican or a Democrat. We have not sought to know whether he was rich or poor. If he would serve the Nation at this time he was our man. And it is a matter of the profoundest pride to me and to every one who knows the facts that the business men of this country have not waited for the call but have volunteered in overwhelming numbers to give of their time and their capacity, without compensation, in this hour of the Government's need.

There is no thought throughout the country that we will not succeed either in raising the money or the men that we need. This country has no doubt of itself. It is the creature of faith. It is greater than any man and greater than any group of men. It is a great adventurous spirit. No man can look as I have done during the last three weeks on the enterprise and the industry and the wealth of this country and think for one moment that we can fail. I have passed through mile after mile of blazing forges. I have seen a solid mountain of the richest copper handled with a steam shovel. I have seen land that yielded sixty bushels of wheat to the acre and more land that yielded four hundred bushels of potatoes to the acre. We will not let our allies starve. We will not let them go without shot for their guns.

This task upon which we are engaged, it must be remembered, is the greatest enterprise that any nation has ever undertaken. For we have not only had to create an army, but we have had to help in the financing of four of the greatest nations of the world, to aid in the reconstruction of their railroads, in supplying them with munitions and with food, and this at a distance of more than three thousand miles. We have had to stimulate our own industries and our own agriculture. We have had to make plans for saving food and saving money, for the protection of our own people as well as others against profiteering. Each day there have been prophecies of failure, but our Navy patrols the sea, and not a man has been lost on his way to France; our Army is housed, clothed, and is in the field drilling, and we are getting rifles for them at the rate of fifteen thousand a day.

The message that the West sends to you is this: Have faith in your country, have faith in your Government, remember that prophecies of evil always fail in the United States. Whatever the temporary conditions may be, the man who is the thoroughbred wins out. We are but beginning to learn the art of coöperation in the United States. We have not exercised the powers as a government that can be exercised for the support and maintenance of the great enterprises and industries of the country which are its arteries, its hands and feet. Go out over the western hills and you will come back, as I have come back, without depression, with a heart full of confidence in the robust spirit, the manly determination and the fine idealism of our people, as well as in their ability to put at the service of the world the unending resources of this great continent. The stock ticker is not a stalwart boy in khaki, filled with courage and proud to do his bit for a country that he loves —no, the stock ticker is a nervous old man who sometimes thinks himself the master of the world and again fears his own shadow. It has not conscience, courage or vision. It may be a thermometer but it is not a seer.

I am here to ask your help in the name of the President and the Secretary of the Treasury in the sale of the new issue of liberty bonds. Our appeal on behalf of the nation is to the people of the nation. This is a fight for Democracy, and we are following democratic methods. A war for Democracy should be supported by the money of Democracy.

We have drafted our young men into our army. The son of the millionaire stands to-day in the ranks alongside the son of the drayman, the lawyer alongside his own baker. We have made no preference and drawn no line of distinction, and when these same men "go over the top" the guns of the enemy will show no preference and draw no distinctions. This nation has been summoned to arms in a cause that is right, and every man and every woman will serve their country in this contest. There is not so much credit in giving our money as in giving our lives, but in a war which is the organized industrialism of all nations the giving of life will be idle without the guns, the food, the aëroplanes, the trains, the ships, the factories—all these resources which money can command. One-half of the men now in camp are volunteers, militia or regular army men; the other half of them drafted. And this same method, a combination of compulsion and voluntary offering, we are following as to our finances. Some of our revenues we take by the stern mandate of the law in the form of taxes, the rest we ask for as a loan from our people.

This war is costing not less than one hundred million dollars a day, but this is the least of its cost. There are five million hospital beds in Europe. These beds have been filled three times since this war began. Fifteen million men, the stalwarts of Europe, have passed over them, and ten millions, blind, armless, or shattered wrecks and remnants of men will live in Europe for years to come to testify to the horrors of this war. Nine million men, three times the number of men the North and South sent into our Civil War, have been killed. And all because a few men who are masters of Germany determined that Germany was to be the master of the world.

This is to be a grim time for us. Let us not delude ourselves or carry any false illusions that the righteousness of our cause, the injustice done to us, the vastness of our resources, or the greatness of our man-power will so touch or overawe the enemy as to make them seek a peace that will make this world safe for Democracy until those who have forced this fight realize that with the world against them they cannot win. Lloyd George said the other day that the United States had never fought a war that it had not won. He might have added that we never fought a war in which we did not know that we were right. This war, however, is to be a supreme test. We are to test the fiber of our people; we are to test our ability to coöperate; we are to test our sense of nationalism; we are to test our loyalty to Democracy; we are to test to the ultimate the resources of our nation, the capacity of our mines and miners, of our farms and farmers, of our mills and millhands. We are to test our vision and the greatness of our own minds—whether we are worthy of a large future or wedded to a little life; we are to test our own conception of this country and its relation to the world.

What is to be the future of the United States? It was not in the nature of things that we could remain isolated. It was our hope that this might be so, but seas have narrowed and interests have been so twisted and intertwined, and our rights are so identical with the right of others that the world had become before this war a great Brotherhood. We made rules to control this relationship. Each people was to determine for itself what its own internal policy should be.

It was not for us to say that the form of government which best pleased us should be adopted by others. But it was for us to say that, notwithstanding we were a democracy, notwithstanding our isolated position, removed from the European and Asiatic world of struggle, we must be treated with full national honors and rights. The first condition of that Brotherhood was that each member of it should regard his given word as a pledge upon which turned his right to recognition and fraternity. Upon entering into this war, Germany violated that pledge by the invasion of Belgium. She tore her treaty up and gave notice to the world that her war necessities were superior to her national word. That was a shock to the conscience of every people. But we stood neutral because we did not realize then, as we did later, that this act was but an evidence of a policy which must sooner or later affect rights in which we were vitally interested. We saw the German army march to within fifty miles of Paris, until old Marshal Joffre stood on the Marne and said: "This has gone far enough." We made no protest at the invasion of the country which had followed our lead into democracy. Then Germany turned to the seas. She sank our boats loaded with American grain, and we contented ourselves with a protest. She sank the *Lusitania* carrying American civilians. We protested that the seas belonged to us as much as to her; that for a thousand years the lives of civilians had been regarded as sacred, even though on an enemy ship. And no apology came. One after another our ships went down and the ships of other neutral nations. Lives by the hundreds were lost. She promised to respect our rights, but after a time, when she had become ready to carry on in more ruthless fashion her predatory war upon the seas, we found that this promise was as worthless to us as her promise to Belgium had been to her. Then, by the power vested in it by the Constitution, Congress declared that war had been made upon us and accepted the challenge which Germany had thrown down. We were no longer to be regarded as a nation of cowards who would not enforce recognition of what all nations had conceded to be our rights. There is no appeal from that decision. It is idle to argue to-day as to the cause of the war. It is equally idle to argue that we should not have entered the war. We have made our decision and we are going forward. We know that we are right. Our conscience would have convicted us of cowardice if we had longer withheld the assertion of our power.

But this war has grown away from a mere invasion of our rights. It is to-day a contest between the principle of empire and the principle of democracy—a contest between the few who believe in government by the soldier and the many who believe in government by the people. It is a contest between those who believe that men are made to serve the government and those who believe that government is made to serve the people. It is a contest between those who believe that the purpose of a government is to enrich itself by extending its boundaries through the use of force, and those who believe that the purpose of government is to insure to the people life, liberty, and the pursuit of happiness. Two systems are in conflict here. The one has come down to us from Cæsar. It believes in mastery, in fear, in power. The other is the outgrowth of a Christian civilization. It believes that no man or set of men have been created by God to master all men.

Why is the world against Germany? Germany does not know that the time of empires and emperors is past. She does not know that the day of arbitrary might has gone by. She will not play the Twentieth Century game under Twentieth Century rules. She asks for friendship, but she dishonors her friends by asking them to do things which they should not do. There was no country more willing to remain neutral than the Argentine Republic. Yet Germany's minister asks the Swedish minister to convey messages to Germany which outline a policy of ruthlessness upon the sea against that Republic which offends the sensibilities of mankind. You say to me that Germany was not hostile to the United States. How can any such statement be made in the face of the Zimmermann note, in which Germany, while we are still at peace with her, called upon Mexico as her friend to invade our territory, promising her as reward part of our own lands and attempting to induce her to involve Japan with her in war against us.

Is a nation at peace with us whose ambassador asks from his country money with which to influence our Congress, as was shown by the recent Bernstorff cable to his government? With what contempt must the government of Germany look upon the American people when they think that our Congress can be made to do as she wills and not as our people will? Government by fear is not to be the master of this earth. If Germany succeeds, that is the only kind of government we will know. We will sail the seas by her consent, carrying our goods where she permits. We will live with a country filled with spies and with our national capital undermined by foreign intrigue. We will never be sure of the word that nations give to us. We will endure life with the horrors of another such war constantly in our minds. We will pay taxes unending and huge to support an army which we do not want but must have. Our sons will be raised with the constant thought in their minds that theirs is not the mission to reclaim the land, to dig the mine, to carry out the experiment, to lay the railroad, to lead the minds of men, to master the forces of unwilling nature; for, from this hope, this dream of usefulness, they may any day be turned aside by the stern necessity of self-protection; and their wives may be raised with the picture continually before their eyes of what has befallen the Belgian women. This is not a life for a self-respecting people. We must know where we are and what our standing is and what our future may be. We must know that we have rights upon this world—rights that do not depend upon sufferance, rights that we can assert. And we must know that while we observe the common laws that govern mankind and keep our pledged word, no nation has in its mind the purpose to make us subject to a government

THE MESSAGE OF THE WEST

that is not of our own making. This is the foundation stone of Americanism.

I ask you, as volunteers in the service of your country, to help in the successful prosecution of this war. I know no people more capable of contributing in small amounts and large to the replenishing of our national treasury. We do not ask for gifts; we are not giving money to our foreign friends—we are making loans to them, and you are making loans to yourselves.

I ask you to do this in the name of our Commander-in-Chief, who sits in the White House, meeting from day to day the problems of conducting the greatest enterprise upon which this Nation has ever been engaged. His is the master mind of our world; he is the leader of liberal thought the world around.

We need your money! Give to your President your silver and gold that he may fashion it into a great spear, and with it overthrow the champion of the Divine Right of Kings, the principle which enables the few to enslave the many. Let Philadelphia be true to her past, and her future is assured!

WOODROW WILSON

THE FOURTEEN POINTS

[The terms upon which Germany could obtain peace were given to the world by President Wilson before the Congress in joint session on January 8, 1918. With Lloyd George's similar utterance it laid the war aims of the Entente Allies for the first time clearly before the world. Though there was some criticism over the alleged vagueness of some of the terms, the press throughout the United States supported him with striking unanimity, and there was an almost unprecedented outpouring of favorable comment in all the Allied countries. Later the fourteen terms, with the exception of the second, were accepted by Great Britain, France, and the defeated nations as a basis for the peace negotiations.]

GENTLEMEN OF THE CONGRESS: Once more, as repeatedly before, the spokesmen of the Central Empires have indicated their desire to discuss the objects of the war and the possible basis of a general peace. Parleys have been in progress at Brest-Litovsk between Russian representatives and representatives of the Central Powers to which the attention of all the belligerents has been invited for the purpose of ascertaining whether it may be possible to extend these parleys into a general conference with regard to terms of peace and settlement. The Russian representatives presented not only a perfectly definite statement of the principles upon which they would be willing to conclude peace, but also an equally definite program of the concrete application of those principles. The representatives of the Central Powers, on their part, presented an outline of settlement which, if much less definite, seemed susceptible of liberal interpretation until their specific program of practical terms was added. That program proposed no concessions at all, either to the sovereignty of Russia or to the preferences of the population with whose fortunes it dealt, but meant, in a word, that the Central Empires were to keep every foot of territory their armed forces had occupied—every province, every city, every point of vantage—as a permanent addition to their territories and their power. It is a reasonable conjecture that the general principles of settlement which they at first suggested originated with the more liberal statesmen of Germany and Austria, the men who have begun to feel the force of their own peoples' thought and purpose, while the concrete terms of actual settlement came from the military leaders who have no thought but to keep what they have got. The negotiations have been broken off. The Russian representatives were sincere and in earnest. They cannot entertain such proposals of conquest and domination.

The whole incident is full of significance. It is also full of perplexity. With whom are the Russian representatives dealing? For whom are the representatives of the Central Empires speaking? Are they speaking for the majorities of their respective Parliaments or for the minority parties, that military and imperialistic minority which has so far dominated their whole policy and controlled the affairs of Turkey and of the Balkan States, which have felt obliged to become their associates in this war? The Russian representatives have insisted, very justly, very wisely, and in the true spirit of modern democracy that the conferences they have been holding with the Teutonic and Turkish statesmen should be held within open, not closed, doors, and all the world has been audience, as was desired. To whom have we been listening, then? To those who speak the spirit and intention of the resolutions of the German Reichstag of the 9th of July last, the spirit and intention of the liberal leaders and parties of Germany, or to those who resist and defy that spirit and intention and insist upon conquest and subjugation? Or are we listening in fact, to both, unreconciled and in open and hopeless contradiction? These are very serious and pregnant questions. Upon the answer to them depends the peace of the world.

But whatever the results of the parleys at Brest-Litovsk, whatever the confusions of counsel and of purpose in the utterances of the spokesmen of the Central Empires, they have again attempted to acquaint the world with their objects in the war and have again challenged their adversaries to say what their objects are and what sort of settlement they would deem just and satisfactory. There is no good reason why that challenge should not be responded to, and responded to with the utmost candor. We did not wait for it. Not once, but again and again we have laid our whole thought and purpose before the world, not in general terms only, but each time with sufficient definition to make it clear what sort of definite terms of settlement must necessarily spring out of them. Within the last week Mr. Lloyd George has spoken with admirable candor and in admirable spirit for the people and Government of Great Britain. There is no confusion of counsel among the adversaries of the Central Powers, no uncertainty of principle, no vagueness of detail. The only secrecy of counsel, the only lack of fearless frankness, the only failure to make definite statement of the objects of the war, lies with Germany and her allies. The issues of life and death hang upon these definitions. No statesman who has the least conception of his responsibility ought for a moment to permit himself to continue this tragical and appalling outpouring of blood and treasure unless he is sure beyond a peradventure that the objects of the vital sacrifice are part and parcel of the very life of society and that the people for whom he speaks think them right and imperative as he does.

There is, moreover, a voice calling for these definitions of principle and of purpose which is, it seems to me, more thrilling and more compelling than any of the many moving voices with which the troubled air of the world is filled. It is the voice of the Russian people. They are prostrate and all but helpless, it would seem, before the grim power of Germany, which has hitherto known no relenting and no pity. Their power apparently is shattered. And yet their soul is not subservient. They will not yield either in principle or in action. Their conception of what is right, of what is humane and honorable for them to accept, has been stated with a frankness, a largeness of view, a generosity of spirit, and a universal human sympathy which must challenge the admiration of every friend of mankind; and they have refused to compound their ideals or desert others that they themselves may be safe. They call to us to say what it is that we desire, in what, if in anything our purpose and our spirit differ from theirs; and I believe that the people of the United States would wish me to respond with utter simplicity and frankness. Whether their present leaders believe it or not, it is our heartfelt desire and hope that some way may be opened whereby we may be privileged to assist the people of Russia to attain their utmost hope of liberty and ordered peace.

It will be our wish and purpose that the processes of peace, when they are begun, shall be absolutely open, and that they shall involve and permit henceforth no secret understandings of any kind. The day of conquest and aggrandizement is gone by; so is also the day of secret covenants entered into in the interest of particular Governments and likely at some unlooked-for moment to upset the peace of the world. It is this happy fact, now clear to the view of every public man whose thoughts do not still linger in an age that is dead and gone, which makes it possible for every nation whose purposes are consistent with justice and the peace of the world to avow now or at any other time the objects it has in view.

We entered this war because violations of right had occurred which touched us to the quick and made the life of our own people impossible unless they were corrected and the world secured once for all against their recurrence. What we demand in this war, therefore, is nothing peculiar to ourselves. It is that the world be made fit and safe to live in; and particularly that it be made safe for every peace-loving nation which, like our own, wishes to live its own life, determine its own institutions, be assured of justice and fair dealings by the other peoples of the world, as against force and selfish aggression. All of the peoples of the world are in effect partners in this interest and for our own part we see very clearly that unless justice be done to others it will not be done to us.

The program of the world's peace, therefore, is our program, and that program, the only possible program, as we see it, is this:

I. Open covenants of peace must be arrived at, after which there will surely be no private international action or rulings of any kind, but diplomacy shall proceed always frankly and in the public view.

II. Absolute freedom of navigation upon the seas, outside territorial waters, alike in peace and in war, except as the seas may be closed in whole or in part by international action for the enforcement of international covenants.

III. The removal, so far as possible, of all economic barriers and the establishment of an equality of trade conditions among all the nations consenting to the peace and associating themselves for its maintenance.

IV. Adequate guaranties given and taken that national armaments will reduce to the lowest point consistent with domestic safety.

V. Free, open-minded, and absolutely impartial adjustment of all colonial claims, based upon a strict observance of the principle that in determining all such questions of sovereignty the interests of the population concerned must have equal weight with the equitable claims of the government whose title is to be determined.

VI. The evacuation of all Russian territory and such a settlement of all questions affecting Russia as will secure the best and freest coöperation of the other nations of the world in obtaining for her an unhampered and unembarrassed opportunity for the independent determination of her own political development and national policy, and assure her of a sincere welcome into the society of free nations under institutions of her own choosing; and, more than a welcome, assistance also of every kind that she may need and may herself desire. The treatment accorded Russia by her sister nations in the months to come will be the acid test of their good-will, of their comprehension of her needs as distinguished from their own interests, and of their intelligent and unselfish sympathy.

VII. Belgium, the whole world will agree, must be evacuated and restored, without any attempt to limit the sovereignty which she enjoys in common with all other free nations. No other single act will serve as this will serve to restore confidence among the nations in the laws which they have themselves set and determined for the government of their relations with one another. Without this healing act the whole structure and validity of international law is forever impaired.

VIII. All French territory should be freed and the invaded portions restored, and the wrong done to France by Prussia in 1871 in the matter of Alsace-Lorraine, which has unsettled the peace of the world for nearly fifty years, should be righted, in order that peace may once more be made secure in the interest of all.

IX. A readjustment of the frontiers of Italy should be effected along clearly recognizable lines of nationality.

X. The peoples of Austria-Hungary, whose place among the nations we wish to see safeguarded and assured, should be accorded the freest opportunity of autonomous development.

XI. Rumania, Serbia, and Montenegro should be evacuated; occupied territories restored; Serbia accorded free and secure access to the sea; and the relations of the several Balkan States to one another determined by friendly counsel along historically established lines of allegiance and nationality; and international guaranties of the political and economic independence and territorial integrity of the several Balkan States should be entered into.

XII. The Turkish portions of the present Ottoman Empire should be assured a secure sovereignty, but the other nationalities which are now under Turkish rule should be assured an undoubted security of life and an absolutely unmolested opportunity of autonomous development, and the Dardanelles should be permanently opened as a free passage to the ships and commerce of all nations under international guaranties.

XIII. An independent Polish state should be erected which should include the territories inhabited by indisputably Polish populations, which should be assured a free and secure access to the sea, and whose political and economic independence and territorial integrity should be guaranteed by international covenant.

XIV. A general association of nations must be formed under specific covenants for the purpose of affording mutual guaranties of political independence and territorial integrity to great and small states alike.

In regard to these essential rectifications of wrong and assertions of right, we feel ourselves to be intimate partners of all the Governments and peoples associated together against the imperialists. We cannot be separated in interest or divided in purpose. We stand together until the end.

For such arrangements and covenants we are willing to fight and to continue to fight until they are achieved; but only because we wish the right to prevail and desire a just and stable peace, such as can be secured only by removing the chief provocations to war, which this program does remove. We have no jealousy of German greatness, and there is nothing in this program that impairs it. We grudge her no achievement or distinction of learning or of pacific enterprise such as have made her record very bright and very enviable. We do not wish to injure her or to block in any way her legitimate influence or power. We do not wish to fight her either with arms or with hostile arrangements of trade, if she is willing to associate herself with us and the other peace-loving nations of the world in covenants of justice and law and fair dealing. We wish her only to accept a place of equality among the peoples of the world—the new world in which we now live—instead of a place of mastery.

Neither do we presume to suggest to her any alteration or modification of her institutions. But it is necessary, we must frankly say, and necessary as a preliminary to any intelligent dealings with her on our part, that we should know whom her spokesmen speak for when they speak to us, whether for the Reichstag majority or for the military party and the men whose creed is imperial domination.

We have spoken now, surely, in terms too concrete to admit of any further doubt or question. An evident principle runs through the whole program I have outlined. It is the principle of justice to all peoples and nationalities, and their right to live on equal terms of liberty and safety with one another, whether they be strong or weak. Unless this principle be made its foundation, no part of the structure of international justice can stand. The people of the United States could act upon no other principle, and to the vindication of this principle they are ready to devote their lives, their honor, and everything that they possess. The moral climax of this, the culminating and final war for human liberty, has come, and they are ready to put their own strength, their own highest purpose, their own integrity and devotion to the test.

SAMUEL GOMPERS

LABOR'S ATTITUDE

[Samuel Gompers, for many years President of the American Federation of Labor, was of great service in rallying the working men of his country to patriotic support of the war. The following speech was given on Washington's Birthday, February 22, 1918, in the Lexington Avenue Theater, New York.]

I DOUBT that there existed, or now exists, in all the world a man who is so pronounced a pacifist as was I. I belonged to every peace society of which I knew anything. An officer in some form or other of each of them, a speaker of nearly all of them, within the sphere of my opportunities. In addition, as a union man, a labor man, an internationalist in spirit, I had believed, came to believe, that it would be impossible for such a war to have occurred at any time after the international understandings and pledge of the workers of nearly all the civilized countries; and I really believed in the pledge, in the spirit of it. . . . I had permitted myself to live in a fool's paradise. I believed that when men solemnly pledged themselves and those in whose name they had the authority to speak, they would go the limit in their own countries to prevent a rupture of international peace. . . . I was so in love with peace that I could have, without flinching, died for the cause of peace. [Applause.]

Almost out of the clear sky came this declaration of war, and I found that the men who had pledged to me and mine, my fellows, flying to the colors of the greatest autocrat of all time, the modern buccaneer of the world, the type of the intellectual scientific murderer, to fly to the colors upon his order, to attack the brothers whose lives they vouched to protect. I awoke. From then until now and until the peace of the world is assured I count myself transformed from an ultra pacificist to a living, breathing, fighting man. [Applause.] No one who has known me fairly intimately has ever accused me of running away from an honorable contest. And it is not of much interest what any one man believes or is, but that which he tries to inculcate upon his fellow-citizens. I believe that in our country we have the greatest opportunities existing of any country upon the face of the globe. [Applause.] America is not perfect; the Republic of the United States is not perfect; it has the imperfections of the human; and inasmuch as we are not perfect, we have not been able to make a perfect, democratic Republic; but it is the best country on the face of the earth. [Applause.]

America is not merely a name. It is not merely a land. It is not merely a country, nor is it merely a continent. America is a symbol; it is an ideal, the hopes of the world can be expressed in the ideal—America. [Applause.] The man in America, with the opportunities afforded, with the right of expression, with the right of determination, with the right of creating a political revolution by well-ordered methods, who will not or does not appreciate that it is his duty to stand by such a country in such stress and in such a storm, who is unwilling to stand up and be counted as a man in this fight for the maintenance of these ideals—is unworthy of the privilege of living in this country.

I have no quarrel with the man or the group of men who differ with me, or the course which I pursue, in anything. I doubt that there is anyone who welcomes expressions of dissent or disapproval more than I do. I am willing to battle with him mentally, argumentatively, in any honorable way that is provided among men, self-respecting men and women. Constructive criticism is of the greatest benefit to those who are criticized. It is the nagger, the mean, contemptible, nagging one that has no purpose other than negative and destructive that is unworthy the consideration of decent men and women. [Applause.]

Who declared war in Germany? Was it even that mugwumpery called the Reichstag? [Laughter and applause.] No; not even that. But who declared war in Germany? Was it the people of Germany? No. It was the Kaiser and his immediate military clique. That autocratic clique by one accord determined that the time for which they had been planning had arrived, and then was the time to strike the blow. Now, you have no need to enter into a full discussion of all the matter which may be of vital interest, and no doubt you know them just as well, if not better, than I do, but here is the point: In the United States of America it was not a Kaiser, a King, or even the President of the United States who declared war; it was the Congress of the United States, the men and women [Laughter] elected by the people of the United States. [Applause.] There must be lodged somewhere in the Government the power to declare that its life is endangered and therefore has the right to strike a blow in the defense of that country. In our Republic that authority is vested in the Congress of the United States—the Congress elected by the people of the United States, the Congress elected, in many States, by the votes of the men and the women of those States. . . .

In truth, the state of war existed from January, 1916, when the attacks were made upon our industrial plants and our transportation lines [Applause], the murdering of our men and women and our children in cold blood. If that did not constitute a state of war I would like to know what did. The point that I want to make clear is this: That it was not an autocrat, it was not the President, but that it was the representatives of the people, elected by the people to the Congress of the United States, the only authority recognized by the Constitution of our country, who realized the situation as it was and declared that a state of war existed between our Republic and the Imperial German Government. That body authorized the President to use all the available means and all the forces of the country to carry into effect and purpose the resolution of the Congress of the United States, and to make good this declaration that the democracy of the United States is not impotent or incompetent to defend itself. [Applause.]

Until the only authority in the country had decided the question whether we should recognize that war existed or not, until that declaration was made it was the privilege, as it was the right of every man to express his own view whether we should recognize this fact and go to war or not. But when the constituted authority in our Republic declared war, that was a decision of the people of this country, and from that decision there is and can be no appeal. [Applause.] To follow the thought that it is now permissible to discuss whether we should continue in the war or to retreat from it reminds me of the situation as it now exists in Russia.

I think that every American, every liberty-loving man and woman throughout the whole world, was thrilled when we learned that the Russian people had overthrown the Czar and his Empire and established a Government based upon some sort of democratic conception. Not long after, under the leadership of so-called radicals, they undertook to institute in the army the democratic thought that before any battle was to be undertaken the soldiers should vote upon it. [Laughter.] In theory that might be fairly good. As an academic discussion, it does not sound bad [Laughter]; but when you have opposed to you a well-organized gang of scientific murderers [Applause], who have their guns leveled at you, that is not the time to discuss whether you should defend yourself or not. That is the time to fight [Applause]. . . . Anarchy prevails in Russia, and the radicalism of the Bolsheviki of Russia has given the people, not land, not bread, not peace; and instead of finding this great people of Russia standing erect and fighting for their homes and for their lives, we find them without power or will, helpless before the Kaiser's hordes and the forces of autocracy, powerless to maintain their own freedom or to realize their own ideals. Yes, this radical, this radical gang there, and those who are showing their heads here, to them must be laid the charge of the undoing of the great people of Russia. If the so-called radicals of America would have their way, you would find in our United States the same condition as it is in Russia now.

I am rather fond of life. I have had 68 years of it, and I am not tired of it at all. [Applause.] I want to live. I don't know of anything better than living. I am not anxious to find out, but I don't want to live when I can't maintain my own self-respect. Indeed, I feel that I could not live in the atmosphere of unfreedom. There have been at least two occasions in my life when I was threatened with imprisonment; on two different occasions, and each for a year, because I undertook to express my judgment, and we were then at peace, not at war. But I undertook to express my judgment, express my opinion as an American citizen against a decree issued by one of our courts in a private controversy between two interests. I merely mention it, as I was willing to take a chance, whatever that may mean, for the maintenance of the principles of freedom of expression and freedom of the press.

So, just imagine—it does not take much to see the point at issue—if the German militarist system could win—it can't, but if it could win, how would that victory be accomplished, or what would its immediate result be? I know that we have been living in the thought that we are so far removed from the whole world that we are perfectly safe. But if it were possible for the German militarist machine to be so efficient that it could conquer France and England, the first result of that conquest would be, without question, the taking over from France and England of their combined navies. Without taking over these navies, as the result of German conquest, she could not be the complete winner; and imagine, with the military forces, the navies of England and France, and her vessels of commerce and transports, what would become of the vaunted safety of the home and fireside of the American people?

Referring to a remark made by Harry Lauder, and of which I was so glad to hear our honored Secretary speak, he said, in speaking to a lot of our boys in the camp: "Don't you for a moment imagine that you are going to send your troops over to save France or to save England. When you send your troops over you will be saving yourselves. Either you must fight over there or you will fight over here." [Applause.]

To me this war has quite a different meaning than almost any other war in history of which I have read. It began through the machinations of the German Kaiser and in the splendid responses made by France and England and Belgium. In Prussia they were all exulting, but when the Republic of the United States entered into this world struggle it ceased to be a war and became at once a crusade for freedom and justice and liberty. [Applause.] I hold it to be the duty of every man to give every ounce of energy in fighting, in producing, in helping in any way that he can, that this crusade shall be a triumph for the world. If we may not be able to abolish war for all time, at least let us make the conditions such that a war of this character may never again occur, or at least shall be long deferred.

For years and years the workers of America, realizing the position in which we are placed in this most favored country of ours, pressed home upon the agencies of government, the agencies of industry, the agencies of all activities, that inasmuch as the workers performed so large a service for society and civilization, the human side of the workers should receive the highest consideration, and that no agency of government or of industry should be constituted without the representative of the workers as part of that agency. [Applause.]

I never have asked anything for myself. I have no favor to ask. I have no personal pleas to make. I speak for a cause. I speak for the masses of the workers as well as the masses of all our people. [Applause.] For, no matter, the meanest of all of them, I consider it my duty and privilege to say a word for him, even when perhaps he might repudiate me. But, as the result of this war or crusade, this principle for which labor has been contending has found recognition in the department of government.

My friends, do you know how thoroughly in sympathy with the high and noble thought and work and associations of the labor movement are the members of the President's Cabinet and the President of the United States himself? That has come and it is coming to a larger extent with every development of our time. Does anyone think that when peace shall have come again to our beloved country and to the people of the world the representatives of these various agencies will be in conflict? Surely not. The principle is recognized. Hence this means while we are fighting for democracy and against autocracy, in France and soon in Belgium and then into Germany [applause], then in the meantime we are fighting to maintain democracy at home. [Applause.]

Let me say to you that, talking of international conferences with representatives of the enemy countries, we are not going to permit ourselves to be lulled into a fancied security and, under the guise of radicalism, go back a hundred years. [Applause.] Why, the Kaiser's minions would not give a passport to anyone unless he would carry out the policy of the autocracy of Germany.

Then, to meet in council with these men, gaining from us our confidence, swerving us from the path of duty, trying to influence us that the governments of these democracies are, after all, only capitalistic. I have said, and I say it in the name of the American labor movement—the convention of which in November declared it unalterably, the executive council of which, in session at Washington last week, affirmed it in most emphatic terms, and the American Alliance for Labor and Democracy reaffirmed it by the resolutions presented here this evening—we all say in essence: "You can't talk peace with us now; you can't talk international conferences with us now. Either you smash your autocracy, or, by the gods, we will smash it for you. [Great applause.] Before you talk peace terms, before you bring about international conferences, get out of France. [Applause.] Get back from Belgium, back to Germany, and then we will talk peace." [Applause.]

One of the great causes of this war was the obsession of this German military caste that democracies are impotent and inefficient; that France was a sort of democracy, with an army that was in a way inefficient because of the long-standing contention of Alsace-Lorraine. Germany knew that if she went to war she would have a rather hard fight with France, but surely would conquer her. She had an extreme contempt for the democracy of Great Britain and for any army Great Britain could raise. To the German mind, as it has been tutored for this last half a century, there is nothing efficient except it is governmental, unless it is directed by an autocratic head. The same contempt the Germans had for America. They believed us to be such devotees and lovers of the almighty dollar that we could never stand for an ideal and make sacrifices for its achievement. That is the great mistake which autocracies have ever made—they do not know. They have never known that once touch the heart, the conscience, and the spirit of the democratic peoples, they will make more sacrifices than any conscripts under compulsion. [Applause.] So we find ourselves in this war, in this crusade.

A month before the war was declared, with some degree of

prescience, the executive council of the American Federation of Labor called a conference of the representative officials of the American labor movement, and there a great discussion ensued, and there a declaration was finally adopted. I am going to ask you to let me read the closing two paragraphs.

We, the officers of the national and international trade-unions of America, in conference assembled, in the Capital of our Nation, hereby pledge ourselves, in peace or in war, in stress or in storm, to stand unreservedly by the standards of liberty and the safety and preservation of the institutions and ideals of our Republic. In this solemn hour of our Nation's life it is our earnest hope that our Republic may be safeguarded in its unswerving desire for peace; that our people may be spared the horrors and the burden of war; that they may have the opportunity to cultivate and develop the arts of peace, human brotherhood, and a higher civilization; but despite all our endeavors and hopes should our country be drawn into the maelstrom of the European conflict, we, with these ideals of liberty and justice herein declared as the indispensable basis for national policies, offer our services to our country in every field of activity to defend, safeguard, and preserve the Republic of the United States of America against its enemies, whomsoever they may be, and we call upon our fellow workers and fellow citizens in the holy name of labor, justice, freedom, and humanity to devotedly and patriotically give like service. [Applause.]

That declaration was adopted by a unanimous vote a month before the declaration of war. At the convention of the American Federation of Labor in November, the President of the United States, that great leader and spokesman of the democracies of the world [great applause] came and delivered a message to labor, and through that body, to the great masses of the people of America, and through them to the liberty loving men and women of the whole world. Did you ever think, my friends, of the curious situation in our country? The Government of the country carrying on this war are unanimously pacifists, from the President, the Secretary of the Navy, the Secretary of War, the Secretary of Labor—all of them ultrapacifists—before the war. [Laughter.]

If a gang of organized assassins were to come into this community, ready to pounce upon the innocent people, and they came upon the block in which you lived, and attacked your neighbor on the corner, what kind of a man would you be if you didn't get up and at them, rather than wait until they came into your own room? That is the situation with our country and our people in this great world struggle. There is not anything that will contribute so much to winning this war as the unity of spirit as well as the unity of action among the people of our country to make, if necessary, the extreme sacrifice that freedom shall live. I know that it may mean much loss and many heartaches, but we know that there were sacrifice and heartaches among the men and the women of our revolutionary times.

Who is there in America to-day who looks back with regret on the sacrifices made when the Declaration of Independence was coined for the world and a new nation created? Who regrets that anyone belonging to them, no matter how near or how remote, sacrificed his life and his all that America should be born? The war of our civilized life, our Civil War, when the struggle was for the maintenance of the Union and the abolition of human slavery, who among the gallant men on both sides, or either side, now regrets that the fight was made and the sacrifices borne in order to make good that this Nation is one and indivisible and that on its shores and under its flag slavery is forever-abolished? [Applause.] Who doubts that? Our war with Spain, small though it was, meant sacrifices. It meant Cuba free and independent. Is there a man or woman in this audience or in this country who regrets the sacrifice that was made that Cuba might be made free?

So the men and the women of the future will regard this struggle as we now look upon those struggles to which I have just referred. They will call us blessed, every man and every woman, who has given something to this great cause of human justice and freedom, to feel the satisfaction, the exultation, the exaltation of youth and energy renewed in them in a great cause, the greatest that has ever been presented to the peoples of any country and in any time. It is a privilege to live in this time and to help in this common fight. [Applause.]

With all my heart and spirit I appeal to my fellow citizens, to my fellow workers, to make this one great slogan, the watchword from now on until triumph shall perch upon our arms: "Unity, solidarity, energy, and the will to fight and to win." [Great applause.]

WOODROW WILSON

FORCE TO THE UTMOST

[The following speech of President Wilson was delivered in the 5th Regiment Armory of Baltimore before an audience of 15,000 on April 6, 1918, the anniversary of our entry into the War. The *New York Times* of the next day declares that "President Wilson brought the multitude to its feet with prolonged cheers when he declared that America accepted Germany's challenge of force. 'Germany has once more said that force and force alone shall decide whether justice and peace shall reign in the affairs of men.' Says the President, 'I accept the challenge.' And he did accept it in words that will hearten the fighting men at the front, that will be read with praise and thanksgiving by the chiefs of the governments associated with us in the war, and lift up the spirits of the people and strengthen them to meet whatever sacrifices war may involve."]

FELLOW CITIZENS: This is the anniversary of our acceptance of Germany's challenge to fight for our right to live and be free, and for the sacred rights of free men everywhere. The Nation is awake. There is no need to call to it. We know what the war must cost, our utmost sacrifice, the lives of our fittest men and, if need be, all that we possess. The loan we are met to discuss is one of the least parts of what we are called upon to give and to do, though in itself imperative. The people of the whole country are alive to the necessity of it, and are ready to lend to the utmost, even where it involves a sharp skimping and daily sacrifice to lend out of meager earnings. They will look with reprobation and contempt upon those who can and will not, upon those who demand a higher rate of interest, upon those who think of it as a mere commercial transaction. I have not come, therefore, to urge the loan. I have come only to give you, if I can, a more vivid conception of what it is for.

The reasons for this great war, the reason why it had to come, the need to fight it through, and the issues that hang upon its outcome, are more clearly disclosed now than ever before. It is easy to see just what this particular loan means because the Cause we are fighting for stands more sharply revealed than at any previous crisis of the momentous struggle. The man who knows least can now see plainly how the cause of Justice stands and what the imperishable thing is he is asked to invest in. Men in America may be more sure than they ever were before that the cause is their own, and that, if it should be lost, their own great Nation's place and mission in the world would be lost with it.

I call you to witness, my fellow countrymen, that at no stage of this terrible business have I judged the purposes of Germany intemperately. I should be ashamed in the presence of affairs so grave, so fraught with the destinies of mankind throughout all the world, to speak with truculence, to use the weak language of hatred or vindictive purpose. We must judge as we would be judged. I have sought to learn the objects Germany has in this war from the mouths of her own spokesmen, and to deal as frankly with them as I wished them to deal with me. I have laid bare our own ideals, our own purposes, without reserve or doubtful phrase, and have asked them to say as plainly what it is that they seek.

We have ourselves proposed no injustice, no aggression. We are ready, whenever the final reckoning is made, to be just to the German people, deal fairly with the German power, as with all others. There can be no difference between peoples in the final judgment, if it is indeed to be a righteous judgment. To propose anything but justice, even-handed and dispassionate justice, to Germany at any time, whatever the outcome of the war, would be to renounce and dishonor our own cause. For we ask nothing that we are not willing to accord.

It has been with this thought that I have sought to learn from those who spoke for Germany whether it was justice or dominion and the execution of their own will upon the other nations of the world that the German leaders were seeking. They have answered, answered in unmistakable terms. They have avowed that it was not justice but dominion and the unhindered execution of their own will.

The avowal has not come from Germany's statesmen. It has come from her military leaders, who are her real rulers. Her statesmen have said that they wished peace, and were ready to discuss its terms whenever their opponents were willing to sit down at the conference table with them. Her present Chancellor has said,—in indefinite and uncertain terms, indeed, and in phrases that often seem to deny their own meaning, but with as much plainness as he thought prudent,—that he believed that peace should be based upon the principles which we had declared would be our own in the final settlement. At Brest-Litovsk her civilian delegates spoke in similar terms; professed their desire to conclude a fair peace and accord to the peoples with whose fortunes they were dealing the right to choose their own allegiances. But action accompanied and followed the profession. Their military masters, the men who act for Germany and exhibit her purpose in execution, proclaimed a very different conclusion. We cannot mistake what they have done,—in Russia, in Finland, in the Ukraine, in Roumania. The real test of their justice and fair play has come. From this we may judge the rest. They are enjoying in Russia a cheap triumph in which no brave or gallant nation can long take pride. A great people, helpless by their own act, lies for the time at their mercy. Their fair professions are forgotten. They nowhere set up justice, but everywhere impose their power and exploit everything for their own use and aggrandizement; and the peoples of conquered provinces are invited to be free under their dominion!

Are we not justified in believing that they would do the same things at their western front if they were not there face to face with armies whom even their countless divisions cannot overcome? If, when they have felt their check to be final, they should propose favorable and equitable terms with regard to Belgium and France and Italy, could they blame us if we concluded that they did so only to assure themselves of a free hand in Russia and the East?

Their purpose is undoubtedly to make all the Slavic peoples, all the free and ambitious nations of the Baltic peninsula, all the lands that Turkey has dominated and misruled, subject to their will and ambition and build upon that dominion an empire of force upon which they fancy that they can then erect an empire of gain and commercial supremacy,—an empire as hostile to the Americans as to the Europe which it will overawe,—an empire which will ultimately master Persia, India, and the peoples of the Far East. In such a program our ideals, the ideals of justice and humanity and liberty, the principle of the free self-determination of nations upon which all the modern world insists, can play no part. They are rejected for the ideals of power, for the principle that the strong must rule the weak, that trade must follow the flag, whether those to whom it is taken welcome it or not, that the peoples of the world are to be made subject to the patronage and overlordship of those who have the power to enforce it.

That program once carried out, America and all who care or dare to stand with her must arm and prepare themselves to contest the mastery of the World, a mastery in which the rights of common men, the rights of women and of all who are weak, must for the time being be trodden under foot and disregarded, and the old, age-long struggle for freedom and right begin again at its beginning. Everything that America has lived for and loved and grown great to vindicate and bring to a glorious realization will have fallen in utter ruin and the gates of mercy once more pitilessly shut upon mankind!

The thing is preposterous and impossible; and yet is not that what the whole course and action of the German armies has meant wherever they have moved? I do not wish, even in this moment of utter disillusionment, to judge harshly or unrighteously. I judge only what the German arms have accomplished with unpitying thoroughness throughout every fair region they have touched.

What, then, are we to do? For myself, I am ready, ready still, ready even now, to discuss a fair and just and honest peace at any time that it is sincerely purposed,—a peace in which the strong and the weak shall fare alike. But the answer, when I proposed such a peace, came from the German commanders in Russia, and I cannot mistake the meaning of the answer.

I accept the challenge. I know that you accept it. All the world shall know that you accept it. It shall appear in the utter sacrifice and self-forgetfulness with which we shall give all that we love and all that we have to redeem the world and make it fit for free men like ourselves to live in. This now is the meaning of all that we do. Let everything that we say, my fellow countrymen, everything that we henceforth plan and accomplish, ring true to this response till the majesty and might of our concerted power shall fill the thought and utterly defeat the force of those who flout and misprize what we honor and hold dear. Germany has once more said that force, and force alone, shall decide whether Justice and Peace shall reign in the affairs of men, whether Right as America conceives it or Dominion as she conceives it shall determine the destinies of mankind. There is, therefore, but one response possible from us: Force, Force to the utmost, Force without stint or limit, the righteous and triumphant Force which shall make Right the law of the world, and cast every selfish dominion down in the dust.

HERBERT HOOVER

FOOD CONTROL—A WAR MEASURE

[Herbert Hoover, born in 1874, was active for many years in large engineering enterprises in various parts of the world. He was in London at the outbreak of the war and soon became the head of the Commission for Relief in Belgium. His services in this difficult task won him world-wide fame, and on America's entry into the war he was appointed food administrator by President Wilson. The following speech indicates the unparalleled crisis which the war had reached in the spring of 1918. Only by greatest efficiency in production and greatest economy in consumption could sufficient food be provided for England. The speech was given before the Pittsburg Press Club, April 18, 1918.]

THE Food Administration is purely a war institution. Its first and primary concern is the feeding of our own people and those of the allies, and thereby the maintenance of the strength of all the men, women, and children both there and here, and thus the strong arm of our soldiers.

The necessity for the creation of food administrations in all the countries at war with Germany arises solely from the situation in overseas shipping. Over one-third of the world's carrying capacity has been diverted directly and indirectly to military purposes, and of the remainder, there has been an unceasing loss during the War. There is an abundance of food accessible to the seas, but there are not the ships to carry it from every point and still to conduct the war.

The first adjustment of this situation has been to isolate the more remote markets. There are to-day abundant stores of food in Australia, the East, and in South America. Ours and Canada's are the nearest supplies to the allies, and better protection from submarines can be given to ships on the Atlantic lane than on other sea routes.

Roughly, every 5,000 tons of food to the allies requires 15,000 tons of shipping from Australia, 10,000 tons from the Argentine, and 5,000 tons from North America. Every steamer we can save from these long journeys means the possibility of an additional shipload of soldiers and munitions to France. If the allies were compelled to go to these more remote markets for their whole food supply today it would require over 2,500,000 tons more shipping than at present in use for this purpose. If North America could next year provide the whole of allied necessities we could save 1,500,000 tons of shipping. Every ship we save is a ship built. The weight of our blow against the Germans will be limited not alone by the ships we build, but by the ships we save. The measure of ships saved by food supplied directly from North America is, until our shipping expands, the measure of ships for our own soldiers.

If the allies were forced to rely wholly upon the remote markets for their food we should have no soldiers in France to-day. Nor will the burden grow less in the near future, for every ship we build will be needed to replace losses and to increase our Army at the front. This is conservation of ships as well as of food.

Therefore the whole war-food problem is simply and solely a determination of the amount of food that can be spared from North America. The marginal amount must be drawn from the more remote markets.

From this spring the broad administrative issues:

First: The amount of food we can send without injury to our people and the method of securing it.

Second: The economic measures we must adopt to protect our people from the disturbance to nutrition and commerce by this drain of supplies.

Any broad consideration of these problems requires a constant reassessment not only of our own food resources but of the food resources of the Allies and of other markets from which food may be brought to the allied world.

North America is the greatest factor in the allied food pool, and in the final analysis it might become necessary for the allies to live practically on North American supplies. It is therefore of importance to review our possibilities in this direction.

Our ability to supply the allied world with food lies in four directions:

First: The United States usually produces a small surplus of food for export over and above our normal consumption. This surplus we can export without economic disturbance.

Second: We have for years exported to other countries than the allies. By partial or complete embargo of these shipments we can slightly increase the supplies available to the allies.

Third: We can expand the area planted, and if our harvests are normal we can thereby enlarge the surplus for export through increased production.

Fourth: Our normal consumption and waste of food are anywhere from 15 to 20 per cent more than is necessary to maintain our own public health and strength, and we can in an emergency restrict the national consumption to our need and thereby increase our exports.

We have thus, so far as the allies are concerned, four marginal resources—our small normal surplus, the embargo, an abnormal surplus to be created by stimulated production, and a further surplus to be created by a reduction in our consumption.

Our resiliency of resources in these four directions, principally the latter, is such that we can, if we have the will to do so, maintain the strength of the allies and our own people, and all talk of famine is mere hysteria. Our world food situation is not to be interpreted as famine, at worst it is to be interpreted in terms of soldiers to France, or, alternatively, it can be interpreted in terms of larger shipbuilding programs.

The reduction of consumption during this year has been vital. To secure it we had three alternatives of action:

First: Rationing.

Second: By bidding up prices in the purchase of allies' supplies until the consumption falls.

Third: By obtaining a voluntary reduction of the individual consumption, simpler living, economy in waste, substitution of commodities we have in greater abundance for those we need export.

1. Rationing.—Any system of positive rationing of the United States bristles with difficulties. Fifty per cent of the population are either producers or live in intimate contact

with the producer, and therefore cannot be restrained in their consumption by any rationing. The consumption of the very poor is not beyond the necessities of their health and strength.

Our industrial population varies greatly in its habit of consumption of any given commodity in different parts of the country. Furthermore, this class of the community varies greatly in its habit in different sections of the United States as to the commodities they consume. For instance, the southern worker consumes perhaps not more than 2 pounds of wheat products per week per capita, whereas in some parts of the North he consumes 8 pounds. Rationing of wheat on any broad national line would increase the consumption beyond necessity in the South and decrease it in the North below necessity. Furthermore, to adopt rationing as a positive system would cost the Government $10,000,000 or $15,000,000 annually for bureaucratic expense, as we should have to place tickets and coupons with every householder, and behind these tickets would have to be erected a vast administrative organization.

2. Price Privation.—It has been believed by many that the best adjustment in consumption would be obtained by increasing price levels in that commodity in which it is desired to reduce consumption by simply bidding up the price for allied supplies. I feel strongly, however, that reduction of consumption to the extent that we require by an increasing price is simply and purely to place certain commodities out of the reach of those classes of the community who have not the purchasing power, and that this whole conception is simply conservation for the rich and against the poor. The adoption of this principle of rising prices would simply mean that the poorer sections of our community would have paid in suffering and the better-to-do classes would have paid in price many score times the cost of any other system of reduction.

Furthermore, if we have to increase the price of our foodstuffs merely to decrease their consumption, we must enter a vicious circle of constant readjustment of wages, for our working people must live.

Beyond this, again, we could no doubt reduce the consumption, for instance, of sugar by 20 per cent if we doubled the price, but to double the price of sugar alone means an annual drain on our population of $600,000,000, and this $600,000,000 would go into the hands of a vast number of middlemen and would give rise at once to profiteering, discontent, and would lay the foundation for social revolution.

3. Voluntary Action.—In considering the whole problem, we determined upon a line not hitherto applied and the success of which we believe will be one of the remembered glories of the American people in this titanic struggle; that is, that we should place the reduction of consumption on a voluntary basis. We felt that we could secure voluntary reduction by savings which would be made—not from the necessities of the poorer classes of the community, but in the saving out of plenty by the better-to-do classes.

Voluntary conservation has as well a moral side, to my mind, of some importance. By it we are appealing directly for the self-sacrifice of the people of the United States to the carrying on of the war. I do not believe that there is another nation in the world in which the proportion of individuals of a willing sense of self-sacrifice is so high as in this people of ours and in which a sufficient voluntary reduction could be obtained. Our program therefore has been a hazard upon the number of people of this kind in the United States. This basis of reduction gave some trepidation to the allies for fear of its failure, but I am happy to say that we shall have performed our national duty, the allies will have been fed during this harvest year, so far as the obligation falls upon us, almost wholly upon a voluntary footing. Far beyond this, it is justifying us in our belief in the high idealism and willingness to sacrifice in the American people.

We have had some criticism from individuals who believe that they should not be called upon to do more than their neighbors willingly do. In response to this, my feeling is that our Army does not fail to go over the top because there may be two or three slackers hiding in the trenches.

Aside from the prime necessity of protecting our independence and our institutions, there is but one possible benefit from the war, and that is the stimulation of self-sacrifice in the people, the lifting of its ideals, and the diversion from its peacetime inclinations toward the purely material things in life to a strengthening of its higher purposes. I do not say that such compensations are full compensations for war, but they are at least an amelioration of the terrible currents that are threatening our existence. Therefore we felt that if there could be brought home to the sense of every American household the necessity of this personal and individual sacrifice we would have spread the opportunity for service beyond those who sacrifice in giving their sons to immolation on the national altar.

To accomplish this requires education, requires an intimate understanding for each man, woman, and child in the United States of the objectives of the Government and the duty that falls upon them. We have called upon the millions of women and men in the United States with an unfailing reply. We have created great numbers of committees who have worked with the utmost devotion. We have penetrated each of our 20,000,000 households periodically with literature and we have plastered the boardings of the country with posters and urging. We have secured the fine coöperation of the manufacturers and distributors of food.

But we could not have attained this had we not had the absolute devotion and teamwork of every newspaper in the United States. Our every appeal has, through this gigantic influence, received an immediate and prompt distribution. Without this incessant, voluntary, liberal support our plan would have been impossible.

There is another side of all this to those of us who have lived behind the German lines. No hour goes by but our hearts are haunted by the scenes of long lines of emaciated women and children who to-day and for three years have gathered in Belgium for their daily bread from America. That pittance—their all—represents scarcely the wastes from American tables. This winter these lines have, for the first time during the war, gathered in the poorer sections of England, France, and Italy. Not only should this pull at our hearts, but beyond this, it is a menace to our very safety. In the presence of a common enemy we sit at a common table with all people defenders. Is the daily call of the Food Administration for less waste, for simpler living, to eat only for strength, not a call to conscience? Is it not a vital call of defense?

But right at this point arises to me a fundamental principle in national war economics. I do not believe that any person in this United States has a right to make one cent more profit out of any employment than he would have made under prewar conditions. I do not care whether this refers to the farmer, to the laborer, to the manufacturer, to the middle-man, or to the retailer; to me, every cent taken beyond this standard is money abstracted from the blood and sacrifice of the American people.

I do not believe that extortionate profits are necessary to secure the maximum effort on the part of the American people in this war. If we are going to adopt that theory, we have admitted everything that has been charged against us of being the most materialistic, the most avaricious, and the most venal of people in this world.

If we are going to admit that the Government, in order to secure the supreme effort of its citizens in production, must bribe them with money to this extra exertion we have admitted a weakness of American character, of American civilization, and of American ideals that puts us on a plane below German kultur.

Moreover, I am not at all convinced that extortionate returns do stimulate production for they sometimes tend to cause relaxation in effort.

Do not mistake that I am saying that prices and wages should return to the prewar normal, because the incidence of war before we joined in it had lifted our costs of operation, and there must be compensation in every direction. Nevertheless, I hold that any man who has made more than his necessary living out of the cost his Nation is giving in the blood of the boys we are sending to France should not stand out as a benefactor to his community.

I have had this statement met before now with the expression that it is dreamy idealism, but I have found no individual who was prepared in his own instance to defend any such line of action.

It is true that this doctrine has been made a law only to the larger food trades. I am confident that profiteering has, from a national point of view, been greatly reduced in the regulated food trades, and, in consequence, my belief is that it should be applied generally to all business in this country, and it is also my belief that before we are finished with this war, that will have been done.

To me this goes much further than the mere case of the individual and the blame that may be attached to him. As I have seen this war develop from an active participation in its backwash and misery since its first day, I have seen growing out of the masses of people in every country aspirations for a great economic change. That change, broadly, will be in the view of extremists that those who work with their hands will obtain a larger portion of this world's goods and those who work with their brains will obtain less, while those who do not work should obtain nothing.

My own view is that hand and brain workers will obtain a larger proportion of that which formerly went to the non-workers—war taxation will do this in any event.

If we are to bring about this economic change in an orderly and American way, and not by convulsions during the period of recuperation from the war, we must lay the foundations for it now. None of us wants a repetition in the United States of the history of the last twelve months of Russia. The proper social development of this country along these lines fills the background of all men's minds and its proper guidance rests upon the liberal and thinking men of the country.

The enforcement of this law against profiteering in the food trades is a considerable part of our anxieties. In order to determine how far we have succeeded—that is, how far the margin between the producer and consumer has been diminished—we maintain positive data in our organization.

To illustrate this, we have calculated a price index based upon the food values of the principal commodities. For instance, a rise of a half dollar a dozen in eggs would be a good headline, but it is not as important to the country as a rise of a cent a loaf in bread. Upon this basis we find that since the Food Administration was founded the price of food commodities has increased 18 per cent to the producer and at the same time it has decreased 12 per cent to the consumer. The margin is thus smaller by 30 per cent; in fact, it is now so narrow that price changes to the producer directly reflect to the consumer, and the Food Administration has to take all of the curses of both sides.

FOOD CONTROL—A WAR MEASURE

This has been accomplished largely by voluntary coöperation of the food trades. Ninety-five per cent of our traders desire to serve the common interest, and the measure of their coöperation is one of the most illuminating proofs of the high sense of service in our people. While isolated instances will occur, I am convinced that at no time in the last three years has there been as little speculation and extortion in the Nation's food as there is to-day.

Another economic theme which the Food Administration has had to pioneer is that of saving. Speaking broadly, we have some 36,000,000 of able-bodied manhood. We have already had to divert 2,000,000 of these men to actual arms. Beyond this, we have had to divert a vast number of men to provide munitions not only for themselves but for the allies. We have had to divert vast numbers of men to the provision of the raw materials for these shops. We have had to set aside larger amounts of our foodstuffs for the allies, and, consequently, there was a diversion of farm production to this purpose.

Altogether, a rough calculation indicates that already we have diverted from eight to ten million men from their normal occupations toward war and the products it requires. That is from one-quarter to one-third of our normal productive units. It is possible that we can increase the exertion of the remainder of our productive population by eliminating non-essential labor, by more intensive labor and longer hours, by the application of woman's labor, by putting the boys into labor earlier than otherwise, and can make up some of the gap in our productive units. We cannot, however, compass the whole, and the deficiency can only be overcome by the reduction in the consumption of commodities.

This does not apply to food alone. It applies to every commodity of which we consume more than necessary for our health and comfort. We must strip to the bone in order that we may afford the economic luxury of the diversion of this portion of our productive power to the destruction of war. If we do not, our exertion in this war will stop short of the task imposed upon us, and we cannot look to victory with any assurance.

When we survey the economic field in detail, we necessarily

find difference in the degree of the essential character of commodities and labor. There are some commodities and some labor that we do not require at all, and all that we can turn to our shipyards, our munition works, and the allied food supply is a contribution to war.

Too much economic thinking is done in terms of money. If we could, like Germany, reach that point of economic balance where the increased productivity of our home population and the decreased consumption of our home population affords the complete supply of men and commodities needed in war, we could fight for the next 50 years without economic loss. Money becomes purely the counters through which distribution of those commodities and labor is obtained.

If we subscribe for one Liberty bond from our normal surplus income we will have furnished the Treasury with some of its necessary counters, but if we subscribe for another Liberty bond from the savings that we make on the consumption of commodities and labor we will have contributed these commodities or this labor to the war, and our second bond will have done two duties. Without it, neither the Treasury will have enough counters nor our fighting men enough supplies.

The subscription of Liberty bonds from surplus income is no sacrifice for the American people. It is a superlative investment. It is the saving that we make in the consumption of commodities and in the employment of labor that is the sacrifice for the winning of this war.

Another prime economic theme by which I am impressed in this war is this: The American ideal in executive work is efficiency, but efficiency does not alone mean the best appliances and the greatest numbers made for the least cost. In war it involves a new factor that transcends all others, and that is speed. Many of our present difficulties arise from our inability to get away from our trodden interpretation of the word "efficiency" and many of them from the fear of our executive officers of criticism if they fail in popular interpretation of this term.

In this light measures taken, results attained cannot be judged by the microscopic inspection of the threads in the tapestry—its broad lines, its inspiration, must be attained quickly, not by years of careful development. It will be of no avail to us if we lose a war, even though it may cost less per unit than any war in history.

There is but one real test. Our game is to win the war, and the test is, Do we keep our eye on the ball? For, friends, this people will be cursed for the next ten generations if we don't. Nor does this test apply to Washington alone. This Government is nothing more than the expression of the people, and if we are to win the war, it will be only because every man, woman, and child charges himself daily and hourly with the test, Does this or that contribute to win the war?

Nor is this the gospel of gloom; it is the gospel of the full health, spirits, and strength of our people in maintaining the last ounce of production, the last atom of economy.

HENRY P. DAVISON

THE AMERICAN RED CROSS

[On May 18, 1918, President Wilson led the great Red Cross parade down Fifth Avenue amid cheering multitudes. In the evening at the Metropolitan Opera House the Red Cross Drive was opened by appeals from President Wilson and Mr. Davison, Chairman of the American Red Cross World Organization, who had just returned from a tour of the war districts of Europe and told of his experiences in the following address. Mr. Davison was a member of the banking firm J. P. Morgan & Co, and was a leader in the financial affairs of the world. He was born in Troy, Pennsylvania, in 1867, and died May 6, 1922.]

It must be admitted that the military situation on the Western front is serious and that the next few months will undoubtedly be the critical months of the War, as Germany is hurling, at all costs, her vast force against the line, determined if possible to divide and smash the armies before we can get there in force. Conscious of this I can say that I have never left Europe more confident of the final success of the Entente, as I have never known the morale as high—all along the line and back of the line, as it is to-day.

I have spoken of the military situation because the work of the American Red Cross is closely allied with it. You must appreciate that it is impossible to give, within a few minutes, any picture of the work it is doing, both at home and throughout the Western front. You have seen our boys don their uniforms. They have given you their leavetaking. They have gone to their camps, and many of them have gone over there! You have resolved that nothing which would protect them from sickness or add to their comfort shall be withheld. Furthermore, you have demanded that a service should be rendered to their families left behind, and to them "over there" for their peace of mind in connection with their families at home, and also that to those unfortunate enough to become prisoners of the enemy every possible service through the Red Cross shall be extended for their health and comfort. The women of the country have not only demanded this of the American Red Cross, but by their patriotism and industry have made it possible to make provisions for their comfort. Of course, it is not conceivable that this work at home, enormous as it is, and requiring every kind of talent and human resource, should be in any sense restricted, but rather enlarged and continued during the war.

If you could have seen during the recent offensive, the rushing by night of Red Cross camions loaded with food to meet the thousands of men, women and children being bombarded out of their homes without notice; if you could have seen them receiving the hot food and drink given to them by the American people as they are on their way they know not where; and if later you could see the thousands and thousands of them who have been helped by the American people to secure lodging, food and clothing, you would then understand the look of gratitude upon their faces—gratitude to the American people.

If you could go throughout those countries into the buildings where thousands of children are being cared for, maternity homes where mothers and their babies are attended, of workshops where thousands of people are given employment to make materials necessary for the destitute of these countries, in the dispensaries and countless villages where with the aid of the Rockefeller Foundation, the greatest war is being carried on against tuberculosis; if you could visit with Red Cross representatives the families of the soldiers whose names are given by the military authorities, to whom direct relief is extended; and could go with the Red Cross representatives in the front line trenches to see them give articles of comfort and serve hot drinks to the soldiers of our allies; if you could go into the Red Cross rest-rooms and canteens and see them care for and feed over 3,000,000 men a month; if you could visit the many hospitals in Europe organized and being run by the Red Cross and knew that in addition supplies are contributed to more than 5000 military hospitals in France and Italy; if you could go through the factories where artificial limbs are being made for our own boys and those of our allies, through the factory where splints are being so scientifically made that they have been put on the wounded men before they have been moved from No Man's Land, thus saving many lives and limbs which otherwise would have been lost—you would then not fully cover the field of Red Cross operations, for there is to-day practically no breach into which Red Cross does not rush. It is in this way that the American people are giving courage not only to the soldiers of our allies, but to their families, and assuring them that they must keep heart whatever happens, as the American forces will soon be there in number and quality to fight with them until the war is won.

My tour on the Continent with the heads of the respective Red Cross commissions was practically an ovation from beginning to end, not to me or to the Red Cross, but to the American people, as we have studiously made clear that the work of the American Red Cross is but an expression from the American people to those who have suffered for us as well as themselves in a common cause.

The continuation of this work will hold and further establish our relations with the peoples of our allies. This should make a recurrence of the present situation, which is not within the power of man to describe, impossible, and will contribute more than any other voluntary act within our power to the winning of the war, to the saving of the lives of our own boys and to the end that this world be made possible to live in which it will never be again until the German military power is crushed.

I hope there are no American men and women who do not realize that the time has come when each must contribute generously and cheerfully with the feeling that their contribution is in no sense a gift but as an act of protection and of justice as well. A Frenchman, prefect of one of the provinces, a picturesque and charming old gentlemen, said to me: "We of France knew of your riches, knew of your power, but it took the war to show us your heart." Now in these tragic weeks of the world's history when all our associates are in the death struggle for freedom let us indeed carry on—carry on and show not only to them—those fighting with us and for us, on and back of the lines, but to our enemies as well—

that there is yet in the world a power of love, a power of sympathy, a power of Christianity and a power of justice which must and shall reëstablish the world for the betterment of all mankind.

RUDYARD KIPLING

THE AMERICAN INVASION OF ENGLAND

[Rudyard Kipling was born in Bombay, India, of British parents in 1865. By the time he was twenty-four his fame was world-wide as a writer of stories. He married an American and for several years lived in this country. Both in his fiction and in his poetry he has interpreted the work of the British Empire and the faith and ideals of the British people. This address was delivered to American troops at Winchester, England, July 21, 1918. Reprinted by permission from the War Volumes published by The New York Times Company.]

SEVERAL years have passed since England was permanently occupied by the armed forces of a foreign nation. On the last occasion—eight hundred years ago—our people did not take kindly to the invaders. I know they did not, because I live a few miles from where the Battle of Hastings was fought, where all the trouble began; and I assure you we are still talking about it. But don't let me take up your time by retailing the local gossip of these parts. Besides, conditions have changed. They will after 853 years—even in England. You may have noticed that we natives do not resent either the presence of your armed forces on our soil, or your buildings such as these—huts, which are one of the visible signs of your occupation. As far as you are concerned, we are a placid, not to say pacifist, community. Why, gentlemen, you could not annoy us if you started in to build pyramids. On the contrary, we should be pleased. We should say: "This looks like business; this looks as if the United States meant to stay till they had done their share of the job thoroughly."

We have been a long time over our present job, and we may be a long time yet. It has been a little bigger than we expected, because this is the first time since the creation that all the world has been obliged to unite for the purpose of fighting the devil. You remember that before the war one of our easy theories was that the devil was almost extinct—that he was only the child of misfortune or accident, and that we should soon abolish him by passing ringing resolutions against him. That has proved an expensive miscalculation. We find now that the devil is very much alive, and very much what he always was—that is to say, immensely industrious, a born organizer, and better at quoting Scripture for his own ends than most honest men. His industry and organization we all can deal with, but more difficult to handle is his habit of quoting Scripture as soon as he is in difficulties.

When Germany begins to realize her defeat is certain we shall be urged in the name of mercy, toleration, loving kindness, for the sake of the future of mankind, or by similar appeals to the inextinguishable vanity of man, who delights in thinking himself holy and righteous when he is really only lazy or tired—I say, we shall be urged on these high grounds to make some sort of compromise with or to extend some recognition to the power which has for its one object the destruction of man body and soul. Yet, if we accept these pleas, we shall betray mankind as effectively as though we had turned our backs upon the battle from the first.

But you, gentlemen, have not come 3000 miles to protect Germany. Your little vanguard is here to help her change her heart, and I read a day or two ago the lines on which you propose to change it: "When we went to war with Germany it was with the resolve to destroy German war power. If that power is inseparable from the German people, then we are resolved upon the destruction of the German people. The alternative is in their hands." That is reasonable and easy to understand. You are going, none too soon, into a world which has been laboriously wrecked by high German philosophy, based on the devil's own creed that there is nothing good or evil in life but thinking makes it so—in other words, that right and wrong are matters of pure fancy.

That belief it will be your privilege to assist in removing from the German's mind. His beliefs are primitive. Except on certain portions of the front, where he has been better educated, he believed that the United States Army does not exist. In the first place, it could not cross the Atlantic; in the second, it was sunk while crossing; in the third, it was no use when it arrived. It is possible that you may be able to persuade him that he has been misinformed on these points.

Meantime, your invasion of England goes forward according to program day by day. Unlike the other invaders we have known, you bring everything you need with you, and do not live upon the inhabitants. In this you are true to the historical vow of your ancestors, when they said to ours, "Millions for defense, but not a cent for tribute." At any other time the nations would be lost in amazement at the mere volume and scope of your equipment, at the terrifying completeness of your preparations, at the dread evidence of power that underlies them. But we have lived so among miracles these last four years that, even though the thing accomplished itself before our very eyes, we scarcely realize that we watch the actual bodily transit of the New World moving in arms to aid in redressing the balance of the Old. We are too close to these vast upheavals and breakings forth to judge of their significance. One falls back on the simpler, the more comprehensible fact that we are all blood-brothers in a common cause, and therefore in that enduring fellowship of loss, toil, peril, and homesickness which must needs be our portion before we come to the victory.

But life is not all grey even under these skies. There is a reasonable amount of fun left in the world still, if you know where to look for it—and I have noticed that the young generally have this knowledge. And there are worse fates in the world than to be made welcome, as you are more than welcome, to the honorable and gallant fraternity of comrades-in-arms the wide world over. Our country and our hearts are at your service, and with these our understanding of the work ahead of you. That understanding we have bought at the price of the lifeblood of a generation.

ENOCH HERBERT CROWDER

BEGIN NOW!

[Enoch Herbert Crowder was born in Missouri in 1859 and graduated from West Point in 1881. When the United States entered the War he was judge advocate general, U. S. A., and was largely responsible for initiating the Selective Draft. He was made Provost Marshal General, U. S. A., and for his services later awarded the distinguished service medal. The following address was given in September, 1918, to Class One, Selective Service Men; later it was read to all men enlisted in the national army.]

You have been selected, by the Congress of the Nation and by the Board of your own community, to fill the ranks of our National Army. Your appointed task is to defend our country from the force and fraud of a ruthless enemy. *Begin now!*

Your call to arms is coming, in due season. But in the meantime your very selection by the Boards of your community marks you as possessing already a privilege and a duty. You are not only to bear arms when the time comes. You are to prepare to be worthy and capable. *Begin now!*

The more you think now about the things which a true soldier must know, the more competent and satisfied you will be when the actual call arrives. What do you know of a soldier's daily duties? What do you know of an army's organization? What do you know of the work and the science of its several branches—Infantry, Cavalry, Artillery, Signal, Quartermaster, Ordnance, and the rest? What do you know of the weapons, the tools, and the materials that each of them uses? What do you know of the geography of the great battlefield of Europe? What do you know of the nations arrayed for and against us? How intelligent are you as to the causes and objects of this war? Do you realize that as a good soldier you have much to learn, and that the sooner you learn it the better soldier you will be when you arrive in camp? *Begin now!*

Do you know the men of this town and county that are to join the ranks with you? Have you reflected that the greatest friendship that one man ever has for another in this world is the friendship that grows up between those who have fought side by side? Have you realized that all of you, here in this county, now form a picked band of brothers in arms destined to see each other through, in many a crisis, in the days to come? Have you made a start of these friendships yet? *Begin now!*

Have you ever thought that our enemy is attacking us, not only in Europe, but at home? Have you realized that his especial trickery consists in seeking to make men disloyal here in our own community? Have you tried to discover and suppress the enemy's work here in the peaceful region of our own homes? Since your appointed task is to act as the defenders of our country, why wait till you are called to camp? Your time for that has come already. *Begin now!*

From now on, regard yourselves as a selected fraternity of active patriots. Strengthen those who are weak. Encourage those who are timid. Inspire the indifferent. Inform the ignorant. Search out the slackers. Begin now to make every one of you into a good soldier, a capable defender of our country, in spirit, in knowledge, and in physical fitness.

There never was a war to which men could give themselves with greater confidence and devotion. There never was a war in which a man had less excuse for holding back. There never was a time when a man could be more desirous to be known as a soldier. There never will be a century in the world's history in which a man's family, his townsmen, and his countrymen, will be prouder to point him out as one of *their* men— one of the men who had the honor of being in the Army.

This is *your* war. You are going to win it by what you are—good Americans and good soldiers. You are good Americans already. It will take some time to make good soldiers out of you. The sooner you start, the sooner you will arrive. *Begin now!*

V. THE PEACE CONFERENCE

[The Peace Conference at Paris lasted for six months, during which there was continuous debate and discussion by the representatives of the participating nations. Since the Conference adjourned the debating and discussion have continued and multiplied. We print the speeches made at the first three general sessions. Apart from the extraordinary interest arising from the occasion the speeches are notable in themselves, each being admirably suited to its particular purpose.

The first General Session of the Peace Conference met at the Quai d'Orsay, on the 18th of January, and after the initial speech by President Poincaré in which, speaking in the name of France, he formally convoked the Conference, President Wilson nominated Premier Clemenceau as President of the Conference. Mr. Lloyd-George and Baron Sonnino seconded the nomination. After a few words of appreciation he stated that the rules of procedure of the Conference would be distributed to all delegates through the Bureau. He then came rapidly to the program immediately before the Conference, and announced that the questions on the order of the day were, first: responsibility of the authors of the war; second: penalties for crimes committed during the war; third: international legislation in regard to labor.

Having hurriedly stated the method of routine, the President then announced that the order of the day for the next sitting would begin with the question of the Society of Nations and declared the Session closed, with a final request that all questions and expressions of opinion should be addressed to the Bureau.

The inaugural speech of President Poincaré, the nomination of Clemenceau as president of the Conference, and M. Clemenceau's opening address to the Peace Conference are given here.

The Session of January. 25 was devoted to the question of the introduction of the League of Nations, with speeches by President Wilson, Mr. Lloyd-George, Signor Orlando and M. Leon Bourgeois.

The Conference accepted the proposals for the creation of the League of Nations in a threefold resolution and appointed a Committee representative of the associated governments to work out the details of the Constitution and functions of the League.

The third General Session was held on February 14, and was called to receive the report of the Commission on the League of Nations, of which President Wilson was Chairman. President Wilson's speech was delivered on this occasion, as in other instances extemporaneously, except for the reading of the text of the Covenant. He was followed by a number of other speakers whose speeches are reproduced here.]

1. OPENING SESSION OF THE PEACE CONFERENCE JANUARY 18, 1919

PRESIDENT POINCARÉ'S INAUGURAL SPEECH

Reprinted from the London *Times,* January 20, 1919.

GENTLEMEN:—France greets and welcomes you and thanks you for having unanimously chosen as the seat of your labors the city which, for over four years, the enemy has made his principal military objective and which the valor of the Allied armies has victoriously defended against unceasingly renewed offensives.

Allow me to see in your decision the homage of all the nations that you represent towards a country which, still more than any others, has endured the sufferings of war, of which entire provinces, transformed into vast battlefields, have been systematically wasted by the invader, and which has paid the heaviest tribute to death.

France has borne these enormous sacrifices without having incurred the slightest responsibility for the frightful cataclysm which has overwhelmed the universe, and at the moment when this cycle of horror is ending, all the Powers whose delegates are assembled here may acquit themselves of any share in the crime which has resulted in so unprecedented a disaster. What gives you authority to establish a peace of justice is the fact that none of the peoples of whom you are the delegates has had any part in injustice. Humanity can place confidence in you because you are not among those who have outraged the rights of humanity.

There is no need of further information or for special inquiries into the origin of the drama which has just shaken the world. The truth, bathed in blood, has already escaped from the Imperial archives. The premeditated character of the trap is to-day clearly proved. In the hope of conquering, first, the hegemony of Europe and next the mastery of the world, the Central Empires, bound together by a secret plot, found the most abominable pretexts for trying to crush Serbia and force their way to the East. At the same time they disowned the most solemn undertakings in order to crush Belgium and force their way into the heart of France. These are the two unforgetable outrages which opened the way to aggression. The combined efforts of Great Britain, France, and Russia broke themselves against that mad arrogance.

If, after long vicissitudes, those who wished to reign by the sword have perished by the sword, they have but themselves to blame; they have been destroyed by their own blindness. What could be more significant than the shameful bargains they attempted to offer to Great Britain and France at the end of July, 1914, when to Great Britain they suggested: "Allow us to attack France on land and we will not enter the Channel"; and when they instructed their Ambassador to say to France: "We will only accept a declaration of neutrality on your part if you surrender to us Briey, Toul, and Verdun"? It is in the light of these memories, gentlemen, that all the conclusions you will have to draw from the war will take shape.

Your nations entered the war successively, but came, one and all, to the help of threatened right. Like Germany, Great Britain and France had guaranteed the independence of Belgium. Germany sought to crush Belgium. Great Britain and France both swore to save her. Thus, from the very beginning of hostilities, came into conflict the two ideas which for fifty months were to struggle for the dominion of the world— the idea of sovereign force, which accepts neither control nor check, and the idea of justice, which depends on the sword only to prevent or repress the abuse of strength.

Faithfully supported by her Dominions and Colonies, Great Britain decided that she could not remain aloof from a struggle in which the fate of every country was involved. She has made, and her Dominions and Colonies have made with her, prodigious efforts to prevent the war from ending in the triumph of the spirit of conquest and the destruction of right.

Japan, in her turn, only decided to take up arms out of loyalty to Great Britain, her great Ally, and from the consciousness of the danger in which both Asia and Europe would have stood, for the hegemony of which the Germanic Empires had dreamt.

Italy, who from the first had refused to lend a helping hand to German ambition, rose against an age-long foe only to answer the call of oppressed populations and to destroy at the cost of her blood the artificial political combination which took no account of human liberty.

Rumania resolved to fight only to realize that national unity which was opposed by the same powers of arbitrary force. Abandoned, betrayed, and strangled, she had to submit to an abominable treaty, the revision of which you will exact. Greece, whom the enemy for many months tried to turn from her traditions and destinies, raised an army only to escape attempts at domination, of which she felt the growing threat. Portugal, China, and Siam abandoned neutrality only to escape the strangling pressure of the Central Powers. Thus it was the extent of German ambitions that brought so many peoples, great and small, to form a league against the same adversary.

And what shall I say of the solemn resolution taken by the United States in the spring of 1917 under the auspices of their illustrious President, Mr. Wilson, whom I am happy to greet here in the name of grateful France, and, if you will allow me to say so, gentlemen, in the name of all the nations represented in this room? What shall I say of the many other American Powers which either declared themselves against Germany—Brazil, Cuba, Panama, Guatemala, Nicaragua, Haiti, Honduras—or at least broke off diplomatic relations—Bolivia, Peru, Ecuador, Uruguay? From north to south the New World rose with indignation when it saw the empires of Central Europe, after having let loose the war without provocation and without excuse, carry it on with fire, pillage, and massacre of inoffensive beings?

The intervention of the United States was something more, something greater, than a great political and military event: it was a supreme judgment passed at the bar of history by the lofty conscience of a free people and their Chief Magistrate on the enormous responsibilities incurred in the frightful conflict which was lacerating humanity. It was not only to protect themselves from the audacious aims of German megalomania that the United States equipped fleets and created immense armies, but also, and above all, to defend an ideal of liberty over which they saw the huge shadow of the Imperial Eagle encroaching farther every day. America, the daughter of Europe, crossed the ocean to wrest her mother from the humiliation of thraldom and to save civilization. The American people wished to put an end to the greatest scandal that has ever sullied the annals of mankind.

Autocratic governments, having prepared in the secrecy of the Chancelleries and the General Staff a map program of universal domination, at the time fixed by their genius for intrigue let loose their packs and sounded the horns for the chase, ordering science at the very time when it was beginning to abolish distances, bring men closer, and make life sweeter, to leave the bright sky towards which it was soaring and to place itself submissively at the service of violence, lowering the religious idea to the extent of making God the complacent auxiliary of their passions and the accomplice of their crimes; in short, counting as naught the traditions and wills of peoples, the lives of citizens, the honor of women, and all those principles of public and private morality which we for our part have endeavored to keep unaltered through the war and which neither nations nor individuals can repudiate or disregard with impunity.

While the conflict was gradually extending over the entire surface of the earth and clanking of chains was heard here and there, and captive nationalities from the depth of their age-long jails cried out to us for help. Yet more, they escaped to come to our aid. Poland came to life again and sent us troops. The Czecho-Slovaks won their right to independence in Siberia, in France, and in Italy. The Jugo-Slavs, the Armenians, the Syrians and Lebanese, the Arabs, all the oppressed peoples, all the victims, long helpless or resigned, of great historic deeds of injustice, all the martyrs of the past, all the outraged consciences, all the strangled liberties revived at the clash of our arms, and turned towards us, as their natural defenders. Thus the war gradually attained the fullness of its first significance, and became, in the fullest sense of the term, a crusade of humanity for Right; and if anything can console us in part at least, for the losses we have suffered, it is assuredly the thought that our victory is also the victory of Right.

This victory is complete, for the enemy only asked for the armistice to escape from an irretrievable military disaster. In the interest of justice and peace it now rests with you to reap from this victory its full fruits in order to carry out this immense task. You have decided to admit, at first, only the Allied or associated Powers, and, in so far as their interests are involved in the debates, the nations which remained neutral. You have thought that the terms of peace ought to be settled among ourselves before they are communicated to those against whom we have together fought the good fight. The solidarity which has united us during the war and has enabled us to win military success ought to remain unimpaired during the negotiations for, and after the signing of, the Treaty.

It is not only governments, but free peoples, who are represented here. Through the test of danger they have learned to know and help one another. They want their intimacy of yesterday to assume the peace of to-morrow. Vainly would our enemies seek to divide us. If they have not yet renounced their customary maneuvers, they will soon find that they are meeting to-day, as during the hostilities, a homogeneous block which nothing will be able to disintegrate. Even before the armistice you placed that necessary unity under the standard of the lofty moral anl political truths of which President Wilson has nobly made himself the interpreter.

And in the light of those truths you intend to accomplish your mission. You will, therefore, seek nothing but justice, "justice that has no favorites," justice in territorial problems, justice in financial problems, justice in economic problems. But justice is not inert, it does not submit to injustice. What it demands first, when it has been violated, are restitution and reparation for the people and individuals who have been despoiled or maltreated. In formulating this lawful claim, it obeys neither hatred nor an instinctive or thoughtless desire for reprisals. It pursues a twofold object—to render to each his due, and not to encourage crime through leaving it unpunished. What justice also demands, inspired by the same feeling, is the punishment of the guilty and effective guaranties against an active return of the spirit by which they were tempted; and it is logical to demand that these guaranties should be given, above all, to the nations that have been, and might again be most exposed to aggressions or threats, to those who have many times stood in danger of being submerged by the periodic tide of the same invasions.

What justice banishes is the dream of conquest and imperialism, contempt for national will, the arbitrary exchange of provinces between states as though peoples were but articles of furniture or pawns in a game. The time is no more when diplomatists could meet to redraw with authority the map of the empires on the corner of the table. If you are to remake the map of the world it is in the name of the peoples, and on condition that you shall faithfully interpret their thoughts, and respect the right of nations, small and great, to dispose of themselves, and to reconcile it with the right, equally sacred, of ethnical and religious minorities—a formidable task, which science and history, your two advisers, will contribute to illumine and facilitate.

You will naturally strive to secure the material and moral means of subsistence for all those peoples who are constituted or reconstituted into states; for those who wish to unite themselves to their neighbors; for those who divide themselves into separate units; for those who reorganize themselves according to their regained traditions; and, lastly, for all those whose freedom you already sanction or are about to sanction. You will not call them into existence only to sentence them to death immediately. You would like your work in this, as in all other matters, to be fruitful and lasting.

While thus introducing into the world as much harmony as possible, you will, in conformity with the fourteenth of the propositions unanimously adopted by the Great Allied Powers, establish a general League of Nations, which will be a supreme guaranty against any fresh assaults upon the right of peoples. You do not intend this International Association to be directed against anybody in future. It will not of set purpose shut out anybody, but, having been organized by the nations that have sacrificed themselves in defense of Right, it will receive from them its statutes and fundamental rules. It will lay down conditions to which its present or future adherents will submit, and, as it is to have for its essential aim to prevent, as far as possible, the renewal of wars, it will, above all, seek to gain respect for the peace which you will have established, and will find it the less difficult to maintain in proportion as this peace will in itself imply greater realities of justice and safer guaranties of stability.

By establishing this new order of things you will meet the aspiration of humanity, which, after the frightful convulsions of these bloodstained years, ardently wishes to feel itself protected by a union of free peoples against the ever-possible revivals of primitive savagery. An immortal glory will attach to the names of the nations and the men who have desired to coöperate in this grand work in faith and brotherhood, and who have taken pains to eliminate from the future peace causes of disturbance and instability.

This very day forty-eight years ago, on January 18, 1871, the German Empire was proclaimed by an army of invasion in the Château at Versailles. It was consecrated by the theft of two French provinces; it was thus vitiated from its origin and by the fault of the founders; born in injustice, it has ended in opprobrium. You are assembled in order to repair the evil that it has done and to prevent a recurrence of it. You hold in your hands the future of the world. I leave you, gentlemen, to your grave deliberations, and I declare the Conference of Paris open.

PRESIDENT WILSON: NOMINATION OF M. GEORGES CLEMENCEAU AS PRESIDENT OF THE CONFERENCE

I HAVE the great honor to propose as definitive president of this conference the French Premier, M. Clemenceau. I shall doubtless do this in conformity with usage. I should do it even if it were only a question of paying homage to the French Republic, but I do it also because I desire, and you certainly desire with me, to pay homage to the man himself. France, as it is, would alone deserve this honor, but we are to-day in her capital, and it is here that this great Conference has met. France, by her sufferings and sacrifices during the war, deserves a special tribute. Moreover, Paris is her ancient and splendid capital, where more than once these great assemblages, on which the fate of the world has depended, have met.

I am happy to think that the meeting which is beginning crowns the series of these meetings. This Conference may be considered in some respects as the final crowning of the diplomatic history of the world up to this day, for never have so many nations been represented at the same time to solve problems which in so high a degree interest the whole world. Moreover, this meeting signifies for us the end of this terrible war, which threatened to destroy civilization and the world itself. It is a delightful sensation for us to feel that we are meeting at a moment when this terrible menace has ceased to exist.

But it is not only to France, it is to the man who is her great servant, that we wish to pay homage and to do honor. We have learned, since we have had relations with him, and since he has been at the head of the French Government, to admire the power of his direction and the force and good sense of his actions. But, more than this, those who know him, those who have worked in close connection with him, have acquired for him a real affection. Those who, like ourselves, have seen him work in these recent times know how much he is united with us, and with what ardor he is working for that which we ourselves desire. For we all desire the same thing. We desire before all to lift from the shoulders of humanity the frightful weight which is pressing on them, so that humanity, released from this weight, may at last return joyfully to work. Thus, gentlemen, it is not only to the Premier of the French Republic, it is to M. Clemenceau that I propose you should give the presidency of this assemblage.

MR. LLOYD GEORGE

GENTLEMEN, it is not only a pleasure for me, but a real privilege, to support in the name of the British Empire the motion which has been proposed by President Wilson. I shall do it for the reasons which the President has just expressed with so much eloquence. It is homage to a man that we wish to pay before all. When I was at school M. Clemenceau was already one of the moving forces in French politics. Already his renown had spread far. And, were it not for this memory of my childhood, I should be tempted to believe the legend which is commonly spread abroad of the eternal youth of M. Clemenceau. In all the conferences at which we have been present the most alert, the most vigorous, in a word, the youngest man, was always M. Clemenceau. By the freshness of his mind and his indefatigable energy he displayed his youth at every moment. He is indeed "the grand young man" of France. But nothing will give us greater pleasure than to see him take the place which we propose that he should accept. No one is better qualified for that place. We have often had discussion together. We have often been in agreement and sometimes we have disagreed, and in that case we have always been in the habit of expressing our opinions with all the force and vigor which belong to two Celts like ourselves.

I believe that in the debates of this Conference there will at first inevitably be delays, but I guarantee from my knowledge of M. Clemenceau that there will be no time wasted. That is indispensable. The world is thirsting for peace. Millions of men are waiting to return to their normal life, and they will not forgive us too long delays. I am sure that M. Clemenceau will not allow useless delays to occur. He is one of the greatest living orators, but he knows that the finest eloquence is that which gets things done and that the worst is that which delays them. Another reason for congratulating him on occupying the place which we are about to give him is his indomitable courage, of which he has given proof in days of difficulty. In these days his energy and presence of mind have done more than all the acts of us others to ensure victory. There is no man of whom one can say that he has contributed more to surmount those terrible difficulties which were so close to the final triumph. He represents the admirable energy, courage and resource of his great people, and that is why I desire to add my voice to that of President Wilson and to ask for his election to the presidency of the Peace Conference.

BARON SONNINO

Gentlemen, on behalf of the Italian Delegation, I associate myself cordially with the proposal of President Wilson, supported by Mr. Lloyd George, and I ask you to give the presidency of the Peace Conference to M. Clemenceau. I am happy to be able in these circumstances to testify to my good will and admiration for France and for the eminent statesman who is at the head of her Government.

[M. Clemenceau was then elected president of the Conference unanimously.]

M. CLEMENCEAU: OPENING ADDRESS

GENTLEMEN, you would not understand it if, after listening to the words of the two eminent men who have just spoken, I were to keep silent. I cannot elude the necessity of expressing my lively gratitude, my deep gratitude, both to the illustrious President Wilson and to the Prime Minister of Great Britain, as well as to Baron Sonnino, for the words which they have uttered. In the past, in the days of my youth—long ago now, as Mr. Lloyd-George has reminded me—when I traveled over America and England, I used always to hear the French blamed for that excess of politeness which led them beyond the boundaries of the truth. Listening to the American statesman and the British statesman, I asked myself whether in Paris they had not acquired our national vice of flattering urbanity.

It is necessary, gentlemen, to point out that my election is due necessarily to lofty international tradition, and to the time-honored courtesy shown toward the country which has the honor to welcome the Peace Conference in its capital. The proofs of "friendship"—as they will allow me to call it —of President Wilson and Mr. Lloyd-George touched me profoundly, because in these proofs may be seen a new force for all three of us which will enable us, with the help of this entire Conference, to carry through the arduous task entrusted to us. I draw new confidence from it for the success of our efforts.

President Wilson has good authority for his remark that we have here for the first time a collection of delegates from all the civilized peoples of the earth. The greater the sanguinary catastrophe which devastated and ruined one of the richest regions of France, the more ample and more splendid should be the reparation—not merely the reparation for material acts, the ordinary reparation, if I may venture to say so, which is due to us—but the nobler and loftier reparation we are going to try to secure, so that the peoples may at last escape from this fatal embrace, which, heaping up ruins and sorrows, terrorizes the populations and prevents them from devoting themselves freely to their work for fear of the enemies who may spring up at any moment. It is a great and noble ambition that has come to us all. We must hope that success will crown our efforts. This can only be if we have our ideas clear-cut and well defined.

I said in the Chamber of Deputies some days ago, and I make a point of repeating the statement here, that success is possible only if we remain firmly united. We have come here as friends. We must pass through that door as brothers. That is the first reflection which I am anxious to express to you. Everything must be subordinated to the necessity for a closer and closer union between the peoples which have taken part in this great war. The Society of Nations has its being here, it has its being in you. It is for you to make it live, and for that there is no sacrifice to which we are not ready to consent. I do not doubt that as you are all of this disposition we shall arrive at this result, but only on condition that we exercise impartial pressure on ourselves to reconcile what in appearance may be opposing interests in the higher view of a greater, happier, and better humanity. That, gentlemen, is what I had to say to you.

I am touched beyond all expression by the proof of confidence and regard which you have been kind enough to give me. The program of the Conference, the aim marked out by President Wilson, is no longer merely peace for the territories, great and small, with which we are directly concerned; it is no longer merely a peace for the continents, it is peace for the peoples. This program speaks for itself; there is nothing to be added to it. Let us try, gentlemen, to do our work speedily and well. I am handing to the Bureau the rules of procedure of the Conference, and these will be distributed to you all.

I come now to the order of the day. The first question is as follows: "The responsibility of the authors of the war." The second is thus expressed: "Penalties for crimes committed during the war." The third is: "International legislation in regard to labor."

The Powers whose interests are only in part involved are also invited to send in memoranda in regard to matters of all kinds—territorial, financial, or economic—which affect them particularly. These memoranda should be addressed to the general secretariat of the Conference. This system is somewhat novel. Our desire in asking you to proceed thus is to save time. All the nations represented here are free to present their claims. You will kindly send in these memoranda as speedily as possible, as we shall then get on with the work which we shall submit for your consideration. You can deal with the third question from the standpoint of the organization of labor.

It is a very vast field. But we beg of you to begin by examining the question as to the responsibility of the authors of the war. I do not need to set forth our reasons for this. If we wish to establish justice in the world we can do so now, for we have won victory and can impose the penalties demanded by justice. We shall insist on the imposition of penalties on the authors of the abominable crimes committed during the war. Has anyone any question to ask in regard to this? If not I would again remind you that every delegation should devote itself to the study of this first question, which has been made the subject of reports by eminent jurists, and of a report which will be sent to you entitled, "An Inquiry into the Criminal Responsibility of the Emperor William II." The perusal of this brochure will, without doubt, facilitate your work. In Great Britian and in America studies on this point have also been published. No one having any remark to make, the program is adopted.

It only remains for me to say, gentlemen, that the order of the day for our next sitting will begin with the question of the Society of Nations. Our order of the day, gentlemen, is now brought to an end. Before closing the sitting, I should like to know whether any delegate of the Powers represented has any question to submit to the Bureau. As we must work in complete agreement, it is to be desired that members of the Conference shall submit all the observations they consider necessary. The Bureau will welcome the expression of all kinds, and will answer all questions addressed to it. No one has anything further to say? The sitting is closed.

2. SESSION OF JANUARY 25

PRESIDENT WILSON
Reprinted from the London *Times,* January 27, 1919.

Mr Chairman:—I consider it a distinguished privilege to be permitted to open the discussion in this Conference on the League of Nations. We have assembled for two purposes: to make the present settlements which have been rendered necessary by this war, and also to secure the peace of the world, not only by the present settlements, but by the arrangements we shall make at this Conference for its maintenance. The League of Nations seems to me to be necessary for both of these purposes. There are many complicated questions connected with the present settlements which perhaps cannot be successfully worked out to an ultimate issue by the decisions we shall arrive at here. I can easily conceive that many of these settlements will need subsequent consideration, that many of the decisions we make shall need subsequent alteration in some degree; for, if I may judge by my own study of some of these questions, they are not susceptible of confident judgments at present.

It is, therefore, necessary that we should set up some machinery by which the work of this Conference should be rendered complete. We have assembled here for the purpose of doing very much more than making the present settlements that are necessary. We are assembled under very peculiar conditions of world opinion. I may say, without straining the point, that we are not representatives of governments, but representatives of peoples. It will not suffice to satisfy governmental circles anywhere. It is necessary that we should satisfy the opinion of mankind. The burdens of this war have fallen in an unusual degree upon the whole population of the countries involved. I do not need to draw for you the picture of how the burden has been thrown back from the front upon the older men, upon the women, upon the children, upon the homes of the civilized world, and how the real strain of the war has come where the eye of government could not reach, but where the heart of humanity beat. We are bidden by these people to make a peace which will make them secure. We are bidden by these people to see to it that this strain does not come upon them, and I venture to say that it has been possible for them to bear this strain because they hoped that those who represented them could get together after this war and make such another sacrifice unnecessary.

It is a solemn obligation on our part, therefore, to make permanent arrangements that justice shall be rendered and peace maintained. This is the central object of our meeting. Settlements may be temporary, but the action of the nations in the interest of peace and justice must be permanent. We can set up permanent processes. We may not be able to set up permanent decisions. Therefore, it seems to me that we must take, so far as we can, a picture of the world into our minds.

Is it not a startling circumstance, for one thing, that the great discoveries of science, that the quiet studies of men in laboratories, that the thoughtful developments which have taken place in quiet lecture-rooms, have now been turned to the destruction of civilization? The powers of destruction have not so much multiplied as gained facility. The enemy whom we have just overcome had at his seats of learning some of the principal centers of scientific study and discovery, and he used them in order to make destruction sudden and complete; and only the watchful, continuous coöperation of men can see to it that science, as well as armed men, is kept within the harness of civilization.

In a sense, the United States is less interested in this subject than the other nations here assembled. With her great territory and her extensive sea borders, it is less likely that the United States should suffer from the attack of enemies than that many of the other nations here should suffer; and the ardor of the United States—for it is a very deep and genuine ardor—for the society of nations is not an ardor springing out of fear or apprehension, but an ardor springing out of the ideals which have come to consciousness in this war. In coming into this war the United States never for a moment thought that she was intervening in the politics of Europe, or the politics of Asia, or the politics of any part of the world. Her thought was that all the world had now become conscious that there was a single cause which turned upon the issues of this war. That was the cause of justice and of liberty for men of every kind and place. Therefore, the United States would feel that her part in this war had been played in vain if there ensued upon it a body of European settlements. She would feel that she could not take part in guaranteeing those European settlements unless that guaranty involved the continuous superintendence of the peace of the world by the associated nations of the world.

Therefore, it seems to me that we must concert our best judgment in order to make this League of Nations a vital thing—not merely a formal thing, not an occasional thing, not a thing sometimes called into life to meet an exigency, but always functioning in watchful attendance upon the interests of the nations, and that its continuity should be a vital continuity; that it should have functions that are continuing functions, and that do not permit an intermission of its watchfulness and of its labor; that it should be the eye of the nations to keep watch upon the common interest, an eye that did not slumber, an eye that was everywhere watchful and attentive.

And if we do not make it vital, what shall we do? We shall disappoint the expectations of the peoples. This is what their thought centers upon. I have had the very delightful experience of visiting several nations since I came to this side of the water, and every time the voice of the body of the people reached me through any representative, at the front of the plea stood the hope for the League of Nations. Gentlemen, the select classes of mankind are no longer the governors of mankind. The fortunes of mankind are now in the hands of the plain people of the whole world. Satisfy them, and you have not only justified their confidence, but established peace. Fail to satisfy them, and no arrangement that you can make will either set up or steady the peace of the world.

You can imagine, gentlemen, I dare say, the sentiments and the purpose with which representatives of the United States support this great project for a League of Nations.

We regard it as the keystone of the whole program which expressed our purposes and ideals in this war and which the associated nations accepted as the basis of the settlement. If we return to the United States without having made every effort in our power to realize this program, we should return to meet the merited scorn of our fellow-citizens. For they are a body that constitutes a great democracy. They expect their leaders to speak their thoughts and no private purpose of their own. They expect their representatives to be their servants. We have no choice but to obey their mandate. But it is with the greatest enthusiasm and pleasure that we accept that mandate; and because this is the keystone of the whole fabric, we have pledged our every purpose to it, as we have to every item of the fabric. We would not dare abate a single item of the program which constitutes our instruction. We would not dare compromise upon any matter as the champion of this thing—this peace of the world, this attitude of justice, this principle that we are the masters of no people, but are here to see that every people in the world shall choose its own masters and govern its own destinies, not as we wish but as it wishes. We are here to see, in short, that the very foundations of this war are swept away.

Those foundations were the private choice of small coteries of civil rulers and military staffs. Those foundations were the aggression of great powers upon small. Those foundations were the holding together of empires of unwilling subjects by the duress of arms. Those foundations were the power of small bodies of men to work their will and use mankind as pawns in a game. And nothing less than the emancipation of the world from these things will accomplish peace. You can see that the representatives of the United States are, therefore, never put to the embarrassment of choosing a way of expediency, because they have laid down for them the unalterable lines of principle. And, thank God, those lines have been accepted as the lines of settlement by all the high-minded men who have had to do with the beginnings of this great business.

I hope, Mr. Chairman, that when it is known, as I feel confident it will be known, that we have adopted the principles of the League of Nations and mean to work out that principle in effective action, we shall by that single thing have lifted a great part of the load of anxiety from the hearts of men everywhere. We stand in a peculiar case. As I go about the streets here I see everywhere the American uniform. Those men came into the war after we had uttered our purposes. They came as crusaders, not merely to win a war, but to win a cause; and I am responsible to them, for it fell to me to formulate the purposes for which I asked them to fight, and I, like them, must be a crusader for these things, whatever it costs and whatever it may be necessary to do, in honor, to accomplish the object for which they fought.

I have been glad to find from day to day that there is no question of our standing alone in this matter, for there are champions of this cause upon every hand. I am merely avowing this in order that you many understand why, perhaps, it fell to us, who are disengaged from the politics of this great continent and of the Orient, to suggest that this was the keystone of the arch, and why it occurred to the generous mind of our President to call upon me to open this debate. It is not because we alone represent this idea, but because it is our privilege to associate ourselves with you in representing it.

I have only tried in what I have said to give you the fountains of the enthusiasm which is within us for this thing, for those fountains spring, it seems to me, from all the ancient wrongs and sympathies of mankind, and the very pulse of the world seems to beat to the surface in this enterprise.

MR. LLOYD GEORGE

M. CLEMENCEAU, I rise to second this resolution. After the noble speech of the American President I feel that no observations are needed in order to commend this resolution to the Conference, and I should not have intervened at all had it not been that I wished to state how emphatically the people of the British Empire are behind this proposal. And if the national leaders have not been able during the last five years to devote as much time as they would like to its advocacy, it is because their time and their energies have been absorbed in the exigencies of a terrible struggle.

Had I the slightest doubt in my own mind as to the wisdom of this scheme it would have vanished before the irresistible appeal made to me by the spectacle I witnessed last Sunday. I visited a region which but a few years ago was one of the fairest in an exceptionally fair land. I found it a ruin and a desolation. I drove for hours through a country which did not appear like habitation of living men and women and children, but like the excavation of a buried province—shattered, torn, rent. I went to one city where I witnessed a scene of devastation that no indemnity can ever repair—one of the beautiful things of the world disfigured and defaced beyond repair. And one of the cruelest features, to my mind, was what I could see had happened: that Frenchmen, who loved their land almost beyond any nation, in order to establish the justice of their cause, had to assist a cruel enemy in demolishing their own homes, and I felt these are the results, only part of the results. Had I been there months ago I would have witnessed something that I dare not describe. But I saw acres of graves of the fallen. And these were the results of the only method, the only organized method, that civilized nations have ever attempted or established to settle disputes amongst each other. And my feeling was: surely it is time, surely it is time that a saner plan for settling disputes between peoples should be established than this organized savagery.

I do not know whether this will succeed. But if we attempt it the attempt will be a success, and for that reason I second the proposal.

PREMIER ORLANDO OF ITALY

I WISH to express my fervent adhesion to the great principles which we are asked to consecrate, and I think that by doing this we shall only fulfill the most solemn obligation we have undertaken towards our people. We asked them to make immense efforts, and the counterpart of the responsibility we took was for them sacrifices, unnamed sufferings, death.

We are only doing our duty by keeping our sacred promise. We must therefore bring into this a full consent of mind and, if I may say so, purity of soul.

No people is more ready to accept in its entirety the principles laid down by President Wilson in his speech than the Italian people. It is with no feeling of vanity that I shall now recall the great juridical tradition of the Italian people. The principle of law is not only a principle of protection and of justice against violence, it is the form guaranteed by the state of what is the vital principle to humanity, social coöperation, solidarity between men. The plan which will now be laid before us must give us not only guaranties against future wars, but must secure coöperation between the nations. This is a great historical day. To-day the right of peoples is born. It is only just that it should be born in this generous country of France which has fought so well by her genius and by her blood to ensure the triumph of the rights of man, and this is a happy omen for the beginning of these debates.

M. LÉON BOURGEOIS

I express my gratitude to the President of the Republic who has appointed me to speak on this great occasion. Was it because of his memory of the part I took in The Hague Conference? Whatever the reason, half of the honor now given to me must go to those of my colleagues present who were at The Hague with me.

The strong expression used by President Wilson that we are not only the representatives of governments, but representatives of peoples, is something we must reflect upon. What do the free peoples of the world wish for? They wish that the terrible experience of the last four and a half years should never be renewed; they wish for the thing so deeply desired by all the victims of this war, all those who died for freedom and the right, the men who died fighting not only for their country but as true crusaders for the liberty of the world.

The striking picture drawn by Mr. Lloyd-George of what

he saw in one of the devastated parts of France is only one instance of a great fact. The devastating effect of an international conflict cannot now be limited to the place near where the conflict started. There is now no possibility of limiting any conflict of this sort. It cannot happen anywhere without putting the whole world in mortal danger. The whole world is interdependent economically, morally, and intellectually.

Another reason makes it impossible for us to face a renewal of such a war. It is the great progress and the great future progress of science, which—against its object, which is all for the benefit of mankind—will be used as it has been used, if we do not find some way out of the difficulty, for purposes of wholesale destruction.

By thinking of what has been done during this war we can imagine what will happen if another war takes place in another forty or fifty years. We have the right to say that the problem before our consciences—how to assure the future of our own country and the future of our common motherland, the world, while making superior its interest—is the problem of general peace.

We can remember the scruples which at The Hague were felt, even by the representatives of the most free and most peaceful countries, when they said that they were obliged to limit the stipulations to what would preserve the honor and the vital interests of their respective countries.

At present the vital interest of all countries is for a universal peace based upon the prevalence of right, and the rights of all our countries separately are dependent upon it. How can we make a reality of what was thought to be a dream of yesterday? How is it that practical statesmen are now around the table with this common thought that will certainly be expressed by your unanimous votes on what we thought only yesterday to be Utopia?

If we look backward to the history of the last thirty years, and especially, if I am permitted to refer to it again, The Hague Conference, we can see that, in spite of the disappointment we have suffered, such meetings as that of The Hague Conference had results. Such a dangerous conflict as that between France and Germany at the time of the Casablanca incident could be solved by a decision respecting the honor of both countries by a process of arbitration.

Why was it not possible to apply the same proceeding to the terrible conflict which has caused the world so much suffering? There are two causes for it, one of which you will deal with presently. It is because the map of the world did not show a state of things in conformity with the principles of right. It was impossible for Frenchmen not to remember that some of their old countrymen were under foreign rule. It was impossible for Italy to forget that some of the fair provinces of Italy were not yet members of their own Mother Country; and there were many other questions I need not mention now.

How can you organize international peace by suppressing a just claim for unredeemed countries and populations? This cannot be done. But after you have arrived at a settlement in conformity with the principles of right and the wishes of the populations themselves, then you will have a firm basis to build up what The Hague Conference was unable to establish.

The second difference between that time and the present time is that you will be able to sit and establish a system of sanctions. At The Hague it was impossible because of the division between the nations there, and that division showed already the same classification which had been shown in this war. The same group of nations was then adhering to every proposal against peaceful settlement, which we had seen since destroying the peace and the happiness of the whole world. At present we are in a position not only to lay down principles, but also to establish a system of penalties.

By this you will be able to do a lasting work, and you will be able to enter with a serene mind into the temple of peace. In the name of the Government of the Republic it is my duty to say that we are ready to attempt and to lend our earnest will to everything that can bring us, as far as possible, on the road which has been pointed out by President Wilson's speech. You will see what measures have to be taken, but you can be certain that it is with deep and sincere fervor that the whole of France will join in the efforts.

President Wilson said that this question is in the heart of all mankind. Well, it is so. He also said that the League of Nations must be the ever watching eye which shall protect mankind against the danger. Well, that is what we tried to do years ago before we were in a position to do so. At The Hague we felt the pulse of mankind beating feebly, but now we are sure that united mankind is born, and we greet its birth.

3. SESSION OF FEBRUARY 15

PRESIDENT WILSON

Reprinted from the New York *Times*, February 15, 16, 17, 1919.

MR. CHAIRMAN: I have the honor, and assume it a very great privilege, of reporting in the name of the Commission constituted by this conference on the formulation of a plan for the Leauge of Nations. I am happy to say that it is a unanimous report, a unanimous report from the representatives of fourteen nations—the United States, Great Britain, France, Italy, Japan, Belgium, Brazil, China, Czecho-Slovakia, Greece, Poland, Portugal, Rumania, and Serbia.

I think it will be serviceable and interesting if I, with your permission, read the document, as the only report we have to make.

[President Wilson read the draft of the Constitution of the League of Nations, commenting on some of the articles. In conclusion he spoke as follows:]

It gives me pleasure to add to this formal reading of the result of our labors that the character of the discussion which occurred at the sittings of the commission was not only of the most constructive but of the most encouraging sort. It was obvious throughout our discussions that, although there were subjects upon which there were individual differences of judgment with regard to the method by which our objects should be obtained, there were practically at no point any serious differences of opinion or motive as to the objects which we were seeking.

Indeed, while these debates were not made the opportunity for the expression of enthusiam and sentiment, I think the other members of the commission will agree with me that there was an undertone of high respect and of enthusiasm for the thing we were trying to do, which was heartening throughout every meeting, because we felt that in a way this conference did intrust unto us the expression of one of its highest and most important purposes, to see to it that the concord of the world in the future with regard to the objects of justice should not be subject to doubt or uncertainty, that the coöperation of the great body of nations should be assured in the maintenance of peace upon terms of honor and of international obligations.

The compulsion of that task was constantly upon us, and at no point was there shown the slightest desire to do anything but suggest the best means to accomplish that great object. There is very great significance, therefore, in the fact that the result was reached unanimously.

Fourteen nations were represented, among them all of those powers which for convenience we have called the great powers, and among the rest a representation of the greatest variety of circumstances and interests. So that I think we are justified in saying that the significance of the result, therefore, has the deepest of all meanings, the union of wills in a common purpose, a union of wills which cannot be resisted, and which, I dare say, no nation will run the risk of attempting to resist.

Now as to the character of the document. While it has consumed some time to read this document, I think you will see at once that it is very simple, and in nothing so simple as in the structure which it suggests for a League of Nations—a body of delegates, an Executive Council, and a permanent secretariat.

When it came to the question of determining the character of the representation in the body of delegates, we were all aware of a feeling which is current throughout the world. Inasmuch as I am stating it in the presence of the official representatives of the various governments here present, including myself, I may say that there is a universal feeling that the world cannot rest satisfied with merely official guidance. There has reached us through many channels the feeling that if the deliberating body of the League of Nations was merely to be a body of officials representing the various Governments, the peoples of the world would not be sure that some of the mistakes which preoccupied officials had admittedly made might not be repeated.

It was impossible to conceive a method or an assembly so large and various as to be really representative of the great body of the peoples of the world, because, as I roughly reckon it, we represent, as we sit around this table, more than twelve hundred million people. You cannot have a representative of twelve hundred million people, but if you leave it to each government to have, if it pleases, one or two or three representatives, though only with a single vote, it may vary its representation from time to time.

Therefore, we thought that this was a proper and a very prudent concession to the practically universal opinion of plain men everywhere that they wanted the door left open to a variety of representation, instead of being confined to a single official body with which they could or might not find themselves in sympathy.

And you will notice that this body has unlimited rights of discussion—I mean of discussion of anything that falls within the field of international relations—and that it is especially agreed that war or international misunderstandings, or anything that may lead to friction or trouble, is everybody's business, because it may affect the peace of the world.

And in order to safeguard the popular power so far as we could of this representative body, it is provided, you will notice, that when a subject is submitted, it is not to arbitration, but to discussion by the Executive Council. It can, upon the initiative of either of the parties to the dispute, be drawn out of the Executive Council into the larger forum of the general body of delegates, because through this instrument we are depending primarily and chiefly upon one great force, and this is the moral force of the public opinion of the world—the pleasing and clarifying and compelling influences of publicity, so that intrigues can no longer have their coverts, so that designs that are sinister can at any time be drawn into the open, so that those things that are destroyed by the light may be promptly destroyed by the overwhelming light of the universal expression of the condemnation of the world.

Armed force is in the background in this program, but it is

in the background, and if the moral force of the world will not suffice, the physical force of the world shall. But that is the last resort, because this is intended as a constitution of peace, not as a league of war.

The simplicity of the document seems to me to be one of its chief virtues, because, speaking for myself, I was unable to see the variety of circumstances with which this League would have to deal. I was unable, therefore, to plan all the machinery that might be necessary to meet the differing and unexpected contingencies. Therefore, I should say of this document that it is not a strait jacket, but a vehicle of life.

A living thing is born, and we must see to it what clothes we put on it. It is not a vehicle of power, but a vehicle in which power may be varied at the discretion of those who exercise it and in accordance with the changing circumstances of the time. And yet, while it is elastic, while it is general in its terms, it is definite in the one thing that we were called upon to make definite. It is a definite guaranty of peace. It is a definite guaranty by word against aggression. It is a definite guaranty against the things which have just come near bringing the whole structure of civilization into ruin.

Its purposes do not for a moment lie vague. Its purposes are declared, and its powers are unmistakable. It is not in contemplation that this should be merely a league to secure the peace of the world. It is a league which can be used for coöperation in any international matter. That is the significance of the provision introduced concerning labor. There are many ameliorations of labor conditions which can be effected by conference and discussion. I anticipate that there will be a very great usefulness in the Bureau of Labor which it is contemplated shall be set up by the League. Men and women and children who work have been in the background through long ages, and sometimes seemed to be forgotten, while governments have had their watchful and suspicious eyes upon the maneuvers of one another, while the thought of statesmen has been about structural action and the larger transactions of commerce and finance.

Now if I may believe the picture which I see, there comes into the foreground the great body of the laboring people of the world, the men and women and children upon whom the great a very recent period thought that it was still too early to hope.

Many terrible things have come out of this war, gentlemen, but some very beautiful things have come out of it. Wrong has been defeated, but the rest of the world has been more conscious than it ever was before of the majority of right. People that were suspicious of one another can now live as friends and comrades in a single family, and desire to do so. The miasma of distrust, of intrigue, is cleared away. Men are looking eye to eye and saying "We are brothers and have a common purpose. We did not realize it before, but now we do realize it, and this is our covenant of friendship."

M. LÉON BOURGEOIS

I RISE to express the deep satisfaction of all, and of France more than any other country, because she is among the countries who have most suffered, to see the unity of our wills and of our hearts in a passionate adhesion to the principles of the League of Nations. That act of faith we shall do in a spirit of cordiality and good will that has been that of the committee. Under the eminent chairmanship of President Wilson the committee has worked with all their hearts to attain this great object.

Lord Robert Cecil has said we now present to the conference and to the world the result of our work, but we do not present it as something that is final, but only as the result of an honest effort to be discussed and to be examined not only by this conference but the public opinion of the world.

We are unanimous in our opinion that this scheme must be presented to the world, and it resulted from our deliberation. We must preserve the character of unanimity which its note has given it. We still retain our rights when further discussions take place to state more definitely our views on some details.

Signor Orlando has said how difficult it seemed at the beginning to conciliate two apparently contradictory principles—that of the sovereignty of nations and that of the limitations that nations must accept in order to secure the reign of right and justice. That conciliation has taken place without effort, and we have demonstrated movement, as Signor Orlando said, by walking.

We rise to prevent the renewal of war like that which we have just seen; we rise at the appeal of all those who have fallen to spare their offspring the renewal of such an ordeal. We are persuaded that no war in the future can be limited to a small area.

The interdependence of the different parts and different interests of the world has become such that no conflict can be limited. It is that the whole world may keep itself from danger that we to-day have ordained that right and justice must be the basis of settlement in all our conferences. In the view of just people there are no small and no great States. All are and all will be equal before the principle of international justice, and in the tribunal that will give the decisions the judges will sit, not as the representatives of one particular nation, but as the representatives of international right.

This is a principle to which we are particularly attached. All the States, in consenting to submit to international justice, take at the same time a definite pledge to guarantee to each other the integrity of their territories as established by the settlement of the present peace treaty, and also to guarantee their political independence against future aggression. This is the object of our scheme. I hope the means which are suggested by it will allow us to attain our object.

We have established a certain number of judicial principles and international organizations binding the States together, binding them to a common work, and binding them to the truce without which their common development would be impossible. These organizations, the creation of which is provided for in the last articles of the covenant, are similar to some which have existed already, but which were scattered through various parts of the world and which had never been brought together to form part of the common body of humanity. The foundation is now laid, and we are certain that the organizations will be multiplied and will help humanity more and more to attain its common aims.

We have been unanimous in proclaiming these principles, and we have felt the force of these principles so much that we have no doubt that a strong light will penetrate even into the darkest ports, that the light radiating from those principles will find its way in lands that seem to be the least open to it.

But it is not enough to proclaim such great principles. We must organize a system of guaranty and a system of action, both judicial and practical. The plan laid down is a clear and simple one. There is a council where all the States are represented equally, each having only one vote, and there is an Executive Committee which is constituted on a different principle. But even in this case, where it has been found necessary for purposes of action to give five votes to the larger Powers, the principle of equality has been secured by giving as much as four votes to the smaller States.

Respect for the decision given by that body will be assured by definite rules, the violation of which shall be considered as an act of war against all the contracting States. If one State (it may be the smallest and most remote of all the States) is attacked without justification, then the whole of the League of Nations is being attacked, and will resist.

But we must go further. In order to secure the execution of international sentences there must be a limitation of armaments. This has been the wish of the world for a great many years. What was formerly so difficult has to-day become possible. Our victory has made it possible, because it has enabled us to disarm the barbaric force that was in the way of such an improvement.

That limitation must be such that no State can be capable of prevailing against the will of the law of nations, but at the same time each State should be strong enough to contribute to the force that will enable the League of Nations to impose its will. There has been unanimity upon all these points.

There are one or two points upon which I wish particularly to insist, because they are connected with dangers that may be of special moment to some of us, dangers that may arise not equal for all.

There are special dangers for countries like France, Belgium, Serbia, and the new States that are in the stage of formation in Central Europe. It is necessary to give them special guaranties, and this has been recognized by the committee, when it states that special account should be taken of the geographical situation of, and the mode of application to, each State in the scale of armaments. Where the frontiers are more exposed it must be possible to have stronger systems of defense, and possibly also greater armaments.

This is all right, but there is no doubt that it will put on the shoulders of the nations who happen to be in that difficult position a special burden. It will hamper them in the peaceful competition that is the life of the world.

And here again two practical questions must be put. To give all nations necessary security, the principle of the limitation of armaments must not only be executed but executed very fast. It has been said (and no one has said it more forcefully than President Wilson) that modern war has become a war of material, that in such a war as the one we have just seen, and such as we hope never to see in the future, what has triumphed has been science turned into barbarism.

Now, it is necessary for us to control the war industries all over the world. The nations, who are the contracting parties of the covenant, pledge themselves mutually to communicate to each other full information about their armaments and their means of production. This is a very good plan, with which I am particularly satisfied.

At the same time, I propose an amendment, which I think I ought to mention. I thought it would be necessary to institute a permanent organization for purposes of inspection, and this amendment was not at the moment embodied in the text. We have accepted the text as it is before you, and we now mention that amendment. It is because—as the whole scheme is going to be discussed by the world—it is better that all the points that have given occasion for important observations should be mentioned.

Here is a second point. Take a State that violates the international covenant. That State is supposed to be in a state of war against all the members of the League, and all are prepared to compel it to execute its obligations. But war is not something that can proceed at once, especially when the question is how to bring together forces belonging to States which are very different from each other and may be at the four corners of the world. Each nation will have to wait in order to act until a certain procedure is gone through and until for each particular nation a vote has been taken by its Parliament—and so on. This means time and delay.

And, supposing that there is on the part of the aggressor a will to precipitate a situation, then we must provide for the possibility. For this purpose it would be desirable to have all the means of resistance studied and concerted action prepared before the occasion arises. This would be the best check against any ill design.

If the would-be aggressor knows that resistance is fully prepared against any action such as he contemplated then he will be restrained. Where, on the other hand, he knows that no such preparation exists and that sudden action on his part would encounter no prepared and well-thought-out resistance, perhaps he would not be restrained and it would be extremely dangerous.

If you do not wish to see the terrible ordeal through which the world has passed renewed in the future, we ought to have a permanent organization to prepare the military and naval means of execution and make them ready in case of emergency.

This has been objected to by some of the members of the committee because it involved some difficult constitutional problems. This is why we have agreed to the text without that amendment, but we think the principle of that proposed amendment ought to be put before public opinion at the same time as the scheme to which we have agreed.

I hope that no one, either here or anywhere in the world, will be mistaken about my intention. I will not say, and I have not said, a word that could weaken the feeling of our complete and hearty unanimity. We have acted with one heart for the triumph of the cause, which is that of our conference, the cause of right against violence, the cause of right against might.

We believe that this scheme that is now before us is an excellent one. We believe in its virtues and its possibilities. The observations we have made on some points will, we hope, be of some value in the further discussions, since we are at the beginning of the examination of the whole plan.

Now we must, at the end, express our deep gratitude toward our colleagues, and our deep gratitude toward President Wilson, who presided over our labors in such a competent way and with such high spirit, and we wish still more to express the sincere wish of France to see that the great pact becomes, possibly with some improvement on the two points I have mentioned, the law of nations.

LORD ROBERT CECIL

MR. PRESIDENT AND GENTLEMEN:—I rejoice very much that the course which has been taken this afternoon has been pursued. It seems to me a good omen for the great project in which we are engaged that before its final completion it should have been published to the world and laid before all its people for their service and for their criticism. The President spoke of the spirit which animated the commission over which he presided with such distinction. I gladly bear my testimony to the complete accuracy, both in letter and in spirit, of everything which he has said about it.

It was, indeed, a pleasure to serve with such colleagues, and but for the common purpose and the common devotion to that purpose, it would have been impossible for us to have accomplished the task set before us within the time which was given to it. For, after all, the problem which we were engaged in solving was one of great difficulty. As I see it, it was to devise some really effective means of preserving the peace of the world consistent with the least possible interference with national sovereignty.

You have heard the covenant and it is unnecessary for me to dwell on its details. We have sought to safeguard the peace of the world by establishing certain principles. The first and chiefest of them is that no nation shall go to war with any other nation until every other possible means of settling the disputes shall have been fully and fairly tried.

Secondly, we lay down that under no circumstances shall any nation seek forcibly to disturb the territorial settlement to be arrived at as the consequence of this peace or interfere with the political independence of any of the States in the world. These are the two great precepts which we seek to lay down for the government of international relations.

And we have recognized that if these principles are really to be acted upon we must go one step further and lay it down that no nation must retain armament on a scale fitted only for aggressive purposes. I do not doubt that the working out of that principle will be difficult, but it is laid down clearly in this document, and the organs of the League are intrusted with the duty of producing for the consideration and support of the world a workable scheme for carrying it into effect.

And, finally, we have thought that if the world is to be at peace it is not enough to forbid war. We must do something more than that. We must try and substitute for the principle of international competition that of international coöperation, and you will find at the end of this document a number of clauses, which point out the various respects in which the world can better discharge its duties by the coöperation of each nation for purposes which are beneficial to the whole of them. They are the examples of what may be done. There are many omissions.

There is one clause which points out that in future international coöperation shall be made subject to and connected with the League of Nations. Certainly I should hope that there are such questions as the opium trade, the white slave traffic, and, in another order of ideas, the regulation of the arteries of the air, which, besides those mentioned in this document, call earnestly for effective international coöperation. Certain it is that if we can once get the nations of the world into the habit of coöperation with one another, you will have struck a great blow at the source or origin of almost all the world wars which have defaced the history of the world.

Those, I believe, are the principles on which we have relied for the safeguarding of Peace.

And as to national sovereignty, we have thought, in the first place, that the League should not in any respect interfere with the international liberties of any nation. I do not regard the clause which deals with labor as any such interference, for it is quite certain that no real progress in ameliorating the conditions of labor can be hoped for except by international agreement. Therefore, although the conditions of labor in a country are a matter of internal concern, yet, under the conditions under which we now live that is not so in truth, and bad conditions of labor in one country operate with fatal effect in depressing conditions of labor in another.

Secondly, we have laid down (and this is the great principle of the delegates except in very special cases and for very special reasons which are set out in the covenant) that all action must be unanimously agreed to in accordance with the general rule that governs international relations. That this will to some extent, in appearance at any rate, militate against the rapidity of action of the organs of the League is undoubted. In my judgment that defect is far more than compensated by the confidence that it will inspire that no nation, whether small or great, need fear oppression from the organs of the League.

Gentlemen, I have little more to say. The President has pointed out that the frame of the organization suggested is very simple. He has alluded to some respects in which some may think it might have been more elaborate, but I agree with him that simplicity is the essence of our plan. We are not seeking to produce for the world a building finished and complete in all respects. To have attempted such a thing would have been an arrogant piece of folly. All we have tried to do—all we have hoped to do—is to lay soundly and truly the foundations upon which our successors may build. I believe those foundations have been well laid out, and it depends upon those who come after us what will be the character and stability of the building erected upon them.

If it is merely a repetition of the old experiments of alliance, designed for however good a purpose, believe me, gentlemen, our attempt is doomed to failure. It must be a practical thing (and this is the real point), instinct with a genuine attempt to achieve the main objects we have in view.

And if those who build on those foundations really believe that the interest of one is the interest of all and that the prosperity of the world is bound up with the prosperity of each nation that makes it up—that goes to compose the family—then only will the finished structure of the League of Nations be what it ought to—a safeguard and a glory for the humanity of the world.

PREMIER ORLANDO OF ITALY

If I have asked to take part in this debate, it is to express my deep satisfaction at having coöperated in the first production of what is going to be one of the great documents of history, and I hope that my present feeling will be fully justified.

We all expect from the discussion and development of the present act a renewal of the whole world, but as the present debate has for its object to bring the whole scheme before the public opinion of the world, I wish to bring to that debate my personal contribution.

I am not going to speak on the general aim of the scheme. This has been formulated by the men who have the highest and noblest right to do it, and I am not here to insist upon the main and fundamental principles. This is what Lord Robert Cecil has done with vigorous lucidity of mind. But I have something to say on the general method upon which our work has been conducted.

Our task, gentlemen, was one of incomparable difficulty. We were faced with two absolute principles, the conciliation of which would seem to be logically impossible—on one side the sovereignty of States, admitting of no limitation, and, on the other hand, a limit, imposed upon the action of States, so that rights might be conciliated and so that the liberty of States should not include the liberty of doing wrong.

Now, we have been able to conciliate these two principles on the basis of self-constraint. The Governments have recognized that limit, and they will make it effective in each case, as there will be the overwhelming pressure of the public opinion of the world.

I do not forget the possibility that such a scheme has been the object of attacks by skeptics, some of them, according to their temper, in sorrowful tones, others in an ironical mood. I will answer them as the Greek philosopher did, when the reality of movement was denied in his presence, and he answered by rising to his feet and walking.

The possibility of collective international action has been

demonstrated by the work of our committee itself, there being eminent statesmen there representing the interests of the most divergent national existences, and they had to face problems which were difficult and puzzling. But even in spite of this we have agreed in a short time and after full discussion, where all the difficulties of solution were shown, and we had an opportunity of seeing which of the solutions was the best and wisest.

We reached our agreement after periods of suspense and reflection. Then we felt that something was growing and ripening, as a grain in the earth, and what has taken place at this time and will take place in the future is but an example of how that idea can work in its reality in a tangible form. If that idea is going to be transformed into a reality it is because of the generous and occult influence of all the blood that has been spilt, of all the terrible bereavement of the whole world.

After great wars in the past men have erected splendid monuments to glorify the fallen heroes, with their names inscribed on the walls. But the greatest monuments of the world, even the pyramids of Egypt, would not be equal, under the present circumstances where millions of men have died for a cause, to this document.

The pact which has been brought here to-day is the monument we intend to erect. This document of freedom and right was not born in vain, and it represents the redemption of humanity by sacrifice.

BARON MAKINO OF JAPAN

I BEG to add another voice to echo the congratulatory speeches that have been made on the presentation of a document which is perhaps the most important document that has been compiled by the hand of man. The great leaders with staunch purpose have personified this great movement, a movement involving intricate problems of divers nations, and they deserve the gratitude of their fellow-men for successfully piloting to this advanced stage a most effective instrument for the maintenance of the world. Their names will be indelibly written on pages of history, and that will be the grateful acknowledgment of humanity for their labors. As I understand there is to be no discussion of the project before us, I will limit myself to these few remarks, observing that, at a later stage in the discussion of this project, I shall have the privilege of addressing certain propositions, which I hope will receive earnest and favorable consideration from the distinguished men who represent the nations assembled here.

MR. GEORGE N. BARNES

Mr. President and Gentlemen: As one whose privilege it is to represent specially the working folk of Great Britain, I want just to make a very few observations. I think I know the mind of the British people on this question of the League of Nations, and I can assure you that it is one of eager expectancy. The people of Great Britain have shouldered their burden during the war, but through all its struggles and sacrifices they have looked eagerly forward for the day when aggressive war shall be no more. That day is dawning and, I believe, has been hastened by the work of the last month. To my mind, Mr. President, there are three outstanding principles in this document which, I believe, will stand out conspicuously as landmarks in the history of mankind.

First of all, the substitution of an altruistic principle for imperialism and violence in the adjustment of international affairs. Nations which have suffered and sacrificed in the acquisition of territory have agreed to the overseership of the League of Nations in the administration of that territory. They have further agreed to the principle that the welfare and assent of the peoples shall be the determining considerations in its administration. There is in this agreement, Mr. President, to my mind, a great advance in the application of the principle of moral idealism, and I can only say that I believe that that will strike the imagination of the world.

Second, they have agreed on the principle of reduction of armaments, a point of national safety, as prescribed by the League of Nations. This I believe to be the essential feature of the condition of permanent peace. If there be excess of guns, there will always be a chance of them getting fired off. Moreover, the nations in the future will be unable in any case to bear the burdens of armaments which have been the feature of our sad history during the last two or three decades. I am, therefore, glad that in this document provision is made for reduction of armaments, thereby, I believe, lessening the risk of war and easing the economic burden upon the people.

The third is a principle to which I wish to call attention in regard to the signatories to this document—they have agreed on a recognition of the evils of private profit in the manufacture of armaments—although, for my part, I should like to have seen a more robust declaration in favor of the abolition of private arms. Abolition I believe to be a step which will ultimately be found necessary, and I further hope that the Executive may be able to devise ways and means by which private profit may be eliminated, and I am perfectly sure that nothing would be more welcome to the mind of working folks.

There are just one or two things, Mr. President, which, to my mind, might have been more explicit, and which, I believe, will have to be grafted on to a League of Nations as the idea of world unity becomes more widely accepted. Let me mention one. I am afraid that when the time comes for the enforcement of decrees—if ever it does come, which God forbid—there may be delay and confusion on the part of the League. What I am afraid of is that an aggressive nation might again try to break through, and win its way to its object before the forces of mankind can be mobilized against it. Therefore, I should have been glad to have seen some provision for the nucleus of an international force which would be ready to strike against an aggressive nation. This, I know, cuts into the idea of the sovereignty of nations, but I hope that there may be future discussion on the part of the affiliated States as to how they can adjust their national life so as to admit of a greater degree of coöperation than is in this document.

Finally, I gladly note the insertion of a clause providing for the formation of international charters of labor. Hitherto nations have endeavored to protect themselves against low-paid labor by the imposition of tariff barriers. I hope we shall in the future, under the authority of the League of

Nations, seek and find a better way by abolishing low-paid labor altogether. We hope to raise life and labor from the mere struggle for bread on to higher levels of justice and humanity. The Commission, Mr. Chairman, which was appointed a few weeks ago to go into this matter is now busily engaged in formulating its detailed plan, and we hope to report in a few weeks' time. I can only say now on behalf of that Commission, that we shall endeavor to bring ourselves into contact with the League of Nations on as many points as we possibly can, and to bring ourselves in line with this epoch-making document which President Wilson has submitted to us to-day, and, through us, to the war-weary world.

M. VENISELOS OF GREECE

THE chairman has done me a great honor by calling upon me to speak, but I feel greatly embarrassed when I think what has been said before. What can I add? I shall be satisfied, being an idealist, and very often criticized as such, to express my enthusiasm.

I think idealism excludes materialism, but it does not exclude realism or reality. Humanity by one step has made a great stride toward its new and better fate. No doubt the plan now before us can be discussed and criticized. On one point I should like to say something, not to enter upon discussion with M. Bourgeois, but just to avoid the impression that might be created that public opinion could be in doubt of the possibilities of the scheme. As it is, we hear that some nations have an objection to the constitution of a permanent international force for constitutional reasons. We hope that it will be possible to raise these constitutional objections, and to find a way around the difficulty. But supposing this cannot be done, we must not say that the League of Nations would then be made powerless. We know that the would-be aggressor would know that behind the sentence—behind the tribunal—there is the League of Nations, that is, the nations here represented and the nations who have shown what they could do—some of them, perhaps, would not be ready at once when the occasion arose, but all showing with what force they could develop in case of need.

This being known, what Power would be inclined to play the part of the aggressor? He would know, whatever success he might attain at the beginning, his efforts would be doomed to failure and his cause to disaster. He would know his aggression would be a hopeless enterprise.

The representative of Japan has very aptly expressed my own thought when he said that the hand of man never wrought a more important document. And Signor Orlando also expressed the feeling that is in all our hearts when he said that we owe the benefits of this great act to the blood of all those who have died for the liberty of the world. We owe it also to the feeling of solidarity that has been created by the coöperation of the nations who have come together from all parts of the world. They are united, and this is the best step they can take toward their great and better future.

MR. WELLINGTON KOO OF CHINA

Mr. President and Gentlemen:—I have no lengthy eulogy to deliver, but I just want to express the very warm sentiment in my heart, and to express it very briefly, also. I have listened with deep pleasure and profound satisfaction to the words of my esteemed colleagues here in commendation of the spirit of the draft constitution which has just been made before us. Just as no people are more anxious than we are to see the League of Nations established, so no people are more gratified than the people of China to see and note the completion of another stage in advance in the movement for the founding of a League of Nations. Representing, as I have the honor to represent, at least one-third of the population represented here in this distinguished assemblage, I believe it is only fitting that I should add a word of satisfaction to those which have already been so eloquently uttered to us. Not only the character of the conditions in this draft, but the spirit permeating all the provisions through and through are of the most inspiring kind to us. We realize there is room for improvement, perhaps, but we also realize that we are making but a beginning now, and that, therefore, I cannot but express the satisfaction of the Chinese Delegation with the spirit underlying this instrument, the spirit of fair-mindedness and friendship, the spirit of concord and conciliation. It is but the natural result of the spirit which has animated the entire membership of the Commission on the League of Nations, and I say it, gentlemen, from my very pleasing experience of the sittings of that Commission of which I have the honor to be a part.

Thanks to the able leadership of President Wilson and also to the mutual coöperation of all members of the Commission, we are now at last in possession of an instrument which, as my distinguished colleague from Japan has already stated, is to be a memorable document in history, a document which, to my mind, will serve as a bulwark against international restlessness and a guaranty of universal peace. Therefore, gentlemen, the rapid and successful completion of the work of the Commission on the League of Nations, to my mind, marks a very distinct milestone on the road upon which mankind has been toiling forward ever from time immemorial in order to attain a goal of a durable peace. It is my privilege and a duty, therefore, to assure the Conference that China will always be ready to coöperate with those who will be members of the League, in order to coöperate with them not only for the organization, but also for the developmennt of this League of Nations, which will be the greatest institution that mankind will ever see.

WILLIAM HOWARD TAFT

THE LEAGUE OF NATIONS

[On March 4, 1919, President Wilson and Mr. Taft spoke in the Metropolitan Opera House in New York on the League of Nations. President Wilson said that he should tell Europe that "an overwhelming majority of the American people was in favor of the League of Nations." Mr. Taft gave a clear, non-partisan analysis of the Articles of the League of Nations, replying to criticisms and showing them to be groundless.

William Howard Taft was born in Cincinnati in 1857. He graduated from Yale in 1878 and from the Cincinnati Law School in 1880. He was first civil governor of the Philippines 1901-1904; Secretary of War 1904-1908; President of the United States from 1909-1913; and was appointed Chief Justice of the United States in 1921. He was president of the League to Enforce Peace and an active advocate of the ratification of the Treaty of Peace and the League of Nations.]

WE are here to-night in the sight of a League of Peace, of what I have ever regarded as the "Promised Land." Such a war as the last is a hideous blot on our Christian civilization. The inconsistency is as foul as was slavery under the Declaration of Independence. If Christian nations cannot now be brought into a united effort to suppress a recurrence of such a contest it will be a shame to modern society.

During my administration I attempted to secure treaties of universal arbitration between this country and France and England, by which all issues depended for their settlement upon legal principles were to be submitted to an international court for final decision. These treaties were emasculated by the Senate, yielding to the spirit which proceeds, unconsciously doubtless, but truly, from the conviction that the only thing that will secure to a nation the justice it wishes to secure is force; that agreements between nations to settle controversies justly and peaceably should never be given any weight in national policy; that in dealings between civilized nations we must assume that each nation is conspiring to deprive us of our independence and our prosperity; that there is no impartial tribunal to which we can entrust the decision of any question vitally affecting our interests or our honor, and that we can afford to make no agreement from which we may not immediately withdraw, and whose temporary operation to our detriment may not be expressly a ground for ending it. This is the doctrine of despair. It leads necessarily to the conclusion that our only recourse to avoid war is competitive armament, with its dreadful burdens and its constant temptation to the war it seeks to avoid.

The first important covenant with reference to peace and war in the Constitution of the League is that looking to a reduction of armament by all nations. The Executive Council, consisting of representatives of the United States, the British Empire, France, Italy, Japan, and of four other nations to be selected by the body of delegates, is to consider how much the armaments of the nations should be reduced, having regard to the safety of each of the nations and their obligations under the League. Having reached a conclusion as to the proportionate limits of each nation's armament, it submits its conclusion to each nation, which may or may not agree to the limit thus recommended; but when an agreement is reached it covenants to keep within that limit until, by application to the Executive Council, the limit may be raised. In other words, each nation agrees to its own limitation. Having so agreed it must keep within it.

The importance of providing for a reduction of armament every one recognizes. It is affirmed in the newly proposed Senate resolution. Can we not trust our Congress to fix a limitation safe for the country and to stick to it? If we can't, no country can. Yet all the rest are anxious to do this and they are far more exposed than we.

The character of this obligation is affected by the time during which the covenants of the League remain binding. There is no stipulation as to how long this is. In my judgment there should be a period of ten years or a permission for any member of the League to withdraw from the covenant by giving a reasonable notice of one or two years of its intention to do so.

The members of the League and the non-members are required, the former by their covenant, the latter by an enforced obligation, to submit all differences between them not capable of being settled by negotiation to arbitration before a tribunal composed as the parties may agree. They are required to covenant to abide the award. Should either party deem the question one not proper for arbitration then it is to be taken up by the Executive Council of the League. The Executive Council mediates between the parties and secures a voluntary settlement of the question if possible; if it fails, it makes a report. If the report is unanimous, the Executive Council is to recommend what shall be done to carry into effect its recommendation. If there is a dissenting vote, then the majority report is published, and the minority report, if desired, and no further action is taken. If either party of the Executive Council itself desires, the mediating function is to be discharged by the body of delegates in which every member of the League has one vote. There is no direction as to what shall be done with reference to the recommendation of proper measures to be taken, and the whole matter is then left for such further action as the members of the League agree upon. There is no covenant by the defeated party that it will comply with the unanimous report of the Executive Council or the Body of the League.

And right here I wish to take up the objection made to the League that under this machinery we might be compelled to receive immigrants contrary to our national desire from Japan or China. We could and would refuse to submit the issue to arbitration. It would then go to mediation. In my judgment the Council as a mediating body should not take jurisdiction to consider such a difference. Immigration by international law is a domestic question completely within the control of the government into which immigration is sought, unless the question of immigration is the subject of treaty stipulation between two countries. If, however, it be said that there is no limitation in the covenant of the differences to be mediated, clearly we would run no risk of receiving from the large body of delegates of all the members of the League a unanimous report recommending a settlement by

THE LEAGUE OF NATIONS 351

which Japanese immigrants shall be admitted to our shores or Japanese applicants be admitted to our citizenship, contrary to our protest. But were it made, we are under no covenant to obey such recommendation. If it could be imagined that all of the other nations of the world would thus unite their military forces to compel us to receive Japanese immigrants under the covenant, why would they not do so without the covenant?

These articles compelling submission of differences either to arbitration or mediation are not complete machinery for settlement by peaceable means of all issues arising between nations. But they are a substantial step forward. They are an unambitious plan to settle as many questions as possible by arbitration or mediation. They illustrate the spirit of those who drafted this covenant and their sensible desire not to attempt more till after actual experience.

The next covenant is that the nations shall not begin war until three months after the arbitration award or the recommendation of compromise, and not then if the defendant nation against whom the award or recommendation has been made shall comply with it. This is the great restraint of war imposed by the covenant upon members of the League and non-members. It is said that this would prevent our resistance to a border raid of Mexico or self-defense against any invasion. This is most extreme construction. If a nation refuses submission at all, as it does when it begins an attack, the nation attacked is released instanter from its obligation to submit and is restored to the complete power of self-defense. Had this objection not been raised in the Senate one would not have deemed it necessary to answer so unwarranted a suggestion.

If the defendant nation does not comply with the award or unanimous report, then the plaintiff nation can begin war and carry out such complete remedy as the circumstances enable it to do. But if the defendant nation does comply with the award or unanimous report, then the plaintiff nation must be content with such compliance. It runs the risk of not getting all it thought it ought to have or might have by war, but as it is asking affirmative relief it must be seeking some less vital interest than its political independence or territorial integrity, and the limitation is not one which can be dangerous to its sovereignty.

The third covenant, the penalizing covenant, is that if a nation begins war, in violation of its covenant, then *ipso facto* that it is an act of war against every member of the League, and the members of the League are required definitely and distinctly to levy a boycott on the covenant-breaking nation and to cut off from it all commercial, trade, financial, personal, and official relations between them and their citizens and it and its citizens. Indeed, the boycott is compound or secondary, in that it is directed against any non-members of the League continuing to deal with the outlaw nation. This is an obligation operative at once on each member of the League. With us the Executive Council would report the violation of the covenant to the President and that would be reported to Congress, and Congress would then, by reason of the covenant of the League, be under an honorable legal and moral obligation to levy an embargo and prevent all intercourse of every kind between this nation and the covenant-breaking nation.

The extent of this penalty and its heavy withering effect when the hostile action includes all members of the League, as well as non-members, may be easily appreciated. The prospect of such an isolation would be likely to frighten any member of the League from a reckless violation of its covenant to begin war. It is inconceivable that any small nation, dependent as it must be on larger nations for its trade and sustenance, indeed for its food and raw material, would for a moment court such a destructive ostracism as this would be.

Other covenants of the penalizing article impose on the members of the League the duty of sharing the expense of a boycott with any nation upon which it has fallen with uneven weight and of supporting such a nation in its resistance to any special measures directed against it by the outlaw nation. But there is no specific requirement as to the character of the support beyond the obligation of the boycott, the contribution of expenses and the obligation of each member of the League to permit the passage through its territory of forces of other members of the League coöperating with military forces against the outlaw nation.

THE LEAGUE OF NATIONS 353

If, however, the boycott does not prove sufficient, then the Executive Council is to recommend the number of the military and naval forces to be contributed by the members of the League to protect the covenants of the League in such a case. There is no specific covenant by which they agree to furnish any amount of force, or, indeed, any force at all, to a League army. The use of the word "recommended" in describing the functions of the Executive Council shows that the question whether such forces shall be contributed and what shall be their amount must ultimately address itself to the members of the League for their discussion and action. There is this radical and important difference, therefore, between the obligation to lay a boycott and the obligation to furnish military force, and doubtless this distinction was insisted upon and reached by a compromise. The term "recommendation" cannot be interpreted to impose any imperative obligation on those to whom the recommendation is directed.

By Article X, the high contracting parties undertake to respect and preserve against external aggression the political independence and territorial integrity of every member of the League, and when these are attacked or threatened the Executive Council is to advise as to the proper means to fulfill this obligation. The same acts or series of acts which made Article X applicable will be a breach of the covenant which creates an outlaw nation under Article XVI, so that all nations must begin a boycott against any nation thus breaking the territorial integrity or overthrowing the independence of a member of the League. Indeed, Article X will usually not be applicable until a war shall be fought to the point showing its specific purpose. Protection against it will usually be necessary in preventing, a treaty of peace, the appropriation of territory or the interference with the sovereignty of the attacked and defeated nation. We have seen this in the construction of the Monroe Doctrine put upon it by Secretary Seward and President Roosevelt. The former, when Spain attacked Chili and Chili appealed to the United States to protect it, advised Spain that under the policy of the United states it would not interfere to prevent the punishment by war of an American nation by a non-American nation, provided it did not extend to a permanent deprivation of its territory or an overthrow of its sovereignty. President Roosevelt, in the Venezuelan matter, also announced that the Monroe Doctrine did not prevent nations from proceeding by force to collect their debts provided oppressive measures were not used which would deprive the nation of its independence or territorial integrity. This furnishes an analogy for the proper construction of Article X.

The fact that the Executive Council is to advise what means shall be taken to fulfill the obligation shows that they are to be such as each nation shall deem proper and fair under the circumstances, considering its remoteness from the country and the fact that the nearer presence of other nations should induce them to furnish the requisite military force. It thus seems to me clear that the question, both under Article XVIII, and under Article X, as to whether the United States shall declare war and what forces it shall furnish, are remitted to the voluntary action of the Congress of the United States under the constitution, having regard for a fair division between all the nations of the burden to be borne under the League and the proper means to be adopted, whether by the enjoined and inevitable boycott alone, or by the advance of loans of money, or by the declaration of war and the use of military force. This is as it should be. It fixes the obligation of action in such a way that American nations will attend to America and European nations will attend to Europe and Asiatic nations to Asia, unless all deem the situation so threatening to the world and to their own interests that they should take a more active part. It seems to me that appropriate words might be added to the pact which should show distinctly this distribution of obligation. This will relieve those anxious in respect to the Monroe Doctrine to exclude from forcible intervention by European or Asiatic nations in issues between American nations until requested by the United States or an executive council of the American nations framed for the purpose.

Objection is made that Great Britain might have more delegates in the Executive Council than other countries. This is an error. The British Empire, which, of course, includes its dominions, is limited to one delegate in the Executive Council.

Provision is made by which upon a vote of two-thirds of the body of delegates new members may be admitted who are independent states or self-governing dominions or colonies. Under this Canada and Australia and South Africa might be admitted as delegates. I presume, too, the Philippines might be admitted. But the function of the body of delegates is not one which makes its membership of great importance. When it acts as a mediating and compromising body its reports must be unanimous to have any effect. The addition of members, therefore, is not likely to create greater probability of unanimity. More than this, the large number of countries who will become members will minimize any important British influence from the addition of such dominions and colonies since they are really admitted because they have different interests from their mother country. The suggestion that Great Britain will have any greater power than other member nations in shaping the policy of the League in really critical matters, when analyzed, will be seen to have no foundation whatever.

A proposed resolution in the Senate recites that the Constitution of the League of Nations in the form now proposed should not be accepted by the United States, although the sense of the Senate is that the nations of the world should unite to promote peace and general disarmament. The resolution further recites that the negotiations on the part of the United States should immediately be directed to the utmost expedition of the urgent business of negotiating peace terms with Germany satisfactory to the United States and the nations with whom the United States is associated in the war against the German government, and that the proposal for a League of Nations to insure the permanent peace of the world should then be taken up for careful and serious consideration. It is said that this resolution will be supported by thirty-seven members of the new Senate, and thus defeated the confirmation of any treaty which includes the present proposed covenant of Paris.

The President of the United States is the authority under the Federal Constitution which initiates the form of treaties and which at the outset determines what subject matter they shall include. Therefore, if it shall seem to the President of the United States and to those acting with him and with similar authority for other nations that a treaty of peace cannot be concluded except with a covenant providing for a League of Nations in substance like that now proposed as a condition precedent to the proper operation and effectiveness of the treaty itself it will be the duty of the President and his fellow delegates to the conference to insert such a covenant in the treaty. If, accordingly, such a covenant shall be incorporated in a treaty of peace, signed by the representatives of the Powers and shall be brought back by the President and submitted by him to the Senate, the question which will address itself to the proponents of this Senate resolution will be not whether they would prefer to consider a League of Nations after the treaty of peace but whether they will feel justified in defeating or postponing a treaty because it contains a constitution of a League of Nations deemed by the President necessary to the kind of peace which all seek.

The covenant of Paris, which is now a covenant only between the nations at war with Germany, including the seven nations who actually won the war, is essential to an effective treaty of peace to accomplish the purposes of the war; for the purposes of the war were to defeat militarism, to make the world safe for democracy, and to secure permanent peace.

Under the informal agreement between the nations who won this war, outlined in the President's message of January 8, 1918, as qualified by the Entente Allies before the armistice, we are to create and recognize as independent states four nations forming a bulwark between Germany and Russia to prevent future intrigues by Germany to secure control of Russia. In the process we are to carve these new nations out of the great autocracies, Russia, Germany, and Austria. We are to give Germany and Austrian Poland to the republic of Poland, to set up the Czecho slovak state of ten million inhabitants between Germany and Austria-Hungary, as well as the Jugoslav state carved out of Austria, and Hungary in the south. We are to fix new boundaries in the Balkans, with Rumania enlarged by Transylvania and Bessarabia, and to make an internationalized government at Constantinople, keeping ward over the passage between the Black Sea and the Ægean, and to establish autonomous dominions in Palestine, Syria, Armenia, and Mesopotamia. This plan for the peace and the reasons for it were set out with great force and vision by Senator Lodge in a speech last January. The chief purpose of the plan is to take away the possibility that Germany shall ever again conceive and carry toward accomplishment her dream of the control of Russia and of a Middle European and Asiatic Empire, reaching from Hamburg to the Persian Gulf.

The plan thus requires not only the establishment but the continued maintenance of seven new republics in Europe and several autonomies in Asia Minor. We are to create twenty nations instead of four; and we are to carve the new ones out of the old ones. The peoples of the new republics will not have had experience in self-government. They are the children of the League of Nations, as Cuba has been our child. The League must continue to be a guardian of their internal stability, if they are to serve their purpose. Their natural resentment for past oppression against the neighboring countries out of which they have been carved and the corresponding hatred of them by the defeated peoples of those countries will at once produce controversies innumerable over the interpretation of the treaty and its application. Even the new countries as between themselves, with their natural lack of self-restraint and their indefinite ideas of their powers, have already come into forced conflict.

Unless there be some means for authoritatively interpreting the treaty and applying it, and unless the power of the League be behind it to give effect to such interpretation and application, the treaty instead of producing peace will produce a state of continued war.

More than this, in the dark background is the threatening specter of Bolshevism, hard, cruel, murderous, uncompromising, destructive of Christian civilization, militant in pressing its hideous doctrines upon other peoples and insidious in its propaganda among the lowest element in every country. Against the chaos and the explosive dangers of Bolshevism, throughout all the countries of Europe, a League of Nations must be established to settle controversies peaceably and to enforce the settlement.

If it be said that the European nations should unite in a league to maintain these independent states and settle the difficulties arising between them and the older states in the sphere of war, as well as to resist Bolshevism, it is sufficient to say that the withdrawal of the United States from the League of Nations will weaken it immeasurably. The disinterestedness of the United States, its position as the greatest Power in the world in view of its people and their intelligence and adaptability, its enormous natural resources, and its potential military power, demonstrated on the fields of France and Belgium, make its membership in the League indispensable. The confidence of the world in its disinterestedness and in its pure democracy will enormously enhance the prestige and power of the League's earnest desire for peace with justice.

For the United States to withdraw would make a league of other nations nothing but a return to the system of alliances and the balance of power with a certain speedy recurrence of war, in which the United States would be as certainly involved as it was in this war. The new inventions for the destruction of men and peoples would finally result in world suicide, while in the interval there would be a story of progressive competition in armaments, with all their heavy burdens upon the peoples of the nations, already oppressed almost to the point of exhaustion. With such a prospect and to avoid such results the United States should not hesitate to take its place with the other responsible nations of the world and make the light concessions and assume the light burdens involved in membership in the League.

No critic of the League has offered a single constructive suggestion to meet the crisis that I have thus summarily touched upon. The resolution of the Senate does not suggest or refer in any way to machinery by which the function of the League of Nations in steadying Europe and the maintaining of the peace agreed upon in the Peace Treaty shall be secured. Well may the President, therefore, decline to comply with the suggestions of the proposed resolution. Well may he say when he returns with the treaty, of which the covenant shall be a most important and indispensable part, "If you would postpone peace, if you would defeat it, you can refuse to ratify the Treaty. Amend it by striking out the covenant and you will have confusion worse confounded, with the objects of the war unattained

THE LEAGUE OF NATIONS

and sacrificed and Europe and the world in dangerous chaos."

Objection is made that the covenant of the League is a departure from the traditional policy of the United States following the advice of Washington in avoiding entangling alliances with European nations. The European war into which we were drawn demonstrates that the policy is no longer possible for the United States. It has ceased to be a struggling nation. It has been made a close neighbor of Great Britain and France and Italy and of all nations of Europe, and is in such intimate trade relations that in a general European war it never can be a neutral again. It tried to be in this war and failed. Whatever nation secures the control of the seas will make the United States its ally, no matter how formal and careful its neutrality, because it will be the sole customer of the United States in food, raw material, and war necessities. Modern war is carried on in the mines and the workshops and on the farm, as well as in the trenches. The former are indispensable to the work in the latter. Hence the United States will certainly be drawn in, and hence its interests are inevitably involved in the preservation of European peace. These conditions and circumstances are so different from those in Washington's day, and are so unlike anything which he could have anticipated, that no words of his having relation to selfish offensive and defensive alliances such as he described in favor of one nation and against another should be given any application to the present international status.

Objection is made that the covenant destroys the Monroe Doctrine. The Monroe Doctrine was announced and adopted to keep European monarchies from overthrowing the independence of and fastening their system upon governments in this hemisphere. It has been asserted in various forms, some of them extreme, and others less so. I presume that no one now would attempt to sustain the declarations of Secretary Olney in his correspondence with Lord Salisbury. But all will probably agree that the sum and substance of the Monroe Doctrine is that we do not propose in our own interests to allow European nations or Asiatic nations to acquire, beyond what they now have, through war or purchase or intrigue, territory, political power, or strategical opportunity from the countries of this hemisphere. Article X of the constitution of the League is intended to secure this to all signatory nations, except that it does not forbid purchase of territory or power.

In some speeches in the Senate intimations have been made which enlarge the Monroe Doctrine beyond what can be justified. Those who would seek to enforce a doctrine which would make the western hemisphere our own preserve, in which we may impose our sovereign will on other countries in what we suppose to be their own interest, because, indeed, we have done that in the past, should not be sustained. Our conquests of western territory, of course, have worked greatly for the civilization of the world and for the usefulness and happiness of those who now occupy that territory; but we have reached a state in the world's history when its progress should be now determined and secured under just and peaceful conditions, and progress through conquest by powerful nations should be prevented.

To suppose that the conditions in America and in Europe can be maintained absolutely separate, with the great trade relations between North America and Europe, is to look backward, not forward. It does not face existing conditions.

The European nations desire our entrance into this League, not that they may control America but to secure our aid in controlling Europe, and I venture to think that they would be relieved if the primary duty of keeping peace and policing this western hemisphere were relegated to us and our western colleagues. I object, however, to such a reservation as was contained in the Hague Conference against entangling alliances, because the recommendation was framed before this war and contained provisions as to the so-called policy against entangling alliances that are inconsistent with the present needs of this nation and of the rest of the world if a peaceful future is to be secured to both. I would favor, however, a recognition of the Monroe Doctrine as I have stated it above by specific words in the covenant, and with a further provision that the settlement of purely American questions should be remitted primarily to the American nations, with machinery like that of the present League, and that European nations should not intervene unless requested to do so by the American nations.

Objection is made to this League on constitutional grounds. This League is to be made by the treaty-making power of the United States. What does the treaty-making power cover? The Supreme Court of the United States, through Mr. Justice Field, in the Riggs case, has held that it covers the right to deal by contract with all subject-matters which are usually dealt with by contract in treaties between nations, except it cannot be used to change our form of government or to part with territory of a State without its consent. The Supreme Court has, over and over again, through Mr. Chief Justice Marshall, indicated that the United States was a nation and a sovereign capable of dealing with other nations as such, and with all the powers inferable from such sovereignty. It is said, however, that the League will change the form of our government. But no function or discretion is taken from any branch of the government which it now performs or exercises. It is asserted that the covenant delegates to an outside tribunal, viz., the Executive Council, the power vested by the Constitution in Congress or the Senate. But the Executive Council has no power but to recommend to the nations of the League courses which those nations may accept or reject, save in the matter of increasing the limit of armament, to which the United States by its Congress, after full consideration, shall have consented. Neither the Executive Council nor the body of delegates in the machinery for the peaceful settling of differences does other than to recommend a compromise which the United States does not under the League covenant to obey. In all other respects these bodies are mere instruments for conference by representatives for devising plans which are submitted to the various governments of the League for their voluntary acceptance and adoption. No obligation of the United States under the League is fixed by action of either the Executive Council or the body of delegates.

Then it is said we have no right to agree to levy an embargo and a boycott. It is true that Congress determines what our commercial relations shall be with other countries of the world. It is true that if a boycott is to be levied Congress must levy it in the form of an embargo, as that which was levied by

Congress in Jefferson's adminstration, and the validity of which was sustained by the Supreme Court, with John Marshall at its head. It is true that Congress might repudiate the obligation entered into by the treaty-making power and refuse to levy such an embargo. But none of these facts would invalidate or render unconstitutional a treaty by which the obligation of the United States was assumed.

In other words, the essence of sovereign power is that while the sovereign may make a contract, it retains the power to repudiate it, if it chooses to dishonor its promise. That does not render null the original obligation or discredit its binding moral force. The nations of Europe are willing to accept, as we must be willing to accept from them, mutual promises, the one in consideration of the other, in confidence that neither will refuse to comply with such promises honorably entered into.

Finally, it is objected that we have no right to agree to arbitrate issues. It is said that we might by arbitration lose our territorial integrity or our political independence. This is a stretch of imagination by the distinguished Senator who made it, at which we marvel. In the face of Article X, which is an understanding to respect the territorial integrity and political independence of every member of the League, how could a board of arbitration possibly reach such a result? More than that, we do not have to arbitrate. If we do not care to arbitrate, we can throw the matter into mediation and conciliation, and we do not covenant to obey the recommendation of compromise by the conciliating body. We have been arbitrating questions for one hundred years.

We have stipulated in treaties to arbitrate classes of questions long before the questions arise. How would we arbitrate under this treaty? The form of the issue to be arbitrated would have to be formulated by our treaty-making power—the President and the Senate of the United States. The award would have to be performed by that branch of the government which executes awards, generally the Congress of the United States. If it involved payment of money, Congress would have to appropriate it. If it involved limitation of armament, Congress would have to limit it. If it involved any duty within the legislative power of Congress under the Constitution,

Congress would have to perform it. If Congress sees fit to comply with the report of the compromise by the conciliating body, Congress will have to make such compliance.

The covenant takes away the sovereignty of the United States only as any contract curtails the freedom of action of an individual which he has voluntarily surrendered for the purpose of the contract and to obtain the benefit of it. The covenant creates no super-sovereignty. It merely creates contract obligations. It binds nations to stand together to secure compliance with those obligations. That is all. This is no different from a contract that we make with one nation. If we enter into an important contract with another nation to pay money or to do other things of vital interest to that nation and we break it, then we expose ourselves to the just effort of that nation by force of arms to attempt to compel us to comply with our obligations. This covenant of all the nations is only a limited and loose union of the compelling powers of many nations to do the same thing. The assertion that we are giving up our sovereignty carries us logically and necessarily to the absurd result that we cannot make a contract to do anything with another nation because it limits our freedom of action as a sovereign.

Sovereignty is freedom of action and nations. It is exactly analogous to the liberty of the individual regulated by law. The sovereignty that we should insist upon, and the only sovereignty we have a right to insist upon, is a sovereignty regulated by international law, international morality, and international justice, a sovereignty enjoining the sacred rights which sovereignties of other nations may enjoy, a sovereignty consistent with the enjoyment of the same sovereignty of other nations. It is a sovereignty limited by the law of nations and limited by the obligation of contracts fully and freely entered into in respect to matters which are usually the subjects of contracts between nations.

The President is now returning to Europe. As the representative of this nation in the conference he has joined in recommending in this proposed covenant a League of Nations for consideration and adoption by the conference. He has, meantime, returned home to discharge other executive duties, and it has given him an opportunity to note a discussion of the

League in the Senate of the United States and elsewhere. Some speeches, notably that of Senator Lodge, have been useful in taking up the League, article by article, criticizing its language, and expressing doubts either as to its meaning or as to its wisdom.

He will differ, as many others will differ, from Senator Lodge in respect to many of the criticisms, but he will find many useful suggestions in the constructive part of the speech which he will be able to present to his colleagues in the conference. They will be especially valuable in revising the form of the covenant and making reservations to which his colleagues in the conference may readily consent, where Senator Lodge or the other critics have misunderstood the purpose and meaning of the words used.

This covenant should be in the treaty of peace. It is indispensable in ending the war, if the war is to accomplish the declared purpose of this nation and the world in that war, and if it is to work the promised benefit to mankind. We know the President believes this and will insist upon it. Our profound sympathy in his purpose and our prayers for his success should go with him in his great mission.

WILLIAM E. BORAH

WILLIAM EDGAR BORAH

THE LEAGUE OF NATIONS

[William Edgar Borah was born in Fairfield, Illinois, in 1865. He has been United States senator from Idaho since 1907. Senator Borah was one of the leading opponents of the ratification of the peace treaty in the United States Senate. This speech was delivered November 19, 1919, when the peace treaty, with many reservations, was before the Senate for final vote.]

MR. PRESIDENT, I am not misled by the debate across the aisle into the view that this Treaty will not be ratified. I entertain little doubt that sooner or later—and entirely too soon—the Treaty will be ratified with the League of Nations in it, and I am of the opinion with the reservations in it as they are now written. There may possibly be some change in verbiage in order that there may be a common sharing of parentage but our friends across the aisle will likely accept the League of Nations with the reservations in substance as now written. I think, therefore, this moment is just as appropriate as any other for me to express my final views with reference to the Treaty and the League of Nations. It is perhaps the last opportunity I shall have to state, as briefly as I may, my reasons for opposing the treaty and the league.

Mr. President, after Mr. Lincoln had been elected President, before he assumed the duties of the office at a time when all indications were to the effect that we would soon be in the midst of civil strife, a friend from the city of Washington wrote him for instructions. Mr. Lincoln wrote back in a single line, "Entertain no compromise; have none of it." That states the position I occupy at this time and which I have, in an humble way, occupied from the first contention in regard to this proposal.

My objections to the League have not been met by the reservations. I desire to state wherein my objections have not been met. Let us see what our attitude will be toward Europe and what our position will be with reference to the other nations of the world after we shall have entered the League with the present reservations written therein. With all due respect to those who think that they have accomplished a different thing and challenging no man's intellectual integrity or patriotism, I do not believe the reservations have met the fundamental propositions which are involved in this contest.

When the League shall have been formed, we shall be a member of what is known as the Council of the League. Our accredited representative will sit in judgment with the accredited representatives of the other members of the League to pass upon the concerns not only of our country but of all Europe and all Asia and the entire world. Our accredited representatives will be members of the assembly. They will sit there to represent the judgment of these 110,000,000 of people, more then, just as we are accredited here to represent our constituencies. We cannot send our representatives to sit in council with the representatives of the other great nations of the world with mental reservations as to what we shall do in case their judgment shall not be satisfactory to us. If we go to the council or to the assembly with any other purpose than that of complying in good faith and in absolute integrity with all upon which the council or the assembly may pass, we shall soon return to our country with our self-respect forfeited and the public opinion of the world condemnatory.

Why need you gentlemen across the aisle worry about a reservation here or there, when we are sitting in the council and in the assembly and bound by every obligation in morals, which the President said was supreme above that of law, to comply with the judgment which our representative and the other representatives finally form? Shall we go there, Mr. President, to sit in judgment, and in case that judgment works for peace join with our allies, but in case it works for war withdraw our coöperation? How long would we stand as we now stand, a great Republic commanding the respect and holding the leadership of the world, if we should adopt any such course?

So, sir, we not only sit in the council and in the assembly

with our accredited representatives, but bear in mind that Article XI is untouched by any reservation which has been offered here; and with Article XI untouched, and its integrity complete, Article X is perfectly superfluous. If any war or threat of war shall be a matter of consideration for the League, and the League shall take such action as it deems wise to deal with it, what is the necessity of Article X? Will not external aggression be regarded as a war or threat of war? If the political independence of some nation in Europe is assailed will it be regarded as a war or a threat of war? Is there anything in Article X that is not completely covered by Article XI?

It remains complete, and with our representatives sitting in the council and the assembly, and with Article XI complete, and with the assembly and the council having jurisdiction of all matters touching the peace of the world, what more do you need to bind the United States if you assume that the United States is a nation of honor?

We have said, Mr. President, that we would not send troops abroad without the consent of Congress. Pass by now for a moment the legal proposition. If we create executive functions, the Executive will perform those functions without the authority of Congress. Pass that question by and go to the other question. Our members of the council are there. Our members of the assembly are there. Article XI is complete, and it authorizes the League, a member of which is our representative, to deal with matters of peace and war, and the League through its council and its assembly deals with the matter, and our accredited representative joins with the others in deciding upon a certain course, which involves a question of sending troops. What will the Congress of the United States do? What right will it have left, except the bare technical right to refuse, which as a moral proposition it will not dare to exercise? Have we not been told day by day for the last nine months that the Senate of the United States, a coördinate part of the treaty-making power, should accept this League as it was written because the wise men sitting at Versailles had so written it, and has not every possible influence and every source of power in public opinion been organized and directed against the Senate to compel it to do that thing? How much stronger will be the moral compulsion upon the

Congress of the United States when we ourselves have indorsed the proposition of sending our accredited representatives there to vote for us?

Ah, but you say that there must be unanimous consent, and that there is vast protection in unanimous consent.

I do not wish to speak disparagingly; but has not every division and dismemberment of every nation which has suffered dismemberment taken place by unanimous consent for the last three hundred years? Did not Prussia and Austria and Russia by unanimous consent divide Poland? Did not the United States and Great Britain and Japan and Italy and France divide China, and give Shantung to Japan? Was that not a unanimous decision? Close the doors upon the diplomats of Europe, let them sit in secret, give them the material to trade on, and there always will be unanimous consent.

How did Japan get unanimous consent? I want to say here, in my parting words upon this proposition, that I have no doubt the outrage upon China was quite as distasteful to the President of the United States as it is to me. But Japan said "I will not sign your treaty unless you turn over to me Shantung, to be turned back at my discretion," and you know how Japan's discretion operates with reference to such things. And so, when we are in the League, and our accredited representatives are sitting at Geneva, and a question of great moment arises, Japan, or Russia, or Germany, or Great Britain will say, "Unless this matter is adjusted in this way I will depart from the League." It is the same thing, operating in the same way, only under a different date and under a little different circumstances.

Mr. President, if you have enough territory, if you have enough material, if you have enough subject peoples to trade upon and divide, there will be no difficulty about unanimous consent.

Do our Democratic friends ever expect any man to sit as a member of the council or as a member of the assembly equal in intellectual power and in standing before the world with that of our representative at Versailles? Do you expect a man to sit in the council who will have made more pledges, and I shall assume made them in sincerity, for self-determination and for the rights of small peoples, than had been made by our

THE LEAGUE OF NATIONS 369

accredited representative? And yet, what became of it? The unanimous consent was obtained nevertheless.

But take another view of it. We are sending to the council one man. That one man represents 110,000,000 people.

Here, sitting in the Senate, we have two from every State in the Union, and over in the other House we have Representatives in accordance with population, and the responsibility is spread out in accordance with our obligations to our constituency. But now we are transferring to one man the stupendous power of representing the sentiment and the convictions of 110,000,000 people in tremendous questions which may involve the peace or may involve the war of the world.

However you view the question of unanimous consent, it does not protect us.

What is the result of all this? We are in the midst of all of the affairs of Europe. We have entangled ourselves with all European concerns. We have joined in alliance with all the European nations which have thus far joined the League, and all nations which may be admitted to the League. We are sitting there dabbling in their affairs and intermeddling in their concerns. In other words, Mr. President—and this comes to the question which is fundamental with me—we have forfeited and surrendered, once and for all, the great policy of "no entangling alliances" upon which the strength of this Republic has been founded for one hundred fifty years.

My friends of reservations, tell me where is the reservation in these articles which protects us against entangling alliances with Europe?

Those who are differing over reservations, tell me what one of them protects the doctrine laid down by the Father of our country? That fundamental proposition is surrendered, and we are a part of the European turmoils and conflicts from the time we enter the League.

Let us not underestimate that. There has never been an hour since the Venezuelan difficulty that there has not been operating in this country, fed by domestic and foreign sources, a powerful propaganda for the destruction of the doctrine of no entangling alliances.

Lloyd-George is reported to have said just a few days before the conference met at Versailles that Great Britain could give up much, and would be willing to sacrifice much to have America withdraw from the policy. That was one of the great objects of the entire conference at Versailles, so far as the foreign representatives were concerned. Clemenceau and Lloyd-George and others like them were willing to make any reasonable sacrifice which would draw America away from her isolation and into the internal affairs and concerns of Europe. This League of Nations, with or without reservations, whatever else it does or does not do, does surrender and sacrifice that policy; and once having surrendered and become a part of the European concerns, where, my friends, are you going to stop?

You have put in here a reservation upon the Monroe Doctrine. I think that, in so far as language could protect the Monroe Doctrine, it has been protected. But as a practical proposition, as a working proposition, tell me candidly, as men familiar with the history of your country and of other countries, do you think that you can intermeddle in European affairs and keep Europe from intermeddling with your affairs?

When Mr. Monroe wrote to Jefferson, he asked him his view upon the Monroe Doctrine, and Mr. Jefferson said, in substance our first and primary obligation should be never to interfere in European affairs; and, secondly, never to permit Europe to interfere in our affairs.

He understood, as every wise and practical man understands, that if we intermeddle in her affairs, if we help to adjust her conditions, inevitably and remorselessly Europe then will be carried into our affairs, in spite of anything you can write upon paper.

We cannot protect the Monroe Doctrine unless we protect the basic principle upon which it rests, and that is the Washington policy. I do not care how earnestly you may endeavor to do so, as a practical working proposition, your League will come to the United States. Will you permit me to digress long enough to read a paragraph from the great French editor upon this particular phase of the matter, Mr. Stephen Lausanne, editor of *Le Matin*, of Paris:

> When the Executive Council of the League of Nations fixes "the reasonable limits of the armament of Peru"; when it shall demand information concerning the naval program of Brazil; when it shall

tell Argentina what shall be the measure of the "contribution to the armed forces to protect the signatures of the social covenant"; when it shall demand the immediate registration of the treaty between the United States and Canada at the seat of the league, it will control, whether it wills or no, the destinies of America. And when the American States shall be obliged to take a hand in every war or menace of war in Europe (art. XI), they will necessarily fall afoul of the fundamental principle laid down by Monroe, which was that Americans should never take part in a European war.

If the League takes in the world, then Europe must mix in the affairs of America; if only Europe is included, then America will violate of necessity her own doctrine by intermixing in the affairs of Europe.

If the League includes the affairs of the world, does it not include the affairs of all the world? Is there any limitation of the jurisdiction of the council or of the assembly upon the question of peace or war? Does it not have now, under the reservations, the same as it had before, the power to deal with all matters of peace or war throughout the entire world? How shall you keep from meddling in the affairs of Europe or keep Europe from meddling in the affairs of America?

Mr. President, there is another and even more commanding reason why I shall record my vote against this treaty. It imperils what I conceive to be the underlying, the very first principles of this Republic. It is in conflict with the right of our people to govern themselves free from all restraint, legal or moral, of foreign powers. It challenges every tenet of my political faith. If this faith were one of my contriving, if I stood here to assert principles of government of my own evolving, I might well be charged with intolerable presumption, for we all recognize the ability of those who urge a different course. But I offer in justification of my course nothing of my own—save the deep and abiding reverence I have for those whose policies I humbly but most ardently support. I claim no merit save fidelity to American principles and devotion to American ideals as they were wrought out from time to time by those who built the Republic and as they have been extended and maintained throughout these years. In opposing the treaty I do nothing more than decline to renounce and tear out of my life the sacred traditions which throughout fifty years have been translated into my whole intellectual and moral being. I will not, I can not, give up my belief that America must, not alone for the happiness of her own people, but for the moral guidance and greater contentment of the world, be permitted to live her own life. Next to the tie which binds a man to his God is the tie which binds a man to his country, and all schemes, all plans, however ambitious and fascinating they seem in their proposal, but which would embarrass or entangle and impede or shackle her sovereign will, which would compromise her freedom of action I unhesitatingly put behind me.

Sir, since the debate opened months ago those of us who have stood against this proposition have been taunted many times with being little Americans. Leave us the word American, keep that in your presumptuous impeachment, and no taunt can disturb us, no gibe discompose our purposes. Call us little Americans if you will, but leave us the consolation and the pride which the term American, however modified, still imparts. Take away that term and though you should coin in telling phrase your highest eulogy, we would hurl it back as common slander. We have been ridiculed because, forsooth, of our limited vision. Possibly that charge may be true. Who is there here that can read the future? Time, and time alone, unerring and remorseless, will give us each our proper place in the affections of our countrymen and in the esteem and commendation of those who are to come after us. We neither fear nor court her favor. But if our vision has been circumscribed it has at all times within its compass been clear and steady. We have sought nothing save the tranquillity of our own people and the honor and independence of our own Republic. No foreign flattery, no possible world glory and power have disturbed our poise or come between us and our devotion to the traditions which have made us a people or the policies which have made us a Nation, unselfish and commanding. If we have erred we have erred out of too much love for those things which from childhood you and we together have been taught to revere—yes, to defend even at the cost of limb and life. If we have erred it is because we have placed too high an estimate upon the wisdom of Washington and Jefferson, too exalted an opinion upon the patriotism of the sainted Lincoln. And blame us not therefore if we have, in our limited vision, seemed sometimes bitter and at all times uncompromising, for the things which we have spoken, feebly spoken, the things which we have endeavored to defend have been the things for which your fathers and our fathers were willing to die.

Senators, even in an hour so big with expectancy we should not close our eyes to the fact that democracy is something more, vastly more, than a mere form of government by which society is restrained into free and orderly life. It is a moral entity, a spiritual force as well. And these are things which live only alone in the atmosphere of liberty. The foundation upon which democracy rests its faith in the moral instincts of the people. Its ballot boxes, the franchise, its laws, and constitutions are but the outward manifestations of the deeper and more essential thing—a continuing trust in the moral purposes of the average man and woman. When this is lost or forfeited your outward forms, however democratic in terms, are a mockery. Force may find expression through institutions democratic in structure equal with the simple and more direct processes of a single supreme ruler. These distinguishing virtues of a real republic you cannot commingle with the discordant and destructive forces of the Old World and still preserve them. You cannot yoke a government whose fundamental maxim is that of liberty to a government whose first law is that of force and hope to preserve the former. These things are in eternal war, and one must ultimately destroy the other. You may still keep for a time the outward form, you may still delude yourself, as others have done in the past, with appearances and symbols, but when you shall have committed this Republic to a scheme of world control based upon force, upon the combined military force of the four great nations of the world, you will have soon destroyed the atmosphere of freedom, of confidence in the self-governing capacity of the masses, in which alone a democracy may thrive. We may become one of the four dictators of the world, but we shall no longer be master of our own spirit. And what shall it profit us as a Nation if we shall go forth to the dominion of the earth and share with others the glory of world control and lose that fine sense of confidence in the people, the soul of democracy?

Look upon the scene as it is now presented. Behold the task we are to assume, and then contemplate the method by which we are to deal with this task. Is the method such as to address itself to a government "conceived in liberty and dedicated to the proposition that all men are created equal"? When this League, this combination, is formed four great powers representing the dominant people will rule one-half of the inhabitants of the globe as subject peoples—rule by force, and we shall be a party to the rule of force. There is no other way by which you can keep people in subjection. You must either give them independence, recognize their rights as nations to live their own life and to set up their own form of government, or you must deny them these things by force. That is the scheme, the method proposed by the League. It proposes no other. We will in time become inured to its inhuman precepts and its soulless methods, strange as this doctrine now seems to a free people. If we stay with our contract, we will come in time to declare with our associates that force—force, the creed of the Prussian military oligarchy—is after all the true foundation upon which rest all stable governments. Korea, despoiled and bleeding at every pore; India, sweltering in ignorance and burdened with inhuman taxes after more than a hundred years of dominant rule; Egypt, trapped and robbed of her birthright; Ireland, with seven hundred years of sacrifice for independence—this is the task, this is the atmosphere, and this is the creed in and under which we are to keep alive our belief in the moral purposes and self-governing capacity of the people, a belief without which the Republic must disintegrate and die. The maxim of liberty will soon give way to the rule of blood and iron. We have been pleading here for our Constitution. Conform this League, it has been said, to the technical terms of our charter and all will be well. But I declare to you that we must go further and conform to those sentiments and passions for justice and freedom which are essential to the existence of democracy. You must respect not territorial boundaries, not territorial integrity, but you must respect and preserve the sentiments and passions for justice and for freedom which God in His infinite wisdom has planted so deep in the human heart that no form of tyranny however brutal, no persecution however prolonged can wholly uproot and kill. Respect nationality, respect justice, respect freedom, and you may have some hope of peace, but not so if you make your standard the standard of tyrants and despots, the protection of real estate regardless of how it is obtained.

Sir, we are told that this treaty means peace. Even so, I would not pay the price. Would you purchase peace at the cost of any part of our independence? We could have had peace in 1776—the price was high, but we could have had it. James Otis, Sam Adams, Hancock, and Warren were surrounded by those who urged peace and British rule. All through that long and trying struggle, particularly when the clouds of adversity lowered upon the cause there was a cry of peace—let us have peace. We could have had peace in 1860; Lincoln was counseled by men of great influence and accredited wisdom to let our brothers—and, thank heaven, they are brothers—depart in peace. But the tender, loving Lincoln, bending under the fearful weight of impending civil war, an apostle of peace, refused to pay the price, and a reunited country will praise his name forevermore—bless it because he refused peace at the price of national honor and national integrity. Peace upon any other basis than national independence, peace purchased at the cost of any part of our national integrity, is fit only for slaves, and even when purchased at such a price it is a delusion, for it cannot last.

But your treaty does not mean peace—far, very far, from it. If we are to judge the future by the past it means war. Is there any guaranty of peace other than the guaranty which comes of the control of the war-making power by the people? Yet what great rule of democracy does the treaty leave unassailed? The people in whose keeping alone you can safely lodge the power of peace or war nowhere, at no time and in no place, have any voice in this scheme for world peace. Autocracy which has bathed the world in blood for centuries reigns supreme. Democracy is everywhere excluded. This, you say, means peace.

Can you hope for peace when love of country is disregarded in your scheme, when the spirit of nationality is rejected, scoffed at? Yet what law of that moving and mysterious force does your treaty not deny? With a ruthlessness unparalleled your treaty in a dozen instances runs counter to the divine law of nationality. Peoples who speak the same language, kneel at the same ancestral tombs, moved by the same traditions, animated by a common hope, are torn asunder, broken in pieces, divided, and parceled out to antagonistic nations. And this you call justice. This, you cry, means peace. Peoples who have dreamed of independence, struggled and been patient, sacrificed and been hopeful, peoples who were told that through this Peace Conference they should realize the aspirations of centuries, have again had their hopes dashed to earth. One of the most striking and commanding figures in this war, soldier and statesman, turned away from the peace table at Versailles declaring to the world, "The promise of the new life, the victory of the great humane ideals, for which the peoples have shed their blood and given their treasure without stint, the fulfillment of their aspirations toward a new international order and a fairer and better world are not written into the treaty." No; your treaty means injustice. It means slavery. It means war. And to all this you ask this Republic to become a party. You ask it to abandon the creed under which it has grown to power and accept the creed of autocracy, the creed of repression and force.

Mr. President, I turn from this scheme based upon force to another scheme, planned one hundred and forty-three years ago in old Independence Hall, in the city of Philadelphia, based upon liberty. I like it better. I have become so accustomed to believe in it that it is difficult for me to reject it out of hand. I have difficulty in subscribing to the new creed of oppression, the creed of dominant and subject peoples. I feel a reluctance to give up the belief that all men are created equal—the eternal principle in government that all governments derive their just powers from the consent of the governed. I cannot get my consent to exchange the doctrine of George Washington for the doctrine of Frederick the Great translated into mendacious phrases of peace. I go back to that serene and masterful soul who pointed the way to power and glory for the new and then weak Republic, and whose teachings and admonitions even in our majesty and dominance we dare not disregard.

I know well the answer to my contention. It has been piped about of late from a thousand sources—venal sources, disloyal sources, sinister sources—that Washington's wisdom was of his day only and that his teachings are out of fashion—things long since sent to the scrap heap of history—that while he was great in character and noble in soul he was untrained in the arts of statescraft and unlearned in the science of government. The puny demagogue, the barren editor, the sterile professor now vie with each other in apologizing for the temporary and commonplace expedients which the Father of our Country felt constrained to adopt in building a republic!

What is the test of statesmanship? Is it the formation of theories, the utterance of abstract and incontrovertible truths, or is it the capacity and the power to give to a people that concrete thing called liberty, that vital and indispensable thing in human happiness called free institutions and to establish over all and above all the blessed and eternal reign of order and law? If this be the test, where shall we find another whose name is entitled to be written beside the name of Washington? His judgment and poise in the hour of turmoil and peril, his courage and vision in times of adversity, his firm grasp of fundamental principles, his almost inspired power to penetrate the future and read there the result, the effect of policies, have never been excelled, if equaled, by any of the world's commonwealth builders. Peter the Great, William the Silent, and Cromwell the Protector, these and these alone perhaps are to be associated with his name as the builders of States and the founders of governments. But in exaltation of moral purpose, in the unselfish character of his work, in the durability of his policies, in the permanency of the institutions which he more than any one else called into effect, his service to mankind stands out separate and apart in a class by itself. The works of these other great builders, where are they now? But the work of Washington is still the most potent influence for the advancement of civilization and the freedom of the race.

Reflect for a moment over his achievements. He led the Revolutionary Army to victory. He was the very first to suggest a union instead of a confederacy. He presided over and counseled with great wisdom the convention which framed the Constitution. He guided the Government through its first perilous years. He gave dignity and stability and honor to that which was looked upon by the world as a passing experiment, and finally, my friends, as his own peculiar and particular contribution to the happiness of his countrymen and to the cause of the Republic, he gave us his great foreign policy under which we have lived and prospered and strengthened for nearly a century and a half. This policy is the most sublime confirmation of his genius as a statesman. It was then, and it now is, an indispensable part of our whole scheme of government. It is to-day a vital, indispensable element in our entire plan, purpose, and mission as a nation. To abandon it is nothing less than a betrayal of the American people. I say betrayal deliberately, in view of the suffering and the sacrifice which will follow in the wake of such a course.

But under the stress and strain of these extraordinary days, when strong men are being swept down by the onrushing forces of disorder and change, when the most sacred things of life, the most cherished hopes of a Christian world seem to yield to the mad forces of discontent—just such days as Washington passed through when the mobs of Paris, wild with new liberty and drunk with power, challenged the established institutions of all the world, but his steadfast soul was unshaken—under these conditions come again we are about to abandon this policy so essential to our happiness and tranquillity as a people and our stability as a Government. No leader with his commanding influence and his unquailing courage stands forth to stem the current. But what no leader can or will do experience, bitter experience, and the people of this country in whose keeping, after all, thank God, is the Republic, will ultimately do. If we abandon his leadership and teachings, we will go back. We will return to this policy. Americanism shall not, cannot die. We may go back in sackcloth and ashes, but we will return to the faith of the fathers. America will live her own life. The independence of this Republic will have its defenders. Thousands have suffered and died for it, and their sons and daughters are not of the breed who will be betrayed into the hands of foreigners. The noble face of the Father of his Country, so familiar to every boy and girl, looking out from the walls of the Capitol in stern reproach, will call those who come here for public service to a reckoning. The people of our beloved country will finally speak, and we will return to the policy which we now abandon. America, disenthralled and free, in spite of all these things, will continue her mission in the cause of peace, of freedom, and of civilization.

VI. THE WASHINGTON CONFERENCE ON THE LIMITATION OF ARMAMENTS

[The Conference on the Limitation of Armaments assembled in Continental Hall in Washington on November 12, 1921, with a full attendance of delegations from the United States, England, France, Italy, Japan, China, Holland, Belgium and Portugal and was formally opened by President Harding in an address of welcome. This first session, expected to consist only of formal addresses of welcome and the interchange of civilities, provided on the contrary, a profound dramatic interest in Secretary Hughes' address.

The addresses following that of Secretary Hughes were given on subsequent days of the Conference, the speeches of Mr. Balfour and Baron Kato on November 15, and the speech of M. Briand on November 21. Before sailing for this country M. Briand repeatedly explained that his decision, though head of the government, to leave Paris for a month was in order that he might present to the Washington Conference and through them to the world, the apologies of France. The United States did not need M. Briand's assurances that France is not a nation carried away by military pride; he spoke in America but he was really addressing his European neighbors.

PRESIDENT HARDING AT THE OPENING OF THE CONFERENCE

Mr. Secretary and Members of the Conference, Ladies and Gentlemen: It is a great and happy privilege to bid the delegates to this Conference a cordial welcome to the Capitol of the United States of America. It is not only a satisfaction to greet you because we were lately participants in a common cause, in which shared sacrifices and sorrows and triumphs brought our nations more closely together, but it is gratifying to address you as the spokesman for nations whose convictions and attending actions have so much to do with the weal or woe of all mankind.

It is not possible to overappraise the importance of such a conference. It is no unseemly boast, no disparagement of other nations which, though not represented, are held in highest respect, to declare that the conclusion of this body will have a signal influence on all human progress—on the fortunes of the world.

Here is a meeting, I can well believe, which is an earnest of the awakened conscience of twentieth century civilization. It is not a convention of remorse, nor a session of sorrow. It is not the conference of victors to define terms of settlement. Nor is it a council of nations seeking to remake humankind. It is rather a coming together from all parts of the earth, to apply the better attributes of mankind to minimize the faults in our international relationships.

Speaking as official sponsor for the invitation, I think I may say the call is not of the United States of America alone; it is rather the spoken word of war-wearied world, struggling for restoration, hungering and thirsting for better relationship; of humanity crying for relief and craving assurances of lasting peace.

It is easy to understand this world-wide aspiration. The glory of triumph, the rejoicing in achievement, the love of liberty, the devotion to country, the pangs of sorrow, the burdens of debt, the desolation of ruin—all these are appraised alike in all lands. Here in the United States we are but freshly turned from the burial of an unknown American soldier, when a nation sorrowed while paying him tribute. Whether it was spoken or not, a hundred millions of our people were summarizing the inexcusable cause, the incalculable cost, the unspeakable sacrifices, and the unutterable sorrows, and there was the ever-impelling question: How can humanity justify or God forgive? Human hate demands no such toll; ambition and greed must be denied it. If misunderstanding must take the blame, then let us banish it, and let understanding rule and make good-will regnant everywhere. All of us demand liberty and justice. There cannot be one without the other, and they must be held the unquestioned possession of all peoples. Inherent rights are of God, and the tragedies of the world originate in their attempted denial. The world to-day is infringing their enjoyment by arming to defend or deny, when simple sanity calls for their recognition through common understanding.

Out of the cataclysm of the World War came new fellowships, new convictions, new aspirations. It is ours to make the most of them. A world staggering with debt needs its burden lifted. Humanity which has been shocked by wanton destruction would minimize the agencies of that destruction. Contemplating the measureless cost of war and the continuing burden of armament, all thoughtful peoples wish for real limitation of armament and would like war outlawed. In soberest reflection the world's hundreds of millions who pay in peace and die in war wish their statesmen to turn the expenditures for destruction into means of construction, aimed at a higher state for those who live and follow after.

It is not alone that the world cannot readjust itself and cast aside the excess burdens without relief from the leaders of men. War has grown progressively cruel and more destructive from the first recorded conflict to this pregnant day, and the reverse order would more become our boasted civilization.

Gentlemen of the Conference, the United States welcomes you with unselfish hands. We harbor no fears; we have no sordid ends to serve; we suspect no enemy; we contemplate or apprehend no conquest. Content with what we have, we seek nothing which is another's. We only wish to do with you that finer, nobler thing which no nation can do alone.

We wish to sit with you at the table of international understanding and good will. In good conscience we are eager to meet you frankly, and invite and offer coöperation. The world demands a sober contemplation of the existing order and the realization that there can be no cure without sacrifice, not by one of us, but by all of us.

I do not mean surrendered rights, or narrowed freedom, or denied aspirations, or ignored national necessities. Our Republic would no more ask for these than it would give. No pride need be humbled, no nationality submerged, but I would have a mergence of minds committing all of us to less preparation for war and more enjoyment of fortunate peace.

The higher hopes come of the spirit of our coming together. It is but just to recognize varying needs and peculiar positions. Nothing can be accomplished in disregard of national apprehensions. Rather, we should act together to remove the causes of apprehensions. This is not to be done in intrigue. Greater assurance is found in the exchanges of simple honesty and directness among men resolved to accomplish as becomes leaders among nations, when civilization itself has come to its crucial test.

It is not to be challenged that government fails when the excess of its cost robs the people of the way to happiness and the opportunity to achieve. If the finer sentiments were not urging, the cold, hard facts of excessive cost and the eloquence of economics would urge to reduce our armaments. If the concept of a better order does not appeal, then let us ponder the burden and the blight of continued competition.

It is not to be denied that the world has swung along throughout the ages without heeding this call from the kindlier hearts of men. But the same world never before was so tragically brought to realization of the utter futility of passion's sway when reason and conscience and fellowship point a nobler way.

I can speak officially only for our United States. Our hundred millions frankly want less of armament and none of war. Wholly free from guile, sure in our minds that we harbor no unworthy designs, we accredit the world with the same good intent. So I welcome you, not alone in good will and high purpose, but with high faith.

We are met for a service to mankind. In all simplicity, in all honesty and all honor, there may be written here the avowals of a world conscience refined by the consuming fires of war, and made more sensitive by the anxious aftermath. I hope for that understanding which will emphasize the guaranties of peace, and for commitments to less burdens and a better order which will tranquilize the world. In such an accomplishment there will be added glory to your flags and ours, and the rejoicing of mankind will make the transcending music of all succeeding time.

CHARLES E. HUGHES, TO THE CONFERENCE

It is with a deep sense of privilege and responsibility that I accept the honor you have conferred.[1]

Permit me to express the most cordial appreciation of the assurances of friendly coöperation, which have been generously expressed by the representatives of all the invited Governments. The earnest desire and purpose, manifested in every step in the approach to this meeting, that we should meet the reasonable expectation of a watching world by effective action suited to the opportunity, is the best augury for the success of the conference.

The President invited the Governments of the British Empire, France, Italy and Japan to participate in a conference on the subject of limitation of armament, in connection with which Pacific and Far Eastern questions also would be discussed. It would have been most agreeable to the President to have invited all the Powers to take part in this conference, but it was thought to be a time when other considerations should yield to the practical requirements of the existing exigency, and in this view the invitation was extended to the group known as the Principal Allied and Associated Powers, which, by reason of the conditions produced by the war, control in the main the armament of the world. The opportunity to limit armament lies within their grasp.

It was recognized, however, that the interest of other powers in the Far East made it appropriate that they should be invited to participate in the discussion of the Pacific and Far Eastern problems, and, with the approval of the five Powers, an invitation to take part in the discussion of those questions has been extended to Belgium, China, The Netherlands and Portugal.

The inclusion of the proposal for the discussion of Pacific and Far Eastern questions was not for the purpose of embar-

[1] The permanent Chairmanship of the Conference.

rassing or delaying an agreement for limitation of armament, but rather to support that undertaking by availing ourselves of this meeting to endeavor to reach a common understanding as to the principles and policies to be followed in the Far East and thus greatly to diminish and, if possible, wholly to remove, discernible sources of controversy. It is believed that by interchanges of views at this opportune time the Governments represented here may find a basis of accord and thus give expression to their desire to assure enduring friendship.

In the public discussions which have preceded the conference, there have been apparently two competing views; one, that the consideration of armament should await the result of the discussion of Far Eastern questions, and another, that the latter discussion should be postponed until an agreement for limitation of armament has been reached. I am unable to find sufficient reason for adopting either of these extreme views. I think that it would be most unfortunate if we should disappoint the hopes which have attached to this meeting by a postponement of the consideration of the first subject.

The world looks to this conference to relieve humanity of the crushing burden created by competition in armament, and it is the view of the American Government that we should meet that expectation without any unnecessary delay. It is therefore proposed that the conference should proceed at once to consider the question of the limitation of armament.

This, however, does not mean that we must postpone the examination of the Far Eastern questions. These questions of vast importance press for solution. It is hoped that immediate provision may be made to deal with them adequately, and it is suggested that it may be found to be entirely practicable through the distribution of the work among designated committees to make progress to the ends sought to be achieved without either subject being treated as a hindrance to the proper consideration and disposition of the other.

The proposal to limit armament by agreement of the powers is not a new one, and we are admonished by the futility of earlier effort. It may be well to recall the noble aspirations which were voiced twenty-three years ago in the imperial rescript of his Majesty the Emperor of Russia. It was then pointed out with clarity and emphasis that, "The intellectual and physical strength of the nations, labor, and capital are for the major part diverted from their natural application and unproductively consumed. Hundreds of millions are devoted to acquiring terrible engines of destruction, which, though to-day regarded as the last word of science, are destined to-morrow to lose all value in consequence of some fresh discovery in the same field. National culture, economic progress and the production of wealth are either paralyzed or checked in their development. Moreover, in proportion as the armaments of each power increase, so do they less and less fulfill the object which the Governments have set before themselves. The economic crises, due in great part of the system of armaments *à l'outrance* and the continual danger which lies in this massing of war materials, are transforming the armed peace of our days in a crushing burden, which the peoples have more and more difficulty in bearing. It appears evident, then, that if this state of things were prolonged it would inevitably lead to the calamity which it is desired to avert, and the horrors of which make every thinking man shudder in advance. To put an end to these incessant armaments and to seek the means of warding off the calamities which are threatening the whole world—such is the supreme duty which is to-day imposed on all States."

It was with this sense of obligation that his Majesty the Emperor of Russia proposed the conference which was "to occupy itself with this grave problem," and which met at The Hague in the year 1899.

Important as were the deliberations and conclusions of that Conference, especially with respect to the pacific settlement of international disputes, its results in the specific matter of limitation of armament went no further than the adoption of a final resolution setting forth the opinion "that the restrictions of military charges, which are at present a heavy burden on the world, is extremely desirable for the increase of the material and moral welfare of mankind," and the utterance of the wish that the Governments "may examine the possibility of an agreement as to the limitation of armed forces by land and sea, and of war budgets."

It was seven years later that the Secretary of State of the

United States, Mr. Elihu Root, in answering a note of the Russian Ambassador suggesting in outline a program of the Second Peace Conference, said: "The Government of the United States, therefore, feels it to be its duty to reserve for itself the liberty to propose to the Second Peace Conference, as one of the subjects for consideration, the reduction or limitation of armaments, in the hope that, if nothing further can be accomplished, some slight advance may be made toward the realization of the lofty conception which actuated the Emperor of Russia in calling the First Conference." It is significant that the Imperial German Government expressed itself as "absolutely opposed to the question of disarmament," and that the Emperor of Germany threatened to decline to send delegates if the subject of disarmament was to be discussed. In view, however, of the resolution which had been adopted at the First Hague Conference, the delegates of the United States were instructed that the subject of limitation of armament "should be regarded as unfinished business, and that the Second Conference should ascertain and give full consideration to the result of such examination as the Governments may have given, to the possibility of an agreement pursuant to the wish expressed by the First Conference." But by reason of the obstacles which the subject had encountered, the Second Peace Conference at The Hague, although it made notable progress in provision for the peaceful settlement of controversies, was unable to deal with limitation of armament except by a resolution in the following general terms: "The Conference confirms the resolution adopted by the Conference of 1899 in regard to the limitation of military expenditure; and, inasmuch as military expenditure has considerably increased in almost every country since that time, the Conference declares that it is eminently desirable that the Governments should resume the serious examination of this question."

This was the fruition of the efforts of eight years. Although the effect was clearly perceived, the race in preparation of armaments, wholly unaffected by these futile suggestions, went on until it fittingly culminated in the greatest war of history, and we are now suffering from the unparalleled loss of life, the destruction of hopes, the economic dislocations, and the widespread impoverishment which measure the cost of the victory over the brutal pretensions of military force.

But if we are warned by the inadequacy of earlier endeavors for limitation of armament, we cannot fail to recognize the extraordinary opportunity now presented. We not only have the lessons of the past to guide us, not only do we have the reaction from the disillusioning experiences of war, but we must meet the challenge of imperative economic demands. What was convenient or highly desirable before is now a matter of vital necessity. If there is to be economic rehabilitation, if the longings for reasonable progress are not to be denied, if we are to be spared the uprising of peoples made desperate in the desire to shake off burdens no longer endurable, competition in armament must stop. The present opportunity not only derives its advantage from a general appreciation of this fact, but the power to deal with the exigency now rests with a small group of nations, represented here, who have every reason to desire peace and to promote amity.

The astounding ambition which lay athwart the promise of the Second Hague Conference no longer menaces the world, and the great opportunity of liberty-loving and peace-preserving democracies has come. Is it not plain that the time has passed for mere resolutions that the responsible Powers should examine the question of limitation of armament? We can no longer content ourselves with investigations, with statistics, with reports, with the circumlocution of inquiry. The essential facts are sufficiently known. The time has come, and this Conference has been called, not for general resolutions or mutual advice, but for action. We meet with full understanding that the aspirations of mankind are not to be defeated either by plausible suggestions of postponement or by impracticable counsels of perfection. Power and responsibility are here and the world awaits a practicable program which shall at once be put into execution.

I am confident that I shall have your approval in suggesting that in this matter, as well as in others before the Conference, it is desirable to follow the course of procedure which has the best promise of achievement rather than one which would facilitate division; and thus, constantly aiming to agree so far as possible, we shall, with each point of agreement, make it easier to proceed to others.

The question, in relation to armament, which may be regarded as of primary importance at this time, and with which we can deal most promptly and effectively, is the limitation of naval armament. There are certain general considerations which may be deemed pertinent to this subject.

The first is that the core of the difficulty is to be found in the competition in naval programs, and that, in order appropriately to limit naval armament, competition in its production must be abandoned. Competition will not be remedied by resolves with respect to the method of its continuance. One program inevitably leads to another, and, if competition continues, its regulation is impracticable. There is only one adequate way out and that is to end it now.

It is apparent that this cannot be accomplished without serious sacrifices. Enormous sums have been expended upon ships under construction, and building programs which are now under way cannot be given up without heavy loss. Yet if the present construction of capital ships goes forward, other ships will inevitably be built to rival them, and this will lead to still others. Thus the race will continue, so long as ability to continue lasts. The effort to escape sacrifices is futile. We must face them or yield our purpose.

It is also clear that no one of the naval Powers should be expected to make these sacrifices alone. The only hope of limitation of naval armament is by agreement among the nations concerned, and this agreement should be entirely fair and reasonable in the extent of the sacrifices required of each of the Powers. In considering the basis of such an agreement and the commensurate sacrifices to be required, it is necessary to have regard to the existing naval strength of the great naval Powers, including the extent of construction already affected in the case of ships in process. This follows from the fact that one nation is as free to compete as another, and each may find grounds for its action. What one may do another may demand the opportunity to rival, and we remain in the thrall of competitive effort. I may add that the American delegates are advised by their naval experts that the tonnage of capital ships may fairly be taken to measure the relative strength of navies, as the provision for auxiliary combatant craft should sustain a reasonable relation to the capital ship tonnage allowed.

It would also seem to be a vital part of a plan for the limitation of naval armament that there should be a naval holiday. It is proposed that for a period of not less than ten years there should be no further construction of capital ships.

I am happy to say that I am at liberty to go beyond these general propositions, and, on behalf of the American delegation acting under the instructions of the President of the United States, to submit to you a concrete proposition for an agreement for the limitation of naval armament.

It should be added that this proposal immediately concerns the British Empire, Japan and the United States. In view of the extraordinary conditions, due to the World War, affecting the existing strength of the navies of France and Italy, it is not thought to be necessary to discuss at this stage of the proceedings the tonnage allowance of these nations, but the United States proposes that this matter be reserved for the later consideration of the Conference.

In making the present proposal the United States is most solicitous to deal with the question upon an entirely reasonable and practicable basis to the end that the just interests of all shall be adequately guarded, and the national security and defense shall be maintained. Four general principles have been applied:

1. That all capital shipbuilding programs, either actual or projected, should be abandoned;

2. That further reduction should be made through the scrapping of certain of the older ships;

3. That, in general, regard should be had to the existing naval strength of the Powers concerned;

4. That the capital ship tonnage should be used as the measurement of strength for navies, and a proportionate allowance of auxiliary combatant craft prescribed.

With the acceptance of this plan the burden of meeting the demands of competition in naval armament will be lifted. Enormous sums will be released to aid the progress of civilization. At the same time the proper demands of national defense will be adequately met and the nations will have ample opportunity during the naval holiday of ten years to consider their future course. Preparation for offensive naval war will stop now.

[Secretary Hughes then detailed the principal features of the proposed agreement.]

MR. BALFOUR

MR. CHAIRMAN, you have invited those who desire to continue the discussion which began on Saturday last. I think it would be very unfortunate if we were to allow the events of Saturday to pass without some further observation on the part of those to whom you, Mr. Chairman, addressed your speech and if, for any reason which I shall venture to explain in a moment, I am the first to take up the challenge, it is because of all the powers here assembled the country which I represent is, as everybody knows, the most intimately interested in naval questions.

Statesmen of all countries are beginning to discover that the labors and difficulties of peace are almost as arduous and require almost as great qualities as those which are demanded for the conduct of a successful war.

This struggle to restore the world to the condition of equilibrium, so violently interfered with by five years of war, is one that taxes and must tax the efforts of everybody. And I congratulate you, if I may, Mr. Chairman, on the fact that you have added the new anniversary which will henceforth be celebrated in connection with this movement toward reconstruction in the same spirit in which we welcomed the anniversary celebrated only a few hours ago, on the day on which hostilities came to an end. If the 11th of November in the minds of the allied and associated powers, in the minds perhaps not less of all the neutrals—if that is a date imprinted on grateful hearts, I think November 12 will also prove to be an anniversary welcomed and thought of in a grateful spirit by those who in the future shall look back upon the arduous struggle now being made by the civilized nations of the world, not merely to restore pre-war conditions, but to see that war conditions shall never again exist.

I count myself among the fortunate of the earth in that I was present, and to that extent had a share in the proceedings of last Saturday. They were memorable, indeed. The secret was admirably kept. I hope that all the secrets, so long as they ought to be secrets, of our discussion, will be as well kept. In my less sanguine mood I have doubts. But, however they may be, the secret in this case was most admirably kept, and I listened to a speech which I thought eloquent, appropriate, in every way a fitting prelude to the work of the conference which was about to open, or which, indeed, had been opened by the President, without supposing that anything very dramatic lay behind. And suddenly I became aware, as I suppose all present became aware, that they were assisting not merely at an eloquent and admirable speech, but at a great historical event. It was led up to him with such art. The transition seemed so natural that when the blow fell, when the speaker uttered the memorable words which have now gone round and found echo in every quarter of the civilized world, it came as a shock of profound surprise: it excited the sort of emotions we have when some wholly new event springs into view, and we felt that a new chapter in the history of world reconstruction had been warily opened.

Mr. Chairman, the absolute simplicity of the procedure, the easy transition and the great dramatic climax were the perfection of art, which shows that the highest art and the most perfect simplicity are very often, indeed very commonly, combined.

Now, I said I would explain, if I was allowed, why I venture to rise first to-day to deal with the subject which is in all our hearts. As I have hinted, it is because the British Empire and Great Britain, these two together, are more profoundly concerned with all that touches matters naval than it is possible for any other nation to be, and this not, believe me, for any reasons of ambition, not for any reasons drawn from history or tradition, but from the hard, brutal necessities of claims and obvious facts.

There never has been in the history of the world a great empire constituted as the British Empire is. It is a fact no doubt familiar to everybody whom I am addressing at the present moment, but has everybody whom I am addressing imaginatively conceived precisely what the situation of the British Empire is in this question?

Most of my audience are citizens of the United States. The United States stands solid, impregnable, self-sufficient, all its lines of communication protected, doubly protected, completely protected from any conceivable hostile act. It is not merely that you are 110,000,000 of population; it is not that you are the wealthiest country in the world; it is that the whole configuration of your country, the geographical position of your country, is such that you are wholly immune from the particular perils to which, from the nature of the case, the British Empire is subjected.

Supposing, for example, that your Western States, for whose safety you are responsible, were suddenly removed 10,000 miles across the sea. Supposing that you found that the very heart of your empire, the very heart of this great State, was a small, a crowded island depending for overseas trade not merely, not chiefly, for its luxuries, but depending upon overseas communication for the raw material of those manufactures by which its superabundant population lives; depending upon the same overseas communication for the food upon which they subsist. Supposing it was a familiar thought in your minds that there never was at any moment of the year within the limits of your State more than seven weeks' food for the population, and that that food had to be replenished by overseas communication. Then, if you will draw that picture, and if you will see all that it implies and all that it carries with it, you will understand why it is that every citizen of the British Empire, whether he comes from the far dominions of the Pacific or whether he lives in the small island in the North Sea, never can forget that it is by sea communication that he lives and that without sea communication he and the empire to which he belongs would perish.

Now, ladies and gentlemen, do not suppose that I am uttering laments over the weakness of my empire. Far from it. We are strong, I hope, in the vigorous life of its constituent parts. We are strong, I hope, in the ardent patriotism which binds us all together. But this strategic weakness is obvious to everybody who reflects; it is present in the minds of our enemies, if we have enemies. Do not let it be forgotten by our friends.

These reflections, with your kindness, I have indulged in

order to explain why it is that I am addressing you at the present time. We have had to consider, and we have considered, the great scheme laid before you by our Chairman. We have considered it with admiration and approval. We agree with it in spirit and in principle. We look to it as being the basis of the greatest reform in the matter of armament and preparation for war that has ever been conceived or carried out by the courage and patriotism of statesmen. I do not pretend, of course—it would be folly to pretend—that this or any other scheme, by whatever genius it may have been contrived, can deal with every subject; can cover the whole ground of international reconstruction. It would be folly to make the attempt and it would be folly to pretend that the attempt has yet been made in any single scheme as was clearly explained by the Secretary of State on Saturday. The scheme deals, and deals only, with three nations which own the largest fleets at present in the world. It therefore, of necessity, omits all consideration for the time being of those European nations who have diminished their fleets, and who at present have no desire, and I hope never will have any desire, to own fleets beyond the necessities that national honor and national defense require.

Again, it does not touch a question which every man coming from Europe must feel to be a question of immense and almost paramount importance. I mean the heavy burden of land armaments. That is left on one side to be dealt with by other schemes and in other ways.

What it does is surely one of the biggest things that has ever yet been done by constructive statesmanship. It does deal with the three great fleets of the world, and in the broad spirit in which it deals with those fleets, in the proportion of disarmament which it lays down for those fleets, the Government of the country which I represent is in the fullest and the heartiest sympathy with the policy which the United States has brought before us for our consideration. They have, as we think most rightly, taken the battle fleet as the aggressive unit which they have in the main to consider; and in the battle fleet you must include those auxiliary ships without which a modern battle fleet has neither eyes nor ears, has little power of defense against certain forms of attack.

and little power of observation, little power of dealing with any equal foe to which it may be opposed.

Taking those two as really belonging to one subject, namely, the battle fleet, taking those two, the battleships themselves and the vessels auxiliary and necessary to a battle fleet, we think that the proportion between these various countries is acceptable; we think the limitations of amounts is reasonable; we think it should be accepted; we firmly believe that it will be accepted.

In my view, the message which has been sent around the world on Saturday is not a message which is going to be received by those most concerned with cool approbation. I believe it is going to be received by them with warm, hearty approval, and with every effort at full, loyal and complete coöperation.

I think it would be ill-fitting on such an occasion as this if I were to attempt to go into any details. There are questions—and I have no doubt that the Secretary of State, our Chairman, would be the first to tell us that there are details which can be adequately dealt with only in committee. At the first glance, for example, and I give it merely as an example, our experts are inclined to think that perhaps too large an amount of tonnage has been permitted for submarines. Submarines are a class of vessels most easily abused in their use and which, in fact, in the late war, were most grossly abused. We quite admit that probably the submarine is the defensive weapon, properly used, of the weak, and that it would be impossible, or, if possible, it might be well thought undesirable, to abolish them altogether. But the amount of submarine tonnage permitted by the new scheme is far in excess, I believe, of the tonnage possessed by any nation at the present moment, and I only throw it out as a suggestion that it may be well worth considering whether that tonnage should not be further limited, and whether, in addition to limiting the amount of the tonnage, it might not be practicable, and, if practicable, desirable, to forbid altogether the construction of those submarines of great size which are not intended for defense, which are not the weapon of the weaker party, whose whole purpose is attack and whose whole purpose is probably attack by methods which civilized nations would regard with horror.

MR. BALFOUR 395

However, there may be other questions of detail, questions connected with replacement, questions connected with cruisers, which are not connected with or required for fleet action. But those are matters for consideration by the technical experts, and however they be decided, they do not touch the main outline of the structure which the United States Government desires erected and which we earnestly wish to help them in erecting.

That structure stands, as it seems to me, clear and firm, and I cannot help thinking that in the broad outline, whatever may happen in the course of these discussions during the next few weeks, that structure will remain as it was presented by its original architects, for the admiration and for the use of mankind.

I have little more to say except this: It is easy to estimate in dollars or in pounds, shillings and pence the savings to the taxpayer of each of the nations concerned which the adoption of this scheme will give. It is easy to show that the relief is great. It is easy to show that indirectly it will, as I hope and believe, greatly stimulate industry, national and international, and do much to diminish the difficulties under which every civilized Government is at this time laboring. All that can be weighed, measured, counted; all that is a matter of figures. But there is something in this scheme which is above and beyond numerical calculation. There is something which goes to the root, which is concerned with the highest international morality.

This scheme after all—what does it do? It makes idealism a practical proposition. It takes hold of the dream when reformers, poets, publicists, even potentates, as we heard the other day, have from time to time put before mankind as the goal to which human endeavor should aspire.

A narrative of all the attempts made, of all the schemes advanced, for diminishing the sorrows of war, is a melancholy one. Some fragments were laid before you by our Chairman on Saturday. They were not exhilarating. They showed how easy it is to make professions and how difficult it is to carry those professions into effect.

What makes this scheme a landmark is that combined with the profession is the practice, that in addition to the expression, the eloquent expression of good intentions, in which the speeches of men of all nations have been rich, a way has been found in which, in the most striking fashion, in a manner which must touch the imagination of everybody, which must come home to the dullest brain and the hardest heart, the Government of the United States has shown its intention not merely to say that peace is a very good thing, that war is horrible, but there is a way by which wars can really be diminished, by which the burdens of peace, almost as intolerable as the burdens of war, can really be lightened for the populations of the world. And in doing that, in doing it in the manner in which they have done it, in striking the imagination not merely of the audience they were addressing, not merely of the great people to whom they belong, but of the whole civilized world, in doing that they have, believe me, made the first and opening day of this congress one of the landmarks in human civilization.

I have said all that I propose to say, but if you will allow me I will read a telegram put into my hands just as I reached this meeting, this congress, from the British Prime Minister:

"Following for Mr. Balfour from Mr. Lloyd-George:

"Many thanks for your telegram. If you think it will serve useful purpose to let them know, message might be published, as follows:

"'Government have followed proceedings at opening session of Conference with profound appreciation and wholeheartedly endorse your opinion that speeches made by President Harding and Secretary of State were bold and statesmanlike utterances, pregnant with infinite possibilities. Nothing could augur better for ultimate success of conference. Please convey to both our most sincere congratulations.'"

BARON KATO

JAPAN deeply appreciates the sincerity of purpose evident in the plan of the American Government for the limitation of armaments. She is satisfied that the proposed plan will materially relieve the nations of wasteful expenditures and cannot fail to make for the peace of the world.

She cannot remain unmoved by the high aims which have

actuated the American project. Gladly accepting, therefore, the proposal in principle, Japan is ready to proceed with determination to a sweeping reduction in her naval armament.

It will be universally admitted that a nation must be provided with such armaments as are essential to its security. This requirement must be fully weighed in the examination of the plan. With this requirement in view, certain modifications will be proposed with regard to the tonnage basis for replacement of the various classes of vessels. This subject should be referred to special consideration by naval experts. When such modifications are proposed, I know that the American and other delegations will consider them with the same desire to meet our ideas as we have to meet theirs.

Japan has never claimed, nor has intention of claiming, to have a general establishment equal in strength to that of either the United States or the British Empire. Her existing plan will show conclusively that she had never in view preparations for offensive war.

M. BRIAND
Reprinted from *New York Times,* November 22, 1921.

GENTLEMEN, you will readily admit that I, as a delegate of France, should feel moved when rising to speak from this full-sounding platform, whence every word that is said goes to the attentive and anxious ear of the world and of all civilized people.

I wish, first of all, to thank my colleagues of the Conference who, on the opening of this public meeting, so kindly allowed me to speak as the representative of my country.

I shall endeavor to make it appear to your eyes and to the eyes of the world with its true, genuine face, as it is, that will show you that she is ready, and I might say perhaps more ready than any other country, to direct her attention and her earnest will to whatever steps may be thought desirable in order to insure final peace for the world. Nothing for my colleagues and myself would be more pleasant than to be able to tell you this: We bring here sacrifices to the fullest extent possible. We have our own security insured. We lay down arms. We should be so happy to be able to make that gesture in order to participate in the final disarmament of the world.

Unfortunately, we cannot speak in this way. I say also, unfortunately, we have not the right to do so. I shall briefly explain later on for what reasons. I shall tell you, for France, that she wants to make peace. If you want to make peace, there must be two people, yourself and the neighbor opposite. To make peace—I am speaking, of course, of land armament—it is not sufficient to reduce effectives and decrease war material. That is the physical side, a physical aspect of things.

There is another consideration which we have no right to neglect in such a problem, that touches vital questions which are of the most serious character for the country concerned. It is necessary that besides this physical disarmament there should be in those same circles what I shall call a general atmosphere of peace. In other words, a moral disarmament is as necessary as the material one.

I have the right to say this, and I hope to be able to prove it to you. And I have the right to say to you that in Europe, as it is at present, there are serious elements of instability, there are such conditions prevailing that France is obliged to face them, and to contemplate the necessary matters from the point of view of her own security.

I am now staying in a country many of the men of which have already enjoyed the opportunity of seeing France and knowing exactly what she is. They came to us in the most critical time of the war. They came and shed their blood—mingled their blood with ours, and they shared our life, and they have seen France, and they now know what France is. And certainly these men have contributed to enlighten their own countrymen, and they have done everything to dispel and drive away those noxious gases which have been spread about, and under which certain people have been trying to mask and to conceal the true face of France.

Here in this country you are living among States which do not know the entangled barriers and frontiers of Europe. Here you live in an immense expanse of space. You do not know any factions on your own land. You have nothing to fear. So that it is rather difficult for some of you—it must be difficult for some of you—to realize what are the conditions at present prevailing in Europe, after war and after victory.

I quite admit that every citizen of the United States should come and tell me this: "The war is won. Peace is signed. Germany has reduced her army to a great extent. Most of her war material has been destroyed. What is it that prevents peace from now reigning in Europe? Why is it that France keeps such a considerable army, abundantly provided with war material?"

Of course, in saying this only certain people have got something at the back of their minds. They suggest that France also has some hidden thought—some hidden design. It has been said that France wanted to install in Europe a sort of military supremacy, and that after all she wanted to be so simply to take the place Germany occupied before the war.

Gentlemen, perhaps this is the most painful, heartrending and cruel thing that a Frenchman can hear.

And for them to say it, after the direful war from which we have just emerged—unprovoked war which we had to undergo—to be again in the cruel necessity to give to the world only the appearance that we have perfidious intentions and military design—this, gentlemen, constitutes, I may say, the most disheartening thing for us.

If we had not the full confidence of those that know my country, those that have seen it—they can testify that not one word of it is true. If there is a country that has deliberately turned her steps toward peace, that wants peace with all her heart, believes in it with her entire faith—if there is a country that does this, gentlemen, it is France.

Since the armistice we have had many disappointments. France has had to wait for certain realizations which she has not been able to get. She has seen Germany digress—haggle over the signature which had been given. Germany has refused to stand by her pledged word. She has refused to pay compensation due for the devastated regions. She has declined to make the gesture of chastisement that, after all, every man of sense would expect after the horrors that we have witnessed. Germany has refused to disarm.

At that time France was strong and Germany could not resist. Public opinion in France was naturally impatient: while under this provocation France remained perfectly cool. There was not one gesture on her part to aggravate the situation. I may say here emphatically in the face of the world, we have no hatred in our hearts, and France will do everything she can. She will use every means to prevent between Germany and herself a recurrence of these bloody conflicts. She wishes for nothing else but that the two peoples should be able to live side by side in the normal conditions of peace.

But, after all, we have no right to forget. We have no right to abandon ourselves. We have no right to weaken our position; and were it only because we must avoid giving rise, in the bosom that would only be ready to take advantage of it, to certain hopes that would be encouraged by our weakness.

Gentlemen, I spoke a few moments ago of the moral aspect of disarmament, and I referred in my remarks to Germany. I do not want to be unjust; nothing is further from my mind. But we know there is in Germany, there is one part of Germany, that is for peace. There are many people, especially among the working classes, who want to work, who have had enough of this war, who have had enough of war altogether, and are most anxious to settle down in peace, and also to set to work. We shall do everything to help that Germany, and if she wants to restore her balance in the bosom of a pacific republic and democratic institutions, then we can help her, and we shall be able to contemplate the future with feelings of security.

But, gentlemen, there is another Germany, a Germany which has not changed her mind and to which the last war has taught no lesson. That Germany keeps thoughts in the back of her mind; she has the same designs which she entertained before the war; she has kept the same preoccupations and she cherishes the same ambitions as the Hohenzollerns did. And how can we close our eyes to this? How can we ignore this state of things?

This, gentlemen, is happening at our very doors; we have only got to look. This is happening but a few miles from us, and we follow the thoughts of the Germans, or certain Germans, and the evolution which is taking place. And more than that, we have witnessed certain attempts to return to the former state of things.

Nobody could be mistaken about the real bearing of what was called the *Kapp Putsch*. We know very well that if it had succeeded, Germany would have returned to her pre-war state, and we do not know what might have happened, or, rather, we know too well what would have been the consequences of such state of things.

Gentlemen, a volume has been published by no less a man than Field Marshal Ludendorff, who still enjoys great authority in many German circles, and who is followed by a great part of the élite in Germany, professors, philosophers, writers, etc. What do we read in this book? Gentlemen, I should not like to make too many quotations. I should not like to prolong this speech, and perhaps draw too much of your attention, but this is part of my brief, and if you are, like me, convinced that the moral elements is of the utmost importance, you will allow me to read just two or three passages. This is the first quotation:

"It is necessary that we should learn to understand that we live in a warlike time, that struggle will remain forever for the single individual, as for the State, a natural phenomenon; and that the struggle is equally on the divine order of the world."

In the same book Marshal Ludendorff produces these terrible words of de Moltke on the 11th of December, 1919:

"Eternal peace is a dream. It is not even a beautiful dream, and war is one of the parts of the order of the world, such as it has been created by God. It is by war that are developed the noblest virtues of man, courage, disinterestedness, devotion to duty and the spirit of sacrifice, up to the abandonment of one's own life. Without war the world would sink in the morass of materialism."

And further, this is Marshal Ludendorff himself speaking now:

"It is for the political education of the German people, and it is an indispensable notion with the knowledge of this fact, that in the future war will be the last and the only decisive means of policy; that thought, completed by the virile life of war, the Entente shall not be able to forbid the German people to entertain, although they are trying to take it away from us. War is the cornerstone of all intelligent policy. It is the cornerstone of every form of future even, and chiefly of the future of the German people."

And, lastly, Marshal Ludendorff says this:
"The warlike qualities of the Prussian and German army have been put to the proof on the bloody battlefields. The German people need no other qualities for their moral renovation. The spirit of the former army must be the germ which will allow this renovation to take place."

Such, gentlemen, are the words used by the highest German authorities who have preserved, and I can quite understand it, the full part, the great part at least, of the confidence of the German people, and that is what we are listening to now. After a war that has caused the death of millions of men, after the sore wounds that have been inflicted and that are still bleeding in the sides of the countries of Europe, that is the sort of thing that is being taught at the very door of France. How can you expect that France should close her eyes to such words?

I now come to the physical aspects of disarmament. I can quite understand that somebody might say it is not sufficient to harbor evil designs; to make war one must have appropriate means, because when it is a question of war enormous effectives are necessary; you must have the officers and non-commissioned officers; you must have plentiful material—rifles, guns, machine guns, artillery, etc.—and Germany has no longer any of these.

Germany, from the point of view of effectives, just emerging from the war, from a war where her men have been fighting for four years—and I should be the last to underestimate the valor of her soldiers—our soldiers have had to face and to fight the German soldiers, and they know to what point the German soldier is able to carry his heroism; but Germany just issuing from the war, still has 7,000,000 men over there in Germany who have made the war. Of course, you will say they are not actually serving under the flag, they are not living in barracks. Certainly. Have these men any officers and non-commissioned officers ready to be marshaled to the field? Is it possible to mobilize such an army to-morrow?

To this question I answer "yes," and I am going to explain it.

Since the war, since the moment peace was signed, Germany has constituted a force, a so-called police force, which was intended for the maintenance of public order. That force is called the *Reichswehr*. It is to include 100,000 men, and, in fact, does include 100,000 men. But what men? They are nearly all officers or non-commissioned officers. I mean, gentlemen, regulars, all having served in or having belonged to the old army. Therefore, the cadres are ready there, the officers and non-commissioned officers are ready to marshal the army of to-morrow.

And what is that army? Is it in conformity with the requirements of the Peace Treaty? Is it only for purposes of public order? No. There are a certain number of those of which I have to express the facts as they are.

According to secret instructions issued by the military authorities, the *Reichswehr* is to prepare not only for police purposes but also for war, and is to train for war, with the necessary rehearsals and maneuvers.

There is something more. Germany has another denomination. There is another group called *Einwohnerwehr*. This group includes almost all the men of good will who are ready to serve their country in time of need, and, instead of using it only to preserve internal order, it might be used for other purposes.

The danger was so real that the Allies were obliged to send an ultimatum to Germany to demand this force should be disarmed.

At another moment, under an organization called the *Orgesch*, which is the organization of war, the *Einwohnerwehr* acquired such strength and became such a threat that the Prime Minister of Bavaria, animated by a spirit of revolt, informed the world that he had at his disposal and he could raise in a short time an army of 300,000, plentifully provided with rifles, machine guns and artillery. Well, that force has been disorganized. The German Government has done its duty, and nobody more than myself is ready to recognize it.

It is only a duty on my part, a mere duty, a mere sense of fair play. I stated it in my own Parliament. I am ready to recognize that the German Chancellor, Chancellor Wirth, is a man of good will, animated by fair purposes, loyal and frank, and that he has applied every endeavor, acting with no small merit on his part, in order to really realize a state of peace, and honor the signature of Germany.

But this Government in Germany is weak. It is being watched. Snares are laid in its path and it may fall at any moment. While I may say that on our side we are ready to do everything in order to allow this great people to return to normal conditions of peace, and the German Government, as I said, dissolves the *Einwohnerwehr,* there is something else, gentlemen.

There is another force, which is called the *Chezheitz Politze.* That is also a police force. It includes 150,000 men. These are enlisted men. The force is composed exclusively of regulars, officers, and non-commissioned officers, or at least non-commissioned officers ready to undergo a new period of military service. We demanded the dissolution of this force, but what happened? The *Chezheitz Politze* disappeared, but another appeared in its place—*Schutz Politzi;* but it was just the same. That included 150,000 men. So that, instead of its being a local police force, it became a general police force at the disposal of the Central Government, that could be used anywhere on German territory; so that we come to a total of 250,000 men, and enough men that are real officers, ready to marshal the troops who are training, to be ready instantly in case of war. These men are constantly watched by the Government.

The Government keeps them under its hands. These 7,000,000 men have not returned to civil life, to civil occupations entirely. They are grouped together in this marvelously ingenious way which the German people always have when they want to achieve their purposes. They are called *Frie Corps,* or former combatants' associations, and what not. Any day, any anniversary—and Germans are rather fond of anniversaries—is favorable in order to convene these men and marshal them, to see that you have got them under your hand ready to do the work that is to be done.

We are Frenchmen. We know that. It is happening at our door. And I will only give you an example to show you how rapidly these organizations might be put on a war footing.

Just one second. When the Upper Silesian question reached a somewhat acute stage recently, within a few weeks, I might almost say within a few days, there were, out of these *Frie Corps* or other bodies, about 40,000 men ready with guns, machine guns, rifles, armored trains, and with most perfect military instruments, so that this force should have its full combatant value.

These are facts, gentlemen. I am not noticing them and bringing them here just to make my case better. They are facts that have been verified, and that everybody can ascertain for himself. Therefore, as a question of fact and from the point of view of effectives, Germany can rise in a few weeks, and perhaps almost in a few days and can begin to raise her 6,000,000 or 7,000,000 men with their officers again, and the non-commissioned officers are ready to do the work.

Now I must ask the great people of the United States, so fond of justice, so noble in their purposes, to answer me when I tell them this: Suppose by your side, oh, American people, a nation which has been for years and centuries in bloody conflict with you; and suppose that this nation, you feel, is still ready, morally and materially, to enter into a new struggle. What would you do?

Would you turn away your eyes? Would you close your eyes to a danger that was threatening you? You that are said to be such a positive, such a precise people, would you close your eyes? Would you not desire to do everything in your power in order to safeguard your life, and, what is more, your honor? Would you do anything to weaken yourselves? No. There is not one citizen in the whole United States who would not answer me: "No, never in the world!"

France is looking upon what is happening. France does not exaggerate. She is only watching and waiting.

I now come to the question of war material. We have been told that there was no more war material. It is true the commissions of control in Germany have done admirable work. A great many guns—artillery, I mean—have been destroyed. Some of the destruction has been supervised by the allied officers. It is real.

Other destruction has taken place, as we have been told. We might have a doubt. We are not quite certain. But we must give the opponents the benefit of the doubt, and we believe the destruction on that side is practically completed.

But the problem of war material is one that can easily be solved. You have seen, in the war, with what promptitude—and that was lucky, because if the help had not come so quickly we might have been down, finally—you have seen how quickly immense armies have come over to us, provided with the most modern material, and fought on our sides upon the battlefields.

Well, what is Germany but a vast country of industry—industrially organized? Germany always had two aims. The first was trade, commerce. And that is only natural. The second was war. All her industries, all her manufactures, have been working to the full during the war, and they have developed since.

Everything is ready in Germany, the plans, the designs and calibers. Everything is there ready to insure a steady manufacturing of guns, machine guns and rifles. Suppose that during a period of diplomatic tension, purposely protracted for a number of weeks, certain of the manufactures, certain of the works, begin to fabricate, just at the beginning, just to start the war, just to set the war going, and then go on manufacturing guns and rifles and artillery; what would happen? It is not only in Germany that industry can work to the full. You can make preparations outside. In fact, preparations have actually taken place. In fact, great captains of industry or great industrial magnates have bought important firms in Scandinavia and in other parts of Europe.

It is easy enough to fabricate these guns without our seeing it, outside of our supervision. You know very well that it is possible to build great railroads. You know very well that it is impossible to bring here the proof that Germany is not actually making or purchasing war materials.

It is different from the navy. It is rather difficult to lay the keel of a ship in the stocks, to prepare the dockyards without the world knowing it. But suppose that was possible, do you think you could launch a capital ship without somebody being on the spot and knowing what was happening? But the guns, the rifles, the machine guns—any instruments used on the field of battle—they can be manufactured and cannot be controlled with any measure of certainty.

Ah, gentlemen, this is not the first time in history that France has had to face a situation of this kind. We have known Prussia disarmed. And disarmed by whom? By Napoleon. Well, that Prussia, which seemed practically disarmed, which was harmless to all intents and purposes, we found her again on the battlefield and we were nearly bled white. How can we forget that?

Of course, we know what is often said of the French people. It is often said that we are a frivolous nation and that naturally, when the danger is past, we turn our minds to other things—just as befits a frivolous people. Evidently, gentlemen, we are not the sort of men to keep our eyes steadily fixed on whatever is sad and depressing.

We have not been doing that since the war, but we have been too deeply wounded, I might almost say murdered, to forget the direful lesson which has just been taught us. Gentlemen, there are too many homes in mourning in the country, there are too many men in the streets that are disabled and maimed. Even if we wanted to forget, we could not.

Therefore, we have not the right and we do not intend to leave France defenseless. France must, to all intents and purposes, protect herself.

Such is the situation as far as we are concerned. You will grant me, gentlemen, that it is serious enough. But that is not all. What about the rest of Europe? Apparently Europe is at peace, although here and there on the ground certain volumes of smoke just arising seem to indicate that the fire is not extinguished everywhere. I might say that this fire is smoldering in certain parts of Europe and if France had not had an army, war would already have broken out in Europe again.

I will just draw your attention to one subject to which I may refer later on, and that is the subject of Russia. Russia is a country of 120,000,000 men, which is actually boiling over with anarchy. They have an enormous standing army, which is in theory 1,500,000 men but which has a practical strength of 600,000 men. What will Russia do? Who can say what will happen on that side?

About a year and a half ago there was a wild rush of Russia on Europe. Russia tried to rush Poland and through Poland to reach Germany, where some people were beckoning to her. Gentlemen, we had at that time terribly anxious hours in France. If the barrier had not held good, if that anarchic army had been able to join the people who were calling them on the other side, what would have happened? Where would France be and where would the rest of Europe be? Happily there was the French Army, which was the soldier of order for its own account and for the sake of the world.

The situation in Russia is far from being settled. It is a sort of permanent anxiety to everybody. What will become of that enormous army? What could, or might, Germany do in order to equip Russia and exploit her? We know not. There are so many problems, economic, financial, etc., with which we have to deal that really, gentlemen, we do not know to which to turn; but the greatest problem of all, the greatest question, is life.

First of all, we must be able to live. That is a sort of question mark in France. Thanks to our allies, to whom our gratitude will remain everlasting—thanks to their efforts, we have been able altogether to insure the life, liberty and dignity of men, but, gentlemen, I trust you will certainly feel the weight of my argument and recognize that we are faced with a very terribly serious situation.

When we say we contemplate a reduction of naval armaments, when we discuss it with ourselves, heart to heart, we could have nothing in our minds. We are speaking between friends. There is no threat of war; if there is any menace to peace it is so far distant that you can hardly conceive it, and yet you have not assumed the right of ignoring this danger altogether. You intend to keep your navies to the extent necessary to defend your liberties and insure your life.

If you do that, gentlemen, on the sea, what shall we do when the danger is there at our doors and hanging over our heads? I may say that I have always been in favor of peace; I have assumed powers for the sake of peace in very difficult conditions. Where my country was feeling natural impatience at the state of things, I formally attached myself to the cause of peace. I fastened my heart on that noble task, and I may say that if ever peace is to be disturbed in the world, I shall not be the one to disturb it. But, gentlemen, precisely because I have urged everybody on the road of peace, because I have done everything in my power in order to obtain peace, I feel all the more the great weight of the responsibility which I have assumed, and if to-morrow, because I had been too optimistic, I saw my country again attacked, trampled under foot, bleeding because I had weakened her, gentlemen, I should be a most despicable traitor.

It is that situation which we have got to take into account, gentlemen, and the weight of the responsibilities with which we are burdened.

Only the other day the course of events turned in such a way that it certainly became acute, as you know, in Upper Silesia. I have already referred to this subject. Germany, which did not think that the French people were ready to undertake a military operation, suddenly informed us that she was going to send the *Reichswehr* to the spot in Upper Silesia in order to preserve order.

These were momentous times for us, and, although I have been through many critical times in my life, I may say that no hour was perhaps of more importance than that, and that I clearly and definitely made up my mind, and I told Germany that such a thing was not possible, and that if Germany undertook a thing of the sort she would have to bear the consequences, and the language was understood.

But, gentlemen, if I had spoken without having the French Army back of me, what would my words have become? And if the event had actually taken place, what would have become of Europe itself? Europe is still in a troublous state. It is composed of young States, newly come to life. Who could say what such conflict might have become?

That is the problem and that was the problem, and the struggle did not take place because it was felt that there was still a sufficient force in Europe and in France to preserve order.

Quite recently another attempt has been made, a certain attempt at the restoring of the old order of things in the center of Europe, that might have set fire to the powder magazine again. Nothing happened, because the Allies were in perfect understanding and the incident was peaceably settled.

Gentlemen, I give you these reflections for you to ponder over. You will see that there is nothing in that that would draw us aside from the path that leads to final peace. I apologize for having been with you so long and for having so trespassed upon your attention. Perhaps at another time the President will be less inclined to allow me to speak.

The thought of reducing the armaments, which was the noble purpose of this Conference, is not one from which we would feel disinterested from the point of view of land armaments. We have shown it already. Immediately after the armistice demobilization began, and demobilization began as rapidly and as completely as possible. According to the military laws of France there are to be three classes of men: that is, three generations of young men under the flag. The law is still extant; that law is still valid. It has not been abrogated yet, and the Government has taken the responsibility to reduce to two years the time spent under the flag, and instead of three classes—three generations of young men—we have only two undergoing military service.

It is therefore an immediate reduction by one-third that has already taken place in the effectives—and I am speaking of the normal effectives of the metropolis, leaving aside troops needed for colonial occupation or obligation imposed by treaty in the Rhineland or other countries and plebiscites.

We do not think that endeavor was sufficient, and in the future we have plans in order to restrict further the extent of our armies. In a few days it is certain that the proposals of the Government will be passed in the Chamber, in order to reduce further the military service by half. That is to say, there will be only one class and a half actually serving. The metropolitan French army would be therefore reduced by half, but if anybody asks us to go further, to consent to other reductions, I should have to answer clearly and definitely that it would be impossible for us to do it without exposing ourselves to a most serious danger.

You might possibly come and tell us "This danger that you are exposed to, we see it, we realize it and we are going to share it with you. We are going to offer you all means—put all means at your disposal in order to secure your safety."

Immediately, if we heard those words, of course, we would strike upon another plan. We should be only too pleased to demonstrate the sincerity of our purpose. But we understand the difficulties and the necessities of the statesmen of other countries. We understand the position of other peoples who have also to face difficult and troublous situations.

We are not selfish enough to ask other people to give a part of their sovereign national independence in order to turn it to our benefit and come to our help. We do not expect it; but here I am appealing to your consciences, if France is to remain alone, facing the situation such as I have described—and without any exaggeration—you must not deny her what she wants in order to insure her security. You must let her do what she has to do, if the need arises and if the time comes.

I should be the last one here to try to restrict the noble endeavors which are being made here in order to limit armament in the Conference which has been convened, with such noble purposes in view, and I should like to be able to say that I foresee no limit, no restriction to your labors and to the results which you may achieve. Any question here can be debated and can be resolved upon, but I must draw your attention to one thing; moral disarmament of France would be very dangerous.

Allow me to say it will be most unjust. We do not enjoy the sufficient condition. We should be ready to do it, but the time has not come yet to give up our defense for the sake of final peace in Europe.

We have to know, however, that France is not morally isolated, that she still has with her the men of good will, and the hearts of all people who have fought with her on the same battlefield. The true condition of a moral disarmament in Germany—I mean to say I am referring to these noxious elements of which I have already spoken—the true condition at this time of disarmament in Germany lies in the fact that it should be known over there that France is not alone, and then I feel quite sure that the poisonous propaganda of which I have spoken will simply run up dead against the wall; that it will not be able to go through, and that nobody anywhere will believe in it.

If those that still harbor evil designs know that, and if

those that entertain happy ideas of peace—this working class that wants to return to a normal state of peace—if it is known in Germany that France is not morally alone, peace will come back much quicker; and the words of anger, the words of revenge, will be simply preached in the wilderness. It will be impossible for Germany to reconstruct a defensive army, and she will be able to install democratic institutions, and then we can all hope for final conditions of peace.

Everything that France can do in this direction she will do. In fact, she has already done much. She did not hesitate to open conversations with the German Government in order to settle this painful question of reparation for the devastated regions. Everything has been done and will be done in order to restore normal conditions, and the hour will come when everything will be settled, but the hour has not come yet.

If by direction given to the labors of the Conference it were possible somewhere over there in Europe—if it were possible to say that the outcome of this Conference is indirect blame and opprobrium cast upon France—if it were possible to point out that France is the only country in the world that is still imperialistic, is the only country that opposes final disarmament, then, gentlemen, indeed this Conference would have dealt us a severe blow; but I am quite sure nothing is further from your minds and from your intentions.

If after listening to this argument, after weighing the reasons which you have just heard, you consider it then as valid, then, gentlemen, you will still be with us and you will agree with me and say that France cannot possibly do anything but what she has actually done.

VII. MEMORIALS

BISHOP GINISTY

VERDUN

[On February 17, 1917, Monseigneur Ginisty, Bishop of Verdun, addressed the *"Société des Conférences"* on the suffering and grandeur of soul of the glorious city of Verdun" which had won the admiration of the world by its heroism and martyrdom. After telling of the months of horror and of glory he closed with the following tribute]:

VERDUN! Sacred soil, drenched in blood and tears; city of horror and of honor, of life and of death, city of desolation and of hope, of devastation and of immortality—Verdun! Ah, yes! for our soldiers and for those who have passed through, it is a very hell of fire and steel, of unspeakable torture, of poignant agony, of privation of all kinds, of cold, of heat, of hunger and of thirst. What am I saying? Hell? No, beloved soldiers, no beloved exiles, it is not hell, in spite of the horror and torture which you have endured in body and soul. Call it rather "the calvary of Verdun," for that is where the safety of the country is won, as the safety of the world was brought about at Golgotha; that is where redeeming blood flows in torrents; where the most noble virtues of the French race flourish, where approaching triumphs and the resurrection of France are being prepared.

The final word about Verdun seems to me to come from Canada, from the New France, which has kept the spirit of the mother country; and this word I gather from the lips of a generous Canadian. She sends it to us with a gift of her compassionate charity. Responding to the appeal of Monseigneur, the Archbishop of Montreal, on behalf of our diocese so sorely tried, she brings him her offering: "Ah! Monseigneur," she says, "Verdun is the Flag!"

Yes it is the Flag, symbol of all France, of the sacred union of all her children; synthesis of all her history; memorial of the past, strength of the present, hope of the future; it is the Flag of the Great War, pierced with shot, mutilated, tatterdemalion, but bearing on its hanging tatters, glorious shreds, names forever famous—Douamont, Vaux, Fleury, Damloup, Thiaumont, the Hill of Poivre, Hill 304, le Mort-Homme and many others. It is the Flag which spreads in the wind of victory and on whose folds the enemy can read "They shall not pass" and all France can see "We shall conquer."

A FRENCH OFFICER

TO THE FIRST AMERICANS WHO FELL IN FRANCE

[The first announcement that American troops had been under fire in Europe was contained in a dispatch dated October 27, 1917, which stated that "on the morning of a recent day somewhere in France" the artillery had fired the first shot. On November 3 an official statement from Washington stated that "before daylight November 3 a salient occupied for instruction by a company of American infantry was raided by Germans. Our losses were three killed, five wounded and twelve captured or missing." The three men killed—the first Americans actually to fall in battle in the war were buried on November 6.

"With a guard of French infantrymen in their picturesque uniforms of red and horizon blue standing on one side and a detachment of American soldiers on the other, the flag-wrapped caskets were lowered into the grave as a bugler blew 'taps' and the batteries at the front fired minute guns. As the guns went off the French Officer commanding the division paid tribute to the fallen Americans."

Reprinted by permission from the War Volumes published by the New York Times Company.

IN the name of the —th division, in the name of the French Army, and in the name of France, I bid farewell to Private Enright, Private Gresham, and Private Hay of the American Army.

Of their own free will they had left a prosperous and happy country to come over here. They knew war was continuing in Europe; they knew that the forces fighting for honor, love of justice and civilization were still checked by the long-prepared forces serving the powers of brutal domination, oppression and barbarity. They knew that efforts were still necessary. They wished to give us their generous hearts, and they have not forgotten old historical memories, while others forget more recent ones.

They ignored nothing of the circumstances, and nothing had been concealed from them—neither the length and hardships of war, nor the violence of battle, nor the dreadfulness of new weapons, nor the perfidy of the foe. Nothing stopped them. They accepted the hard and strenuous life; they crossed the ocean at great peril; they took their places on the front by our side, and they have fallen facing the foe in a hard and desperate hand-to-hand fight. Honor to them. Their families, friends and fellow-citizens will be proud when they learn of their deaths.

Men! These graves, the first to be dug in our national soil, and but a short distance from the enemy, are as a mark of the mighty bond we and our allies firmly cling to in the common task, confirming the will of the people and the army of the United States to fight with us to a finish, ready to sacrifice as long as is necessary until final victory for the most noble of causes, that of the liberty of nations, the weak as well as the mighty. Thus the deaths of these humble soldiers appear to us—with extraordinary grandeur.

We will, therefore, ask that the mortal remains of these young men be left here, left with us forever. We inscribe on the tombs, "Here lie the first soldiers of the Republic of the United States to fall on the soil of France for liberty and justice." The passerby will stop and uncover his head. Travelers and men of heart will go out of their way to come here to pay their respective tributes.

Private Enright, Private Gresham, Private Hay! In the name of France I thank you. God receive your souls. Farewell!

ADMIRAL BEATTY

COMRADES OF THE MIST

[Sir David Beatty, First Earl, Admiral of the Fleet, was born in 1871. He entered the navy in 1884. He has been Commander of the Grand Fleet since 1916, and Admiral of the Fleet since 1919. He was decorated for his services in the War in 1914 and 1915 and again for his victory in the battle of Jutland Bank, 1916. The following address was delivered on board the U. S. S. *New York* before a detachment of the American Sixth Battle Squadron from the Grand Fleet on December 1, 1918. The London *Times* comments on the address as follows:

"One of the difficulties of this Armistice time—every one in English-speaking countries has felt it—is to express the feelings that demand expression. Latin peoples, more fortunate in this than we, seem to find little difficulty in putting their sentiments into words. With us it is immensely difficult; witness the matter-of-fact and blunt farewell of Sir David Beatty to the American 6th Battle Squadron from the Grand Fleet on December 1, 1918. There is no eloquence about it; it does not attempt eloquence, but all the same it is thoroughly characteristic and characteristic as much of the American as of the British people. The American 6th Battle Squadron, Admiral Beatty tells them, was 'the straw that broke the camel's back'—a homely phrase by which he means to say that their arrival so strengthened the English fleet that the prestige of the combined fleets of the Allies brought about the surrender of the German fleet without a battle. No rhetoric could have hit nearer the mark."]

I COULD not let the Sixth Battle Squadron go without coming on board the *New York* and saying something of what I feel at this moment of your departure. I had intended to ask Admiral Rodman to permit me to say something to representatives of all the ships of the Sixth Battle Squadron on board his flagship, but the exigencies of the service did not permit me. Therefore, as Admiral Rodman has said, what I say to you, I hope you will promulgate to your comrades in other ships and also to your comrades of the Atlantic Fleet. What I say, I hope you will understand comes from the heart, not only my heart, but the hearts of your comrades of the Grand Fleet.

I want first to thank you, Admiral Rodman, the Captains, Officers and Ships' Companies of this magnificent Squadron for the wonderful coöperation and loyalty you have given me and my Admirals, and the assistance you have given us in every duty you had to undertake. The support which you have shown is that of true comradeship and in the time of stress that is worth a very great deal. As somebody said the other day, "Fighting is now over, talking is going to begin." Therefore I do not want to keep you here any longer, but I want to congratulate you for having been present upon a day unsurpassed in the naval annals of the world. I know quite well that you, as well as your British comrades, were bitterly disappointed at not being able to give effect to that efficiency you have so well maintained. It was a most disappointing day. It was a pitiful day to see those great ships coming in like sheep being herded by dogs to their fold without an effort on anybody's part, but it was a day everybody could be proud of.

I have received messages from several people offering sympathy to the Grand Fleet, and my answer was, "We do not want sympathy. We want recognition of the fact that the prestige of the Grand Fleet stood so high it was sufficient to cause the enemy to surrender without striking a blow." I had always certain misgivings, and when the Sixth Battle Squadron became part of the Grand Fleet those misgivings were doubly strengthened, and I knew then they would throw up their hands. Apparently the Sixth Battle Squadron was the straw that broke the camel's back. However, the disappointment that the Grand Fleet was unable to strike their blow for the freedom of the world is counteracted by the fact that it was their prestige alone that brought about this achievement. During the last twelve months you have been with us we have learned to know each other very well. We learned to respect each other.

I want you to take back the message to the Atlantic Fleet that you have left a very warm place in the hearts of the Grand Fleet, which cannot be filled until you come back or send another squadron to represent you. You have given us a sample of the Atlantic Fleet which I think it will try the Atlantic Fleet, efficient as it is, hard to reproduce. I understand you are now going to Portland where you are to get leave. After that you have the duty to perform of bringing your President to these waters, and then you will return to your own shores. And I hope in the sunshine which Admiral Rodman tells me always shines there, you will not forget your "comrades of the mist" and your pleasant associations of the North Sea. This is a queer place, as you found, but you were not the first to find it out. There was a great explorer, Marco Polo, who, after traveling over the world for thirty years, one day found himself in the North Sea and then went home and went to bed and did not travel any more. I trust it will not have the same effect on any of you, but I can say this, that those of you whom I have seen during the last twelve months seem to have improved in many ways, if that is possible, and I think the North Sea has a health-giving quality which must be put against all the bad points, of which it has so many.

I thank you again and again and again for the great part the Sixth Battle Squadron has played in bringing about the greatest naval victory in history. I hope you will give this message to your comrades. "Come back soon. Good-by and good luck."

ARTHUR TWINING HADLEY

COMMEMORATION ADDRESS

[Arthur Twining Hadley, born in New Haven, Conn., in 1856, was president of Yale University from 1899 to 1920. The following address was delivered at the Commemoration Service for the Yale men who fell in the War, which was held during the Commencement, June 15, 1919. It is reprinted here by permission from "The Moral Basis of Democracy," copyright 1919, Yale University Press.]

Two years ago this place was filled with men in uniform, eager in their enthusiam for the work that was before them. A year ago they had left us; and among those who remained the spirit of enthusiasm had given place to one of solemn resolution. To-day those who went out have returned in triumph to lay aside their uniforms and to resume the work of peace. The spirit of the day is one of rejoicing.

But not all of those who went have come back. Two hundred Yale men have given their lives in their country's service. Some had the joy and the glory of being killed in action. The runner has ended his last race on the fields of France. The oarsman has fought his best contest to a finish in the waves of the English Channel. The scholar has in a single immortal day set forth more of the true meaning of what

Yale had to teach than others, less privileged, have done in a lifetime. And side by side with those who have thus borne public testimony of their devotion, there is a large number called to bear the yet heavier burden of lingering death from wounds or from disease. Theirs has been the greater sacrifice, with the lesser visible good and to them belongs to-day the fullest measure of recognition.

These men have fought their fight; ours remains before us. Fifty years ago Abraham Lincoln pointed out the way—the only way—in which the living can worthily commemorate the dead. It is for us to see that these heroic dead shall not have died in vain. The visible memorials which we may erect, whatever their usefulness or their beauty, are but symbols of our gratitude and affection. The gratitude and the affection themselves are manifested in seeing that the work of the dead is not left half done.

The need of this admonition is even greater to-day than it was when Lincoln spoke; for the dangers to freedom are more immediate and more complex to-day than they were fifty years ago. At the close of our Civil War we faced the comparatively simple problem of preserving freedom for men already trained in the principles of law and morals on which free institutions had been based. To-day we have to secure freedom to men of many races, with many standards of law and morals, more accustomed to despotic authority than to the exercise of self-government. Liberty is threatened from below as well as from above. Those who died have protected democracy against the attacks of those who conceived themselves to be above the law. To us remains the harder task of protecting it against the machinations of those who conceive themselves to be beneath it.

It is one of history's plainest lessons that democracy is based upon self-control; that a people cannot remain free unless its members will voluntarily use their freedom for the purposes of the community under a system of moral law. Yale has taught this lesson in the past. May she continue to do so in the future; and may we, as Yale men, take our part in the teaching! Thus shall we render to the dead the highest honor that is in our power, by keeping our hand day and night upon the maintenance of the work to which they have given their lives.

GENERAL PERSHING
TO THE UNITED STATES SENATE

[John Joseph Pershing was born in Lynn County, Missouri, in 1860. He graduated from West Point in 1886 and from the Law School of the University of Nebraska in 1893. He entered the United States Cavalry in 1886 and became Major General twenty years later. On October 6, 1917, he was appointed General, U. S. A., and commanded our expeditionary force in France. This speech was delivered September 18, 1919, before the United States Congress when he was formally received and thanked by Congress.]

THE might of America lay not only in her numbers and her wealth, but also in the spirit of her people and their determination to succeed at whatever cost. While every man who went to France courageously did his part, behind him were millions of others eager to follow, all supported by a loyal people who deprived themselves to sustain our armies and succor our allies. Whether billeted in French, Belgian or Italian villages or in the camps of England our young men have left behind them a standard of frankness, of integrity, of gentleness and of helpfulness, which will give the other nations of the world a firm belief in the sincerity of our motives.

The benefits flowing from the experience of our soldiers will be broadly felt. They have returned in the full vigor of manhood strong and clean. In the community of effort men from all walks of life have learned to know and to appreciate each other. Through their patriotism, discipline, and association they have become virile, confident and broad-minded. Rich in the consciousness of honorable public service, they will bring into the life of our country a deeper love for our institutions and a more intelligent devotion to the duties of citizenship.

To you, gentlemen of the Congress, we owe the existence and maintenance of our armies in the field. With a clear conception of the magnitude of the struggle, you adopted the draft as the surest means of utilizing our man power. You promptly enacted wise laws to develop and apply our resources to the best effect. You appropriated the fabulous sums required for military purposes. Many of your members visited the armies in the field and cheered us by their interest and sympathy. You made possible the organization and operation by which victory was achieved.

Throughout the war the President reposed in me his full confidence and his unfailing support simplified my task. The Secretary of War made repeated visits to the front, and I am deeply grateful for his wise counsel. Under him the various staffs, bureaus and departments, with all their personnel, are deserving of especial acknowledgment for the ability with which their problems were met. The officers and soldiers who served at home are entitled to their full share in the victory. There existed a unity of purpose between our government in all its branches and the command of the troops in the field that materially hastened the end.

Our navy performed a brilliant part in transporting troops and supplies and in maintaining our sea communication. The army was convoyed overseas with the maximum of safety and comfort and with incredibly small loss. In this arduous service the generous assistance of the seamen of Great Britain deserves our lasting appreciation.

A special tribute is due to those benevolent men and women who ministered to the needs of our soldiers at home and abroad. The welfare societies maintained by a generous public gave us invaluable aid. In our hospitals the surgeons and nurses, both permanent and temporary, served with a skill and fidelity that will ever be worthy of our grateful remembrance.

Business and professional men abandoned their private interests and gave their service to the country. Devoted men, women and even children, often in obscure positions, zealously labored to increase the output of ships, munitions, war material and food supplies while the press and the pulpit stimulated patriotic enthusiasm.

Our admiration goes out to our war-worn allies, whose tenacity, after three years of conflict made possible the effectiveness of the effort. Through their loyal support and hearty coöperation a general spirit of comradeship sprang up among us, which should firmly unite the peoples as it did their armies.

The cheerfulness and fortitude of our wounded were an inspiration and a stimulus to their comrades. Those who are disabled should become the affectionate charge of our people, whose care they have richly earned. Let us in sympathy remember the widows and the mothers who to-day mourn the loss of their husbands and sons.

Our hearts are filled with reverence and love for our triumphant dead. Buried in hallowed ground which their courage redeemed, their graves are sacred shrines that the nation will not fail to honor.

The glorious record made in the fight for our treasured ideals will be a precious heritage to posterity. It has welded together our people and given them a deeper sense of nationality. The solidity of the republic and its institutions in the test of a world war should fill with pride every man and woman living under its flag. The great achievements, the high ideals, the sacrifices of our army and our people belong to no party and to no creed. They are the republic's legacy, to be sacredly guarded and carefully transmitted to future generations.

MARSHAL FOCH

TO THE FRENCH ACADEMY

[On February 5, 1920, Marshal Foch received the highest honor France can pay to her men of achievement when he was formally received as a member of the French Academy. The following tribute of Marshal Foch to his soldiers preceded the eulogy of his predecessor, a customary part of the ceremony. In his speech of welcome M. Poincaré, President of France, recounting the events of Marshal Foch's life and particularly his triumphant career in the Great War said, "It was for you to make war; it is not for you to make peace. You had, however, the right to say what you thought that peace should be in order to prevent a recurrence of war. Let us hope the world will never repent of only partially following your judgment. Marshal of France, Field Marshal of Great Britain, respected soldier, not only of all the Entente Nations, but also of your enemies of yesterday, you will remain for France and all friendly countries the most farseeing and precious of counselors."]

ABOVE my head you have acclaimed the glorious forces who for more than four years, through the rigors of the seasons, at the price of hitherto unknown sacrifices, waged the most violent and most long continued battle. In this greatness of

FERDINAND FOCH

duty accepted by all, this persistent tenacity, this unanimous determination to conquer at all cost, you saw the soul of the country soar upward. And to render homage to the source of this nobility, the army, you have taken into your midst yet another soldier after the illustrious leader who, far from despairing of the safety of his country, broke the invasion and conquered on the Marne.

I thank you for having immortalized in this way the champions of the Marne, the Oise, the Somme and the Yser,—of Artois, of Champagne, of Verdun, of the Somme again, of the Aisne and of Flanders; and those allied legions who in 1918 launched a furious assault from the North Sea to the Vosges to drive the enemy out of France, gain the Rhine and end the peril of the country. You have glorified once more this type of the French soldier, constantly great throughout the ages, with his noble disregard of danger and his lofty ideals—the soldier of the old monarchy, of the revolution, of the empire and the one whom the war of 1914 found greater still; that immortal crusader of the eternal crusade of right and liberty against oppression and force. The story of his ability will astonish the world; by continuous effort for four years of a gigantic struggle, through situations many times desperate, he achieved the safety of the nation in complete victory.

PRESIDENT MILLERAND

SEMICENTENNIAL OF THE FRENCH REPUBLIC

[On November 11, 1920, two great anniversaries were celebrated in France with impressive and solemn ceremonies—the fiftieth anniversary of the French Republic and the second anniversary of the Armistice. In the morning M. Millerand, President of France, made the following address at the Panthéon where a large audience had gathered to do honor to the Unknown French Soldier and the heart of Gambetta, the French patriot. After the ceremony at the Panthéon followed the simple burial beneath the Arc de Triomphe.]

WHAT events have happened, what a transformation has taken place in the half century from September 4, 1870, to September 4, 1920!

Crushed in disaster the Empire fell. The Republic rose up, having for its program the title of the new government: The National Defense. This program is typified by a single man—the tribune whose grateful country has just borne his heart side by side with the nameless and glorious remains of one of his soldiers to the Panthéon.

With an unconquerable faith in the destiny of France, Gambetta did not limit himself—together with his colleagues, the representatives of Alsace and of Lorraine—to the affirmation of the certain revenge of justice at the very hour when force was triumphant. To render possible that revenge which the voice of Paul Déroulède constantly demanded, he consecrated the twelve short years reserved to him by destiny to the work of rebuilding France, to utilize all the resources of most glowing eloquence and flexible policy in order to raise up and develop his party to the point where it should include the entire country; to discipline the party and to transform it from a party of opposition to a party of government; and, simultaneously with the restoration of France, to establish the Republic on unshakable foundations. His work is completed. Under these vaults I salute the representatives of reconstructed France and of the triumphant Republic.

Certainly we deny nothing of what belongs to the French patrimony. The sons of the revolution are truly "the zealots of Jeanne d'Arc." It does not diminish the grandeur of past ages to hold that the nineteenth century—the century of disquietude, of preparation and of research—is one of the most stirring and pathetic.

The period from 1870 to 1920 was hard, but its painful labors themselves attach us the more closely to the soil we tread. Now that the danger has passed, a new and closer bond unites us to those who led us through the perilous situation and who have saved us. Of that order are the indissoluble bonds which to-day attach France to the Republic.

At Rome, it was a mark of honor and nobility to have the right to keep the images of ancestors in the atrium and to have them borne in certain solemn ceremonies. The Republic has won its patent of nobility. On this anniversary it has the right to have borne before it the images of those who have guided it and who, in tragic circumstances, have supplied it with the power to live and to grow. In time of need it has always been the marvelous destiny of France to see rise from its soil the men indispensable to her safety. We will only name the dead; Gambetta, Jules Ferry, Waldeck-Rousseau. Have not all those who succeeded them been, if not always pupils of their methods, at least disciples of their thought?

Gambetta, who in 1870 was the great organizer of the national defense; Gambetta, who, after the treaty of Frankfort, looked forward to the revenge of immanent justice; Gambetta, whose enthusiasms, warmth of heart and spiritual impulse were, on the morrow of the catastrophe, the song of hope rising above the ruins! Gambetta, of whom my illustrious predecessor, in the beautiful book that he consecrated to him a few months ago, said, "his name forms part of the religion of France"; Gambetta who had, in fine, the signal honor of personifying the very fortune of our country to the eyes of the foreigner! Immediately after the funeral of the great patriot Jules Ferry wrote, "Let us allow our conquerors to persuade themselves that Gambetta has carried to his tomb the last remnant of the spirit of revenge; it is well, it is useful that they believe it, but not one of those who have seen and understood the great and consoling spectacles of these incomparable days will dare to blaspheme the heart of France." "To blaspheme the heart of France"—one understands what such words signify; one hears the secret echoes that they express of the soul of him who pronounced them.

Jules Ferry felt the heart of France beat in his own breast; he felt it bleed from the wounds of yesterday and palpitate for all that with hopes for future life. To that resurrection he consecrated himself. With a tenacity, seemingly indifferent but nevertheless profoundly sensitive to the most furious and unjust attacks, without faltering because it was not he but the country that was in jeopardy, he followed the program that he had laid out, a program of national reconstruction, of national education and of national expansion. On the fields of battle in Flanders and on the Somme, on the Marne and on the Meuse, at Ypres as at Verdun, everywhere where you, our Marshals, have led the allied armies, we have seen not heroism alone, but the very soul of those young men who were pupils of Jules Ferry; we have seen the exploits of those soldiers from Africa and Asia whom Jules Ferry has given us.

On the 4th of July, 1899, in the Chamber of Deputies, in a most serious crisis President Waldeck-Rousseau cried "The Republic will live" and was applauded by the majority. Waldeck-Rousseau! The Minister of Commerce of 1900 could not evoke without emotion the figure of the great statesman who, at one of the most critical epochs of French life, had the courage to accept governmental power and was able, through his serenity, poise and ability to reëstablish peace in the minds of the people as well as in the streets of the capital. "The Republic will live," he cried. The Republic has lived. The Republic has conquered. The Republic still lives.

Those republicans were admirable who had the strength of mind never to despair, who suffered in their hearts from the disquietudes born of tragic events and of violent attacks upon them, and who nevertheless remained calm and were able to dissimulate their anguish and suffering, fully determined to reach the goal they knew must be attained. But those men, whatever their importance might be, would not have been sufficient for the task if they had been alone. Demosthenes was unable to accomplish anything against Philip. Their strength was in the people on whom they relied and the essential worth of the Republic is shown by the fact that it made it possible for this people to develop, to expand, and if one may so express it, to rise to the height of the occasion.

Immediately after the victory of the Marne, that five-day battle during which a world filled with foreboding had seen, with astonishment, admiration and delight, an army supposed to be defeated and in flight turn about suddenly and force into retreat a victorious army that believed that it already held definite triumph in its hands, General Joffre telegraphed to the government: "The Republic can be proud of the army it has organized." By this understand: the Republic can be proud of the people it has raised, for was it not the whole French people who were under arms, who fought and held firm and conquered with the aid of its allies?

Fifty years have doubtless not passed without weakness and the commission of faults. To err is human and we are men; but even when we erred, there was something that never weakened—the love of France.

The deep love of country, the passionate desire to make each day more noble and more splendid, more prosperous and more just, to restore its natural frontiers, to guarantee it against fresh crimes; the impassioned desire to bring it about that in sweet France life be made daily easier and more humane,—is not that the sentiment that will forever inspire us all? It matters little that methods differ, the unique goal is there and may not be forgotten.

Look at the position of France on September 4, 1870; look at the position of France on September 4, 1920. We should call to mind the sad voyage of M. Thiers in Europe during that cruel winter of 1870, in search of support that everywhere eluded him. Recall, on the other hand, the Belgians, the British, the Italians, the Russians, the Americans and the volunteers of all races and all tongues who threw themselves forward from 1914 to 1918 to shed their blood on French soil for a cause, at the same time our cause and that of civilization. Call to mind the army of 1870 and its six months calvary. It saved our honor. It added to the anthology of our glory new names and immortal pages: Reichshoffen, Gravelotte, Bazeilles, Chanzy, Faidherbe, Denfert-Rochereau. What an abyss, however, between the army of 1870 and the French Army of 1914, 1915, 1916, 1917 and 1918!

Let us recall the continuity of the foreign policy of the Republic that was able to prepare, organize and maintain those friendships and alliances that we were to find ready in the day of peril.

Let us think of the soldiers from Asia and Africa, whom I invoked just now with the memory of Jules Ferry. It was the colonial policy of the Republic that made it possible for us to acquire and preserve these magnificent overseas domains, where, in the midst of a general unheaval, peace has not ceased to reign. Remember the sad meeting of March 1, 1871, at Bordeaux, where was heard the pathetic protest of the deputies from Alsace and Lorraine; remember the incomparable days of November and December, 1918, in Alsace and Lorraine and say whether the Republic has not brought to success its impassioned effort for the grandeur of France.

But the redemption of France has not been brought about only in the military and political sense. It has been accomplished in all the branches of human activity, in agriculture, in public works, in commerce and in industry.

In social legislation we should recall the measures taken for the protection of child labor, for the regulation and limitation of working hours, from the point of view of hygiene and of safety; for assistance to minors, the aged and infirm; the great laws on labor accidents, on the weekly holiday, on the housing of laborers and the development of mutual aid. Under the action of two laws, those of March 21, 1884, and July 1, 1901, syndicates and associations have multiplied. Also the prodigious development of social conceptions and accomplishments has been one of the features of this period. Though for these grave problems made its way into all parties. It has given to parliamentary eloquence two of the orators who have reflected the highest brilliancy on the French tribune—Jean Jaurès and Albert de Mun. All the moral values, all the social values and all the spiritual values that make up the grandeur of a people have had occasion to manifest and affirm themselves in that space of fifty years. The Republic can rightly take glory in them; and to future generations we do not present ourselves empty-handed.

The coming generations have been the object of constant thought to the governments that have succeeded each other since 1870. If, in the constitution of the Year III there is inscribed the obligation of the state to watch over national education, our Republic has not evaded this duty. There are no cares that it has not given to this work; material cares, intellectual cares, administrative cares. And among its best workers, beside and not far from the name of Jules Ferry, it is only just to inscribe the name of René Goblet. There was construction of schools in all districts of France, organization of girls' education, development of primary, secondary and higher education, and creation of professional education.

The value of that education we have judged by the results it has obtained.

In the life of a people, there is something more, and there ought to be something more than the quest for material prosperity. Men have need of an ideal to guide them, to sustain them in their daily troubles, to enable them to rise above their troubles. Is not the double purpose of education fulfilled when, at the end of school, the young people are equally equipped for action and for thought? And if the young people of France have proved of what they are capable in action, have they not also proved of what they are capable in thought? They have had illustrious masters of whom it can be said that without them the world would not have been raised to its present level. They have followed these masters, and, if it has been sometimes claimed that science has no country, it can never be denied that there is a manner of conceiving science that is peculiarly French.

The names of Pasteur, Berthelot, Henri Poincaré and Pierre Curie are universal but they are above all French by that clarity, that boldness, that breadth, that confidence and that quality of thought that are truly our own. Is it not the same quality that is found in our artists, and is anything more admirable than the surprising mixture of realism and of lyricism, that marvelous life whose disinterestedness is a perpetual lesson, contained in works like those of Rodin in sculpture, of César Franck and Debussy in music, of Puvis de Chavannes and Carrière, of Renoir and Cézanne in painting? And finally in literature, philosophy and history, in criticism and romance, in poetry and drama, from Taine and Renan to Charles Péguy, the movement of ideas has been so rapid, so abundant that it is easy to follow therein the moral history of the generations of the Third Republic.

After the war of 1870 there was a sort of uneasiness; one saw the generations that had lived through the war clutched, as it were, by despondency toward life, taking refuge in the ivory towers, and seeking that ideal whose pain each Frenchman feels in symbols sometimes obscure but whose inspiration affirms its worth. Others pleased themselves with mental activity. Pessimism had its day. But, one morning, rumors from without penetrated the ivory towers. A moment always comes when, weary of the dream in which one is wrapped, the window is opened to the outside air. Through the open window suddenly enter the voices of life which has resumed full strength. While some slept in dreams, others toiled. The song of labor resounds. The isolated dreamer then feels that he ought to add his effort to the universal effort, his verse to the universal song, that he ought to labor to realize that ideal which he had believed could be cultivated only in a secluded retreat.

Sometimes the ideal changes but it is always the ideal. It is not a question of knowing whether these poets, novelists, dramatists and historians are republicans or not, it is not a question of knowing whether they were revolutionists or reactionaries, catholics or free thinkers. It is enough to establish that, by their care for moral, social and religious questions, they have disengaged themselves from that dilettantism whose disintegrating charm is more harmful to a people than the violence of prejudice.

Generations of the beginning of the twentieth century, who were so keen in battle and who entered the arena with such ardor, whose cruel wounds are so deplored, we may ask ourselves to-day if we should not congratulate ourselves on those struggles that were struggles for an ideal, so that in 1905, when external danger appeared abruptly to all eyes, the parties commenced to unite so as to make but one French party. Generations that reached the age of manhood with the war, we must appeal to them in this academic quarter which they left to go to the front with that youthful enthusiasm which detracts nothing from good judgment—they have understood in advance, they have comprehended, they have acquiesced.

1870 to 1920—what a period of accomplishment! In philosophy and in history, in criticism and in romance, in the drama and even in poetry is manifested unceasingly that thought for those lofty problems that make the honor and the grandeur of mankind. It is true that, among these philosophers and these historians, among these critics and these novelists, among these dramatists and these poets, all do not celebrate the Republic; but the Republic celebrates all of them for it is precisely its glory to have made it possible for them all to make known their thoughts, which sometimes they clothed in magnificent language; and if we cannot foresee what judgment posterity will render on our era, we can feel assured that if it does not retain certain names it will nevertheless retain the memory of an epoch of free and unpassioned seeking for truth and beauty.

ARTHUR MEIGHEN

The work is not finished. If, as Gambetta wished, France has preserved intact and ever present the memory of the dear lost provinces, it has never occurred to the thought of any of the governments that it could take the responsibility of appealing to force to attempt to regain the property that had been ravished from it. Immanent justice has decreed that the war, as a result of which just reparation should come, should be initiated by the very perpetrators of the crime.

Aggression interrupted the peaceful work of hands and brain. After more than four years of a terrible war this work has been resumed. New duties have been added to our duties. We have ruins to restore, reparations to assure and guaranties to maintain. May the past give us confidence for the future!

Oh, unknown soldier, nameless and triumphant representative of the heroic host of poilus; Ye dead who sleep your last sleep under the soil of Flanders, of Champagne, of Verdun, of so many famous or unknown battlefields; young heroes who rushed from beyond the Atlantic, from the British Isles, from far off Dominions, from Italy, from Belgium, from Serbia, from all parts of the world to offer your lives for the preservation of the ideal that once again France typified, sleep in peace.

You have fulfilled your destiny.

France and civilization are saved.

ARTHUR MEIGHEN

THE GLORIOUS DEAD

[Delivered at Thelus Military Cemetery, Vimy Ridge, at the unveiling of the Cross of Sacrifice, July 3, 1921.]

The Great War is past; the war that tried through and through every quality and mystery of the human mind and the might of human spirit; the war that closed, we hoped forever, the long, ghastly story of the arbitrament of men's differences by force; the last clash and crash of earth's millions is over now. There can be heard only sporadic conflicts, the moan of prostrate nations, the cries of the bereaved and desolate, the struggling of exhausted peoples to rise and stand and move onward. We live among the ruins and the echoes of Armageddon. Its shadow is receding slowly backward into history.

At this time the proper occupation of the living is, first, to honor our heroic dead; next, to repair the havoc, human and material, that surrounds us; and, lastly, to learn aright and apply with courage the lessons of the war.

Here in the heart of Europe we meet to unveil a memorial to our country's dead. In earth which has resounded to the drums and tramplings of many conquests, they rest in the quiet of God's acre with the brave of all the world. At death they sheathed in their hearts the sword of devotion, and now from oft-stricken fields they hold aloft its cross of sacrifice, mutely beckoning those who would share their immortality. No words can add to their fame, nor so long as gratitude holds a place in men's hearts can our forgetfulness be suffered to detract from their renown. For as the war dwarfed by its magnitude all contests of the past, so the wonder of human resource, the splendor of human heroism, reached a height never witnessed before.

Ours we thought prosaic days, when the great causes of earlier times had lost their inspiration, leaving for attainment those things which demanded only the petty passing inconveniences of the hour. And yet the nobility of manhood had but to hear again the summons of duty and honor to make response which shook the world. Danger to the treasury of common things—for common things when challenged are the most sacred of all—danger to these things ever stirred our fathers to action, and it has not lost its appeal to their sons.

France lives and France is free, and Canada is the nobler for her sacrifice to help free France to live. In many hundreds of plots throughout these hills and valleys, all the way from Flanders to, Picardy, lie fifty thousand of our dead. Their resting-places have been dedicated to their memory forever by the kindly grateful heart of France, and will be tended and cared for by us in the measure of the love we bear them. Above them are being planted the maples of Canada, in the thought that her sons will rest the better in the shade of trees they knew so well in life. Across the leagues of the Atlantic the heart-strings of our Canadian nation will reach through all time to these graves in France; we shall never let pass away the spirit bequeathed to us by those who fell; "their name liveth for evermore."

GENERAL PERSHING

TO THE UNKNOWN BRITISH WARRIOR

[At a simple and beautiful ceremony in Westminster Abbey on October 17, 1921, General Pershing laid the Congressional Medal of Honor on the grave of the Unknown British Warrior. As he conferred the highest military honor which can be bestowed by the United States Government, General Pershing made the following brief address.]

ONE cannot enter here and not feel an overpowering emotion in recalling the important events in the history of Great Britain that have shaped the progress of the nations. Distinguished men and women are here enshrined who through the centuries have unselfishly given their services and their lives to make that record glorious. As they pass in memory before us there is none whose deeds are more worthy and none whose devotion inspires our admiration more than this Unknown Warrior. He will always remain the symbol of the tremendous sacrifice by his people in the world's greatest conflict. It was he who without hesitation bared his breast against tyranny and injustice. It was he who suffered in the dark days of misfortune and disaster, but always with admirable loyalty and fortitude. Gathering new strength from the very force of his determination, he felt the flush of success without unseemly arrogance. In the moment of his victory, alas! We saw him fall in making the supreme gift to humanity. His was ever the courage of right and the confidence of justice. Mankind will continue to share his triumph and with the passing years will come to strew fresh laurels over his grave. As we solemnly gather about this sepulcher, the hearts of the American people join in this tribute to their English-speaking kinsman. Let us profit by the occasion and under its inspiration pledge anew our trust in the God of our fathers, that He may guide and direct our faltering footsteps into paths of permanent peace. Let us resolve together in friendship and in confidence to maintain toward all peoples that Christian spirit that underlies the character of both nations.

And now, in this holy sanctuary, in the name of the President and the people of the United States, I place upon his tomb the Medal of Honor conferred upon him by special Act of the American Congress in commemoration of the sacrifices of our British comrade and his fellow countrymen and as a slight token of our gratitude and affection toward this people.